Image-Based Evidence in International Criminal Prosecutions

Image-Based Evidence in International Criminal Prosecutions

Charting a Path Forward

JONATHAN W. HAK, KC

OXFORD
UNIVERSITY PRESS

OXFORD
UNIVERSITY PRESS

Great Clarendon Street, Oxford, OX2 6DP,
United Kingdom

Oxford University Press is a department of the University of Oxford.
It furthers the University's objective of excellence in research, scholarship,
and education by publishing worldwide. Oxford is a registered trade mark of
Oxford University Press in the UK and in certain other countries

First Edition published in 2024

Published in the United States of America by Oxford University Press
198 Madison Avenue, New York, NY 10016, United States of America

British Library Cataloguing in Publication Data

Data available

Library of Congress Control Number: 2023948483

ISBN 978–0–19–888953–3

DOI: 10.1093/oso/9780198889533.001.0001

Printed and bound by
CPI Group (UK) Ltd, Croydon, CR0 4YY

Preface

I think it is fair to say that writing this book was inevitable, though I was not aware of that fact until more recently. This work is the culmination of many years of using image-based evidence in the prosecution of serious and violent crime in Canada, teaching image-based evidence law internationally, extensive research at Leiden University and the International Criminal Court (ICC) while living in The Hague, and my PhD work at Leiden. I became acutely aware of the value of image-based evidence when prosecuting homicides and relying upon images drawn from public and private CCTV, smartphones, drones, aircraft mounted cameras, and earth observation satellites. It was in this context that I also learned the value that forensic imagery experts can bring to the search for the truth.

Using image-based evidence and forensic imagery expertise in the courtroom led to teaching image-based evidence law in Canada, the US, the UK, Hong Kong, Singapore, Italy, and the Netherlands through courses, conference presentations, and guest lectures. While performing these teaching duties, it became apparent that there was not a comprehensive resource available to international criminal law practitioners to assist them in the use of image-based evidence in the investigation and litigation of atrocity crimes. Creating this resource was the impetus for my research at the ICC and my PhD at Leiden.

This is the first book-length work that critically examines the use of image-based evidence in international criminal prosecutions. It systematically explores how image-based evidence can be used for probative and didactic purposes; it provides commentary on the authentication, interpretation, and reliability of images; and it charts a sound path for the effective use of image-based evidence in the search for truth. It provides a novel approach for how and when images should be evaluated for admissibility. This work also investigates emerging technical frontiers in image-based evidence and the potential uses for virtual reality, immersive virtual environments, and augmented reality as part of advanced visual representations in the international courtroom. It argues that advanced visual representations may have sufficient probative value to warrant their use for substantive and demonstrative purposes and proposes necessary parameters when delving into this potentially controversial method of depicting scenes and events.

The book draws upon litigation experiences in international and domestic criminal law from Nuremberg to the present day and is highly relevant to the practice of international criminal law and the academic study of image-based evidence. While the focus of this work is on international criminal prosecutions for atrocity crimes, the core substance and discussions contained herein transcend international criminal prosecutions and are also relevant to domestic prosecutions for violation of international criminal law under the principles of territoriality, active or passive personality, and universal jurisdiction. It is intended to serve as a resource for all counsel who contemplate using image-based evidence in the presentation of a case and opposing counsel who must respond to it; academics who focus on criminal law, evidence, and technology law; forensic imagery experts; investigators; and judges who must evaluate the evidence to discern its full meaning as part of the search for the truth. The work also has broader implications and may be of interest to human rights organizations, NGOs, public outreach organizations, and for public consumption. Collectively, this work seeks to chart a path forward for the use of image-based evidence in international criminal justice.

While reference is periodically made to different stages of the international criminal law process where image-based evidence is utilized, the primary focus of this book is the trial phase. It is, however, important to note that there is also a broader context for image-based evidence. Images have relevance and value beyond their role in litigation as they can help to fuel a broader truth and evaluative history discussion among scholars, human rights and other international organizations and NGOs, nation builders, governments, and other interested parties. For example, the mission of the Nuremberg trial was much broader than just determining whether the defendants were guilty of the charges they faced. While that determination was pivotal in many respects, prosecutors also needed to document Nazi atrocities for the historical record and to inform the world of what had taken place. Image-based evidence was effectively used as a graphical and poignant method of writing history. More broadly, image-based evidence also plays a role in international criminal justice by creating a visual historical record of atrocities, the events that led up to them, the context in which they occurred, and in some cases, the people responsible for them. The common theme acknowledged in this book is that while image-based evidence is frequently foundational to an international criminal prosecution, it is also part of broader important conversations beyond the courtroom.

This book has benefited from many conversations with forensic imagery experts in North America, the UK, and Europe. I have learned immense amounts of valuable information from their practical application of forensic imagery expertise in criminal and civil cases and judicial inquiries, always in search of the truth. Special thanks in this regard go to Grant Fredericks, Scott Kuntz, and John Kennedy for their longstanding support and exemplary forensic practices. I am also grateful to Carsten Stahn and Jens Iverson in the Grotius Centre for International Legal Studies at Leiden University, whose insightful commentary, constructive criticism, and suggestions elevated this book to a higher level than it otherwise would have achieved.

I am very grateful to Fiona Briden at Oxford University Press who saw promise in this project and supported it from the outset. Without her shepherding it through the approval process, this book may never have existed. Thanks also to the excellent team at OUP, especially Lindsay Glick, my Project Editor, who took all my words and made them into a book.

Most importantly, I owe an immeasurable debt of gratitude to my wife AmyLynn who has long been my north star. She engaged in countless (and perhaps seemingly endless) discussions about this project from the outset. Without her encouragement and support I dare say this book would not exist. Thank you so very much!

I hope that this book will serve as a useful resource for all those who rely upon image-based evidence in the search of the truth in international criminal justice.

The Hague
November 2023

Contents

Table of Cases

IMAGE-BASED EVIDENCE IN INTERNATIONAL CRIMINAL PROSECUTIONS

INTERNATIONAL INSTRUMENTS

JURISPRUDENCE

International Criminal Court

International Criminal Tribunal for Rwanda

International Criminal Tribunal for the former Yugoslavia

Special Tribunal for Lebanon

OTHER AD HOC CRIMINAL TRIBUNALS

DOMESTIC STATUTORY INSTRUMENTS

Domestic Case Law – Canada

Domestic Case Law – Hong Kong

Domestic Case Law – Israel

Domestic Case Law – Sweden

Domestic Case Law – United Kingdom

Domestic Case Law – United States

Introduction

Prosecutions for atrocity crimes before international criminal tribunals and courts are among the most complex and high-profile criminal cases in the modern era.[1] Ranging from the tribunals established to try war crimes committed during World War II,[2] to ad hoc and hybrid tribunals and courts established and operational for varied periods of time during the 1990s through to the 2020s,[3] to the broader reach of the International Criminal Court (ICC), these cases deal with the gravest of crimes before a global audience.[4] Prosecutions for the mass extermination of people, crimes of utmost depravity, political assassinations, and other conduct that beggars the imagination are in a category well apart from most domestic criminal prosecutions.

This was aptly illustrated by Chief Prosecutor Jackson when, in preparation for the *Trial of the Major War Criminals Before the International Military Tribunal, Nuremberg, 14 November 1945–1 October 1946*, he advised US President Truman that the prosecution 'must establish incredible events by credible evidence'.[5] Put another way, extraordinary claims require extraordinary proof. While the approach

[1] Each international criminal tribunal and court draws its jurisdiction from its foundational Charter or statute, which defines the specific criminal offences over which the tribunal or court has jurisdiction. For example, Art. 5 of the *Rome Statute of the International Criminal Court 1998*, UN Doc. A/CONF.183/9, 2187 UNTS 90 ('*Rome Statute*'), which is the foundational document creating the International Criminal Court (ICC), grants the court jurisdiction over the crime of genocide, crimes against humanity, war crimes, and the crime of aggression, each of which is defined in greater detail in Arts. 6–8 *bis*. For ease of reference, I will refer to the crimes prosecuted before international criminal tribunals and courts collectively as 'atrocity crimes' and when referring specifically to cases before the ICC, I will also use the term 'ICC crimes'.

[2] For example, the International Military Tribunal for Nuremberg (IMT) and the International Military Tribunal for the Far East (IMTFE), also known as the Tokyo War Crimes Tribunal.

[3] Including the International Criminal Tribunal for the former Yugoslavia (ICTY), the International Criminal Tribunal for Rwanda (ICTR), the Special Panels for Serious Crimes in East Timor (Special Panels), the Special Court for Sierra Leone (SCSL), the Extraordinary Chambers in the Courts of Cambodia (ECCC), the Special Tribunal for Lebanon (STL), and the United Nations International Residual Mechanism for Criminal Tribunals (MICT).

[4] The ICC has the broadest reach of all international criminal tribunals and courts, with jurisdiction to investigate and prosecute ICC crimes pursuant to a referral from a state party (*Rome Statute*, Art. 14), a referral by the United Nations Security Council acting under Chapter VII of the *Charter of the United Nations* (Art. 13(b)), or where the Prosecutor initiates an investigation *proprio motu* (Art. 15).

[5] 'Report from Mr. Justice Jackson, Chief Counsel for the United States in the Prosecution of Axis War Criminals', US National Archives and Records Administration, Military Agency Records RG 226, Entry 90, B 12, F 126, 3 (quoting Christian Delage, 'Bringing History into the Present Through Film: An Historian in the Archives of Nuremberg', *CINEASTE* (Winter 2011): 34–9, at 36). There were a series of trials held in Nuremberg with the *Major War Criminals Trial* being the first and most widely referenced. Trials of less high-profile war criminals followed. For ease of reference, I will refer to the *Major War Criminals Trial* as the 'Nuremberg trial'.

Image-Based Evidence in International Criminal Prosecutions. Jonathan W. Hak, KC, Oxford University Press.
 DOI: 10.1093/oso/9780198889533.001.0001

taken in domestic criminal prosecutions is worthy of study and selected incorporation, international criminal prosecutions for atrocity crimes require a more specialized approach, more attuned to the situations under examination and the varied audiences that have an interest in both the substance of the prosecution and the outcome.

Proving extraordinary claims in an effective and compelling manner requires considerable foresight and planning. Traditionally, counsel rely heavily upon *viva voce* and documentary evidence, supplemented with photographs, film, and video as deemed necessary. Differing approaches to the selection and presentation of evidence are contingent upon the perceived needs in individual cases and the preferences of counsel. In the Nuremberg trial, the prosecution shied away from death camp survivor testimony, and based their case primarily on documents, 90% of which were sourced from Nazi archives.[6] Significantly, the prosecution also made strategic and effective use of filmic evidence.[7] Conversely, in the Eichmann trial, extensive use was made of survivor testimony and documentary evidence, with minor reference to filmic evidence.[8] Different cases, different approaches.

Viva voce evidence has been the evidential standard bearer in criminal prosecutions for centuries. Eyewitnesses are often indispensable in substantively unfolding the narrative before the court. Augmented by direct and cross examination by counsel and questioning by the court, the reliability of testimonial evidence can be assessed, and prevaricating witnesses can be challenged. Judges, juries, and counsel are somewhat equipped for this important though difficult task, likely more by instinct than formal training. While acknowledging the diverse merits of eyewitness testimony, it is also replete with considerable challenges. Erroneous evidence given by honest, well-meaning witnesses has been extensively studied and documented.[9] Reliance upon translators for the interpretation of witness testimony, a common feature in atrocity crime prosecutions, creates problems when the testimony as interpreted does not accord with the testimony given.[10] Further, numerous factors involving the acquisition (perception of an event), retention (the period between

[6] Guénaël Mettraux, 'Trial at Nuremberg', in *Routledge Handbook of International Criminal Law*, edited by William Schabas and Nadia Bernaz (London: Routledge, 2013), 5–32.

[7] Filmic evidence refers to film-based visual depictions, commonly part of filmmaking or cinematography. 'filmic, adj' (*OED Online*, OUP August 2023), www.oed.com accessed 7 August 2023.

[8] *Attorney-General of the Government of Israel v. Adolf Eichmann*, Criminal Case 40/61, Judgment, 11 December 1961. Even though some of the evidence had little probative value regarding the specific indictment Eichmann faced, it served an important didactic role in the preservation of Holocaust memory and the creation of a historical record; Joseph Powderly, 'The Trials of Eichmann, Barbie and Finta', in *Routledge Handbook of International Criminal Law*, edited by William Schabas and Nadia Bernaz (London: Routledge, 2013), 33–49; see also Gideon Hausner, *Justice in Jerusalem* (New York: Schocken Books, 1966).

[9] See Section 1 of Chapter 1.

[10] Nancy Combs, *Fact-finding Without Facts: The Uncertain Evidentiary Foundation of International Criminal Convictions* (New York: CUP, 2010), 70–8, 124–5; Nancy Combs, 'A New Look at Fact-Finding at the ICTR: Advances in Judicial Acknowledgment', *Criminal Law Forum* 26 (2015): 387–401, at 390–1, 400–1. This miscommunication challenge is discussed in Chapter 5.

the event and the recollection), and retrieval (recollection of the stored event) impact the accuracy of eyewitness identification and event narration.[11]

These concerns have been readily noted in international criminal prosecutions. Witnesses in atrocity crime prosecutions often have great difficulty providing reliable and consistent testimony on dates, time, distances, numbers, and the details and duration of events in question. Some witnesses are unable to evaluate and comment upon two-dimensional depictions of three-dimensional scenes as those representations are not part of their lexicon.[12] Judges must take these inaccuracies and inconsistencies into account when assigning weight to the evidence of witnesses. There may be occasions when there is no eyewitness evidence available on a key point due to there being no living, locatable, or cooperative witness, or when witnesses may be too afraid to testify for fear of reprisal, rendering the presentation of alternate forms of evidence crucial.

Reliance upon *viva voce* evidence and documents has its place in most international criminal prosecutions. However, a veritable treasure trove of valuable evidence resides in the image-based realm.[13] Image-based evidence may be original, derivative, or demonstrative in form and function. Original image-based evidence is first-hand evidence, shown in its original form and includes film, video recordings, and images obtained from remote sensing satellites, unmanned aerial vehicles, and ground-based cameras operated by individuals or computers.[14] Derivative image-based evidence is a transmogrified visual representation of original image-based data for analytical purposes and includes terrestrial laser scanning representations, digital three-dimensional (3D) models, forensic simulations, advanced visual representations, video timelines, etc. Demonstrative image-based evidence is merely the visual representation of a party's theory of how an event occurred and is not strictly derived from original sources, unlike original and derivative image-based evidence, which is admissible substantive evidence capable of being weighed by the court. A typical demonstrative example is a forensic animation, which may or may not bear allegiance to proven facts.

While *viva voce* evidence will rightly continue to retain an important foothold in international criminal prosecutions, the court is more likely to remember and internalize evidence if a visual component is involved.[15] Further, visual representations tend to have a greater impact upon viewers than words alone because images

[11] Elizabeth Loftus, *Eyewitness Testimony* (Cambridge, MA: Harvard University Press, 1979). See Section 1 of Chapter 1.

[12] e.g. maps, diagrams, sketches, photographs, and other images.

[13] Image-based evidence includes film, video recordings, photographs, three-dimensional digital models created by terrestrial laser scanning, forensic reconstructions in the form of animations and simulations, remote sensing images, advanced visual representations, and other forms of evidence with visual form.

[14] This includes original evidence that has been clarified or enhanced to provide additional detail.

[15] Eryn Newman and Neal Feigenson, 'The Truthiness of Visual Evidence', *Jury Expert* 25, no. 5 (2013): 9–14.

are more vivid and strike viewers differently than textual information. Therefore, when presenting their case in court, taking advantage of multimodal learning by weaving image-based evidence into the trial narrative should be a central consideration for counsel. The use of image-based evidence found an early foothold in international criminal prosecutions, primarily because the work of the tribunals was fundamentally different from that of most domestic courts. The tribunals were not focussed on isolated events in one location but rather crimes of untold proportions that frequently crossed national borders. Considering the subject matter, image-based evidence was typically an essential component of the prosecution's case. Filmic evidence such as *Nazi Concentration Camps* featured prominently in the Nuremberg trial, not for the shock value that it clearly possessed, but because words alone could not possibly convey to the tribunal the depth and breadth of the atrocities committed by the Nazi war machine.[16]

The most common type of image-based evidence used in early war crime and atrocity prosecutions was photographic and filmic evidence which typically showed graphic scenes, including films shot by the Nazis themselves for the purpose of documenting their reign of terror on civilian populations, as well as interviews of soldiers and survivors by Allied forces. In more recent years, the use of image-based evidence has expanded to include analogue and digital video; digital images obtained from remote sensing satellites, unmanned aerial vehicles, and ground-based cameras; terrestrial laser scanning representations; digital 3D models; forensic simulations; advanced visual representations with interactive visualization; etc. These images can be used as independent evidence to supplement, illustrate, or contradict the evidence of witnesses, or to show things that witness testimony cannot fully deliver.

Image-based evidence is not without its complexities and much like an iceberg, these technical and epistemic challenges frequently lie below the surface. What may at first glance appear simple may indeed be straightforward and, conversely, what appears simple may bely complexities beyond the understanding of counsel and the court without expert assistance. Most image-based evidence presented in court today is digital in nature, which can present concerns of reliability and authenticity.[17] As investigations and prosecutions become more technical, there is a corresponding responsibility by counsel to present such evidence in a manner that the court can properly assess, interpret, and apply to the task at hand. It is erroneous for counsel to present image-based evidence in a manner that presupposes that the import of the evidence will be transparent and unequivocal to all viewers. This can manifest itself in the presentation of evidence with no supporting

16 The use of this and other filmic evidence in the Nuremberg trial is discussed throughout this book and introduced in detail in Section 3.1 of Chapter 1.

17 Digital evidence is binary data that is created, utilized, stored, or transmitted by a computer. It has no independent visual presence and requires a computer to give it visual form.

witnesses, or with supporting witnesses not equipped for the task. Either approach sets the stage for uninformed decision-making. Image-based evidence plays an important role in virtually all international criminal prosecutions, yet there are few standards and guidelines governing its use and little uniformity in how it is presented and assessed by the court.[18]

Image-based evidence may appear deceptively self-evident, leading viewers to think that because they can see it, they therefore understand it. While some images are readily understandable to unassisted viewers, others require interpretation by witnesses familiar with the image content or by an expert well versed in both the content and its method of creation. To fully understand images, content and meaning must be teased from them. They must be confronted by people armed with the necessary technical expertise and contextual knowledge to properly assess them. Words must be used to evaluate their content, with the express caveat that pictures cannot necessarily be reduced to words.[19] It is often necessary to interrogate images. Using digital video as an example, this type of interrogation involves an in-depth examination of the image metadata for the purpose of assessing its integrity, authenticity, and technical attributes such as image compression, frame rate, resolution, and aspect ratio.[20]

Images then need to be interpreted for the purpose of determining what they fairly depict and narrated for the court so that viewers understand the full parameters of the evidence. Showing images to the court without effective narration by a witness with knowledge does a disservice to the media, assumes an interpretive ability not likely possessed by viewers (let alone one equally possessed by all viewers), and risks a disconnect between what the images show and what unassisted viewers perceive them to show. Images are not unmediated portrayers of facts, nor will they reveal their full content without viewer effort. Seeing should not automatically lead to believing, nor do pictures necessarily speak for themselves. The essence of image-based evidence is that it allows viewers to see (and sometimes hear) something, but assistance may be required to truly comprehend what is being shown.

The responsibility of counsel for the prosecution in assimilating, organizing, and presenting a comprehensive and compelling case for the court to evaluate and rule upon is immense. The obligation of the defence to thoroughly examine and

[18] For example, no common international standards exist for gathering, handling, preserving, and presenting social media and other open source evidence in international and national courts. UC Berkeley School of Law Human Rights Center, 'The New Forensics: Using Open Source Information to Investigate Grave Crimes' (2018), https://humanrights.berkeley.edu/sites/default/files/publications/bellagio_report_july2018_final.pdf, 3 ('The New Forensics'). A similar lack of international standards applies to image-based evidence generally, with rulings being made on a case-by-case basis, while grounded on general principles of reliability and probative value.

[19] Neal Feigenson, 'The Visual in Law: Some Problems for Legal Theory', *Law, Culture and the Humanities* 10, no. 1 (2014): 13–23, at 12, 14.

[20] See Section 2 of Chapter 6 for a discussion of these technical attributes.

challenge the prosecution evidence, and where applicable, present a defence case, is equally important. Many lawyers have a less than comprehensive understanding of technical evidence when they commence a career in international criminal litigation. The learning curve for the use of technical evidence is rather steep but achieving a level of understanding so that technical evidence can be led and argued effectively is essential.

Constant technological advancements continue to create new forms of image-based evidence. Some of these advancements are highly advantageous and will help to shed light on dark deeds. Others are insidious, pernicious, and serve to obfuscate the truth (e.g. deepfake videos). Atrocity crime investigations and prosecutions have profited greatly from the evidence that has emerged from high-quality satellite imagery, the exponential proliferation of smartphones and the video recordings and photographs their users have generated, and the widespread use of social media and other sites to share images and other data.[21] Provided it is properly evaluated, analysed, interpreted, and presented, image-based evidence can be of considerable value to counsel and the court in discovering the truth, thereby assisting the court in determining whether the prosecution has met its burden of proof.[22]

In contrast to *viva voce* evidence generally, image-based evidence has the potential to be a more neutral arbiter of truth, though it is not without its challenges.[23] The current trend shows a tacit (and sometimes necessary) reliance upon non-investigators to gather video recordings and photographic images of key events and scenes, and this gives rise to serious authentication and reliability concerns. If counsel and the court are not fully equipped to assess authentication due to a lack of targeted expert examination and testimony, these concerns become even more acute. Further, the potential for selectivity in evidence creation and submission is palpable and exacerbates the potential mischief that can be created with image-based evidence, as the agendas and biases of the parties can impact their selection of images in favour of a narrative that may support *a* truth, though not necessarily *the* truth. While the democratization of evidence gathering and submission offers laudable benefits, there is often a price to be paid for relying upon evidence gathered by civilians.

Transcending the determination of authenticity are considerations of the interpretive acumen of viewers and their understanding of what is being presented. Attaining suitable visual literacy on the part of counsel and the court is central to the proper interpretation of image-based evidence. Equating mere vision with

[21] Elena Radeva, 'The Potential for Computer Vision to Advance Accountability in the Syrian Crisis', *Journal of International Criminal Justice* 19, no. 1 (2021): 131–46, at 132.

[22] The truth discovery function of international criminal justice is discussed in Section 1.1 of Chapter 2.

[23] This is not to suggest that civilian testimony is wholly unreliable but rather recognizes that witness testimony is often fluid and may tend to gravitate towards the interests of witnesses and their supporters.

a sophisticated visual literacy intuitively able to understand technical issues and properly interpret images is folly. While vision is a gateway to visual literacy, it is not a substitute. Courts often need expert assistance to understand and incorporate technical evidence that is outside the realm of common knowledge. Some image-based evidence comfortably resides in this category. Assessing the reliability and meaning of image-based evidence and its correlation with other evidence should not necessarily be left to counsel and the court as that may do a disservice to the evidence and those who must evaluate it. When counsel and the court are left to determine the meaning of image-based evidence without appropriate assistance, they may not appreciate the full import of the evidence, may misinterpret it, or may reach the wrong conclusion based on their erroneous interpretation. It is problematic when counsel and the court do not have the expert interpretive assistance they require. It is even more problematic when they do not realize they need expert assistance.

Judges do not typically bring a wealth of scientific and technical knowledge to the bench, nor is that a requirement. Further, they are required to decide cases based on evidence presented by the parties, not their own personal knowledge.[24] It therefore falls upon the parties to educate the court with competent, knowledgeable witnesses and in this regard expert witnesses should play an important role in the exposition and interpretation of image-based evidence in a case. The failure of counsel to present necessary expert evidence does not permit the court to conduct its own analysis to fill in the evidential lacuna even in a hybrid inquisitorial environment. When counsel fail to lead requisite expert evidence and leave important issues unresolved, the temptation to solve for X may be irresistible even though it may not withstand appellate scrutiny. Avoiding appellate intervention for lack of due diligence by counsel at trial is essential.

Though extensive reference is made in this book to tribunals and courts that preceded and paralleled the ICC, the dominant focus is on the ICC as it is the predominant adjudicative body involved in investigating and prosecuting atrocity crimes today.[25] For this reason, brief mention of the ICC's approach to the trial process is instructive to provide some context for the assessment of evidence.

[24] An exception to this principle is facts within common knowledge, of which judicial notice can be taken. In the ICC context, this is contained in RPE Art. 69(6). See also Gideon Boas, James Bischoff, Natalie Reid, and Don Taylor, *International Criminal Procedure* (Cambridge: CUP, 2011), 361–6. A further exception is the curious practice utilized by the ad hoc tribunals of taking judicial notice of adjudicated facts from other cases. Yvonne McDermott, 'Strengthening the Evaluation of Evidence in International Criminal Trials', *International Criminal Law Review* 17 (2017): 682–702, at 693. This practice creates the risk of unfairness to the parties as they must contend with findings of fact from other cases in which they had no input.

[25] The ICC is a treaty-based court, deriving its existence from a treaty (the *Rome Statute*), which member states ratify or accede to and are then obligated to perform designated duties while also enjoying certain rights. The Court is independent of the UN as it was not created by nor is it an organ of the UN Security Council. David Scheffer, 'The International Criminal Court', in *Routledge Handbook of International Criminal Law*, edited by William Schabas and Nadia Bernaz (London: Routledge, 2013), 67–83.

Drawing upon the significant experience of the International Criminal Tribunal for the former Yugoslavia (ICTY), the International Criminal Tribunal for Rwanda (ICTR), and other ad hoc tribunals, the ICC has the most developed rules of evidence among the predecessor and contemporary tribunals and tends to gravitate to an adversarial model, though retaining some inquisitorial features.[26] The *Rome Statute*, which resulted from extensive negotiations by the member states, grants the ICC the authority to request the submission of all evidence that it considers necessary for the determination of the truth, subject to an assessment of relevance.[27] Assuming relevance is established, a probative value versus prejudicial effect assessment is undertaken to achieve trial fairness.[28] The ICC's primarily adversarial approach holds the proposed evidence of the prosecution and defence to the same standard in this weighing exercise.[29]

As the title suggests, this book articulates guidelines and recommendations for the use of image-based evidence in international criminal prosecutions.[30] Beyond this foundational guidance is a recommendation regarding the development of a more robust formal repository by the ICC Office of the Prosecutor (OTP) for the acquisition, assessment, and archiving of image-based evidence submitted by individuals and organizations other than OTP investigators.[31] Such a repository will require the increased use of artificial intelligence and machine learning to address the volume of evidence that would need to be evaluated. Significantly, this book argues that the use of image-based evidence is at a tipping point and that positive

[26] The Anglo-Saxon justice system is generally referred to as the adversarial model. In this system, there is effectively a contest between two equal parties who present their cases (a prosecution case and a defence case) to the court. The prosecution presents it case through witnesses and other evidence and carries the burden of proof. The defence challenges the prosecution case and if it chooses, presents its own case. In this party-driven approach, the judge's aim is to deliver justice. The judges have no active role in the investigation of a case or the collection of evidence, aside from granting judicial authorizations for search and seizure, and the use of certain investigative techniques. Their primary role is to conduct trials, receive and rule upon evidence, and serve as a balance for the adversaries. Håkan Friman, 'Inspiration from the International Criminal Tribunals When Developing Law on Evidence for the International Criminal Court', *The Law and Practice of International Courts and Tribunals* 3 (2003): 373–400. Conversely, Continental Europe utilizes the inquisitorial or inquiry model, a system wherein the examining judge plays an active role in the investigation and pre-trial phases, separate from the trial judge who presides over the trial itself. The inquisitorial model is judge-driven and there is one case under examination, not a prosecution and defence case. There are no prosecution or defence witnesses, only court witnesses, and the role of the judge is to find the truth. Kai Ambos, 'International Criminal Procedure: "Adversarial", "Inquisitorial" or Mixed?' *International Criminal Law Review* 3 (2003): 1–37, at 3.

[27] Evidence is considered relevant if it makes the existence of a fact in issue more or less probable. *Prosecutor v. Katanga and Ngudjolo Chui*, ICC-01/04-01/07-2635, Decision on the Prosecutor's Bar Table Motions, 17 December 2010, para. 16.

[28] Arts. 69(3) and (4). Probative value refers to the ability of tendered evidence to establish a stated fact. Assessing probative value may include an examination of the reliability, authenticity, and importance of evidence in the case. *Prosecutor v. Bemba*, ICC-01/05-01/08-2299-Red, Public Redacted Version of 'Decision on the Prosecution's Application for Admission of Materials into Evidence Pursuant to Art. 64(9) of the Rome Statute' of 6 September 2012, 8 October 2012, paras. 7–12.

[29] Evidence tendered by counsel for the victims is held to a similar standard.

[30] See Section 1 of Chapter 9.

[31] See Section 2 of Chapter 9.

steps must be taken to transcend the status quo and push image-based evidence to the next level in the search for truth.[32] In this regard, three specific recommendations are articulated as part of the necessary commitment to maximize the use of image-based evidence. These recommendations focus on comprehensively addressing social media and open source image-based evidence, expanding the use of more technically advanced image-based evidence and digital representations for scene and event analysis, and fully engaging the use of forensic imagery experts to interrogate, evaluate, analyse, and present image-based evidence in court. Collectively, this book explores the significant value that image-based evidence can bring to the pursuit of truth and a just result. It articulates why the status quo is lacking and charts a path forward for the more comprehensive and sound use of image-based evidence in international criminal prosecutions.

[32] See Section 4 of Chapter 9.

PART I

IMAGE-BASED EVIDENCE IN INTERNATIONAL CRIMINAL PROSECUTIONS

1
Image-Based Evidence as a Method of Proof

Introduction

Lights! Camera! Action! The critical success of a movie is often dependent upon the work of the director. Casting, location, camera angles, lighting, and special effects shape the feel and substance of the production and its receptivity by the audience. Though there are no awards for 'Best Atrocity Crime Prosecution of the Year', the parallels between the importance of a movie's director and the prosecutor in a criminal trial are undeniable. Decisions made by the prosecutor in the selection of evidence and the way the case is presented can make the difference between a marginal case and a compelling case.[1] Though the focal point in this chapter is the case for the prosecution, these comments apply equally to the defence and victim's counsel. Primary reference to the prosecution is reflective of the fact that the burden of proof is on the prosecution throughout a trial and the reality that the prosecution typically presents most of the evidence in court.

Securing an indictment against a defendant is one thing, proving the allegations underlying it is quite another. Having alleged criminality, it falls squarely upon the prosecution to present a case that is sufficiently cogent to merit conviction. The role of the prosecution in the collection, organization, selection, and presentation of evidence at trial cannot be understated.[2] Though courts retain an important supervisory role regarding evidence presentation, the pivotal task of building the prosecution's case is generally within the discretion of counsel.[3] An important caveat though—the selection and presentation of evidence by the prosecution must be fair, transparent, and aimed at eliciting the truth.[4] Within that framework,

[1] Evidence is defined as that which tends to prove the existence or non-existence of a fact. Jonathan Law, *A Dictionary of Law*, 9th ed. (Oxford: OUP, 2018). The means by which any alleged matter of fact, the truth of which is submitted for investigation, is established or disproved. Henry Black, *Black's Law Dictionary*, 5th ed. (Minnesota: West Publishing, 1979).

[2] While investigators are primarily responsible for the collection of evidence, prosecutors perform an important function in the evaluation and integration of the evidence collected.

[3] Art. 64 of the *Rome Statute* and Rules 132 *bis* and 134 of the ICC Rules of Procedure and Evidence (RPE) provide a supervisory role for the Trial Chamber. Collectively, the Pre-Trial Chamber and Trial Chamber have sweeping powers over the length of the prosecution and defence cases, the number of witnesses they may call, how witnesses are examined, and the evidence they can lead. Gideon Boas, James Bischoff, Natalie Reid, and Don Taylor, *International Criminal Procedure* (Cambridge: CUP, 2011), 263–6.

[4] For a discussion of the role of truth discovery in international criminal justice, see Section 1.1 of Chapter 2.

Image-Based Evidence in International Criminal Prosecutions. Jonathan W. Hak, KC, Oxford University Press.
 DOI: 10.1093/oso/9780198889533.003.0001

the choices made by the prosecution regarding the selection and presentation of evidence are integral to the effective unfolding of their case. This requires an assessment of the triable issues, examination of the available evidence, and parsing out the relevant evidence specific to each issue.

Atrocity crime prosecutions are lengthy, complex, and involve many different forms of evidence, including eyewitness testimony, statements, and affidavits; expert testimony and reports; documentary evidence; image-based evidence; and physical exhibits. Informed, thoughtful evidence selection and consideration of how it can be efficaciously presented is crucial to the development of a compelling case. Following a discussion of the role of testimonial evidence, this chapter hones its focus on the effective incorporation of image-based evidence in the presentation of the prosecution and defence cases, as this type of evidence often constitutes a vital component in the proof cadre of atrocity crime prosecutions.

1. The Role of *Viva Voce* Evidence

Intuitively, a prosecution for atrocity crimes would seem incomplete without the presentation of *viva voce* evidence, sometimes referred to as eyewitness testimony, although case strategy might dictate otherwise.[5] For example, in conducting the Einsatzgruppen trial, US Army Chief Prosecutor Benjamin Ferencz opted not to present powerful death camp survivor testimony and instead based the prosecution's case upon SS generated documentary evidence.[6] This strategy allowed the prosecution case to be completed in two days, ultimately resulting in convictions for most of the defendants.[7] While this approach was effective in terms of the result, it represents an aberration in international criminal prosecutions, which tend to rely less on a clinical documentary case in favour of a broader approach, incorporating different types of evidence, including image-based evidence.[8] Before focusing on this latter form of evidence, it is important to contextualize the use of *viva voce* evidence.

[5] *Viva voce* is Latin and means 'with the living voice', referring to evidence given by a witness orally as opposed to evidence given in written form, such as an affidavit. 'viva voce, adv, adj, and n' (*OED Online*, OUP August 2023), www.oed.com accessed 7 August 2023.

[6] Formally referred to as the *Trials of War Criminals before the Nuremberg Military Tribunals, United States v. Ohlendorf et al.* [1949] 4 TWC 3, conducted in Nuremberg in 1947–48. The defendants were commanders of the Einsatzgruppen units, which were mobile SS death squads operating behind the front lines in Nazi-occupied Eastern Europe and responsible for over one million murders. Benjamin Ferencz and Donald Ferencz, 'Criminalizing the Illegal Use of Force', in *The Cambridge Companion to International Criminal Law*, edited by William Schabas (Cambridge: CUP, 2016), 230–52.

[7] 'The Accountant of Auschwitz', A Documentary Channel Production, TLNT Productions Inc., 2018; Benjamin Ferencz, 'The Biggest Murder Trial in History', https://benferencz.org/stories/1946-1949/the-biggest-murder-trial-in-history/.

[8] This is also reflective of the relative dearth of documentary evidence available to post-Holocaust prosecutors. Boas, Bischoff, Reid, and Taylor (n 3) 352.

Words have traditionally been the preeminent pedagogical tool in the presentation of evidence. They can be very descriptive, evocative, and powerful in painting a picture for the court of what the witness observed or endured. Effectively delivered words can transport the witness back to the event being described and leave listeners breathless as the words wash over them. However, as captivating as eyewitness testimony can be, it is frequently unreliable. I am not casting aspersions on honest well-meaning witnesses who are trying their best, but rather acknowledge the well-documented frailties associated with the acquisition, retention, and retrieval of memory.[9]

In her seminal work, *Eyewitness Testimony*, Loftus evaluated the acquisition or perception phase of memory and noted that event and witness factors impact a witness's ability to encode information.[10] Event factors include the length and frequency of exposure, the level of detail and type of facts involved, and the presence of violence. Witness factors include stress, cultural expectations, personal biases and prejudices, and perceptual focus. She noted that the retention phase, which is the period between the event and the time the witness is asked to recall it, is affected by the length of the retention period and intervening events.[11] Since memories are constructed from stored and available information, gaps are subconsciously filled with inferences and intervening fragments to form a memory. Finally, she examined the retrieval phase which involves how the information is obtained from the witness, focusing on environment, the questioner, and the manner of questioning.[12] A stressful environment and suggestive or aggressive questioning can impact the veracity of the information received, even from an honest witness.

Loftus found that witnesses have considerable difficulty accurately encoding information about time, speed, distance, and duration of an event, especially if the event involved some level of violence. Combs found similar deficits among atrocity crime witnesses testifying before the International Criminal Tribunal for Rwanda (ICTR), the Special Court for Sierra Leone (SCSL), and the Special Panels.[13] What is striking about the research that was undertaken independently by Loftus and Combs is that Loftus conducted her studies using willing test subjects who

[9] See generally Elizabeth Loftus, *Eyewitness Testimony* (Cambridge, MA: Harvard University Press, 1979); Nancy Combs, *Fact-finding Without Facts: The Uncertain Evidentiary Foundation of International Criminal Convictions* (New York: CUP, 2010); Jed Rakoff and Elizabeth Loftus, 'The Intractability of Inaccurate Eyewitness Identification', *Dædalus, The Journal of the American Academy of Arts and Sciences* 147, no. 4 (2018): 90–8.

[10] Loftus (n 9) 20–51.

[11] Retention phase factors are significant in the atrocity crime context as witnesses may not be asked to formally describe an event for months or years after it occurred and in the interim, they may have learned information from other witnesses or investigators that can enhance, change, or compromise existing memories, or cause witnesses to invent new memories. See Loftus (n 9) 52–87. Carsten Stahn, *Justice as Message: Expressivist Foundations of International Criminal Justice* (Oxford: OUP, 2020), 290.

[12] Loftus (n 9) 88–109.

[13] Combs (n 9); Nancy Combs, 'A New Look at Fact-Finding at the ICTR: Advances in Judicial Acknowledgment', *Criminal Law Forum* 26 (2015): 387–401.

observed preplanned non-violent or *faux* violent events in clinical laboratory settings in 1970s America and found substantial obstacles to accurate memory encoding.[14] Combs studied the testimony of witnesses to atrocity-related events and noted similar memory impediments as well as relevant witness deficits that place many atrocity witnesses in a different category than the Loftus volunteers.[15] In short, if eyewitness evidence is unreliable in non-stressful clinical settings, as Loftus found, one can certainly expect unreliable testimony in the surreal environment of atrocity crimes. Despite these misgivings, I do not suggest that *viva voce* evidence has no place in atrocity crime prosecutions. There remains a general preference for eyewitness testimony at the tribunals and the International Criminal Court (ICC).[16] For all its imperfections and foibles, *viva voce* evidence has earned a seat at the table.

2. The Value of Image-Based Evidence for Proof Purposes

Words have value and they will remain a mainstay in the trial forum, yet research in education and psychology has shown that the manner in which evidence is presented can have diverse impacts on the audience.[17] Evidence that has visual form is better integrated and remembered compared to pure testimonial evidence.[18] Images are generally more influential and informative than non-visual expressions

[14] Crime simulations do not entail the degree of personal threat or alarm that an individual may experience during actual life-threatening events and findings must be contextualized accordingly. In a controlled experiment involving 509 military personnel experiencing actual stress, Morgan et al. found that eyewitness memories encoded during events that are personally relevant, highly stressful, and realistic may be subject to substantial error. Charles Morgan, Gary Hazlett, Anthony Doran, Stephan Garrett, Gary Hoyt, Paul Thomas, Madelon Baranoski, and Steven Southwick, 'Accuracy of Eyewitness Memory for Persons Encountered During Exposure to Highly Intense Stress', *International Journal of Law and Society* 27 (2004): 265–79, at 274.

[15] These deficits include inferior education levels (most prominent), literacy, limited life experiences, cultural norms and taboos, and interpretation challenges owing to the frequent need to translate into French and then into English. Also noted is the difficulty of many witnesses to comprehend two-dimensional depictions of three-dimensional scenes (e.g. maps, diagrams, and photographs). Combs (n 9) 22–39, 63–100.

[16] Combs (n 9) 191–2; Nancy Combs, 'Evidence', in *Routledge Handbook of International Criminal Law*, edited by William Schabas and Nadia Bernaz (London: Routledge, 2013), 323–4.

[17] Neal Feigenson and Richard Sherwin, 'Thinking Beyond the Shown: Implicit Inferences in Evidence and Argument', *Law, Probability and Risk* 6 (2007): 295–310, at 297–8, 309; Richard Sherwin, Neal Feigenson, and Christina Spiesel, 'What Is Visual Knowledge, and What Is It Good For? Potential Ethnographic Lessons from the Field of Legal Practice', *Visual Anthropology* 20 (2007): 143–78, at 156–7; Elizabeth Porter, 'Taking Images Seriously', *Columbia Law Review* 114 (2018): 1687–782, at 1752–3.

[18] In Carole Powell, 'Computer Generated Visual Evidence: Does Daubert Make a Difference?', *Georgia State University Law Review* 12, no. 2 (1996): 577–600, at 579, the author cites the Weiss-McGrath Report which found that juror retention doubled if a visual presentation was used, and that retention increased by 650% if both a visual and oral presentation was used rather than solely an oral presentation. See also Betsy Fiedler, 'Are Your Eyes Deceiving You?: The Evidentiary Crisis Regarding the Admissibility of Computer Generated Evidence', *New York Law School Law Review* 48, no. 1–2 (2003): 295–322, at 302; Eryn Newman and Neal Feigenson, 'The Truthiness of Visual Evidence', *Jury Expert* 25, no. 5 (2013): 9–14, at 9.

of the same visual content.[19] Even the most fluent linguist may not be able to convey by words alone the full meaning of an image, not because the linguist is at a loss for words but rather because images are more vivid than words alone can effectively express.[20] Images strike us differently than words by connecting to internal narratives that inform our perceptions of the world around us.[21] While a witness or counsel may orally describe every visible aspect of an image, they cannot convey the emotions or feelings the image may engender in viewers, nor could they, as the visceral response is deeply personal. In this respect, choosing to describe a scene with words alone will always leave things unsaid.

Our brains process visual information differently from text and sound.[22] Images are processed in several channels instead of one, giving the brain a more in-depth and meaningful encoding experience.[23] Visualization reduces the number of steps viewers must take to understand what is being presented; that is, visual information requires less imagination than words and is more direct.[24] It connects to prior knowledge, thereby improving comprehension and memory.[25] A differentiation may need to be drawn between still and moving images because a plausible claim can be made that moving images may imprint in our brain in ways so similar to a lived experience that they may be easily conflated.[26] Moving images make the experience seem more real, providing the quasi-illusion of viewers having been present and actually witnessing the event.[27] They also tend to stimulate cognitive and emotional responses approximating those encountered when actually experiencing the event, thereby engaging the theatre of the mind.[28]

[19] Richard Sherwin, *Visualizing Law in the Age of the Digital Baroque* (London: Routledge, 2011) 59.

[20] Sherwin, Feigenson, and Spiesel (n 17) 156; Feigenson and Sherwin (n 17) 297.

[21] Vincenzo Sainato, 'Evidentiary Presentations and Forensic Technologies in the Courtroom, The Director's Cut', *Journal of the Institute of Justice and International Studies* 9 (2009): 38–52, at 45–7; Francis Mootz, 'Law Among the Sight Lovers', *New York Law School Law Review* 57, no. 1 (2012): 61–76, at 71.

[22] Lisanne van Weelden and Tessa van Charldorp, 'Communications Perspective on the Use of Visualisations in Dutch Court for Minor Felonies', *Utrecht Law Review* 15, no. 1 (2019): 26–37, at 31.

[23] Christina Spiesel, 'Reflections on Reading: Words and Pictures and Law', *International Journal of Law in Context* 2, no. 3 (2006): 305–20, at 317; Neal Feigenson, 'Visual Evidence', *Psychonomic Bulletin & Review* 17, no. 2 (2010): 149–54, at 151.

[24] Sainato (n 21) 45. Damian Schofield and Ken Fowle, 'Technology Corner—Visualizing Forensic Data: Evidence (Part 1)', *Journal of Digital Forensics, Security and Law* 8, no. 1 (2013): 73–90, at 74–5; Elizabeth Porter, 'Imagining Law: Visual Thinking Across the Law School Curriculum', *Journal of Legal Education* 68, no. 1 (2018): 8–14, at 9–10.

[25] In Damian Schofield, 'Animating Evidence: Computer Game Technology in the Courtroom', *Journal of Information Law and Technology* 1 (2009): 1–21, at 5, the author cites several US studies which showed that people retain vastly more information when it is presented visually rather than orally. See also Newman and Feigenson (n 18) 9.

[26] A dream of sitting on the beach, a film of sitting on the beach, and the experience of sitting on the beach could all reside in our brain in similar ways. See Jessica Silbey, 'Persuasive Visions: Film and Memory', *Law, Culture and the Humanities* 10, no. 1 (2018): 24–42, at 39.

[27] Jennifer Mnookin and Nancy West, 'Theaters of Proof: Visual Evidence and the Law in *Call Northside 777*', *Yale Journal of Law and the Humanities* 13, no. 2 (2001): 329–90, at 386–7.

[28] Richard Serwin, 'Visual Jurisprudence', *New York Law School Law Review* 57, no. 1 (2012): 11–40, at 14. In Rebecca Tushnet, 'Worth a Thousand Words: The Images of Copyright', *Harvard Law Review*

Consumption of visual information in motion occurs faster, more viscerally, and with a perception of increased understanding.[29] Consider the difference between reading a book and seeing a movie based upon the book. Readers must imagine scenery, characters, and events. Conversely, little imagination is required of viewers when presented with images that have been selected by the director. The director's vision may be more expansive than receiving information solely through words. When this effect occurs in the courtroom, counsel and the court experience what Delage refers to as 'the richness of inscribing film into a judicial process'.[30] For these reasons, taking advantage of multimodal learning should be foremost for counsel when structuring the trial narrative.

Domestic criminal prosecutions in America incorporated images hesitantly at first and more often as the twentieth century progressed.[31] International criminal prosecutions incorporated image-based evidence from the outset, in part because the technology was more commonplace, but primarily because the task of the tribunals was more expansive than that of domestic courts. Judges were not hearing about isolated events in one location but rather crimes of epic proportions that frequently crossed national boundaries and for which words were not enough.[32] Images have fundamental importance in international criminal justice.[33] They are advantageous because counsel can show the court the actual scene or event, rather than relying upon what might be imagined solely from *viva voce* evidence.[34]

Images are an attractive tool for storytelling, especially considering the intimacy they can evoke and their production of a common experience or response.[35] Through their selection of evidence, counsel in effect tell the court about their case

125, no. 3 (2012): 683–759, at 691, the author asserts that pictures can trigger emotions more reliably than words can, are processed more quickly, and are easier to remember.

[29] Sherwin, Feigenson, and Spiesel (n 17) 156; Porter (n 17) 1752.

[30] Christian Delage, *Caught on Camera: Film in the Courtroom from the Nuremberg Trials to the Trials of the Khmer Rouge* (Philadelphia: University of Pennsylvania Press, 2014), 5.

[31] The first documented US jury trial involving photographic evidence occurred in 1859; Sainato (n 21) 39. Photographs and other technically produced images are now commonly used in American courtrooms. Jennifer Mnookin, 'The Image of Truth: Photographic Evidence and the Power of Analogy', *Yale Journal of Law and the Humanities* 10, no. 1 (1998): 1–74, at 2–4. This would apply to most developed countries.

[32] Lindsay Freeman, 'Digital Evidence and War Crimes Prosecutions: The Impact of Digital Technologies on International Criminal Investigations and Trials', *Fordham International Law Journal* 41, no. 2 (2018): 283–335, at 298.

[33] They serve as evidence of atrocities, tools for media reporting, and outreach materials used in international criminal justice. Immi Tallgren, 'Come and See? The Power of Images and International Criminal Justice', *International Criminal Law Review* 17 (2017): 259–80, at 263.

[34] Susan Sontag, an American writer and filmmaker said of photographs generally, 'Photographs furnish evidence. Something we hear about, but doubt, seems proven when we're shown a photograph of it.' Susan Sontag, *On Photography* (New York: Farrar, Straus, and Giroux, 1979), 5.

[35] Silbey suggests that, 'We make sense of a unique past recorded on film by situating it in a shared present. In this way, making sense of what is recorded in photographs or film justifies a communal judgment of guilt (and punishment) or innocence (and absolution).' Jessica Silbey, 'Evidence Verité and the Law of Film', *Cardozo Law Review* 31 (2010): 1257–99, at 1265.

through a complex version of storytelling. Viewers become voyeurs, studying images that reveal private, intimate, and disturbing scenes, and become unexpected witnesses to events that deeply affected the parties portrayed. As Tallgren notes, images of '[p]ain, suffering, and horror send captivating messages . . . '[36] The value of images is their ability to bring into the present that which might otherwise be absent.[37]

There appears to be a relationship between viewing an image and belief in its content because content impacts interpretation. For example, an image with aesthetic appeal may generate a greater sense of understanding and acceptance, leading to increased belief.[38] Cognitive psychologists assert that understanding what we see, hear, or read is essential to forming a belief, and vividness and emotional response to what is depicted enhances our belief in the truth of the images.[39] Seeing and simultaneously experiencing images engenders a perception of verisimilitude, even if what is depicted may not be accurate or true.[40] Images capture and frame the outside world and bring it before the court for consideration. They may however prove to be equivocal in meaning, causing viewers to assign truth to their content, whether justified or not.[41] This is more problematic if the image has struck an emotive chord because once there is an emotional basis for belief, viewers are less likely to be swayed by the urgings of opposing counsel to adopt a different interpretation.[42]

There can be little quarrel with the proposition that images are powerful tools of persuasion, especially given the tendency to believe what is shown.[43] One of the benefits of using images for the purposes of proof is that images are able to provide information globally, with greater efficiency than words alone. Conversely, one of the interpretive dangers is that untrained viewers may be inclined to fill in any missing parts so that the image makes more sense.[44] But untrained viewers are not equipped to properly interpret and understand all image content. The willingness to fill in visual information gaps illustrates the paradox between the considerable education required to learn to read words versus the absence of any training in

[36] Tallgren (n 33) 266.

[37] Emma Sandon, 'Law and Film', in *Arcs of Global Justice*, edited by Margaret deGuzman and Diane Amann (New York: OUP, 2018), 501–20.

[38] Sherwin (n 28) 31–2.

[39] Sainato (n 21) 44–7; Sherwin (n 28) 28.

[40] Sherwin notes studies that have shown that the use photographs at trial significantly increases the conviction rate compared to when no photos are shown (up to 38% from only 8.8%). Sherwin (n 28) 30. See also David Bright and Jane Goodman-Delahunty, 'Gruesome Evidence and Emotion: Anger, Blame, and Jury Decision-Making', *Law and Human Behavior* 30 (2006): 183–202, at 186–9; Yvonne McDermott, Alexa Koenig, and Daragh Murray, 'Open Source Information's Blind Spot', *Journal of International Criminal Justice* 19, no. 1 (2021): 85–106, at 99.

[41] Mnookin (n 31) 65.

[42] Richard Sherwin, 'Visual Literacy for the Legal Profession', *Journal of Legal Education* 68, no. 1 (2018): 55–63, at 58–9.

[43] This topic is more fully addressed in Chapter 5.

[44] Porter (n 17) 1753.

how to read images.[45] In the judicial context, the naïve belief that all images can be understood correctly without assistance can lead to erroneous interpretations and injustice. Further, psychologists have found that perception and interpretation of images can be significantly affected by context; more specifically, the tendency to see what we expect to see (observer effects) and the belief that we have always seen or known something once we know it to be true (hindsight bias).[46] Semi-legible images may heighten susceptibility to these cognitive biases.[47]

Image-based evidence can reveal, circumvent, or hide the truth. Perspective, selective recording and editing, and other technical issues can lead viewers away from the truth. Naïve realism, the belief that image-based evidence is more informative than it really is, posits that once we comprehend what we see, we tend to believe it.[48] Images provide both a structure to interpret them and a reminder of the key facts relevant to making an appropriate decision, yet an image cannot show the broader social, legal, and political context that gave rise to incidents depicted.[49] Experience has shown that images should be carefully scrutinized to test whether they stand for the proposition the tendering party urges upon the court.[50] For example, watching video in real-time will often deprive viewers of much needed detail,[51] whereas frame-by-frame analysis provides a more salient environment to probe deeper into each image.[52] Visual literacy gained by education and experience is needed to adequately understand images and to discern their truth.[53] Sight alone does not equate to visual literacy but is a necessary precondition for it.

3. Storytelling: Constructing a Visual Trial Narrative

Criminal trials and the imposition of punishment serve powerful pedagogical and expressivist roles, where public exposition of criminality and the imposition of punishment can both shame and stigmatize.[54] Quintessentially, this dramaturgical

[45] ibid. On this point, Mnookin and West urge caution, asserting that visual evidence relies on a kind of illusion, '... a willingness to ignore the mechanisms by which visual evidence is made, shaped, and constructed'. See Mnookin and West (n 27) 334.

[46] Jennifer Mnookin, 'Semi-Legibility and Visual Evidence: An Initial Exploration', *Law, Culture and the Humanities* 10, no. 1 (2014): 43–65, at 63–4.

[47] Mnookin defines semi-legible visual evidence as evidence that is neither entirely legible nor impossible to read. Understanding it requires effort and sometimes expertise. ibid 47–8.

[48] Richard Sherwin, 'Manifesto for Visual Legal Realism', *Loyola of Los Angeles Law Review* 40, no. 2 (2007): 719–44, at 726.

[49] David Tait, 'Rethinking the Role of the Image in Justice: Visual Evidence and Science in the Trial Process', *Law, Probability and Risk* 6, no. 1-4 (2007): 311–18, at 313; Hedi Viterbo, 'Seeing Torture Anew: Transnational Reconceptualization of State Torture and Visual Evidence', *Stanford Journal of International Law* 50, no. 2 (2014): 281–318, at 283.

[50] Jessica Silbey, 'Images in/of Law', *New York Law School Law Review* 57, no. 1 (2012): 171–84, at 176.

[51] Real-time refers to watching video in a motion format that approximates the actual passage of time of the event, rather than watching the images one at a time.

[52] van Weelden and van Charldorp (n 22) 29–30.

[53] Mootz (n 21) 67.

[54] Mark Drumbl, *Atrocity, Punishment, and International Law* (Cambridge: CUP, 2007), 17.

process facilitates storytelling wherein the prosecution presents its case as a complex narrative of the events and characters that gave rise to the crimes alleged.[55] Storytelling is an integral method of proof in criminal prosecutions though the rules of evidence constrain the telling within legal bounds.[56] Immanent in this process are considerations of how best to tell the story in court, appreciating that the learning curve may be steep and that the manner in which a case is presented has epistemic significance.[57] Prosecutors and defence counsel must consider how to utilize available evidence to present a logical, linear, informative, and interesting story.[58] This is especially important for an audience with limited or no knowledge of the case facts.[59] Presenting evidence is not merely an exposition of facts for later use; it is the weaving of a compelling narrative that sets up themes to be explored and integrated into final arguments for the court's consideration.

Image-based evidence is a key component of most complex cases and has proven to be an integral element in the strategy of persuasion.[60] It helps tell a powerful story to draw in and emotionally engage the court.[61] Visual storytelling efficiently delivers content and sets the stage for interpretation and critique.[62] But counsel must consider the context in which the images were obtained and their intended purpose. They must also consider whether everyone will see the same thing, whether an expert witness is necessary to interpret and narrate the images, whether multiple interpretations are available, and whether the probative value of the images outweighs their prejudicial effect.

It is folly to use image-based evidence simply because it exists. There must be a point in introducing it, whether to advance the narrative, to aid in answering an issue in the case, or to advance the search for the truth.[63] It should be used as part of the prosecution's narrative to corroborate, contradict, or call into question the evidence of eyewitnesses, bearing in mind the obligation to fairly present their case. An eyewitness may give an account that is corroborated or contradicted by

[55] I do not use the word 'story' in a pejorative sense. All cases tell a story, even if the story is horrific. Osiel posits that the prosecution narrative is one of morality play while the defence offers a tragedy for consumption. Neither case can be pegged so narrowly in my view. See Mark Osiel, *Mass Atrocity, Collective Memory, and Law* (New Brunswick: Transaction Publishers, 1997), 3.

[56] Stahn (n 11) 260–1, 289–92.

[57] Stahn notes that the content of a criminal trial is informed by legal storytelling, which serves to give an abstract argument feeling. Carsten Stahn, 'Legacy in International Criminal Justice', in *Arcs of Global Justice*, edited by Margaret deGuzman and Diane Amann (New York: OUP, 2018), 271–85; Stahn (n 11) 15, 160–1, 260–1.

[58] Research has shown that mock jurors understand evidence better when it is presented in chronological order. Sainato (n 21) 46–7.

[59] ICC prosecutors have a significant advantage in that the Trial Chamber typically has a reasonable command of some of the prosecution evidence due to pre-trial applications and rulings, in contrast with domestic adverserial courts which typically have limited knowledge of the prosecution's case.

[60] Tait (n 49) 312.

[61] Silbey (n 35) 1289–90.

[62] Sherwin (n 28) 16.

[63] Naomi Mezey, 'The Image Cannot Speak for Itself: Film, Summary Judgment, and Visual Literacy', *Valparaiso University Law Review* 48, no. 1 (2013): 1–40, at 17.

image-based evidence, thus impacting the theories presented by counsel. Seeing an event from different perspectives and vantage points can assist in evaluating what occurred. Images can shine a light on details that might otherwise suffer from a crisis of credulity when the only proponent of those details is an interested party. Defence counsel may similarly utilize visual evidence to advance their narrative and challenge the prosecution's theory.

Given the multi-perspectival depictions of events in some international criminal prosecutions, where images may come from investigators, police, military personnel, human rights groups, combatants, and victims, image-based evidence allows investigators, counsel, and the court to evaluate the narrative put forth by the parties from different vantage points. This may lend credibility to one version of events over another or lead to the development of a new version. Claims of justification for lethal shootings by police and military personnel are brought into question when observers and victims record these conflicts and share them with the public, the media, and human rights organizations, potentially corroborating the claims of authorities, discounting them, or showing a different perspective.[64] Setting aside prevaricating witnesses who are determined to obfuscate the truth, honest witnesses can legitimately have different yet seemingly valid perspectives of the same event. Eyewitnesses often provide as many versions of the event as there are eyewitnesses. This makes the role of counsel doubly important when incorporating image-based evidence into a cohesive, logical, and evaluative narrative for the court.

Counsel may use image-based evidence for multifarious purposes, sometimes to ascertain the truth, other times to obscure it. The defence, whose duty is to advance the interests of the defendant by providing an effective defence, may launch counter-narratives, and may not always be interested in presenting the complete truth because the truth may not tend to lessen the perceived accountability of their client.[65] So too might an unscrupulous prosecutor, focused on winning at all costs, use image-based evidence to unfairly support the prosecution's version of the truth. Moreover, prosecutors may use upsetting images for the primary purpose of engendering strong emotional reactions from the court, which would be inappropriate and contrary to their obligation to present their case fairly, and to ensure that the probative value of image-based evidence outweighs its prejudicial effect.

When counsel proffer varied or competing interpretations of image-based evidence, the court must decide which interpretation is tenable and most consistent with other reliable evidence. One would be naïve to believe that video images of an event, even multi-perspectival, can tell the whole story. Each camera view shows

[64] Jay Aronson, McKenna Cole, Alex Hauptmann, Dan Miller, and Bradley Samuels, 'Reconstructing Human Rights Violations Using Large Eyewitness Collections: The Case of Euromaidan Protester Deaths', *Journal of Human Rights Practice* (2018): 1–20, at 2.

[65] Set out for the ICC in the *Code of Professional Conduct for Counsel*, Arts. 13–15. See also Stahn (n 11) 294–7.

only what occurred within its field of view for as long as the camera recorded. We do not know what happened before or after the camera recorded its footage or whether the camera captured all that matters. Generally, the more recordings available from different vantage points and sources, the more reliably the court will be able to assess the events portrayed, after considering the disparate interpretations offered by the parties.[66] Using image-based evidence as proof requires an honest accounting of what happened before and after the recording as well as what occurred outside the field of view, thereby acknowledging the importance of context. Images supplement the telling of the story, but rarely do they capture the entire story. These issues must be considered by counsel when constructing their trial narrative.

3.1 The Nuremberg Trial: Pictorial Depiction of the Holocaust

The Nuremberg trial prosecutors determined that it was neither feasible nor advisable to attempt to convey to the International Military Tribunal for Nuremberg (IMT) the horrors of the Holocaust by words and documents alone. Though there was considerable pressure to call Holocaust survivors to the witness stand, Chief Prosecutor Jackson largely rejected that approach, preferring instead to base the prosecution primarily upon an objective presentation of overwhelming evidence without resort to overt emotional pandering.[67] Without imprinting images upon the minds of the judges, the prosecution risked fostering a cognitive dissonance wherein the atrocities being described orally and reflected in Nazi documents might not fully correspond with the seemingly dystopian events that actually transpired.

Understanding the tandem need to create a historical record and educate the IMT judges, the American War Department sent a directive to US Army Signal Corps officials to obtain 'an immediate and complete coverage, by motion pictures and still pictures, of atrocities, enemy prisoners of war, concentration camps and persons who were there at the time of liberation'.[68] The result was the approximately one-hour long film entitled *Nazi Concentration Camps*, which begins with the following statement:[69]

[66] Aronson, Cole, Hauptmann, Miller, and Samuels (n 64) 2–3.

[67] Freeman (n 32) 299. Survivor testimony was presented but in a limited way compared to the Eichmann trial. I use the word 'objectively' advisedly as there is considerable subjectivity involved in images, as will be discussed in Chapters 3 and 4.

[68] Cited in Delage (n 30) 49.

[69] US Army, 'Nazi Concentration Camps' (1945), https://archive.org/details/nazi_concentration_camps_mp4.

AUGUST 28, 1945

THIS IS AN OFFICIAL DOCUMENTARY REPORT COMPILED FROM FILMS MADE BY MILITARY PHOTOGRAPHERS SERVING WITH THE ALLIED ARMIES AS THEY ADVANCED INTO GERMANY. THE FILMS WERE MADE PURSUANT TO AN ORDER BY GENERAL DWIGHT D. EISENHOWER, SUPREME COMMANDER, ALLIED EXPEDITIONARY FORCES.

ROBERT H. JACKSON
UNITED STATES
CHIEF OF COUNSEL

A map of Europe is shown with the location of dozens of concentration camps and prisons, while the narrator states, 'These are the locations of the largest concentration and prison camps maintained throughout Germany and occupied Europe under the Nazi regime. This film report, covering a representative group of such camps, illustrates the general conditions which prevailed.' Thereafter, images from twelve concentration camps and prisons are shown. Excepting statements made by an American prisoner of war, a Royal Air Force officer describing the liberation of Bergen-Belsen, and a German physician who was a prisoner at Belsen, only the narrator speaks. The images are deeply disturbing and capture only a fraction of the horror that transpired in the camps, yet they attempt to reflect, as much as could be done in film, the historicity of Nazi atrocities.[70]

To understand the epistemic value of the *Nazi Concentration Camps* film and other films shown, it is important to contextualize the purposes of the Nuremberg trial, which had a mission broader than just determining whether the defendants were guilty of the charges they faced. Prosecutors needed to document Nazi atrocities for the historical record and inform the world of what had taken place. *Nazi Concentration Camps* introduced the use of film in a courtroom as a method of communicating the magnitude of the atrocities under investigation in an unforgettable and evocative manner, in an attempt to both represent and judge the horrors of the Holocaust.[71] Film was effectively used as a form of testimony.[72]

Consider the strategic decision on the part of the prosecution to show *Nazi Concentration Camps* in the opening days of the trial. It served to fix in everyone's minds the indisputable legal and historical significance of the case, and to set the

[70] There is academic debate about whether these images were able to effectively communicate the enormity of the trauma suffered by the prisoners. See Sandon (n 37) 501–20.

[71] Lawrence Douglas, *The Memory of Judgment: Making Law and History in the Trials of the Holocaust* (New Haven: Yale University Press, 2001), 5, 28. Stahn describes the showing of this film as one of the breaking points in the trial. Stahn (n 57) 271–85.

[72] Peter Burke, *Eyewitnessing: The Use of Images as Historical Evidence* (London: Reaktion Books, 2019), 189.

stage for the evidence to follow. In his Opening Speech, Chief Prosecutor Jackson said:[73]

> We will show you these concentration camps in motion pictures, just as the Allied armies found them when they arrived, and the measures General Eisenhower had to take to clean them up. Our proof will be disgusting and you will say I have robbed you of your sleep. But these are the things which have turned the stomach of the world and set every civilized hand against Nazi Germany.
>
> Germany became one vast torture chamber. Cries of its victims were heard round the world and brought shudders to civilized people everywhere. I am one who received during this war most atrocity tales with suspicion and scepticism. But the proof here will be so overwhelming that I venture to predict not one word I have spoken will be denied. These defendants will only deny personal responsibility or knowledge.

No words, no German documents about planning, carrying out, and tallying up the Final Solution could be as evocative as the images the IMT was shown in this and other films. Non-fictional images can be met with incredulity when they present incredible images, as must have been the case for the images shown of the concentration camps.[74] By showing these films, the prosecution set the stage for a 'collective gaze' on the images, thereby bringing the force of the present to bear on the past, creating a narrative that made judgement possible.[75]

Nazi Concentration Camps was shown to the IMT on 29 November 1945, the fifth day of trial.[76] Not only were the Nazi atrocities unprecedented, aside from any personal involvement in World War I or World War II, most people had never been exposed to images as powerful as those shown in the film.[77] What was shown was truly novel and crucial to the prosecution's didactic mission in educating the IMT and the world audience about the facts of the case; it also reflected the pedagogic nature of the prosecution.[78] Thomas Dodd, Executive Counsel to the American prosecution team, articulated the reason for showing the film thusly, '... this film which we offer represents in a brief and unforgettable form an explanation of what

[73] Robert Jackson, 'Opening Speech for the Prosecution at the Nuremberg Trials, November 21, 1945', in *Historical Dictionary of the 1940s*, edited by James Ryan and Leonard Schlup (New York: Routledge, 2006).

[74] Tallgren (n 33) 271–2.

[75] Silbey (n 35) 1271.

[76] Christian Delage, 'Bringing History into the Present Through Film: An Historian in the Archives of Nuremberg', *CINEASTE* (Winter 2011): 34–9.

[77] Douglas describes it as, '... creating an irrefutable imprint upon the mind, a trauma of sight'. Lawrence Douglas, 'Film as Witness: Screening Nazi Concentration Camps Before the Nuremberg Tribunal', *Yale Law Journal* 105, no. 2 (1995): 449–82, at 473.

[78] 'On no occasion should film get in the way of knowledge of the politics of concentration and extermination. Rather it was supposed to allow everyone, inside and outside the courtroom, to begin to understand it.' Delage (n 30) 82.

the words "concentration camp" imply . . . '[79] This approach utilized the camera as a mechanism through which the prosecution could reconstruct the past and situate it in the present.[80]

Nazi Concentration Camps was not the only film shown during the Nuremberg trial. The Nazis also created their own filmic record, which Chief Prosecutor Jackson referred to in his Opening Speech:[81]

> We will not ask you to convict these men on the testimony of their foes. There is no count in the Indictment that cannot be proved by books and records. The Germans were always meticulous record keepers, and these defendants had their share of the Teutonic passion for thoroughness in putting things on paper. Nor were they without vanity. They arranged frequently to be photographed in action. We will show you their own films. You will see their own conduct and hear their own voices as these defendants re-enact for you, from the screen, some of the events in the course of the conspiracy.

The American prosecution team also showed a film entitled *Original German Film (8 mm) of the Atrocities Against the Jews*, which in contrast to the Signal Corps film showed the actual infliction of violence against helpless victims. Depicted are naked and half-naked women being chased through streets and others being subjected to various indignities. The film is one minute long, created by the SS during the liquidation of a ghetto, and was used as an example of how the SS conducted its operations upon the civilian population. It represents an early example of films made by defendants being used against them at trial. Soviet prosecutors showed *Film Documents on the Atrocities of the German Fascist Invaders*, which showed women in their bunks at Birkenau and children showing their tattoos to liberating forces.[82] Other films shown included *The Nazi Plan*, containing excerpts from Nazi propaganda and newsreel films showing long-term planning and war preparation as the Nazis gained power; *Destruction of the Art of Museums of National Culture Perpetrated on the Territory of the USSR*; and *U.S. Army Film of Materials That Were Found in Reichsbank Vaults, Taken in Frankfurt When the Allied Forces Captured That City*.[83] The use of filmic evidence in the Nuremberg trial allowed counsel and the court to view, analyse, and judge the crimes charged.[84]

[79] *Trial of the Major War Criminals Before the International Military Tribunal, Nuremberg*, Volume II, 14 November 1945–1 October 1946, proceedings of 29 November 1945, 431–2.

[80] Silbey (n 26) 30.

[81] Jackson (n 73).

[82] Douglas (n 71) 67–9; Delage (n 30) 97–8.

[83] Delage (n 30) 275; Samantha Greenfield, 'Social Media Platforms: Preserving Evidence of International Crimes', *International Comparative, Policy Ethics Law Review* 2, no. 3 (2019): 821–48, at 831–2.

[84] Delage (n 76) 36.

Viewers interpret images through their own lens, armed with the knowledge and experience they have at that moment. It follows that without prior visualization of Nazi atrocities, the showing of *Nazi Concentration Camps* would have been very powerful for all observers including the IMT judges.[85] This evidence was presented for the pedagogic purpose of informing the IMT, as much as images could, of the enormity of what the Nazis had done.[86] Images such as these do not lose power over time and thus it would be erroneous to conclude that powerful images would be less cogent today given the widespread visualization of violence in the news and popular culture. The polysemic nature of photographic and video images helps to challenge the suggestion that images lose their capacity to shock.[87] It is one thing to see powerful images that have no connection to viewers, yet quite another when viewers are charged with the responsibility of considering them in the context of a trial.

In the Nuremberg trial, the images helped counsel and the court develop an understanding of the fragility and mortality of human life within their confined juridical setting.[88] The images were so independently evocative, neither the *viva voce* evidence of victims nor perpetrators could have dislodged their truth.[89] While the filmic evidence spoke more graphically than witnesses ever could, the film itself could not be cross examined.[90] The admissibility of powerful images such as *Nazi Concentration Camps* in modern-day atrocity prosecutions would be contingent upon successfully undergoing a probative value versus prejudicial effect analysis.[91]

Powerful images can impact everyone in the courtroom.[92] Shown early in the Nuremberg trial, they would have served as a visceral lens through which the entire

[85] Observers in the courtroom noted that the judges were silent after the film concluded and left the courtroom without formally adjourning court for the day. Susan Twist, 'Evidence of Atrocities or Atrocious Use of Evidence: The Controversial Use of Atrocity Film at Nuremberg', *Liverpool Law Review* 26 (2005): 267–302, at 280; Stephan Landsman, *Crimes of the Holocaust: The Law Confronts Hard Cases* (Philadelphia: University of Pennsylvania Press, 2005), 26.

[86] Writing about atrocious images of evil inflicted by humans upon other humans, Sontag notes the power that images have to shock and haunt viewers. Susan Sontag, *Regarding the Pain of Others* (New York: Farrar, Straus, and Giroux, 2003), 115. As Delage eloquently states, '... the presence in court of filmic traces of the acts being tried before the judges lends to the reconstitution of the past a powerful effect of cinematic realism tinted with the foreignness of time gone by'. Delage (n 30) 244. Douglas notes that, 'To view *Nazi Concentration Camps* today gives an imperfect idea of what the tribunal saw fifty years ago. It was novel then—the atrocities shown.' Douglas (n 71) 27.

[87] Sontag (n 86) 23; Judith Butler, 'Photography, War, Outrage', *PMLA* 120, no. 3 (2005): 822–7, at 823–5; Aoife Duffy, 'Bearing Witness to Atrocity Crimes: Photography and International Law', *Human Rights Quarterly* 40 (2018): 776–814, at 779.

[88] Butler (n 87) 825.

[89] The images also served to militate against anticipated challenges from revisionists. Landsman (n 85) 27.

[90] Twist (n 85) 270–1.

[91] While Art. 69(3) of the *Rome Statute* permits the Chamber to receive relevant evidence for the determination of the truth, Art. 69(4) provides for the weighing of probative value and prejudicial effect in respect of any piece of evidence when assessing trial fairness. Inflammatory images could affect trial fairness absent direct and substantial relevance to the counts before the court. A further issue would be whether the prosecution can produce witnesses who could be cross examined on their content.

[92] In jurisdictions that utilize juries, some jurors have been diagnosed with post-traumatic stress disorder and other conditions because of images they were required to view in court. Michelle Lonergan,

case was viewed, offering a view of ground zero, documenting atrocities for the historical record and for juridical proof.[93] Elie Wiesel, in *Night*, referred to concentration camps starkly as 'factories of death'.[94] *Nazi Concentration Camps* helped to visualize that written description.[95] By 1945, aside from personal wartime experience, most people would have had little or no exposure to images depicting extreme violence and cruelty and so the images shown at the Nuremberg trial would have been particularly disturbing and effective.[96] These films turned courtroom viewers into virtual witnesses. By the time these images were shown at the Eichmann trial in 1961, they occupied a less prominent role having been shown two months into the proceedings, but they still had importance in illustrating Eichmann's control over Jewish concentration camp prisoners.[97] The images also helped to create a more fulsome historical record.[98] Years after Nuremberg, they still had power—Chief Prosecutor Hausner wrote that after *Nazi Concentration Camps* was shown, the judges had tears in their eyes and they rose abruptly and left the courtroom.[99]

3.2 Damning Images and Defendants

Though consideration of the impact of powerful images is usually focused on the court, the defendant's reaction, if any, to such images can have a subconscious effect on the courtroom participants. Even though the Nuremberg defendants were

Marie-Ève Leclerc, Mélanie Descamps, Sereena Pigeon, and Alain Brunet, 'Prevalence and Severity of Trauma and Stressor-Related Symptoms Among Jurors: A Review', *Journal of Criminal Justice* 47 (2016): 51–61; Makiko Haragi, Rutsuko Yamaguchi, Tsuyoshi Okuhara, and Takahiro Kiuchi, 'Questionnaire Survey of a Mock Jury on Their Impressions of Medical-Legal Illustrations Aimed at Reducing Trauma and PTSD of Jurors', *Journal of Visual Communications in Medicine* 43, no. 2 (2020): 67–75. While images have cogent value as a didactic tool, there may be an intangible price to be paid by viewers for the education received.

93 Mnookin and West refer to 'ground zero' as the location where a recorded event occurred. Mnookin and West (n 27) 385–6.

94 Elie Wiesel, *Night* (New York: Bantam, 1960) 64.

95 Referring to images of concentration camps, Sontag wrote, 'Nothing I have seen—in photographs or in real life—ever cut me as sharply, deeply, instantaneously. Indeed, it seems plausible to me to divide my life into two parts, before I saw those photographs (I was twelve) and after . . . When I looked at those photographs, something broke. Some limit had been reached, and not only that of horror . . . '. Sontag (n 34) 17–18.

96 Even though my Dutch parents were in the Netherlands for all of World War II and had ample exposure to German invaders taking prisoners, abusing the civilian population, appropriating property, and bombing cities and other strategic locations, they had no conception of the true extent of Nazi atrocities.

97 Twist (n 85) 296.

98 The Eichmann trial marked a resurgence in the value of survivor testimony with over 100 survivors giving evidence. Stahn (n 11) 302. Corroborating their personal experience with filmic evidence was an excellent use of image-based evidence.

99 Hausner preferred the use of *viva voce* evidence over film as he believed that the testimony of survivors would help people visualize the tragedy of the Holocaust. Though there were historical reasons for recording survivor testimony, its lasting impact may be more transient than images. Gideon Hausner, *Justice in Jerusalem* (New York: Schocken Books, 1966), 348.

charged with the worst crimes imaginable, in the prisoners' dock, they looked like ordinary men wearing suits, not the monsters their conduct would suggest. In his Opening Speech, Chief Prosecutor Jackson said:[100]

> In the prisoners' dock sit twenty-odd broken men. Reproached by the humiliation of those they have led, almost as bitterly as by the desolation of those they have attacked, their personal capacity for evil is forever past. It is hard now to perceive in these miserable men as captives the power by which as Nazi leaders they once dominated much of the world and terrified most of it.

Chief Prosecutor Ferencz described the Einsatzgruppen defendants as 'very ordinary looking men'.[101] Eichmann Chief Prosecutor Hausner said that when the defendant first appeared in court, he 'almost felt like searching him for fangs and claws', noting that without his uniform, he looked 'paltry and insignificant' as did all of the top Nazis that had been tried.[102] It is difficult to dehumanize a defendant when his actual appearance in the courtroom is rather pedestrian.[103] To use a domestic example, one of the reasons for the many conspiracy theories surrounding the assassination of US President Kennedy in 1963 is that many people could not accept that Lee Harvey Oswald, a commoner, could kill a king.[104] It is in part to address the cognitive dissonance that sometimes exists between the crimes being tried and the appearance of the defendant in the courtroom that image-based evidence finds a foothold. Beyond proof of the crimes themselves, this dissonant gap can be expunged with powerful images.

An interesting dynamic sometimes occurs in a courtroom when images are shown which depict the defendant during the commission of the crime, before or after it was committed, or the aftermath of the crime itself. Observers look not just at the images on the screen but also at the defendant's reaction to them. Though not tangible in the sense that it becomes explicit evidence, the court cannot help but subconsciously note such visible reactions.[105] Some defendants steadfastly deny

[100] Jackson (n 73).

[101] Benjamin Ferencz, 'Opening Statement at Nuremberg', *Trial of the Major War Criminals*, vol. IV, 494.

[102] Hausner (n 99) 309–10.

[103] Though not addressing the Holocaust prosecutions specifically, Allot paints an apt picture when he writes, 'Feeble old men and their seedy subordinates shuffle into the courtroom, shrunken figures bearing no physical relationship to the physical scale of suffering for which they are responsible.' Philip Allot, *The Health of Nations: Society and Law Beyond the State* (Cambridge, CUP, 2002), 67. See also Sofia Stolk, 'A Sophisticated Beast? On the Construction of an "Ideal" Perpetrator in the Opening Statements of International Criminal Trials', *European Journal of International Law* 29, no. 3 (2018): 677–701, at 696.

[104] Vincent Bugliosi, *Reclaiming History: The Assassination of President John F. Kennedy* (New York: W.W. Norton and Company, Inc., 2007), xxvii.

[105] 'Even when the defendant does not admit to his crimes, his reactions when confronted with the footage constitute a sort of avowal that jeopardizes his chances of acquittal... They can undermine spurious arguments from the defence as well as serve as an instrument for elucidating the truth.' Delage

Figure 1.1 German war crimes defendants in the prisoners' dock at the Nuremberg trial on 20 November 1945. Among them are Herman Goering and Rudolf Hess (front left). (Photo by Mondadori Portfolio by Getty Images)

viewers the satisfaction of any visible reaction but at times they may be unable to do so, and their reaction can be palpable. Such responses are not uncommon as defendants are not just viewing the event, they are reliving it. Those observations can be instructive and useful in cross examination and can serve as intangible evidence of guilt. This occurred during the Nuremberg trial, where participants and observers looked for some sort of response or non-verbal acknowledgement from the defendants regarding the horrors depicted.[106] The behaviour of the defendants was observed and documented by US Army psychologist Capt. Gilbert. Upon showing *Nazi Concentration Camps*, Gilbert noted that while not all defendants had a visible response, some gasped, cried, shuddered, turned away, and issued denials.[107] An example of this is shown in Figure 1.1.

(n 30) 188. Delage notes a high profile 1984 Canadian case wherein a defendant on trial for opening fire in the Quebec National Assembly reportedly 'cracked' upon seeing video of the shooting spree.

[106] Duffy (n 87) 781.

[107] Gustave Gilbert, *Nuremberg Diary* (New York: The New American Library, 1947 (quoting Douglas (n 71) 106–7); Landsman (n 85) 26.

Hermann Göring said, 'And then they showed that awful film, and it just spoiled everything.'[108] Once in the prisoners' dock, the defendants cannot physically hide and their conduct in the dock becomes noteworthy.[109]

4. Common Types of Image-Based Evidence

Whether as a method of proof, for didactic purposes, or to create a historical record, image-based evidence in the form of film, video, and photographs is an integral component in presenting the prosecution's case. It also has significance for the defence as visual evidence may be presented in the defence case to challenge the prosecution's narrative or at least to show a different perspective. The use of filmic evidence in the Nuremberg trial heralded a much more expansive method of presenting the case for the prosecution, an approach that has gained continued favour in the tribunals and courts that followed the IMT.

This section focuses on specific types of image-based evidence that can be used for the purposes of proof and contends that some aspects of complex prosecutions must be presented visually to convey the full data set to the court. It is helpful to first diverge briefly to comment on the value of counsel and the court viewing the *locus in quo* in person.[110] Counsel and the court cannot attend active atrocity crime scenes for reasons of safety and because investigations and decisions to indict defendants take considerable time. Yet there may still be epistemic value for a *locus in quo* visit during the trial to develop a true sense of the location and its features and to fill informational gaps created from *viva voce* evidence that is unclear or lacking in detail.[111]

The International Criminal Tribunal for the former Yugoslavia (ICTY), ICTR, and ICC have occasionally taken advantage of these visits for fact-finding purposes. In *Prosecutor v. Bagilishema*, all three ICTR Trial Chamber judges visited Kibuye Prefecture in Rwanda '... in order to see the locations of certain alleged events of relevance in the case, and thus to better appreciate the evidence to be adduced during the trial'.[112] This was the first *locus in quo* visit undertaken by an ICTR Trial Chamber. The ICTY Trial Chamber, in *Prosecutor v. Blagojević and Jokić*, conducted a *locus in quo* visit and was able to visualize and confirm witness

[108] Gilbert (n 107) 11.

[109] 'The aim was to force Nazi leaders to acknowledge as their own, in camera and before a court of law, crimes for which they were accountable or responsible. Because of their physical presence in the room, the accused had to accept being seen juxtaposed to the images projected in the courtroom.' Delage (n 30) 108.

[110] Latin for 'the place in which' and referring to the scene of a crime or event. 'locus in quo, n' OED (n 5) accessed 7 August 2023.

[111] Damaška notes the value of judicial visits as a method of gaining information independent of the parties. Mirjan Damaška, *The Faces of Justice and State Authority: A Comparative Approach to the Legal Process* (New Haven: Yale University Press, 1986), 137. See also Combs (n 9) 281–2.

[112] ICTR-95-1A-T, Judgment, 7 June 2001, para. 10.

testimony on several key points.[113] Similar visits have occurred in other ICTR and ICTY cases,[114] as well as in ICC cases.[115]

However, if the prosecution is successful in visualizing locations of interest with image-based evidence, the likelihood of the need for a *locus in quo* visit by the court is reduced. While such visits have epistemic value, they also serve to delay proceedings and present security concerns. For example, in *Prosecutor v. Galić*, in responding to the Prosecution's Motion for the Trial Chamber to Travel to Sarajevo, the Chamber noted the value of being able '. . . to observe certain landmarks and places in order to get a tri-dimensional impression of these locations and to improve its ability to understand and interpret the evidence presented in court about these locations, including evidence which seems to contain contradicting elements'.[116] However, the Chamber also noted the major security measures that would be required and the impossibility of guaranteeing the safety of the Chamber, court staff, counsel, and the defendant. The Chamber noted that it had the substantial benefit of photographs and maps of the locations of interest, relevant video evidence, and eyewitness testimony including witnesses using sketches, such that a *locus in quo* visit was unnecessary.[117]

Despite the value of *locus in quo* visits, they are infrequent events and provide only limited information. The only way to adequately convey to the court what an atrocity crime scene looked like while it was still a crime scene with bodies and other evidence *in situ* is with image-based evidence. This has been essential to atrocity crime prosecutions since Nuremberg.[118] The use of such evidence to display scenes and incident data is the focus in the balance of this section.

[113] IT-02-60-T, Judgment, 17 January 2005, para. 316, n. 1158 and 1159.

[114] *Prosecutor v. Karera*, ICTR-01-74-T, Judgment, 7 December 2007, para. 133; *Prosecutor v. Brdinan*, IT-99-36-T, Judgment, 1 September 2004, para. 614, n. 1556; *Prosecutor v. Strugar*, IT-01-42-T, Judgment, 31 January 2005, para. 316.

[115] *Prosecutor v. Ngudjolo*, ICC-01/04-02/12-3-tENG, Judgment Pursuant to Article 74 of the Statute, 18 December 2012, paras. 68–70; *Prosecutor v. Katanga*, ICC-01/04-01/07, Judgment Pursuant to Article 74 of the Statute, 7 March 2014, paras. 106–108.

[116] IT-98-29-T, Decision on Prosecution's Motion for the Trial Chamber to Travel to Sarajevo, 4 February 2003, para. 8.

[117] ibid paras. 17–19.

[118] In his 7 June 1945 report to President Truman in preparation for the Nuremberg trial, Chief Prosecutor Jackson said, 'We must not forget that when the Nazi plans were boldly proclaimed they were so extravagant that the world refused to take them seriously. Unless we write the record of this movement with clarity and precision, we cannot blame the future if in days of peace it finds incredible the accusatory generalities uttered during the war. We must establish incredible events by credible evidence.' Report from Mr. Justice Jackson, Chief Counsel for the United States in the Prosecution of Axis War Criminals (NARA, RG 226, E 90, B 12, F 126, at 3) (quoting Delage (n 76) 36). Filmic evidence was one of the key components to the credible evidence needed.

4.1 Film, Video, and Photographs

The use of film, video, and photographs as evidence is well established in international criminal prosecutions.[119] Images can constitute a graphic portrayal of what might otherwise be presented by *viva voce* evidence and can transcend their role as evidence of history to become historical themselves.[120] There is often strategic value in using images to supplement testimony and other forms of evidence. Counsel must consider whether still or moving images will be more effective in conveying visual information, when both formats are available.[121] In part, this choice is dependent upon the information sought to be conveyed, as some information is better presented by way of still images, particularly when evaluating detailed image content is critical. Conversely, moving images often engender greater viewer comprehension as they provide certain communicative efficiencies over still images.[122] Studies consistently show that viewers are more able to interpret emotional content when the images are moving, rather than static.[123] Moving images also serve to improve recognition of targeted individuals as the viewer is given a more fluid view of the target.[124]

Film was the primary mode of images in the tribunals until the 1990s when the convenience and technological capability of analogue video replaced it, soon followed by digital video. Video evidence can be obtained from numerous sources, including eyewitnesses, victims, defendants, enemy combatants, broadcast news organizations, and third-party observers such as human rights organizations and other non-governmental organizations (NGOs), and are typically recorded by handheld or tripod mounted video cameras and smartphones. Closed circuit television (CCTV) video may be collected by government organizations, the police, businesses, and private individuals, though rarely in the atrocity crime context, although the destruction of cities in Ukraine by Russian forces may offer CCTV footage of value. CCTV video typically employs mounted cameras, either static or capable of directed movement, that record to a local digital video recorder or to an offsite server.[125] In many domestic jurisdictions, police agencies record video

[119] Film is a thin flexible strip of celluloid, plastic, etc., coated with light-sensitive emulsion that is used in photography and cinematography to record a series of images. Video is a recording of moving images stored on magnetic tape or in digital format. Photographs (still images) can be derived from both film and video. 'film, n' and 'video, n' OED (n 5) accessed 7 August 2023.

[120] Burke (n 72) 29.

[121] If the image was originally captured as a still image (e.g. a single photograph), it must be shown in that format. If the original recording is digital video, single images can be parsed out for display. Still images can also be parsed out from film and analogue video, especially once digitized.

[122] Sherwin (n 42) 57.

[123] Sainato (n 21) 45.

[124] ibid.

[125] Directed movement refers to a camera's ability to pan (left-right), tilt (up-down), and zoom (in-out), as directed by a person or via computer algorithm.

from police vehicle dashcams and body worn cameras, usually uploaded to a cloud storage system.

Images can also be obtained from an aerial vantage point, allowing for a more expansive perspective and the ability to see things not readily discernible from the ground.[126] In recent years, investigators have made considerable use of small, unmanned aircraft systems, commonly called drones. Drones can go where investigators cannot and can obtain excellent quality high-resolution images of scenes, activities, and individuals. They provide not only a live feed but also create a digital record which can be accessed later and used in court.[127] The use of embedded drone images in interactive 360° visual representations in international criminal prosecutions has proven to be valuable.[128]

Commercially available drones used by law enforcement record high definition (HD) video at a minimum of 1,920 pixels of horizontal resolution locally to a small secure digital (SD) card. Most drones record two video streams per camera, one at lower resolution which is transmitted to the pilot on the controller which can be viewed live while flying, and the second is a high-resolution file which is only visible when downloaded from the drone. Drones also record flight telemetry and navigation data which provides tangible proof as to the location of the drone when the video was recorded. Should a drone be compromised by an outside force and crash, it may still be possible to recover video from it. Drones may be audibly undetectable from the ground depending on the height of the aircraft, wind speed, and other ambient noise, giving rise to its use for surveillance purposes as well as recording scenes. Military drones have enhanced capabilities over commercially available versions.[129] Aerial images can also be obtained from cameras in commercial aircraft conducting non-investigative visual surveys, and which may fortuitously have relevance to a criminal investigation.

I conclude this section with a brief word about presentation strategy when video and digital images are used in court. The use of hard copy (printed) digital images and LCD projectors and screens to show video and still images should be avoided due to poor image quality. While a hard copy may be a convenient reference, digital images that are printed on paper lose fine detail that would otherwise be viewable on a high-quality computer monitor or HD presentation screen. By presenting images electronically, greater accessibility can be achieved including the ability to enlarge portions of an image for more detailed examination in court.[130] Further, with

[126] The focus here is on near-earth cameras. Images obtained from remote sensing satellites will be discussed in Section 4.2.

[127] Freeman (n 32) 330.

[128] Discussed in Section 5.1 of Chapter 8.

[129] Email from Deputy Sheriff Scott Kuntz, Dane County Sheriff's Office, Madison, Wisconsin, US, a FAA licensed sUAS pilot, to author (29 March 2020).

[130] Focusing on specific portions of images can increase their impact. Evelyn Marcus, 'The New Razzle Dazzle: Questioning the Propriety of High-tech Audiovisual Displays in Closing Argument', *Vermont Law Review* 30, no. 2 (2006): 361–92, at 382; Frederic Lederer, 'Wired: What We've Learned About Courtroom Technology', *Criminal Justice* 24, no. 4 (2010): 18–25.

annotation software, a witness can visibly mark an image shown on the witness's monitor to point out areas or items of relevance, such markings being visible on all courtroom monitors and capable of being recorded or printed for exhibit purposes. Other platforms such as SMART Board and ELMO Visual Presenter fulfil a similar function. Projecting images with a LCD projector onto a screen guarantees loss of detail and image resolution as the image travels through dust particles in the air and must then contend with screen micro-contours. Additional impediments include the quality of the bulb and lens in the projector, the lighting in the courtroom, and the location of the screen relative to the fact-finders. The hard copy and LCD projection approaches to the presentation of image-based evidence does a significant disservice to the images. Electronic presentation using high-quality monitors and HD presentation screens should be the norm for displaying image evidence.

4.1.1 Application to Atrocity Crime Prosecutions

Given the proliferation of smartphones and other cameras used by eyewitnesses, victims, defendants, enemy combatants, broadcast news organizations, and third-party observers, it is not surprising that video and photographic imagery has featured prominently in atrocity crime prosecutions. It has been a feature in all the tribunals and courts, though for this section I will focus on its use in the ICTY, ICTR, and ICC. This section is not intended to be an exhaustive catalogue of case law as that is well beyond the scope of this book, rather it is designed to illustrate that image-based evidence has taken a firm foothold in atrocity crime prosecutions.

Video and photographic images may be shown as individual exhibits, as part of larger media compilations, or as integral parts of a multimedia presentation. They have been used as evidence to document and establish the crime base of a case or as linkage evidence to tie the defendant to specific incidents.[131] Example of images being used as crime base evidence include the depiction of locations where specific events occurred;[132] the location of mass graves;[133] the presence of

[131] Crime base evidence and linkage evidence are distinctions utilized in international criminal procedure. The former relates to evidence which proves the crime itself, with an emphasis on the crime scene, while the latter focuses on determining the people most responsible for the crime (accountability). Mark Klamberg, *Evidence in International Criminal Trials* (Leiden: Martinus Nijhoff Publishers, 2013), 117–18.

[132] *Prosecutor v. Halilović*, IT-01-48-T, Judgment, 16 November 2005; *Prosecutor v. Bizimungu et al.*, ICTR-99-50-T, Judgment and Sentence, 30 September 2011; *Prosecutor v. Karadzić*, IT-95-5/18-T, Judgment, 24 March 2016.

[133] *Blagojević and Jokić* (n 113); *Prosecutor v. Delić*, IT-04-83-T, Judgment, 15 September 2008; *Prosecutor v. Renzaho*, ICTR-97-31-T, Judgment and Sentence, 14 July 2009; *Prosecutor v. Popović*, IT-05-88-T, Judgment (Volume I), 10 June 2010; *Prosecutor v. Kanyarukiga*, ICTR-2002-78-T, Judgment and Sentence, 1 November 2010; *Prosecutor v. Dordević*, IT-05-87/1-T, Judgment, 23 February 2011; *Prosecutor v. Stanisić and Simatović*, IT-03-69-T, Judgment, 30 May 2013; *Prosecutor v. Gbagbo*, ICC-02/11-01/11-656-Red, Decision on the Confirmation of Charges Against Laurent Gbagbo, 12 June 2014; *Prosecutor v. Ongwen*, ICC-02/04-01/15-1762-Red, Judgment, 4 February 2021.

roadblocks or checkpoints;[134] the presence of weapons;[135] injuries;[136] the identification of people;[137] the identification of vehicles;[138] executions of civilians, opposing soldiers, and prisoners, often recorded by the perpetrators themselves;[139] troop movements;[140] the presence and movement of refugees;[141] people killed by soldiers;[142] Dutch Battalion soldiers being held hostage;[143] combat operations;[144] sniper fire and sniper nests;[145] and the use of and apparent age of child soldiers,[146] amongst other relevant topics.

Example of images being used as linkage evidence include video images of speeches being made by defendants, illustrating the context in which they were made and to show the defendant's apparent status;[147] defendants associating with fellow defendants;[148] and to illustrate that the defendant had a command position.[149] Images may be used to corroborate or challenge *viva voce* evidence.[150]

[134] *Halilović* (n 132); *Prosecutor v. Ngirabatware*, ICTR-99-54-T, Judgment and Sentence, 20 December 2012.

[135] *Halilović* (n 132); *Prosecutor v. Taylor*, SCSL 03-01-T, Judgment, 18 May 2012; *Katanga* (n 115).

[136] *Prosecutor v. Delalić et al.*, IT-96-21-T, Judgment, 16 November 1998; *Katanga* (n 115).

[137] *Katanga* (n 115); *Taylor* (n 135).

[138] *Prosecutor v. Gbagbo*, ICC-02/11-01/11-656-Red, Decision on the Confirmation of Charges Against Laurent Gbagbo, 12 June 2014.

[139] *Prosecutor v. Bagosora et al.*, ICTR-98-41-T, Judgment and Sentence, 18 December 2008; *Prosecutor v. Al-Werfalli*, ICC-01/11-01/17, Warrant for Arrest, 15 August 2017; *Prosecutor v. Gbagbo and Blé Goudè*, ICC-02/11-01/15-1263-Conf-AnxB, Reasons of Judge Henderson, 16 July 2019. A powerful example of this occurred during the *Milosević* trial when during the cross examination of a defence witness, the prosecution introduced a video recording which showed the execution of six men by members of the Scorpions paramilitary unit (part of the MUP) in the aftermath of the Srebrenica massacre. This was done to support the prosecution's theory that Serbia was an active participant in the war in Bosnia, not merely a supporter of the Bosnian Serbs, and to counter the evidence of the witness that no Serbian MUP units were present during the massacre. On the same day, portions of the video were broadcast on Serbian television and helped to change the popular conception of Serbian soldiers. Ivan Zveržhanovski, 'Watching War Crimes: The Srebrenica Video and the Serbian Attitudes to the 1995 Srebrenica Massacre', *Southeast European and Black Sea Studies* 7, no 3 (2007): 417–30, at 424–5. Zveržhanovski opined that using this short video as evidence advanced the mission of the ICTY more than the investigations and trials themselves (at ibid 428).

[140] *Prosecutor v. Bemba*, ICC-01/05-01/08-3343, Judgment Pursuant to Article 74 of the Statute, 21 March 2016.

[141] *Blagojević and Jokić* (n 113); *Delić* (n 133); *Renzaho* (n 133); *Prosecutor v. Perisić*, IT-04-81-T, Judgment, 6 September 2011.

[142] *Blagojević and Jokić* (n 113); *Halilović* (n 132); *Prosecutor v. Haradinaj et al.*, IT-04-84-T, Judgment, 3 April 2008; *Perisić* (n 141); *Popović* (n 133); *Stanisić and Simatović* (n 133).

[143] *Blagojević and Jokić* (n 113); *Perisić* (n 141).

[144] *Stanisić and Simatović* (n 133).

[145] *Prosecutor v. Galić*, IT-98-29-T, Judgment, 5 December 2003; *Prosecutor v. Milosević*, IT-98-29/1-T, Judgment, 12 December 2007; *Karadzić* (n 132).

[146] *Prosecutor v. Lubanga*, ICC-01/04-01/06-2842, Judgment Pursuant to Article 74 of the Statute, 14 March 2012; *Katanga* (n 115).

[147] *Perisić* (n 141); *Lubanga* (n 146); *Karadzić* (n 132); *Gbagbo and Blé Goudè* (n 139).

[148] *Lubanga* (n 146).

[149] *Delalić et al.* (n 136); *Delić* (n 133); *Ngudjolo Chui* (n 115).

[150] *Prosecutor v. Zigiranyirazo*, ICTR-01-73-T, Judgment, 18 December 2008; *Prosecutor v. Nyiramasuhuko et al.*, ICTR-98-42-T, Judgment and Sentence, 24 June 2011; *Prosecutor v. Bemba*, ICC-01/05-01/08-2012, First Decision on the Prosecution and Defence Requests for the Admission of Evidence, 9 February 2012; *Lubanga* (n 146); *Bemba* (n 140).

They may also prove to be helpful in scientific endeavours such as determining bullet, missile, and mortar trajectories.[151]

4.2 Remote Sensing Technology: Geospatial Evidence

Earth observation (EO) technologies generate continually expanding sources of high quality images for use as evidence in international criminal justice.[152] EO satellites are a type of remote sensing technology that is used to acquire information about geography and objects from a distance.[153] They have proven to be remarkable sources of visual information capable of showing significant surface detail.[154] They can show a larger geographic area than drones and can depict locations otherwise inaccessible by ground.[155] EO technologies encompass a broad range of tools for the collection, management, presentation, and analysis of location-based, geographically positioned data.[156] Not only are satellites able to capture visible imagery, some are able to provide infrared images, which can be helpful in tracking the movement of vehicles and people.[157]

Government agencies and military forces have long embraced the use of satellites, unmanned aerial vehicles, and other cutting-edge remote sensing technologies for intelligence gathering and combat strategy.[158] The commercialization of satellite imagery by government agencies and private companies has existed for

[151] *Karadzić* (n 132).

[152] Ray Purdy and Denise Leung, 'Introduction', in *Evidence from Earth Observation Satellites*, edited by Ray Purdy and Denise Leung (Leiden: Martinus Nijhoff Publishers, 2013), 1–8, at 1.

[153] Remote sensing may collect data via active or passive sensors mounted on satellites, manned aircraft, or unmanned aerial vehicles. Theresa Harris, Jonathan Drake, Jessica Wyndham, Susan Wolfinbarger, Stephen Lott, and Michael Lerner, 'Geospatial Evidence in International Human Rights Litigation: Technical and Legal Considerations', *AAAS Scientific Responsibility, Human Rights and Law Program* (2018), doi: 10.1126/srhrl.aau6090, 42. Most EO satellites occupy an orbit of between 500 and 900 km above the earth. Ray Harris, 'Science, Policy and Evidence in EO', in *Evidence from Earth Observation Satellites*, edited by Ray Purdy and Denise Leung (Leiden: Martinus Nijhoff Publishers, 2013), 43–61, at 57.

[154] Very high resolution (VHR) sensors produce images comparable to aerial photographs. Harris (n 153) 51. See also Maureen Williams, 'Satellite Evidence in International Institutions', in *Evidence from Earth Observation Satellites*, edited by Ray Purdy and Denise Leung (Leiden: Martinus Nijhoff Publishers, 2013), 195–216, at 207.

[155] 'International Bar Association Report', *IBA ICL Perspectives: Evidence Matters in ICC Trials* (August 2016) https://www.ibanet.org/document?id=Evidence-matters-in-icc-trials, 19–20.

[156] Harris, Drake, Wyndham, Wolfinbarger, Lott, and Lerner (n 153) 4.

[157] Shaida Johnston, 'Technical Introduction to Satellite EO', in *Evidence from Earth Observation Satellites*, edited by Ray Purdy and Denise Leung (Leiden: Martinus Nijhoff Publishers, 2013), 11–42, at 13. Johnston does not address this type of tracking, but IR has long been used to track heat sources.

[158] Ben Wang, Nathaniel Raymond, Gabrielle Gould, and Isaac Baker, 'Problems from Hell, Solution in the Heavens?: Identifying Obstacles and Opportunities for Employing Geospatial Technologies to Document and Mitigate Mass Atrocities', *Stability: International Journal of Security & Development* 2, no. 3 (2013), 1–18, at 1–2.

many years.[159] These geospatial technologies have also become an important source of evidence in atrocity crime prosecutions, with civilian (and sometimes military) high-resolution satellites being made available to investigators since 1999. For example, satellite imagery has been co-opted for use by NGOs as a method of gathering evidence of atrocity crimes, although its use is somewhat limited due to significant cost, limited availability due to EO commercial precedence requirements, and cloud and ground cover which can be significant geographic and seasonal impediments.[160] Additional limitations impacting EO imagery use include coverage area, image resolution, government restrictions, and ethical (privacy) considerations.[161]

Satellite imagery offers two key types of evidence: the identification of observable objects at a given point in time, and documentation of observable changes in the position and condition of those objects over time.[162] This evidence thereby allows viewers a reconnaissance of both the past and present.[163] Satellite observations can take different *postures* when monitoring a conflict area.[164] The *detection posture* is used by analysts to predict whether threats to civilians exist by identifying signs indicative of amassing ground forces and related infrastructure. During the early stages of atrocities a *deterrence posture* can be utilized, which is designed to warn civilians of pending attacks. Post-atrocity, analysts can assume a *documentation posture* by gathering visual evidence such as images of mass graves, burned structures, and the detritus of conflict. Because satellite images are comprised of digital data, they can be analysed mathematically with Geographic Information Systems (GIS) software, which reveals complex spatial and temporal patterns that even skilled GIS analysts may be unable to discern.[165]

Satellite imagery is not without its potential limitations. Images obtained from EO satellites are more difficult to discern because they show vegetation and other topographic features that can impede comprehension of a scene—in short, they may provide more data than necessary if the goal is merely one of location orientation. Further, while satellites provide valuable visual information, it is at a macro

159 Eya Macauley, 'The Use of EO Technologies in Court by the Office of the Prosecutor of the International Criminal Court', in *Evidence from Earth Observation Satellites*, edited by Ray Purdy and Denise Leung (Leiden: Martinus Nijhoff Publishers, 2013): 217–40, at 240.

160 Wang, Raymond, Gould, and Baker (n 158) 5.

161 Harris, Drake, Wyndham, Wolfinbarger, Lott, and Lerner (n 153) 6–7.

162 Wang et al. define an 'observable' as 'a term for anything contained in the imagery with a distinctive shape and size which may be of interest to the analyst. Examples of these points of interest may include aircraft, ships, tanks, artillery, camps for displaced persons or armed actors, and shelling craters or other evidence of damage.' Wang, Raymond, Gould, and Baker (n 158) 6.

163 Burke (n 72) 192.

164 Wang, Raymond, Gould, and Baker (n 158) 3.

165 Geographic Information Systems are computer systems used for capturing, storing, editing, analysing, and displaying location-based data. They can layer datasets upon other datasets, produce maps, calculate distances between observable features, and perform spatial statistical analysis. Harris, Drake, Wyndham, Wolfinbarger, Lott, and Lerner (n 153) 2, 43.

level and thus evidence at ground level is essential to provide micro data, e.g. to identify responsible parties.

Experts recommend caution when using EO data, citing concerns that it can be manipulated with no possibility of detecting *ex post facto* changes.[166] This is especially pertinent given that satellites do not take conventional pictures but rather capture binary data that is processed to form a picture. The British Institute of International and Comparative Law recommended that standards be adopted regarding the use of satellite data in international courts, and articulated concerns regarding accuracy and variance in interpretation.[167] Other experts recommend that the collection and analysis of satellite data be developed into a structured discipline with established guidelines and procedures, operated by neutral experts.[168] This latter point cannot be overemphasized—the involvement of competent experts utilizing robust operating procedures is essential in reaching an accurate and informed judgement based upon technology generated evidence. Despite its limitations, the potential value offered by satellite images in atrocity crime prosecutions is clear.

4.2.1 Application to Atrocity Crime Prosecutions

Atrocity crime investigations and prosecutions have profited greatly from the evidence that has emerged using high-quality satellite images.[169] These images have provided considerable value to investigators, counsel, and the court because they can be used to conduct a macro analysis of locations, including the depiction of permanent or semi-permanent landform and architectural features, as well as transitory features such as vehicles, equipment, and people. By comparing satellite imagery over time, changes may be discerned which may corroborate ground-based accounts of atrocity crime activity.

By 2010 ICC Office of the Prosecutor (OTP) investigators had commenced discussions with human rights organizations regarding the use of satellite technology to gather evidence for ICC prosecutions.[170] This is reflective of the fact that satellite images are frequently associated with international conflict locations where investigators typically face significant delays in gaining access to sites of interest. As a result, there may be limited or no ability to gain timely aerial images of relevant sites using drones before marked changes have occurred. This contrasts with many

[166] Williams (n 154) 215.

[167] 'Final Report of the BIICL Study Group', *Earth Observation Data in the Legal Sector*, 19 May 2001, 75 (quoting Williams (n 154) 199).

[168] Wang, Raymond, Gould, and Baker (n 158) 15–16.

[169] Elena Radeva, 'The Potential for Computer Vision to Advance Accountability in the Syrian Crisis', *Journal of International Criminal Justice* 19, no. 1 (2021): 131–46, at 132.

[170] Alexa Koenig, Felim McMahon, Nikita Mehandru, and Shikha Bhattacharjee, 'Open Source Fact-Finding in Preliminary Examinations', in *Quality Control in Preliminary Examination*, Vol. 2, edited by Morten Bergsmo and Carsten Stahn (Brussels: Torkel Opsahl Academic EPublisher, 2018), 681–730, at 694–5.

domestic investigations where access to relevant sites often occurs much quicker and with the ability to visually document scenes while they remain relatively intact. Therefore, the ability to obtain targeted or routine satellite imagery can be pivotal in the atrocity crime context.

There is broad application for satellite imagery in atrocity crime prosecutions. For example, the OTP routinely considers the applicability of satellite imagery in its cases and is well aware of their value for proof purposes.[171] Satellite (and aerial) imagery has been used in various investigations and prosecutions for myriad purposes, including documenting the location of mass graves and to show before and after images of towns destroyed by aerial bombardments, e.g. as evidence against perpetrators of the Srebrenica massacre (ICTY);[172] and to show before and after images of mausoleums and mosques destroyed by criminal actions (ICC).[173] These cases represent only a small proportion of cases wherein satellite (and aerial) imagery has been relied upon but present a reasonable cross-section of their value in fact-finding. Satellite imagery is also of value in detecting attacks against humanitarian and peacekeeping missions, the movement of troops and refugees, and large demonstrations in conflict situations; and for identifying military installations and personnel, bomb craters, and road blockades in conflict situations, amongst other items of interest.[174] For court purposes, satellite imagery has proven to be an effective adjunct in interactive 360° visual representations, which are discussed in Section 5.1 of Chapter 8.

Satellite imagery is proving to be a pivotal source of visual documentation in the 2022 Russian invasion of Ukraine. This is shown in Figures 1.2 and 1.3 which illustrate the destruction of buildings in Bakhmut.

They are also being used to show the human cost of conflict as exemplified in Figures 1.4 and 1.5.

These are examples of the many satellite images that may be used in the investigation and prosecution of atrocity crimes. Satellite imagery is also proving to be valuable in visually documenting the 2023 Israel–Gaza conflict. Hiding such large-scale activity is very difficult given the presence of this important form of image-based evidence.

[171] Macauley (n 159) 226.

[172] *Prosecutor v. Krstić*, IT-98-33-T, Judgment, 2 August 2001; *Blagojević and Jokić* (n 113); *Prosecutor v. Limaj et al.*, IT-03-66-T, Judgment, 30 November 2005; *Popović et al.* (n 133); *Prosecutor v. Tolimir*, IT-05-88/2-T, Judgment, 12 December 2012. See also Freeman (n 32) 286–7.

[173] *Prosecutor v. Al Mahdi*, ICC-01/12-01/15-171, Judgment and Sentence, 27 September 2016.

[174] Macauley (n 159) 227–8.

Figure 1.2 Bakhmut, Ukraine, 8 May 2022. Maxar satellite imagery showing before bombing images of Bakhmut theatre and stores. (Satellite image (c) 2023 Maxar Technologies/Getty Images)

Figure 1.3 Bakhmut, Ukraine, 15 May 2023. Maxar satellite imagery showing after bombing images of Bakhmut theatre and stores. (Satellite image (c) 2023 Maxar Technologies/Getty Images)

Figure 1.4 Satellite imagery dated 19 March 2022 showing field prior to the creation of the mass grave site on the northwestern edge of Manhush, Ukraine. (Satellite image (c) 2022 Maxar Technologies/Getty Images)

Figure 1.5 Satellite imagery dated 3 April 2022 showing the expansion of the mass grave site on the northwestern edge of Manhush, Ukraine. (Satellite image (c) 2022 Maxar Technologies/Getty Images)

Conclusion

Through evidence selection and storytelling, counsel create the trial narrative that will be presented to the court. While there will always be a role for *viva voce* evidence, given its well documented frailties and the additional challenges faced by some atrocity crime witnesses, allegations of serious criminality are more likely to be afforded weight by the court if victim or eyewitness testimony can be corroborated by image-based evidence.[175] Judges may be more reluctant to unreservedly accept *viva voce* evidence on its face when not materially corroborated by image-based evidence—not as a matter of law, but as a matter of fact. Counsel must factor this perceived judicial preference for visual proof into their trial narrative.

Image-based evidence is valuable not only to corroborate other evidence but as an independent method of proof. Images have long been used as essential components in international criminal prosecutions ranging from Nuremberg to current ICC prosecutions. Images can do what other forms of evidence cannot. They have demonstrable power to convey scene and event data that cannot be adequately reduced to words. Images are at once efficient, informative, and evocative. They should form an integral part of every atrocity crime prosecution. Doing so requires that counsel be familiar with available imagery and assess how it can be used to address issues before the court and advance the trial narrative.

I would be remiss if I did not note that image-based evidence is not necessarily a proof panacea. Challenges in the creation, evaluation, and interpretation of images render them a form of evidence that must be approached with caution. These issues will be developed throughout the following chapters along with measures designed to provide for a more visually literate appreciation of their benefits and limitations.

[175] McDermott notes the concern of some investigators that the increased prevalence of open source information in atrocity crime prosecutions may serve to devalue those parts of a case that are mostly dependent on witness testimony. McDermott, Koenig, and Murray (n 40) 20. While there is merit to this view, perhaps a sounder perspective is to view open source evidence as something capable of corroborating or challenging *viva voce* evidence, concordant with the goal of finding the truth. *Viva voce* evidence can be buttressed by open source evidence as well as denigrated.

2

Image-Based Evidence as a Didactic Tool

Introduction

At its most basic level, a criminal trial is founded upon the specific allegations that have been levied by the prosecution against the defendant. The function of the trial is to test narratives and evaluate the evidence tendered by the prosecution and defence for the purposes of determining the truth of the allegations and whether the defendant bears criminal responsibility. Image-based evidence is an integral component in proving the case for the prosecution and in presenting the case for the defence and is valuable for both corroborating or contradicting *viva voce* evidence and as an independent source of proof. However, a clinical presentation of evidence bereft of consideration for the intended audience may result in a technically correct exposition of facts but ultimately a failure to effectively deliver the message.

Counsel tender evidence at trial to prove or disprove propositions, e.g. images may be led to prove that the defendant was at a specific location on a certain date and time or that the defendant engaged in criminality. Similarly, images may be tendered to show the harm caused to people or the damage caused to buildings of cultural significance. There can be little doubt that the matter of proof is the core business of evidence that is led at trial, but evidence can also serve salutary parallel purposes. The focus of this chapter is on the use of image-based evidence as a didactic tool, evidence that is used to teach the court and perhaps a broader audience about the case.[1]

Contextualizing the role of evidence requires an exploration of the messages that international criminal justice strives to deliver, with an emphasis on truth discovery and the creation of a historical record. Image-based evidence plays an important role in both realms, yet academic and judicial tensions exist regarding the ability of international criminal justice to ascertain the truth and whether the creation of a historical record should be part of the court's mandate. This chapter posits the view that truth discovery and contribution to the historical record are unavoidable and essential elements of atrocity crime trials, and that image-based evidence has a role to play in both objectives. Used as a didactic tool, image-based

[1] Broader audiences are engaged because atrocity crime allegations concern not only to the wrongs done to the victims, but to society generally. That is why criminal prosecutions are conducted by a public prosecutor. Carsten Stahn, *Justice as Message: Expressivist Foundations of International Criminal Justice* (Oxford: OUP, 2020), 274.

Image-Based Evidence in International Criminal Prosecutions. Jonathan W. Hak, KC, Oxford University Press.
 DOI: 10.1093/oso/9780198889533.003.0002

evidence in the form of filmic, photographic, and video images, computer generated reconstructions, and other advanced visual representations can deepen the search for truth and can be used to create a meaningful historical record.

1. Contextualizing Diverse Goals of International Criminal Justice

There is considerable academic debate about the proper purposes of international criminal justice, revealing a list of putative aims that are at once aspirational and impossible to deliver in their entirety. A detailed discussion of the purposes of international criminal justice is well beyond the scope of this book but a summative introduction is helpful to contextualize the goals that relate to the use of image-based evidence for didactic purposes. Some of the more altruistic objectives are found in the expressivist view that law has value because of its ability to convey social meaning, to articulate and reinforce social norms, and send messages to varying audiences.[2] These audiences include not only the people present in the courtroom but also those currently engaged in criminality, potential perpetrators, the community in which the crimes were committed, and the world at large.

Stated objectives include global outreach to educate the world as to the presence of atrocity crimes and the power of international criminal justice to introduce some semblance of order into a legal and moral void.[3] Tied in with this latter objective is the opportunity to engage in moral ministrations where the value of good over evil is preached.[4] The Nuremberg and *Eichmann* prosecutions have been defended as necessary for didactic purposes, '... by establishing an impartial account of the past and for teaching younger generations of the dangers involved in particular

[2] ibid 6, 7, 19. Expressivism may be defined as the process of creating meaning through communicative actions and representational practices, including symbolic expression.

[3] Gideon Hausner, *Justice in Jerusalem* (New York: Schocken Books, 1966), 291; Lawrence Douglas, *The Memory of Judgment: Making Law and History in the Trials of the Holocaust* (New Haven: Yale University Press, 2001) 3; Lawrence Douglas, 'Truth and Justice in Atrocity Trials', in *The Cambridge Companion to International Criminal Law*, edited by William Schabas (Cambridge: CUP, 2016), 34–51.

[4] International criminal justice establishes moral and legal responsibilities and articulates moral and legal wrongs. Stahn (n 1) 6, 19, 85, 287. Courts cannot avoid moral instruction as trials are in part morality plays, pedagogically ministering to society at large about forbidden conduct and the consequences for violating social norms and laws. Friedman said, 'The criminal justice system is also a teacher and preacher. It announces, by word and deed, a code of behavior and marks the moral behavior of society... It is, in short, didactic theater.' Lawrence Friedman, 'On Stage: Some Historical Notes About Criminal Justice', in *Social Science, Social Policy and the Law*, edited by Patricia Ewick, Robert Kagan, and Austin Sarat (New York: Russell Sage Foundation, 1999), 68–100, at 69–70. Morality messaging was evident in the Einsatzgruppen trial when in his opening address Chief Prosecutor Ferencz said, 'Vengeance is not our goal, nor do we seek merely a just retribution. We ask this Court to affirm by international penal action man's right to live in peace and dignity regardless of his race or creed. The case we present is a plea of humanity to law.' Benjamin Ferencz, 'Opening Statement at Nuremberg', *Trial of the Major War Criminals*, vol. IV, 494; *United States v. Ohlendorf et al.* [1949] 4 TWC 3, at 30.

policies'.[5] Further objectives include creating opportunities for the transformation of society and individuals by sparking discussions aimed at fostering toleration, moderation, and respect, while also giving a voice to victims of atrocities.[6] Equally ambitious objectives include providing truth, accountability, and healing to victims.[7] The restoration of peace and achieving reconciliation in post-conflict situations are also aims of international criminal justice.[8]

A further objective with popular appeal is that of delivering justice.[9] In reality, achieving or delivering true justice is a Sisyphean task which will deliver satisfaction to few.[10] Conceptions of a just result are highly subjective and for victims of atrocity crimes, no court can right such monumental wrongs. Stahn cautions that while international criminal justice is fundamentally about expressing justice, it may not be able to deliver it in the form of retribution.[11] There is soundness in this

[5] Martti Koskenniemi, 'Between Impunity and Show Trials', *Max Planck Yearbook of United Nations Law* 6 (2002): 1–36, at 4–5.

[6] Mark Osiel, *Mass Atrocity, Collective Memory, and Law* (New Brunswick: Transaction Publishers, 1997), 2; Mirjan Damaška, 'What Is the Point of International Criminal Justice?', *Chicago-Kent Law Review* 83, no. 1 (2008): 329–68, at 331. The ICC Office of Public Counsel for Victims plays an important role because it creates a procedural mechanism for victims to have a represented voice in the proceedings. This is a necessary adjunct to granting the right itself.

[7] Barrie Sander, 'The Expressive Limits of International Criminal Justice: Victim Trauma and Local Culture in the Iron Cage of the Law', *International Criminal Law Review* 19 (2019): 1014–45, at 1018–19. Sander notes that formal recognition as a victim may restore a sense of the dignity and worth, and that participation is cathartic and may lead to closure. I suggest that international criminal proceedings can only partially assist in achieving these goals. Legal results can be achieved, but courts are not in the closure business. It is simply too tall an order for criminal proceedings to deliver to most victims of atrocities. Landsman notes the argument that society cannot forgive what it cannot punish. If this is true, then prosecution is an important step in fostering healing. Stephan Landsman, 'Alternative Responses to Serious Human Rights Abuses: Of Prosecution and Truth Commissions', *Law and Contemporary Problems* 59, no. 4 (1996): 81–92, at 84.

[8] Stahn cites the 2003 *Report of the Secretary-General on the Rule of Law in Conflict and Post-Conflict Societies* as promulgating the restoration of peace as one of the justifications for international criminal justice though he argues that trials cannot be expected to create peace and security. Stahn's view is more realistic, though less optimistic. Carsten Stahn, 'Legacy in International Criminal Justice', in *Arcs of Global Justice*, edited by Margaret deGuzman and Diane Amann (New York: OUP, 2018), 271–85. Damaška notes that international criminal courts have espoused a goal of stopping ongoing conflict but asserts that this exceeds the capacity of courts to achieve; Damaška (n 6) 331. I suggest that any cessation of conflict would have only tangential or coincidental connection to any prosecution as the ability of the courts to reach non-litigants is very limited. See also Payam Akhavan, 'The Rise, and Fall, and Rise, of International Criminal Justice', *Journal of International Criminal Justice* 11 (2013): 527–36, at 532.

[9] Hannah Arendt, *Eichmann in Jerusalem: A Report on the Banality of Evil* (New York: Viking, 1963), 253; Frederic Mégret, 'The Anxieties of International Criminal Justice', *Leiden Journal of International Law* 29, no. 1 (2016): 197–221, at 209. International criminal tribunals and courts have often been criticized for representing and delivering victor's justice wherein only those who lose conflicts tend to be prosecuted even though both sides may have committed atrocity crimes. See Margaret deGuzman, 'Criminal Law Philosophy in William Schabas's Scholarship', in *Arcs of Global Justice*, edited by Margaret deGuzman and Diane Amann (New York: OUP, 2018), 155–72, at 166 (regarding the IMT, IMTFE, and ad hoc tribunals). Shannon Fyfe, 'The Office of the Prosecutor: Seeking Justice or Serving Global Imperialism?', *International Criminal Law Review* 18 (2018): 988–1014, at 990 (a criticism of international criminal justice generally).

[10] 'Justice, like beauty, is never fully present, and it is felt most vividly in those moments where the absence is profound and yet ineffable.' Francis Mootz, 'Law Among the Sight Lovers', *New York Law School Law Review* 57, no. 1 (2012): 61–76, at 69.

[11] Stahn (n 1) 408.

caution as no quantum of retribution can right an irreversible wrong, but it can express messages about empowerment and agency. Similarly, international criminal justice may not avoid future atrocities but may help move societies in that direction.[12] Though likely not the final word, expressivism has developed into one of the leading theories to understand the foundations of international criminal justice.[13]

More traditional expressions of international criminal justice find purchase in the largely parallel objectives of accountability, retribution, punishment, incapacitation, and denunciation.[14] Prosecutions may also help to establish or re-establish the rule of law.[15] Expressivists assert that punishment affirms the value of the law, fosters communal solidarity, and elevates moral consensus.[16] Another expressivist message is deterrence, which is punishment's capacity to dissuade would-be criminals from committing crimes because they fear the punitive and broader social consequences of conviction.[17] Expressive deterrence, which focuses on the secondary stigmatizing effects of punishment, is founded on the premise that if the international community expresses its disapproval strongly enough, that disapproval will dissuade others from engaging in atrocity crimes because the downfall and humiliation of conviction as a war criminal impacts the offender's future political viability. This is dependent upon adequate stigmatization and consequences that are severe enough to make criminality worth avoiding. Empirically, it is difficult to determine the efficacy of deterrence, but I suggest that those inclined to commit atrocity crimes are not burdened by the risk of punishment.[18]

Some goals of international criminal justice are more immediate and amenable to delivery, including truth discovery and determining whether the allegations made by the prosecution can be proven. Both of these goals enjoy wide though qualified support, but a more contested role for international criminal justice is that of creating a historical record. Image-based evidence plays a significant role in matters of proof and in the documentation of history because it provides a level of depth and detail that cannot necessarily be delivered solely through words.

[12] ibid.

[13] ibid 7.

[14] Hausner (n 3) 292; Damaška (n 6) 331, 347; Stahn (n 8) 9.

[15] Landsman (n 7) 83.

[16] Mark Drumbl, *Atrocity, Punishment, and International Law* (Cambridge: CUP, 2007), 17.

[17] Chief Prosecutor Ferencz said, 'I could not possibly do justice to the million people who had been killed, but if I could establish a rule of law which could protect humankind in the future, that would make this trial more meaningful than whatever I would do with this handful of murderous [sic]... Did we seek to do justice? Of course not. Because we would still be there trying Nazis to this day, so you try to make a statement of principle. The principle is, "Don't do this—it's a crime against humanity. Stop doing it. If you insist upon doing it, we'll try to catch you if you are a leader and put you away so you won't do it again and others will be deterred from doing it."' 'The Accountant of Auschwitz', A Documentary Channel Production, TLNT Productions Inc, 2018.

[18] International criminal trials likely have little deterrent effect as atrocity crimes involve 'radical evil' of the sort not affected by the fear of future punishment. Koskenniemi (n 5) 7–8.

1.1 Truth Discovery

The truth discovery function of international criminal justice is the prime directive upon which any other expressivist goals are premised because it is only after we know the truth that questions of criminal accountability and punishment can be profitably addressed in a juridical setting.[19] The truth must be pursued, however unwelcome it may be to some when it is found. Though it may seem axiomatic that once we know the facts, we will know the truth, practical experience does not universally bear this out. An adamantine link between facts and truth may prove illusive as facts can be malleable and may give rise to competing explanations, perspectives, theories, and realities. The entire truth may be unknowable though parties can strive to get as near to it as possible.[20] The complete truth may be illusory due to missing, prevaricating, or imperfect witnesses; equivocal evidence; the absence of evidence; facts that legitimately give rise to multiple interpretations; or vast chasms of the unknown between known facts. Though it would be optimistic to rely upon the trial process to conclusively determine the facts, and despite what is often a rather steep quest, replete with roadblocks, rabbit holes, and diversions, the goal must be to learn the truth of the matter.[21]

The search for the truth can be a daunting, sometimes unresolvable task, but without knowing what happened and who is responsible, there can be no attempt at achieving justice, however illusive that goal may be in reality.[22] The healing process can only begin once the truth has been declared and publicly recognized.[23] In this respect, prosecutions serve an important role in educating affected parties about the nature and extent of prior criminality.[24] Selecting, leading, and challenging evidence should therefore be aimed at ascertaining the truth.[25] Truth is not just an esoteric academic precept—the goal of ascertaining the truth is well established in

19 There is broad support for the proposition that findings of fact bear particular importance in international criminal trials. McDermott notes that the purposes of international criminal justice include not only determining whether criminal liability has been established, but also establishing indisputable findings of fact. Yvonne McDermott, 'Strengthening the Evaluation of Evidence in International Criminal Trials', *International Criminal Law Review* 17 (2017): 682–702, at 683.

20 Friedland argues that there is no such thing as absolute truth in human affairs or science and thus truth is a matter of probability. Martin Friedland, 'Searching for Truth in the Criminal Justice System', *Criminal Law Quarterly* 60, no. 4 (2014): 487–521, at 487. I believe absolute truth exists and can sometimes be ascertained.

21 Neither international nor domestic prosecutions require absolute proof but rather proof beyond reasonable doubt. See e.g. *Rome Statute*, Art. 66(3).

22 'Truth, while no guarantee of justice, is an essential precondition for it.' Shannon Fyfe, 'Truth, Testimony, and Epistemic Injustice in International Criminal Law', in *Philosophical Foundations of International Criminal Law: Foundational Concepts*, edited by Morten Bergsmo and Emiliano Buis (Brussels: Torkel Opsahl Academic EPublisher, 2019), 269–308, at 294, citing Larry Laudan.

23 Koskenniemi (n 5) 4.

24 Landsman (n 7) 83.

25 Lindsay Farmer, 'Whose Trial? Comments on "A Theory of the Trial"', *Law and Social Inquiry* 28, no. 2 (2003): 547–52, at 549; Mark Klamberg, *Evidence in International Criminal Trials* (Leiden: Martinus Nijhoff Publishers, 2013), 58–9. Douglas, 'Truth and Justice in Atrocity Trials' (n 3).

domestic courts,[26] the tribunals,[27] and the International Criminal Court (ICC).[28] In *Prosecutor v. Bemba*, the Pre-Trial Chamber stated that 'the search for the truth is the principal goal of the Court as a whole'.[29] And in *Prosecutor v. Gbagbo and Blé Goudé*, Judge Tarfusser said:[30]

> If, for any Prosecutor as a public and independent party to criminal proceedings, there is an obligation to genuinely search for the truth and to request the acquittal when the evidence at trial turns out not being sufficient for a conviction, these obligations are even more crucial for the ICC Prosecutor, in light of the statutory obligation to 'investigate incriminating and exonerating circumstances equally' pursuant to article 54(1)(a) of the Statute.

Rationally, armed with the facts, the court should be able to divine the truth. It may be convoluted and difficult to ascertain, but there should ultimately be one truth, acknowledging the cautionary admonition of the Israel Supreme Court in acquitting Ivan Demjanjuk of the allegation that he was 'Ivan the Terrible', an operator of the gas chambers at Treblinka, 'The matter is closed—but not complete. The complete truth is not the prerogative of the human judge.'[31]

It has been argued that facts are rarely given at trial but rather are produced through the process of adjudication and that the value of the trial process is that competing narratives can be tested for soundness.[32] Holistically, this argument has

[26] See e.g. Larry Laudan, *Truth, Error, and Criminal Law* (New York: CUP, 2006), 1–3; Lindsay Farmer, 'With All the Impressiveness and Substantial Value of Truth: Notable Trials and Criminal Justice, 1750–1930', *Law and Humanities* 1, no. 1 (2007): 57–78, at 71–2; Ralph Grunewald, 'Comparing Injustices: Truth, Justice, and the System', *Albany Law Review* 77, no. 3 (2013): 1139–1200 (examining the importance of truth determination in the US and German systems of criminal law). See also *Tehan v. U.S.*, 383 U.S. 406, at 416 (1966), where the US Supreme Court said, 'The basic purpose of a trial is the determination of the truth.'. *R. v. Nikolovski*, [1996] 3 S.C.R. 1197, para. 13, where the Supreme Court of Canada said, 'The ultimate aim of any trial, criminal or civil, must be to seek and to ascertain the truth.'

[27] e.g in *Prosecutor v. Brdanin and Talić*, IT-99-36-T, Order on the Standards Governing the Admission of Evidence, 15 February 2002, para. 25, the Chamber referred to a trial as 'an often complex journey in search for the truth'. In *Prosecutor v. Halilović*, IT-01-48-T, Motion for Judicial Notice, 1 March 2005, para. 9, the Chamber noted that one of the purposes of the tribunal was to look for the truth of the events in the former Yugoslavia. See also *Rutaganda v. Prosecutor*, ICTR-96-3-A, Judgement, 26 May 2003, paras. 62–63, 75. One of the purposes of the ECCC was to establish collective memory through truth-finding. Stahn (n 1) 175.

[28] The determination of the truth is a foundational underpinning for all ICC prosecutions, as set out in Arts. 54(1)(a) and 69(3) of the *Rome Statute*, noted for example in *Prosecutor v. Katanga*, ICC-01/04-01/07 OA 13, Appeals Chamber Judgment, 27 March 2013, para. 104; *Prosecutor v. Katanga*, ICC-01/04-01/07, Judgment Pursuant to Article 74 of the Statute, 7 March 2014, para 59; *Prosecutor v. Bemba*, ICC-01/05-01/08-3343, Judgement, 21 March 2016, para. 232.

[29] ICC-01/05-01/08-55, Decision on the Evidence Disclosure System and Setting a Timetable for Disclosure between the Parties, 31 July 2008, para. 11.

[30] *Prosecutor v. Gbagbo and Blé Goudé*, ICC-02/11-01/15-1263-AnxA, Opinion of Judge Tarfusser, 16 July 2019, para. 104.

[31] *Demjanjuk v. Israel*, Crim. App. No. 347/88, at 41.

[32] Stahn states that trials seek to reflect and reproduce real events, to reveal what happened. Stahn (n 1) 253, 260.

merit, but I assert that facts indeed emerge from witnesses and other evidence that are then analysed for the purpose of ascertaining truth.[33] Stahn argues that international criminal trials do not merely reflect the truth—they produce it, striving to show what happened and why, and that truth 'emerges through communication, validation, and judgment'.[34] I agree with this view but caution that truth may not be a solitary construct. The objective theory of truth posits that there is only one accurate account of an event and that the goal should be to find it whereas the subjective theory allows for multiple accounts of an event that could each accurately explain it.[35] This gives rise to the prospect of multiple truths about an event or at least layers of truth.[36] Indeed, expressivism recognizes that justice is not necessarily built upon a single truth but rather several truths.[37]

Even though the prosecution is obliged to investigate exonerating as well as incriminating circumstances and to fairly present their case, support for the prosecution theory can still be skewed.[38] While subjectivity remains inherent in both the prosecution and defence cases, the goal should be to seek true and honest justice, not just the façade of justice. However, given that a relentless search for the truth would entail delay and fair trial considerations, international criminal justice must strive for optimum fact-finding bearing in mind those restrictions. An effective adjudication must result in as much factual input as legally possible for truth determination, at least to the criminal standard of proof.

While truth is important in all cases, atrocity crimes particularly cry out for an objective assessment and determination of the facts that led up to their commission. Establishing the truth matters not just to the survivors but to the community, the country, and often the global audience. For example, truth determination will be a prime goal for any international criminal prosecutions that arise from Russia's February 2022 invasion of Ukraine and the atrocity crimes committed thereafter. Misleading claims by Russia that it invaded Ukraine to stop an ongoing genocide and to 'de-nazify' the country will be tested by an objective non-partisan lens. Pro-Russia online reports claimed that posted video images of the invasion were either staged or from a different conflict years ago and these reports were in competition with other media reports from Ukraine supporters which at times also used images from unrelated conflicts.[39] Misleading and fraudulent stories often achieve viral popularity but are anathema to accurate depictions of conflict.

[33] Our differences in perspective are more likely based on semantics than substance.

[34] Stahn (n 1) 266.

[35] Fyfe (n 22) 288–9.

[36] Stahn (n 1) 267.

[37] Carsten Stahn, 'Between "Faith" and "Facts": By What Standards Should We Assess International Criminal Justice?', *Leiden Journal of International Law* 25 (2012): 251–82, at 272.

[38] *Rome Statute*, Art, 54(1)(a); Stahn (n 37) 272.

[39] Alistair Coleman, 'Ukraine Conflict: Further False Images Shared Online' *BBC News* (25 February 2022) https://www.bbc.com/news/60528276; Kayleen Devlin and Shayan Sardarizadeh, 'Ukraine Invasion: Misleading Claims Continue to Go Viral' *BBC News* (28 February 2022) https://www.bbc.

Similarly, the MH17 trial in Amsterdam, stemming from the 17 July 2014 shooting down of Malaysian Airlines flight MH17 over Ukraine, sought to determine whether the pro-Russian separatist defendants were responsible for this crime.[40] While the creation of an accurate historical record is not the primary role of international criminal justice, a fulsome trial record and judgment may put a damper on the promulgation of revisionist history. In summary, finding the truth in atrocity crime prosecutions has an impact far beyond the courtroom.

Image-based evidence proved to be invaluable in the MH17 investigation and prosecution for identifying and tracking the missile launching system that shot down the commercial airliner. The plethora of images emanating from the Russian invasion of Ukraine will no doubt prove to be an important part of any arsenal aimed at finding the truth of what occurred and who is responsible.

1.2 Creating a Historical Record

Perhaps more controversial is the role of international criminal justice in creating a historical record of atrocities, what led up to them, the context in which they occurred, and naming those responsible for them. There is certainly support for the proposition that courts operate as recorders and rapporteurs of history, if not the arbiters of it. In many cases, it is necessary to place a trial in the appropriate historical context and so evidence must be led not just on the elements of the offences before the court, but about the historical milieu in which the alleged offences took place.[41] Not only does this provide context in the juridical environment, it helps to create a historical record.[42] Such was the task facing the multinational team of prosecutors conducting the Nuremberg trial. In what became one of the most significant atrocity crime trials in history, the prosecutors knew that much more was involved than just leading evidence in support of the charges facing the defendants. They also had to make history.[43]

com/news/60554910; Shayan Sardarizadeh and Olga Robinson, 'Ukraine Invasion: False Claims the War Is a Hoax Go Viral' *BBC News* (8 March 2022) https://www.bbc.com/news/60589965.

[40] For further details on the use of image-based evidence in this investigation, see Section 1 of Chapter 3.

[41] Stahn outlines three views of trials and their treatment of history. First, a historical function used to contextualize an event and form collective memory. Second, a focus on criminal liability, not history. The middle ground approach asserts that historical clarification is a useful by-product of a trial and there must be some historical and political analysis to properly conduct a trial. Stahn (n 1) 263–4.

[42] Douglas refers to this as 'the power of the criminal trial to galvanize collective interest in the past'. Douglas, *The Memory of Judgment* (n 3) 4. Friedman refers to trials as 'significant documents of social history'. Friedman (n 4) 77.

[43] A key goal of the Nuremberg and *Eichmann* trials was to produce a 'powerful documentary record [of] the immensity of the Nazi regime's crimes.' Landsman (n 7) 81–2.

The Nuremberg trial produced a detailed record of historical events that occurred in Europe over several years, providing contextualization for the International Military Tribunal for Nuremberg (IMT) and contributing to the historiography of World War II.[44] Images were used as a method of writing history.[45] One of the most significant aspects of the Nuremberg trial was the use of filmic evidence as a didactic tool. Successfully incorporating evocative and shocking films into the trial narrative created an important precedent as it carved out a place for image-based evidence in international criminal law. This important work served to regularize the use of images in subsequent prosecutions.

While the immediate purpose of the 1961 *Eichmann* trial was to determine guilt, the overriding purpose was to create history.[46] Chief Prosecutor Hausner was critical of the Nuremberg trial approach, which involved limited survivor testimony, claiming that it 'failed to reach the hearts of men'.[47] It was his view that, '... we needed more than a conviction; we needed a living record of a gigantic human and national disaster ... '[48] He wanted the people of Israel to know as much as possible about what happened in the Holocaust, so that they might achieve understanding and reconciliation with the past.[49] Thus, the *Eichmann* prosecution was focused less on judging Eichmann as a person than on establishing the truth of the events leading up to and during the Holocaust.[50] It was for this reason that Hausner presented substantial survivor testimony which he believed would help people visualize the tragedy of the Holocaust better than a more clinical presentation.[51] This produced a far more comprehensive treatment of the traumatic history of the Holocaust than was presented at Nuremberg.[52] Douglas makes a compelling point that the Holocaust perpetrator trials collectively served as pedagogic tools of historical instruction.[53]

44 Koskenniemi (n 5) 21.

45 Peter Burke, *Eyewitnessing: The Use of Images as Historical Evidence* (London: Reaktion Books, 2019), 192.

46 *Attorney-General of the Government of Israel v. Adolf Eichmann*, Criminal Case 40/61.

47 Hausner (n 3) 291.

48 ibid.

49 Douglas cautions that collective memory has little to do with historical accuracy. Lawrence Douglas, 'History and Memory in the Courtroom: Reflections on Perpetrator Trials', in *The Nuremberg Trials: International Criminal Law Since 1945*, edited by Herbert Reginbogin, Christoph Safferling, and Walter Hippel (Munich: K.G. Saur, 2006): 95–104, at 96.

50 Koskenniemi (n 5) 3. As such, Eichmann's fate was of secondary importance.

51 Hausner later acknowledged that the prosecution could have presented their case based solely on documentary evidence, but that would not have captured the imagination and conscience of Israel or the world. Douglas (n 50) 97. By placing the destruction of European Jewry at the fore of the *Eichmann* trial, it revised and refined the history of Nazi extermination that had been presented in an incomplete fashion at Nuremberg; Douglas, 'Truth and Justice in Atrocity Trials' (n 3). By including survivor testimony Hausner reframed victim identity in the public consciousness thus adding value to the *Eichmann* proceedings and giving voice to the victims. Stahn (n 1) 50, 172.

52 Douglas (n 49) 100.

53 ibid 95. Douglas cites Robert Kempner, a leading war crimes prosecutor, who described the Nuremberg trials as 'the greatest history seminar ever held'.

Regarding the criminal tribunals that emerged in the 1990s, in *The Rule of the Law and Transitional Justice in Conflict and Post-Conflict Societies*, the Secretary-General of the UN stated that one of the purposes of the tribunals was to establish a record of past events, and noted that criminal trials can establish detailed and well-substantiated records of particular incidents and events.[54] One of the stated goals of the International Criminal Tribunal for the former Yugoslavia (ICTY) was to create an accurate historical record in an effort to prevent historical revisionism.[55] More broadly, the desire for international criminal prosecutions to establish an accurate historical record has reasonable support.[56]

International criminal trials allow for the presentation of sometimes diverse historical narratives from the prosecution, defence, and in some venues, victims. Courts then have the unenviable task of attempting to carve out a judicially approved narrative for trial purposes.[57] Survivors of atrocity crimes may thereby gain intrinsic value from a comprehensive judicially created historical record from which they can learn truths that may otherwise never be told. There is also a broad benefit in promulgating a public understanding of what occurred.[58] An objective assessment of historical truth is especially important to combat misinformation campaigns where detractors deny the very existence of atrocities.[59] A caveat to note is that judicial determinations of what led up to a conflict and specific incidents are governed by rules of evidence and procedure, which may have a limiting effect. Historians do not face the same restrictions and may be more adept at providing a

[54] UN Doc. S/2004/616, paras. 38–39. See also William Schabas, 'Building the Narrative: The UN Tribunals for the former Yugoslavia, Rwanda and Sierra Leone', in *The Scene of the Mass Crime: History, Film, and International Tribunals*, edited by Christian Delage and Peter Goodrich (Oxford: Routledge, 2013), 23–39; Stahn (n 8).

[55] Asserted by the first President of the ICTY, Antonio Cassese, in his presentation to the UN General Assembly (UN Doc. A/52/PV.44, p. 2). Noted in Schabas (n 55) 23–39.

[56] Fyfe asserts that international criminal prosecutions have a 'special responsibility' regarding truth and that they are responsible for establishing an accurate historical record. Fyfe (n 22) 299. Damaška confirms the desire of tribunals and courts to set the historical record straight, in the hope that this will assist in reconciliation and the avoidance of future conflict, as well as the practical need to establish historical context to situate individual activity within the reach of international criminal law. But he acknowledges that this is difficult to achieve given time and resource limitations. Damaška (n 6) 335–7. Wilson urges a reconsideration of the longstanding view that the pursuit of justice and the writing of history are inherently irreconcilable, particularly in respect of the work of the ICTY. He notes that international criminal law relies upon historical contextualization to secure convictions. Richard Wilson, 'Judging History: The Historical Record of the International Criminal Tribunal for the Former Yugoslavia', *Human Rights Quarterly* 27, no. 3 (2005): 908–42, at 909, 917–18, 922, 940.

[57] Judicial narratives may not be uniformly received among audiences beyond the courtroom, in particular the affected community. The information may be filtered by local officials or the media to distort judicial rulings and place their own spin on the findings. Barrie Sander, 'The Method Is the Message: Law, Narrative Authority and Historical Contestation in International Criminal Courts', *Melbourne Journal of International Law* 19, no. 1 (2018): 299–334, at 303–6.

[58] Jessica Levy and Paul Williams, 'Documentation for Accountability', *Case Western Reserve Journal of International Law* 52 (2020): 451–66, at 458; Stahn (n 1) 254.

[59] Levy and Williams (n 58) 458. Showing the Scorpions Srebrenica video of civilians being executed during the ICTY trial of Milošević helped to counter Milošević's propaganda that the Srebrenica massacre was fiction. See also Stahn (n 37) 273.

broader context for conflict, though not necessarily to the same high standard as a court.

Conversely there is also strong support for the view that it is not the role of international tribunals or courts to create a historical record.[60] Douglas argues that because the rules of evidence and procedure limit what information is presented to the court, didactic trials fail to do justice to history.[61] Their role as the arbiters of historical truth has been contested since Nuremberg and Tokyo.[62] Arendt, in *Eichmann in Jerusalem*, said, 'The purpose of a trial is to render justice, and nothing else; even the noblest of ulterior purposes ... can only detract from the law's main business: to weigh the charges brought against the accused, to render a judgment, and to mete out due punishment.'[63] Courts have also expressed reticence at being responsible to construct a historical record, beyond their more pressing task of assessing the criminal accountability of defendants.[64] Equally, it has been stated that judgments cannot be given in a vacuum, without contextual references.[65]

Sander makes the important point that 'historical narratives constructed within international criminal judgments are neither static nor final, but subject to a process of ongoing contestation and evolution over time'.[66] While there may be an expectation that an international criminal court can promulgate a historical narrative which ushers in finality and closure, that is not realistic and is quite likely impossible. Historical findings by courts are subject to revision on appeal and even within trial and appellate judgments there may be dissenting judgments, giving rise to narrative pluralism.[67] Judgments from different courts covering the same conflict may produce inter-court narrative pluralism.[68] Pluralist narratives may

[60] e.g. Stahn (n 37) 271–4; Nancy Combs, 'Deconstructing the Epistemic Challenges to Mass Atrocity Prosecutions', *Washington and Lee Law Review* 75, no. 1 (2018): 223–300, at 226.

[61] Douglas (n 49) 98. Douglas concedes that didactic trials 'are not well equipped to render history in its complexity; nor are they structured self-consciously to acknowledge the limitations of their representation of the past'. (ibid 101) But he argues that little follows from that concession. Indeed, he notes persuasively that the *Eichmann* trial served to transform cultural understandings of Nazi genocide. 'No longer simply a horrific episode of mass killing, the Holocaust emerged from the Eichmann trial as an emblematic act of the twentieth century—an act no longer continuous with the history that proceeded it, but radically disruptive of it.' (ibid 102).

[62] Schabas (n 54); Stahn (n 1) 45, 51, 262–3.

[63] Arendt (n 9) 253.

[64] *Prosecutor v. Kupreskić*, IT-95-16-T, Judgement, 14 January 2000, para. 756; *Prosecutor v. Nikolić*, IT-94-2-S, Sentencing Judgement, 18 December 2003, para. 122 ('... this Tribunal is not a final arbiter of historical facts. That is for historians.').

[65] *Prosecutor v. Kayishema et al.*, ICTR-95-1-T, Judgement, 21 May 1999, paras. 31–33; *Prosecutor v. Bizimungu et al.*, ICTR-99-50-T, Decision on the Prosecutor's Motion and Notice of Adjudicated Facts, 10 December 2004, paras. 14–15.

[66] Sander (n 57) 549.

[67] ibid 551.

[68] ibid 551–4. Sander points out the contrasting judgments in the *Eichmann* prosecution and the Nuremberg trial. The *Eichmann* prosecution's survivor-centric approach varied considerably from the Nuremberg prosecution's largely documentary approach, resulting in different narratives in the respective judgments. Further, as the IMT was required by the Nuremberg Charter to examine Nazi atrocities in a war crimes environment, racially motivated persecution occupied a lesser role, in contrast to the *Eichmann* trial, which was based on the *Nazis and Nazi Collaborators (Punishment) Law*, thereby

also arise from different cases adjudicated by the same international criminal tribunal or court. This intra-court narrative pluralism may arise given that mass atrocities often take place over extended periods of time and each case may focus on different aspects within a broader narrative.[69] The evidence led in each case and the specific incidents being examined may give rise to varied factual findings. Further, later prosecutions may have the benefit of additional and superior evidence compared to earlier prosecutions.

There is broad support for the proposition that trials are not the ideal mechanism for resolving disparate views of history and conclusively determining the political causes for conflict.[70] Trials may inadvertently distort history, largely because they focus on specific events without being able to fully integrate the context in which those events occurred.[71] It is also worthy of note that judicial truth and historical truth may not coincide.[72] Judicial truth is affected by issues of crime nexus, relevance, admissibility, and procedural rules, and therefore historians should not rely upon judges to write a comprehensive history of conflict and crime.[73]

Even though the law serves an important role as a fact-finding tool, the creation of a comprehensive historical record should not be the role of international criminal justice. Historians are better placed to examine the political, ethnic, and cultural milieu in which atrocities were committed. Courts should focus on ascertaining the truth of the evidence presented and determining the criminal culpability for the specific charges alleged against the defendant. Seeking to write history dilutes these prime directives. Courts cannot be expected to create an accurate and thorough historical record. It is not feasible given resource limitations, concerns of relevance, probative value versus prejudicial effect, evidence selection, and time constraints, nor is it necessary for judgment.

allowing the Holocaust to take centre stage. Sander refers to the *Eichmann* judgment as 'the deliberate historical reopening of the Nuremberg judgment'.

69 ibid 554–9.

70 Stahn (n 8); Damaška (n 6). Damaška says that it is too complex and costly to create a historical record, and it gives rise to an expectation by victims that all atrocities should be included, noting the experience of the ICTY. He argues that judges should focus on what they do best—assessing the evidence presented for the purpose of determining criminal liability.

71 Atrocity crime trials tend to exaggerate the role of the defendants in events of greater historical significance by transforming the defendant into someone responsible for broader atrocities, whether correct or not. Douglas 'Truth and Justice in Atrocity Trials' (n 3). See also Damaška (n 6) where the author notes that the ICTR prosecutions did not reflect the fact that one million people were involved as perpetrators or accomplices and that by individualizing responsibility, the tribunal created an inaccurate historical record of responsibility.

72 Koskenniemi (n 5) 11–12.

73 Pieter Lagrou, '"Historical Trials": Getting the Past Right—Or the Future?' in *The Scene of the Mass Crime: History, Film, and International Tribunals*, edited by Christian Delage and Peter Goodrich (Oxford: Routledge, 2013), 9–22. Lagrou argues that judges are more focused on contributing to the history of the courtroom than making history. See also Schabas (n 54), where the author asserts that tribunals and courts contribute to historical narratives but provide a version that is flat and lacking in nuance.

Even though individualizing responsibility through truth determination and creating a historical record are disparate aspirations, every judgment forms a historical record, perfect or not.[74] Further, the historical value of a trial comes not just from the judgment but from opening statements; *viva voce*, image-based, and documentary evidence; exhibits; and closing statements.[75] While the Trial Chamber in *Nikolić* noted that it was not the final arbiter of historical facts, the Chamber nonetheless played a role in creating a historical record of conflict and atrocity.[76] Every trial delves into history and casts judgment upon it, at least insofar as the specific events and allegations against the defendant are concerned. Even though the creation of a comprehensive historical record should not be the role of international criminal justice, some measure of historical context is required for the court to render judgment.

1.3 The Nuremberg Trial: Truth for Trial, History Forever

While the immediate purpose of the Nuremberg trial was to determine whether the defendants were guilty of the allegations levied against them, much more was in play as the parties presented their cases. The presentation of image-based evidence such as the *Nazi Concentration Camps* film and other films did not strictly address the elements of the offences for which each defendant was indicted, nor did they depict any of the defendants committing the crimes charged.[77] The images alone were not a path to conviction. Yet, they served two dominant purposes. First, they portrayed in a most visceral manner the German occupation of much of Europe and the horrors the Nazi war machine inflicted upon the citizenry, thereby helping to establish the truth. Second, they created a powerful and permanent record of some of the Nazi atrocities perpetrated on their captives.[78] Further, the images served an extra-judicial sociological function of indicting Germany as a whole.[79]

[74] Wilson (n 56) 918. Gaynor notes that, '[a]ny trial involving top military or political leaders, where the trial record incorporates thousands of documents and the testimony of hundreds of witnesses, can hardly avoid creating a historical record'. Fergal Gaynor, 'Uneasy Partners—Evidence, Truth and History in International Trials', *Journal of International Criminal Justice* 10 (2012): 1257–75, at 1262.

[75] Trials cannot avoid creating history as they produce images, narratives, and views of the past. They frame historical discourse. Stahn (n 8).

[76] *Nikolić* (n 64).

[77] Susan Twist, 'Evidence of Atrocities or Atrocious Use of Evidence: The Controversial Use of Atrocity Film at Nuremberg', *Liverpool Law Review* 26 (2005): 267–302, at 271, 288–9.

[78] These films denoted a change in the use of evidentiary film in the courtroom. They were used as proof of atrocities but also for broader exposition of the Holocaust. Emma Sandon, 'Law and Film', in *Arcs of Global Justice*, edited by Margaret deGuzman and Diane Amann (New York: OUP, 2018), 501–20.

[79] The images starkly illustrated that the camps arose out of an environment wherein the German people either actively supported Hitler or tacitly assented to the atrocities through their silence. Stephan Landsman, *Crimes of the Holocaust: The Law Confronts Hard Cases* (Philadelphia: University of Pennsylvania Press, 2005), 28.

As time passes, few people will remember who the defendants were, let alone the specific basis upon which they were found guilty. The defendants have become mere footnotes of history. Nor will people recall in any detail the survivor accounts, the mountain of German Final Solution documents entered as exhibits, or the testimony of the defendants themselves. They will however remember the shocking images of the Holocaust presented during the trial; images that have been emblazoned upon the psyche of the world.

The Allied prosecution teams presented more evidence than was strictly necessary to secure a conviction. The extensive use of image-based evidence was intended for far more loftier goals than a successful prosecution. To be sure, the images presented during the Nuremberg trial were presented for the pedagogic purpose of informing the IMT judges, as much as images could, of the enormity of what the Nazis had done. In this regard, the evidence served admirably as a didactic tool to help establish the truth of Nazi atrocities. Beyond that, the loftier didactic goal achieved by the prosecution was that the evidence itself became history and the Nuremberg trial remains to this day one of the most powerful historical records of Nazi atrocities committed during World War II.

2. Using Image-Based Evidence as a Didactic Tool at Trial

All prosecutions fundamentally involve pedagogy as they teach the court about the prosecution and defence theories and the evidence relied upon to support them. Counsel must consider how to present their evidence in the most effective manner because depending on the complexity of the material, the learning curve can be significant. While entertainment value is surely not the goal, so too must banality be avoided. Words will be required, but at times the points sought to be made are ineffable, such that words cannot adequately convey the true meaning of the evidence. It is in these darker corners where image-based evidence can serve a didactic purpose, casting much needed light. This section focuses on the use of image-based evidence to help convey complex facts as part of counsel's mission to educate the court about the case before it.

Understanding the value of images is essential since they are comprehended differently than words and may be digested more efficiently along with a heightened, though not necessarily justified, sense of understanding. They are generally remembered better than words and may also import emotion more readily.[80] These benefits favour using image-based evidence to explain certain evidential complexities to the court in a more concise and memorable manner. The more complex the material, the more image-based evidence may aid in comprehension.[81] How

[80] Elizabeth Porter, 'Taking Images Seriously', *Columbia Law Review* 114 (2014): 1687–1782, at 1752.

[81] Russell Carney and Joel Levin, 'Pictorial Illustrations *Still* Improve Students' Learning from Text', *Educational Psychology Review* 14, no. 1 (2002): 5–26, at 21; Richard Sherwin, 'Manifesto for Visual

information is presented, interpreted, and understood is dependent upon what information has been selected, to whom it is being shown, and the purposes for showing it.[82] Counsel must therefore consider how to weave image-based evidence into their case narrative in a manner that makes the telling of the story more complete, more impactful, and that does justice to the evidence.

Thorough pre-trial preparation will allow counsel to have command of often complex image-based evidence they intend to lead at trial, but the court will not have that same familiarization benefit. Since counsel only gets one opportunity to convey their evidence to the court, it is essential that the presentation be didactically effective. It must appear to observers and participants alike to be seamless, surgical, informative, and efficient. This approach is paradigmatic of the benefit of using image-based evidence as part of the trial narrative. Effective multimedia presentations convey evidential complexity with greater efficiency than words alone and may assist counsel and experts to convey the case narrative more effectively.

When viewers invest time and effort to interpret and understand complex visual evidence, they may believe more strongly in their interpretation because of the effort expended. An image that one must be taught to see and comprehend may achieve heightened credence as a result.[83] An expert witness who teaches complex material effectively using image-based evidence can induce that lightbulb moment when the epistemic competence of the viewers is improved. International criminal prosecutions invariably involve complex evidence that must be presented in such a way as to educate the court to ensure full comprehension and an understanding of the probative value of the evidence. Visual depiction is an essential component of that pedagogic exercise. Examples of the effective use of image-based evidence as didactic tools follow.

2.1 Visual Timelines

Few crimes are committed without substantial antecedents and post-offence events. Counsel must consider how to present such compendious data such that it will allow the court to understand how each piece of evidence fits into the overall case. The court can often gain a better appreciation for the significance of individual pieces of evidence if it is shown the big picture. Presentation of such data with an

Legal Realism', *Loyola of Los Angeles Law Review* 40, no. 2 (2007): 719–44, at 730; Damian Schofield, 'Animating Evidence: Computer Game Technology in the Courtroom', *Journal of Information Law and Technology* 1 (2009): 1–21, at 3.

[82] Damian Schofield and Ken Fowle, 'Technology Corner—Visualizing Forensic Data: Evidence (Part 1)', *Journal of Digital Forensics, Security and Law* 8, no. 1 (2013): 73–90, at 76.

[83] Jennifer Mnookin, 'Semi-Legibility and Visual Evidence: An Initial Exploration', *Law, Culture and the Humanities* 10, no. 1 (2014): 43–65, at 64–5.

effective visual timeline approach lends pedagogic value to the evidence, far exceeding what might be accomplished with a more sterile piecemeal exhibition.

A timeline is a longitudinal visual depiction of the chronology of a case. It may be used to provide an overview of the entire case, a detailed analysis of a specific incident or aspect of the case, or the role of a defendant. Visual timelines wherein longitudinal and contemporaneous case data is displayed in a comprehensive pictorial manner is of considerable value to counsel and the court. Timelines that are meticulously accurate and reflect admissible independently proven evidence are very useful in explaining the longitudinal precursors to critical incidents as well as relevant contemporaneous and subsequent events.

Because most crime does not follow a straight line from origin to conclusion, a timeline can show the occurrence of specific events along the way, as well as the introduction of individuals, objects, and locations.[84] An effective timeline should incorporate still images (ground-based, aerial, or satellite) and video images and may also utilize embedded interactive 360° visual representations. An effective timeline has substantial pedagogic value and can elevate the presentation of evidence from show-and-tell to show-and-teach.

2.2 Three-Dimensional (3D) Terrestrial Laser Scanning

Accurate and detailed depictions of crime scenes, areas of interest, and objects provide investigators, counsel, and the court with data necessary to comprehend available evidence more fulsomely and to understand what occurred. Scene measurements, including the location of objects and features within a scene, are central to a proper scene reconstruction, especially given that scenes are transient and ephemeral and that what may seem unimportant at the outset could take on greater significance at trial.[85] While photographs and video are common methods of documenting a scene, computers can also be used to incorporate data points to create visualized 3D scenes and objects in a digital visually appealing form.[86] Computer-based 3D modelling is particularly helpful when vertical dimensions of geographic, scene-based, or other features are important.[87] There is support for

[84] In experiments using mock juries in complex cases, jurors reported that timelines setting out when certain events occurred helped them to visualize temporal aspects of the case. Samuel Solomon, 'How Jurors Make Decisions: A Practical and Systematic Approach to Understanding Jury Behavior', *Sedona Conference Journal* 4 (2003): 175–96, at 189.

[85] Kayleigh Sheppard, John Cassella, and Sarah Fieldhouse, 'A Comparative Study of Photogrammetric Methods Using Panoramic Photography in a Forensic Context', *Forensic Science International* 273 (2017): 29–38, at 29–30.

[86] Schofield (n 82).

[87] Theresa Harris, Jonathan Drake, Jessica Wyndham, Susan Wolfinbarger, Stephen Lott, and Michael Lerner, 'Geospatial Evidence in International Human Rights Litigation: Technical and Legal Considerations', *AAAS Scientific Responsibility, Human Rights and Law Program* (2018), doi: 10.1126/srhrl.aau6090, 44.

the proposition that 3D modelling can be effective in adding clarity to expert testimony and in increasing viewer comprehension.[88]

Light detection and ranging (LiDAR) technology is a remote sensing technology that measures distance by illuminating a target with a laser and analysing the reflected light. Terrestrial LiDAR scanning devices, also referred to as terrestrial laser scanning (TLS) devices, emit laser beams into the selected environment while rotating horizontally and vertically. The scanner measures the distances and angles from the intensity of the reflected beams and computes the 3D coordinates of all reflected targets to create a 3D point cloud. These points produce a detailed and highly accurate visual 3D depiction of the scene.[89]

Two-dimensional depictions of scenes limit the ability of viewers to accurately assess spatial relationships of the overall scene and features and objects located within it.[90] They are also less suitable for reconstructing scenes and events using computer-generated animations or virtual reality walkthroughs.[91] Three-dimensional laser scanning allows investigators to capture the entire geometry of a scene, including objects and other relevant aspects that may not have been noted when the evidence was gathered, thus ensuring the longevity and preservation of the scene for a subsequent comprehensive examination.[92] The efficiency that TLS affords in documenting a scene saves investigators valuable on-site time. Multiple scanning technologies can be used to accurately measure outdoor and indoor scenes as well as vehicles and other objects. Combining different tiers of scanning technology provides a varied perspectival view of an event, maximizing the data that can be obtained from it.[93]

[88] In mock jury trials, jurors were better able to understand technical anatomical and medical language used by an expert witness when evaluating cause of death in a mock fatality when they were presented with 3D digital models (88%) and 3D-printed replicas (94%) of the victim's damaged cranium, rather than photographs alone (79%). David Errickson, Hannah Fawcett, Tim Thompson, and Andrew Campbell, 'The Effect of Different Imaging Techniques for the Visualization of Evidence in Court on Jury Comprehension', *International Journal of Legal Medicine* (2019): 1–5; Waltraud Baier, Jason Warnett, Mark Payne, and Mark Williams, 'Introducing 3D Printed Models as Demonstrative Evidence at Criminal Trials', *Journal of Forensic Sciences* 63, no. 4 (2018): 1298–1302, at 1302.

[89] Ursula Buck, Beat Kneubuehl, Silvio Näther, Nicola Albertini, Lars Schmidt, and Michael Thali, '3D Bloodstain Pattern Analysis: Ballistic Reconstruction of the Trajectories of Blood Drops and Determination of the Centres of Origin of the Bloodstains', *Forensic Science International* 206 (2011): 22–8, at 23. Forensic Technology Center of Excellence, 'Meeting Report: Terrestrial LiDAR Scanning Working Group for Criminal Justice Applications, First Meeting' (July 2020) https://forensiccoe.org/private/5fdb5d3d0b04d, 1.

[90] `Petra Urbanová, Mikolás Jurda, Tomás Vojtísek, and Jan Krajsa, 'Using Drone-Mounted Cameras for On-Site Body Documentation: 3D Mapping and Active Survey', *Forensic Science International* 281 (2017): 52–62, at 53, 60.

[91] ibid 53.

[92] Forensic Technology Center of Excellence, 'Landscape Study on 3D Crime Scene Scanning Devices (with 2018 Update)' https://forensiccoe.org/private/5dd6ad2d0ffeb, 10 of 2016 study.

[93] Waltraud Baier, Michael Donnelly, Mark Payne, and Mark Williams, 'A Holistic Multi-Scale Approach to Using 3D Scanning Technology in Accident Reconstruction', *Journal of Forensic Sciences* 65 (2020): 1774–8, at 1776.

Crime scenes can be documented three-dimensionally in addition to other conventional methods.[94] TLS devices can quickly scan large areas, buildings, rooms, and vehicles, generating point clouds with millions of points with accuracy ranges up to one millimetre.[95] This data can be used to create virtual reality scene walkthroughs, a topic that will be discussed in Chapter 8.[96] Three-dimensional scans have been used to visualize injuries for the purpose of determining the mechanism of injury, the location of mass graves, and ballistic reconstruction (bullet trajectory), amongst other purposes.[97]

At both the investigation and trial stage, this method of visual representation has clear application depending upon the locations involved. Increasingly, investigators and experts alike are utilizing, when economically and logistically feasible, 3D laser scanning technology for both scene capture and measurement, thereby combining laser scanner surveying and digital photography.[98] These visual presentation methods require expertise and considerable resources to produce but can be effective in depicting areas of interest. They can provide detailed depictions of static scenes, the recreation of an occurrence by showing the chronological sequence of events as they unfolded and may also permit the ability to move throughout the scene to view it from different perspectives. Three dimensional reconstructions have the advantage of increasing viewer comprehension and retention of complex data more efficiently than other presentation methods by more effectively capturing the attentiveness of the viewer and are more persuasive than non-visual evidence.[99]

Disadvantages in the use of 3D depictions include the inequality of arms that can arise when only one party uses such evidence and the risk of conscious or subconscious bias influencing the depiction of the measured data. A further concern is that there may be a reduction in the perceived need for critical appraisal by viewers as they may be inclined to accept a compelling visual presentation more readily.[100] Caution is required as 3D visualizations have a subjective element, and the court is shown what the creators have chosen to include and represent.[101]

As with the visual presentation of any evidence, validation of the underlying data and the presentation itself is essential for the court to utilize the evidence.

[94] Till Sieberth, Akos Dobay, Raffael Affolter, and Lars Ebert, 'Applying Virtual Reality in Forensics—A Virtual Scene Walkthrough', *Forensic Science, Medicine and Pathology* 15 (2018): 41–7, at 41.

[95] ibid.

[96] Eros Agosto, Andrea Ajmar, Piero Boccardo, Fabio Tonolo, and Andrea Lingua, 'Crime Scene Reconstruction Using a Fully Geomatic Approach', *Sensors* 8 (2008): 6280–6302, at 6281.

[97] Baier, Warnett, Payne, and Williams (n 93); Rachael Carew and David Errickson, 'An Overview of 3D Printing in Forensic Science: The Tangible Third-Dimension', *Journal of Forensic Sciences* 65, no. 5 (2020): 1752–60, at 1753–5.

[98] Schofield and Fowle (n 82) 78–9.

[99] ibid 83–4.

[100] ibid.

[101] 'International Bar Association Report', *IBA ICL Perspectives: Evidence Matters in ICC Trials* (August 2016) https://www.ibanet.org/document?id=Evidence-matters-in-icc-trials, 28–9.

Scientific validity and reliability remain the watchwords and data generated by TLS devices must be authenticated to be admissible, meaning that the party seeking to introduce the representation must establish that it is accurate and reliable. Errors in measurement, calibration, forensic workflow, and insufficient technical knowledge by TLS operators can result in the irreversible loss of evidence.[102] TLS data errors can result from systematic error and human error. Systematic errors involve erroneous coordinate values whereas human error concerns the generation of inaccurate measurements.[103] Digital evidence is fragile and may fall prey to intentional or inadvertent alteration during acquisition or subsequent processing.[104] Further, determining the intended evidential status for 3D evidence is essential as it impacts how counsel and the court evaluate the evidence.[105] Visual evidence that is tendered as demonstrative evidence may be subjected to less critique than evidence tendered for substantive purposes.

Details regarding the capture, storage, and transmission of digital scene data must be adequately documented, preserved, and available for review by interested parties. These are essential components of integrity verification.[106] Digital scene data should not be altered between the time of collection and its use in court, and should any alteration occur, it must be fully documented. Access to original data must be restricted to qualified individuals who understand the need to preserve the integrity of the data. Further, proper chain of custody documentation requires an accounting of the chronological history of the evidence with all steps from creation to presentation noted. Therefore, a comprehensive audit trail documenting the digital lifespan of the measurement data should be maintained and available for review. All data gathered from TLS scanning devices requires interpretation by an expert.[107] Where data is gathered by a device operator and then given to an analyst for detailed evaluation and further processing, the analyst must be qualified as an expert witness, specifically in the evaluation, interpretation, and processing of data gathered by TLS devices.

[102] Urbanová, Jurda, Vojtísek, and Krajsa (n 90) 59.

[103] Ryan Andrew Mullins, 'Virtual Views: Exploring the Utility and Impact of Terrestrial Laser Scanners in Forensics and Law (MA thesis, University of Windsor 2016), 14.

[104] Halil Bulbul, Guclu Yavuzcan, and Mezut Ozel, 'Digital Forensics: An Analytical Crime Scene Procedure Model', *Forensic Science International* 233 (2013): 244–56, at 245.

[105] IBA Report (n 101) 28–9.

[106] Integrity verification is the process of ensuring that the data used for analytical and presentation purposes is an accurate rendition of the original data. This may be accomplished with a hash value verification between the two iterations. Scientific Working Group on Digital Evidence, 'SWGDE Best Practices for Image Authentication (2018) https://drive.google.com/file/d/1IhMWleu-i-jW4LBSOIQIJnejNOfdCdJs/view, 4.

[107] Baier, Donnelly, Payne, and Williams (n 93) 1776.

2.3 Computer Generated Visualizations: Animations and Simulations

Computer-generated visualizations produce an image, diagram, graphic, or animation that represents underlying data and are designed to aid in the visual comprehension of the data by depicting what happened in a specific event or what is believed to have happened.[108] They represent a computer-based method of visually exploring the significance of collected data and are particularly helpful when an event is difficult to otherwise visualize, cannot be physically reproduced, is technically complex, when facts are disputed, and when timing is critical to evaluating the event.[109] These visualizations can represent with clarity and precision factual details and variations thereof that might be challenging to imagine relying upon verbal descriptions alone.[110] They can improve the viewer's ability to comprehend dynamic events, especially when supplemented with oral narration.[111] When evidence is animated, memory retention by viewers is heightened significantly.[112] Collectively, computer-generated visualizations represent a paradigmatic shift from the use of photography and video images to depict an event or scene.[113]

Computer-generated visualizations can be used to produce a forensic reconstruction, wherein events are portrayed three-dimensionally using underlying data from a particular event. They may take the form of animations or simulations. An animation is a reconstruction based on the input of known data. The visual result is essentially a digitally created movie destined for the courtroom, designed to present a party's narrative in a visually compelling format, based upon evidence independently proven to be admissible.[114] It can be based upon eyewitness testimony or an expert's theory of how an event occurred.[115] The reliability of the animation is wholly dependent upon the soundness of the source data.

Even though animations are classified as demonstrative evidence with no independent probative value, they can augment and visualize *viva voce* evidence. Animations that depict one party's view of how an event occurred with the added benefit of a temporal element can influence how viewers assesses the facts because

[108] Schofield and Fowle (n 82) 83–5.

[109] Carole Powell, 'Computer Generated Visual Evidence: Does Daubert Make a Difference?', *Georgia State University Law Review* 12, no 2 (1996): 577–600, at 581–2.

[110] Richard Sherwin, Neal Feigenson, and Christina Spiesel, 'What Is Visual Knowledge, and What Is It Good For? Potential Ethnographic Lessons from the Field of Legal Practice', *Visual Anthropology* 20 (2007): 143–78, 156–7; Richard Sherwin, 'Visual Literacy for the Legal Profession', *Journal of Legal Education* 68, no. 1 (2018): 55–63, at 57.

[111] Neal Feigenson, 'Visual Evidence', *Psychonomic Bulletin & Review* 17, no. 2 (2010): 149–54, at 151.

[112] Schofield (n 81) 5.

[113] Vincenzo Sainato, 'Evidentiary Presentations and Forensic Technologies in the Courtroom, The Director's Cut', *Journal of the Institute of Justice and International Studies* 9 (2009): 38–52, at 38.

[114] ibid 41.

[115] Betsy Fiedler, 'Are Your Eyes Deceiving You?: The Evidentiary Crisis Regarding the Admissibility of Computer Generated Evidence', *New York Law School Law Review* 48, no 1–2 (2003): 295–322, at 297.

they incorporate various data into a cohesive narrative.[116] Domestically, animations have been used in criminal and civil cases to recreate murders, motor vehicle collisions, airline crashes, and other events that have movement as their basis.[117] Animations provide a visually appealing didactic platform to present theories and arguments to the court.

In contrast to animations, simulations are generally categorized as real evidence as they are based upon case related data and rely upon mathematical calculations and physics formulas to produce a mathematically accurate portrayal of an event.[118] Simulations can be very helpful in explaining difficult concepts, especially in circumstances where multiple actions are involved, where timing is critical, and when different permutations must be considered. Because they constitute scientific evidence with probative value, simulations must be proven to be scientifically valid and reliable. The tendering party must be able to qualify the expert witness, establish the reliability and validity of the computer hardware and software that produced the simulation, prove the validity and accuracy of the data input and mathematical calculations, and the corresponding accuracy of the ultimate presentation media.[119] Expert testimony must also address the proper interpretation of the simulation—and any limitations inherent in the depiction—and must withstand cross examination and opposing expert testimony in order to have epistemic evidential merit.

Computer-generated visualizations offer important advantages for counsel and the court. They can be used to observe and examine a re-enacted scene for the purpose of teaching the court about the event.[120] They assist in making complex facts and technical details more understandable for viewers, thereby injecting needed clarity and illumination, because they capitalize on the value of data visualization.[121] They are also helpful for counsel when presenting their theories of the case during the trial and in final argument. To have epistemic value and to achieve admissibility, visualizations must fairly and accurately represent the evidence they purport to explain.[122]

[116] Meghan Dunn, Peter Salovey, and Neal Feigenson, 'The Jury Persuaded (and Not): Computer Animation in the Courtroom', *Law and Policy* 28, no. 2 (2006): 228–48, at 229–31; Schofield (n 81) 3–5.

[117] Sainato (n 113) 42–3; Dunn, Salovey, and Feigenson (n 116) 230.

[118] Christopher O'Connor, 'Computer-Generated Visual Evidence', *Advocate (Vancouver Bar Association)* 53, no. 3 (1995): 421–6, https://www.expertinstitute.com/resources/insights/computer-simulations-in-the-courtroom-an-expert-perspective/, at 422.

[119] O'Connor (n 118) 424–5; Fiedler (n 115) 298–302; Wayne Gardner, 'Explanations and Illustrations: Demonstrative Evidence in the Criminal Courtroom', *Criminal Law Quarterly* 38, no. 4 (1996): 425–6, at 438–40; Jennifer Mnookin, 'Repeat Play Evidence: Jack Weinstein, "Pedagogical Devices," Technology, and Evidence', *DePaul Law Review* 64, no. 2 (2015): 571–600, at 575–6.

[120] Fiedler (n 115) 302.

[121] Schofield and Fowle (n 82) 83–5.

[122] David Santee, 'More Than Words: Rethinking the Role of Modern Demonstrative Evidence', *Santa Clara Law Review* 52, no 1 (2012): 105–44, at 125.

Visualizations are not without their disadvantages. Visually powerful presentations can predominate and overwhelm the court's assessment of evidence, drawing on vividness and emotional appeal, especially when juries are involved.[123] Additionally, entertainment value may subvert accuracy for uninformed viewers, causing them to accept the information presented as true, even when it is not.[124] This danger is even more palpable if the presentation's underlying data is in dispute, does not cover all possible interpretations, or is presented in a biased or misleading manner.

As with all visual evidence, the probative value of the animation or simulation must exceed its prejudicial effect.[125] This takes on more importance when considering that the way the data is presented can subtly affect how it is perceived by the viewer.[126] Equality of arms may be an issue when only one party has the resources to produce impressive visualizations of key evidence, though whether that should result in disallowing the advantaged party from using such evidence is debatable.[127] Aside from an equality issue, it is often the case that only the prosecution has the need to visually depict an event.[128] A related consideration is whether a visually compelling presentation is unnecessarily overwhelming and should therefore be disallowed in circumstances where the event depicted is not in issue. For example, the defence may not take issue with the crime base (the atrocity itself), instead focusing on the crime linkage issue of whether the defendant is liable for the atrocity crime. In such cases, a powerful visual presentation may have limited probative value on the true issue and inject unfair prejudice.

3. Demonstrative Evidence

Demonstrative evidence is evidence addressed directly to the senses without the intervention of testimony.[129] It includes non-verbal evidence that is not tendered as real evidence.[130] Significantly, it possesses no independent probative value and takes the form of an object or visual depiction that is used to explain, illustrate, or assist in the comprehension of other admissible evidence in a more effective

[123] Mnookin (n 119) 576.

[124] Fiedler (n 115) 297.

[125] Dunn, Salovey, and Feigenson (n 116) 229.

[126] Fiedler references Gestalt psychology which focuses on how people perceive images and how the area, closeness, proximity, continuation, and symmetry of an image can be manipulated by its creator, sometimes to the unfair advantage to one party over another. Fiedler (n 115) 305–6.

[127] Mnookin suggests that this may be the appropriate judicial levelling response; Mnookin (n 119) 576. I disagree that otherwise admissible and helpful evidence should be excluded solely to level the playing field as the court should have the best evidence.

[128] Traditionally, it is the prosecution who presents a visual narrative, with the defence challenging it, though not necessarily producing a new visual narrative.

[129] Henry Black, *Black's Law Dictionary*, 5th ed. (Minnesota: West Publishing, 1979).

[130] Santee (n 122) 111.

manner.[131] For example, a 3D animation of an event does not prove that the event occurred in the manner depicted. That must be proven through substantive, not demonstrative evidence. However, even though demonstrative evidence lacks probative value, it is often more compelling than the underlying data used to create the demonstrative exhibit, especially when assessing scientific evidence.[132]

Demonstrative evidence is typically secondary in nature, used for the derivative purpose of illustration only. It is evidence that is designed to illustrate *viva voce* and other forms of evidence by way of a visual recreation.[133] It may take the form of photographs, video images, diagrams, charts, maps, 3D models, 3D scans, and computer-generated animations, and may also be used to show competing perspectives of an event.[134] In cases with complex scenes and events such as *Prosecutor v. Ayyash et al.*, demonstrative evidence can be used as a way of injecting clarity and order to vast amounts of data that would otherwise have been very difficult to comprehend.[135]

Demonstrative evidence hovers awkwardly on the boundary between illustration and proof.[136] As a matter of law, it has no independent evidential or probative value, or so counsel argue when tendering it. Demonstrative evidence is sometimes an ersatz label used to cover any number of sins, where counsel seek to tender evidence with no independent basis for admissibility and paint it with the demonstrative evidence brush to get it before the court. For example, in *Prosecutor v. Ongwen*, the prosecution justified a request for delayed disclosure of 'electronic visual representations of the four attack locations derived from the use of drone photography/ video and three dimensional laser scanning' on the basis that they were 'not of primary evidentiary value', yet later sought to have them admitted as full evidentiary exhibits.[137] While perhaps not intending to mislead, the prosecution's inability to properly categorize evidence creates uncertainty for the defence and the court as proper classification dictates the level of scrutiny to be applied. Compelling

131 Gardner (n 119) 445; Santee (n 122) 109; Stephanie Green, '50 Shades of Prejudicial: Reexamining Demonstrative Evidence Through State v. Jones', *University of Toledo Law Review* 45, no. 2 (2014): 319–46, at 325.

132 Green (n 131) 343; Angela Jones and Margaret Kovera, 'A Demonstrative Helps Opposing Expert Testimony Sensitize Jurors to the Validity of Scientific Evidence', *Journal of Forensic Psychology Practice* 15, no. 5 (2015): 401–22.

133 Jennifer Mnookin, 'The Image of Truth: Photographic Evidence and the Power of Analogy', *Yale Journal of Law and the Humanities* 10, no. 1 (1998): 1–74, at 67–70; Sainato (n 122) 39.

134 Santee (n 122) 112.

135 In addition to visualizing the scene of the explosion through satellite images, photographs, and 3D reconstructions, extensive visualization of cell phone and tower data was used as didactic tools to explain billions of call data records; STL-11-01/T/TC R273784, Decision on Five Prosecution Motions on Call Sequence Tables and Eight Witness Statements and on the Legality of the Transfer of Call Data Records to UNIIIC and STL's Prosecution, 6 May 2015, para. 2.

136 Mnookin (n 133) 70.

137 ICC-02/04-01/15-438, Prosecution Submissions in Accordance with the Scheduling Order of 4 May 2016, 18 May 2016, para 8; ICC-02/04-01/15-T-25-ENG ET WT 23-05-2016, Transcript, 23 May 2016, 19–20.

demonstrative evidence may cause viewers to forget that it is merely a visual representation of a witness's evidence.[138]

Demonstrative evidence may venture closer to the unduly prejudicial end of the spectrum and farther away from probity if the viewer is not adequately cautioned that seeing should not necessarily equate with believing.[139] Even then it would be naïve to expect such intellectual rigour, at least on the subconscious level. Judges generally have extensive legal training from their prior legal career and ongoing judicial training and are thus more attuned to compartmentalizing evidence appropriately. Conversely, jurors receive their formal legal training only during the trial itself and are much less likely to be able to section off evidence into proof/non-proof silos. Image-based evidence can be very powerful and emotionally evocative, such that an appealing animation or other visual depiction may be viewed as truth, no matter what admonitions and cautions are given.[140] When a jury is instructed to disregard evidence they should not have received, it serves to highlight the impugned evidence rather than abrogate its existence.

Even though demonstrative evidence may be subjected to less stringent admissibility standards given that it is not tendered as proof, it must still be an accurate representation of the facts.[141] Therefore, admissibility is contingent upon a showing of relevance, authenticity, accuracy, and reliability.[142] When using a forensic animation as a demonstrative tool, there is merit in displaying a disclaimer indicating that the evidence is for demonstrative purposes only.[143] This caution applies to all forms of demonstrative evidence and the court should be constantly reminded that such evidence has no independent value. Image-based evidence offered merely for demonstrative purposes may be intended as subconscious proof disguised by banal nomenclature. Mindful that once rung, a bell cannot be unrung, courts must be cautious in ascertaining the true nature of the evidence tendered and the specific purpose counsel intends to make of it.

Conclusion

Central to this chapter and the book overall is the proposition that atrocity crime prosecutions are in a category that sets them apart from most domestic prosecutions. They involve complexities borne of multiple events occurring over a long period of time covering a broad geographic area and sometimes involving multiple

[138] Santee (n 122) 108–9.
[139] Green (131) 320, 327–8.
[140] Eryn Newman and Neal Feigenson, 'The Truthiness of Visual Evidence', *Jury Expert* 25, no. 5 (2013): 9–14.
[141] Baier, Warnett, Payne, and Williams (n 93) 1299.
[142] Gardner (n 119) 445; Green (n 131) 325.
[143] Sainato (n 113) 49.

defendants. The evidence that is collected and generated for use in court must be given special consideration by counsel and the court and must be presented in a way that sufficiently educates the court as to the import of the evidence and its role in truth discovery. The evidential complexity attendant with these major prosecutions compels a didactic approach in the courtroom. Leading evidence is not simply a disgorgement process; rather counsel must teach their case to the court.

Image-based evidence is a powerful tool for proof and truth purposes but also for the didactic purpose of teaching the case to the court. At its most basic level, the use of photographic, video, and other images can be used to depict scenes and events. A more analytical approach to complex scenes and events may compel a digital recreation using 3D visualization technologies. As will be developed in Chapter 8, atrocity crime prosecutions may lend themselves to the use of sophisticated teaching techniques such as advanced visual representations in the form of virtual reality and immersive virtual environments.

For image-based evidence that requires expert analysis and presentation, such as 3D scene reconstructions, animations, and simulations, it is worth considering whether the expert witness educates the court to be able to comprehend the evidence presented or conversely whether the court simply defers to the expert's authoritative statements regarding the evidence.[144] Does the court really see what the expert is describing or does it merely subconsciously accede to the expert's position? By teaching the court to interpret semi-legible visual evidence, judges may attempt their own interpretation, without the expert's further guidance.[145] For this reason, it is essential that counsel educate the court through the presentation of expert evidence as to the acceptable parameters for which the evidence can be used to prevent the court from drawing more conclusory value from the evidence than is warranted or failing to see alternative interpretations. The dichotomous position where judges either reject technical evidence because they do not understand it or accept it without qualification must be avoided as neither position is tenable.[146] When judges and counsel gain more visual literacy, they are better able to discern what information can fairly be obtained from image-based evidence and to evaluate those findings in the context of other evidence.[147]

[144] Mnookin (n 83) 61.

[145] 'Semi-legible' refers to visual displays that are only partially decipherable by a lay viewer (e.g. poor quality photographs and video images, complex visual reconstructions, fingerprints, x-rays, MRIs, etc.).

[146] Lindsay Freeman, 'Digital Evidence and War Crimes Prosecutions: The Impact of Digital Technologies on International Criminal Investigations and Trials', *Fordham International Law Journal* 41, no. 2 (2018): 283–335, 312.

[147] Neal Feigenson and Richard Sherwin, 'Thinking Beyond the Shown: Implicit Inferences in Evidence and Argument', *Law, Probability and Risk* 6 (2007): 295–310, at 309.

3

The Democratization of Image-Based Evidence

Introduction

A violent crime occurs. The police are called. Police officers arrive and investigate. A forensic team arrives to gather evidence. At the domestic level, serious and violent crime tends to be investigated relatively promptly. Conversely, atrocity crime investigations face substantial delay as international investigators contend with impediments caused by bureaucratic procedures, government interference, and security concerns over the presence of continued conflict. Civilian images of atrocities and ISIS videos of beheadings will not generate an ideal rapid response as investigators cannot be omnipresent. It is within this milieu that locally sourced image-based evidence documenting allegations of criminality has taken a firm foothold in atrocity crime investigations.

There is a clear trend and pressing need in atrocity crime investigations to utilize images obtained by non-investigators as investigative leads or as methods of proof.[1] Atrocity crime investigations are different from most domestic investigations and those differences impact the ability of investigators to obtain valuable evidence in a timely manner. Democratizing the gathering of image-based evidence therefore plays a key role in atrocity crime investigations though it has its disadvantages, including the concern that civilian media may not objectively portray recorded events.[2] A further consideration is how civilian media is transmitted to investigators, whether directly or indirectly through intermediaries, social media, open source sites, and dedicated evidence gathering applications, and how those methods of transmission may affect the integrity of the evidence.

[1] For ease of reference and as more fully discussed in Section 1, I will refer to all forms of images obtained by non-investigators as civilian visual evidence or civilian media. Almost all civilian visual evidence consists of digital video and photographs. Jessica Levy and Paul Williams, 'Documentation for Accountability', *Case Western Reserve Journal of International Law* 52 (2020): 451–66.

[2] When members of the public assume responsibility to gather evidence that would normally be gathered by investigators or the state, this important task is thereby made accessible to a wider range of people and made less elitist. In short, it has been democratized. 'democratise, v', adj' (*OED Online*, OUP August 2023), www.oed.com accessed 7 August 2023. It has also been referred to as 'crowdsourcing'. Mary Fan, 'Democratizing Proof: Pooling Public and Police Body-Camera Videos', *North Carolina Law Review* 96, no. 5 (2018): 1639–80, at 1643.

Image-Based Evidence in International Criminal Prosecutions. Jonathan W. Hak, KC, Oxford University Press.
 DOI: 10.1093/oso/9780198889533.003.0003

Civilian visual evidence has been used in atrocity crime prosecutions at tribunals and the International Criminal Court (ICC), and domestic prosecutions for international crimes. One of the most pernicious issues that arise when civilian visual evidence is uploaded to social media and other sites is that the photographer may be unknown and therefore access to important contextual and technical information is absent. Given the liberally inclusive approach to admissibility adopted by the tribunals and the ICC, the use of anonymous civilian visual evidence poses fair trial concerns.

1. The Role of Civilian Visual Evidence in Atrocity Crime Investigations

Serious and violent crime committed at the domestic level tends to be reported promptly, which allows investigators to gather evidence relatively expeditiously, while there is still an active crime scene and physical evidence remains *in situ*. In the early stages of an investigation, evidence gathering is paramount. While investigators may have preliminary theories of what occurred and who is responsible, objective and thorough documentation of the scene with image-based, physical, and forensic evidence is critical. Delayed attendance impacts the ability of investigators to perform a detailed scene examination, as time and intervening events may result in evidence spoliation and scene changes. Scenes may also prove to be largely inaccessible to investigators due to remoteness or security risks. As such, the ICC Office of the Prosecutor (OTP) and other investigators often face impediments in the efficacious gathering of evidence that set their investigations apart from their domestic counterparts.[3]

OTP investigators face significant hurdles when investigating atrocity crimes, with delay being a common factor. Investigating incidents that occurred long ago is much more exacting because the passage of time rarely benefits the search for evidence—and truth. A common feature in international criminal investigations is that the cases are often cold and the evidence old.[4] Even in a post-conflict environment, access to the crime scene may be delayed by months or years due to the need to secure a legal right of access from the state's government or from the UN Security Council.[5] During the ensuing delay, perpetrators have the opportunity to destroy or conceal evidence, an option that has been exercised over the years.[6]

[3] I will primarily focus on the ICC as it is the OTP that is responsible for many international atrocity crime investigations and prosecutions today, though my comments are also applicable to the tribunals.

[4] Thijs Bouwknegt, 'Investigating International Crimes: Pitfalls, Problems and Promises', in *Quality Control in Criminal Investigation*, edited by Xabier Agirre, Morten Bergsmo, Simon De Smet, and Carsten Stahn (Brussels: Torkel Opsahl Academic EPublisher, 2020), 67–113, at 76.

[5] Anni Pues, 'Towards the "Golden Hour"? A Critical Exploration of the Length of Preliminary Examinations', *Journal of International Criminal Justice* 15 (2017): 435–53, at 438–9.

[6] For example, the Japanese destroyed documents prior to the Tokyo trial, as did the Khmer Rouge when Vietnamese soldiers entered Cambodia, and to hamper investigation of the Srebrenica massacres,

Evidence may also be lost for non-nefarious reasons such as the death or incapacity of witnesses; the loss of documents and other tangible evidence; and deterioration in the forensic value of scenes, human remains, and other items of interest. When *viva voce* evidence is available, it will be affected by the endemic challenges associated with human memory, recall, and reporting.[7] The common theme is that the destruction and degradation of evidence caused by delay often results in a stark paucity of primary and corroborative evidence.

Government interference with OTP investigations is another significant impediment to gathering evidence of atrocity crimes, especially given the fact that many large-scale conflicts involve government officials. There are situations where the OTP's ability to gather evidence within the impugned state is simply not feasible because of danger or remoteness.[8] For example, Burundi has denied OTP access to its territory since the OTP commenced a preliminary investigation in 2016.[9] The OTP's ability to investigate allegations of atrocity crimes in Darfur, Sudan, the first situation the UN Security Council referred to the ICC for investigation, has been effectively thwarted as OTP personnel and anyone suspected of being associated with them have been threatened with death by the Sudanese government.[10] The American government openly expressed its opposition to the ICC conducting any investigation of its activities in Iraq and Afghanistan, including denying entry to the US for ICC staff.[11] Even in situations where OTP investigators are allowed access, their ability to gather the best evidence may be hampered. For example, impediments in conducting a thorough investigation were asserted by an OTP investigator in *Prosecutor v. Lubanga*, who testified regarding the presence of armed groups at the time of the investigation and threats to investigators and anyone believed to be cooperating with them.[12] These examples are reflective of government and local impediments facing investigators.

the Serbs buried victims in mass clandestine graves. Discussed in Nancy Combs, 'Deconstructing the Epistemic Challenges to Mass Atrocity Prosecutions', *Washington and Lee Law Review* 75, no. 1 (2018): 223–300, at 249–50.

[7] Discussed in Section 1 of Chapter 1.

[8] Theresa Harris, Jonathan Drake, Jessica Wyndham, Susan Wolfinbarger, Stephen Lott, and Michael Lerner, 'Geospatial Evidence in International Human Rights Litigation: Technical and Legal Considerations', *AAAS Scientific Responsibility, Human Rights and Law Program* (2018) doi: 10.1126/srhrl.aau6090, 1.

[9] Combs (n 6) 252.

[10] *Prosecutor v. Harun & Kushayb*, ICC-02/05-01/07-48-Red, Public Redacted Version of Prosecution Request for a Finding on the Non-Cooperation of the Government of the Sudan, 19 April 2010, paras. 33–36; Rebecca Hamilton, 'User Generated Evidence', *Columbia Journal of Transnational Law* 57, no. 1 (2018): 1–61, at 13–14; Combs (n 6) 252.

[11] ICC Press releases (11 June 2020) https://www.icc-cpi.int/Pages/item.aspx?name=200611-icc-statement; (2 September 2020) https://www.icc-cpi.int/Pages/item.aspx?name=pr1535. See also Leila Sadat, 'Reforming the International Criminal Court: "Lean in" or "Leave"', *Washington University Journal of Law & Policy* 62 (2020): 51–76, at 57–8. After US President Trump left office in January 2021, restrictions against ICC staff entering the US lessened.

[12] ICC-01/04-01/06, Deposition of Witness DRC-OTP-WWWW-0582, 16 November 2010, 34–40; cited in Hamilton (n 10) 12–13.

A further hindrance to evidence gathering occurs when atrocity crime allegations involve regions undergoing active conflict, which renders the attendance of investigators very difficult and unsafe, especially when the government is antagonistic towards the investigation.[13] When OTP investigators commenced their investigation in the Democratic Republic of the Congo (DRC), they were not able to attend certain regions due to security concerns.[14] Libya poses similar challenges.[15] Difficulties accessing conflict zones and security concerns when in attendance mean that investigators often work through local intermediaries.[16] They may also rely on reports written by the UN or NGOs.[17] Even when investigators are able to enter a conflict zone, multiple attacks within the same area make it more difficult for investigators to differentiate what evidence is associated with what attack.[18]

These investigative challenges have created an evidential vacuum which is increasingly being filled by members of the public. Image-based evidence that emanates from people other than investigators and state actors has been referred to as 'citizen journalism',[19] 'mobile witnessing',[20] and 'user-generated evidence',[21]

[13] Xavier Laroche and Eric Baccard, 'International Courts and Forensic Science', in *Encyclopedia of Forensic Sciences*, 2nd ed., edited by Jay Siegel and Pekka Saukko (Waltham: Academic Press, 2013), 488–95, at 489–90; Xabier Aranburu and Morten Bergsmo, 'Investigative Bottlenecks and the Mindset of Quality Control', in *Quality Control in Criminal Investigation*, edited by Xabier Agirre, Morten Bergsmo, Simon De Smet, and Carsten Stahn (Brussels: Torkel Opsahl Academic EPublisher, 2020), 1–34, at 9–10.

[14] Combs (n 6) 246.

[15] In her *Eleventh Report of The Prosecutor of the International Criminal Court to the United Nations Security Council Pursuant to UNSCR 1970 (2011),* the Prosecutor noted, 'The Office underscores that due to the prevailing instability and current security situation, it is impossible for investigators to undertake investigative activities in Libya. While the Office continues to successfully collect some of the available evidence from outside Libya, a substantial body of the evidence required to augment the investigations and prosecutions can only be accessed in Libya.' (26 May 2016) https://www.icc-cpi.int/itemsDocuments/otp_report_lib_26052016-eng.pdf, para. 11.

[16] 'An intermediary is someone who comes between one person and another; who facilitates contact or provides a link between one of the organs or units of the Court or Counsel on the one hand, and victims, witnesses, beneficiaries of reparations and/or affected communities more broadly on the other.' 'ICC Guidelines Governing the Relations Between the Court and Intermediaries for the Organs and Units of the Court and Counsel Working with Intermediaries' (March 2014) https://www.legal-tools.org/doc/e0f990/pdf, 5. The use of intermediaries is essential but has at times backfired when it came to light that they improperly influenced witnesses. In *Prosecutor v. Lubanga*, ICC-01/04-01/06-2842, Judgment Pursuant to Article 74 of the Statute, 14 March 2012, paras. 482–483, the Trial Chamber was highly critical of the evidence intermediaries gathered and criticized the prosecution for using them. For a helpful analysis of intermediaries, see Emily Haslam and Rod Edmunds, 'Managing a New "Partnership": "Professionalization", Intermediaries and the International Criminal Court', *Criminal Law Forum* 24 (2013): 49–85.

[17] Nancy Combs, 'Grave Crimes and Weak Evidence: Fact-Finding Evolution in International Criminal Law', *Harvard International Law Journal* 58, no. 1 (2017): 47–126, at 123.

[18] Even when the state is cooperative, inadequate local resources and forensic infrastructure are also problematic. Laroche and Baccard (n 13) 488–95.

[19] See e.g. Brianne Leyh, 'Changing Landscapes in Documentation Efforts: Civil Society Documentation of Serious Human Rights Violations', *Utrecht Journal of International and European Law* 33, no. 84 (2017): 44–58, at 46.

[20] See e.g. Anna Reading, 'Mobile Witnessing: Ethics and the Camera Phone in the "War on Terror"', *Globalizations* 6, no. 1 (2009): 61–76, at 65.

[21] See e.g. Hamilton (n 10) 3.

collectively referring to people who in a non-appointed investigative capacity take an active part in documenting and transmitting images of conflict. Included in this category are civilian witnesses, victims, combatants, perpetrators, third-party observers, and members of civil society.[22] Civilians have long answered the clarion call to record images that are of value in criminal cases.[23] For example, civilians provide highly relevant probative videos and photographs for use in investigations and prosecutions before tribunals and the ICC.[24] The advent of the Apple iPhone in 2007 and its competitors resulted in millions of people gaining the ability to document atrocities at unprecedented levels.[25] This evidence has probative value not just as crime base evidence but also as linkage evidence. Combining the pervasiveness of mobile technology with access to the internet and the increasing number of civilians documenting ICC crimes means that prosecutors do not have to rely exclusively upon evidence gathered directly by investigators.[26] While developing nations may have less civilian visual evidence than developed nations, caused in part by differences in the access to technology, the camera has found its place in atrocity crime and human rights violation documentation just the same.[27]

[22] Civil society may be defined as being constituted from all public spheres, separate from the state and economic market, which fosters political participation and discursive interaction. It involves political and social action characterized by a diverse range of actors with different, sometimes competing, agendas and repertoires of action, and includes organizations, institutions, and other entities which mediate between the individual and the state. Paul Gready and Simon Robins, 'Rethinking Civil Society and Transitional Justice: Lessons from Social Movements and "New" Civil Society', *The International Journal of Human Rights* 21, no. 7 (2017): 956–75, at 958. The authors argue that a new civil society has emerged, associated with events such as the Arab Spring and austerity protests in Southern Europe, sometimes rejecting mainstream NGOs, but still focusing on human rights and transitional justice. The UN Office of the High Commissioner for Human Rights defines civil society actors as 'individuals and groups who engage in forms of public participation and actions around shared interest, purposes or values that are compatible with the goals of the UN: the maintenance of peace and security, the realization of development, and the promotion and respect of human rights'. See UN High Commissioner for Human Rights, 'Civil Society and the United Nations Human Rights System: A Practical Guide for Civil Society' (2014) https://www.ohchr.org/en/publications/policy-and-methodological-publications/civil-society-space-and-united-nations-human.

[23] The use of 'civilian' in this broader context is a helpful demarcation intended to refer to people who are not part of any official investigative team. This includes members of civil society groups, many of whom have targeted evidence collection training and may occupy a higher status as a result.

[24] Lonneke van der Velden, 'Forensic Devices for Activism: Metadata Tracking and Public Proof', *Big Data & Society* (July-December 2015): 1–14, at 1; Jay Aronson, 'The Utility of User-Generated Content in Human Rights Investigations', in *New Technologies for Human Rights Law and Practice*, edited by Molly Land and Jay Aronson (Cambridge: CUP, 2018), 129–48, at 131; Levy and Williams (n 1) 455.

[25] Rebecca Hamilton, 'Social Media Platforms in International Criminal Investigations', *Case Western Reserve Journal of International Law* 52 (2020): 213–24, at 216; UC Berkeley School of Law Human Rights Center, 'Digital Lockers: Archiving Social Media Evidence of Atrocity Crimes' (2021) https://humanrights.berkeley.edu/sites/default/files/digital_lockers_report5, 2 ('Digital Lockers').

[26] Róisín Costello, 'International Criminal Law and the Role of Non-State Actors in Preserving Open Source Evidence', *Cambridge International Law Journal* 7, no. 2 (2018): 268–83, at 269; Levy and Williams (n 1) 461–2; Christof Heyns, 'Report of the Special Rapporteur on Extrajudicial, Summary or Arbitrary Executions', UN Doc. A/HRC/29/37 (24 April 2015) para. 39.

[27] See generally Sandra Ristovska, 'The Rise of Eyewitness Video and its Implications for Human Rights: Conceptual and Methodological Approaches', *Journal of Human Rights* 15, no. 3 (2016): 347–60; Jay Aronson, McKenna Cole, Alex Hauptmann, Dan Miller, and Bradley Samuels, 'Reconstructing Human Rights Violations Using Large Eyewitness Collections: The Case of Euromaidan Protester Deaths', *Journal of Human Rights Practice* (2018): 1–20, at 2; Aoife Duffy, 'Bearing Witness to Atrocity

By default, there has been a silent devolution of evidence gathering from state and OTP investigators to civilians, not as part of any explicit or tacit agreement but as a sheer matter of necessity. Resulting from limited investigative resources, delay, interference, and security concerns, investigators are reliant upon third parties for the collection and provision of certain evidence.[28] This is not to suggest that OTP investigators have shifted the responsibility to investigate atrocities to others in abdication of their investigative role. Rather, it reflects the reality that evidence of ICC crimes is often temporally tenuous and if not captured by civilians, it may be lost to the ages. Aside from execution videos recorded by aggressors themselves for trophy and propaganda purposes, likely the only image-based evidence showing active criminality is civilian media provided to investigators either directly, through an intermediary, or uploaded to purpose-built evidence gathering applications created by human rights organizations or as open source video to myriad internet sites including Facebook, YouTube, and TikTok.[29] This rising tide of civilian visual evidence is readily apparent in the 2022 Russian invasion of Ukraine.

Civilian visual evidence has proven to be an unexpectedly rich source of information in other international contexts as well. For example, the MH17 Joint Investigation Team (JIT), which investigated the deliberate downing of a civilian airliner (Malaysia Airlines Flight MH17) over eastern Ukraine on 17 July 2014 resulting in the deaths of all 298 people onboard, relied heavily upon an extensive library of social media images taken over several days which documented a Russian convoy of military vehicles travelling from the 53rd Anti-Aircraft Missile Brigade in Kursk, Russian Federation, to eastern Ukraine. By examining the open source imagery, investigators were able to identify the specific BUK TELAR surface to air missile launcher used to shoot down MH17 as it made its way to eastern Ukraine as part of the military convoy. This was documented in a video presentation produced by the JIT as part of an appeal for witnesses and information from the public.[30] In

Crimes: Photography and International Law', *Human Rights Quarterly* 40 (2018): 776–814, at 784–5; Samantha Greenfield, 'Social Media Platforms: Preserving Evidence of International Crimes', *International Comparative, Policy Ethics Law Review* 2, no. 3 (2019): 821–48.

[28] Carsten Stahn, 'From Preliminary Examination to Investigation: Rethinking the Connection', in *Quality Control in Criminal Investigation*, edited by Xabier Agirre, Morten Bergsmo, Simon De Smet, and Carsten Stahn (Brussels: Torkel Opsahl Academic EPublisher, 2020), 37–66, at 43.

[29] Open source media consists of media that is uploaded to social media sites, information sharing websites, traditional mass media publications, the dark web, and other publicly accessible internet sites. Office of the United Nations High Commissioner for Human Rights and the Human Rights Centre at the University of California, Berkeley, School of Law, 'Berkeley Protocol on Digital Open Source Investigations' (2020) https://www.ohchr.org/sites/default/files/2022-04/OHCHR_BerkeleyProtocol.pdf, 3 ('Berkeley Protocol').

[30] Joint Investigation Team MH17, 'Witness Appeal Video' https://www.youtube.com/watch?v=rhyd875Qtlg.

convicting three of the four defendants on 17 November 2022, the District Court of The Hague relied in part upon these images and others obtained from civilians.[31]

The MH17 investigation is an interesting example of the public becoming engaged in evidence gathering. Ukrainian Interior Minister Aven Avakov posted a thirteen second video clip showing a BUK M-1 missile launcher (the same type of launcher implicated in the downing of MH17) travelling through an urban location at a relevant time.[32] Investigative journalism agency Bellingcat undertook the task of corroborating this video and the location depicted with Google Earth imagery as well as civilian media, CCTV, and dashcam video from various open sources to create a compelling narrative of the missile launcher travelling from the Russian Federation into eastern Ukraine and then back again.[33] This is an example of democratizing evidence gathering—taking seemingly disparate images and analysing it with a view to producing a compelling narrative presentation. I do not suggest that such presentations should be viewed as being the objective truth without the need for further inquiry, but they are worthy of consideration by investigators.

1.1 The Value of Civilian Visual Evidence

Given the grave nature of atrocity crimes, it is imperative that they be well documented to assist the ICC in its mission to hold responsible parties accountable. Democratizing the gathering of image-based evidence has several laudable benefits, with scope being among the most important. Because images are being gathered by a far broader array of people in widely disparate circumstances and locations, with varying vantage points, a larger, richer pool of potential evidence becomes available to investigators.[34] Considering that investigators cannot be at most conflict locations while ICC crimes are actively being committed, there would be far less and sometimes no timely visual evidence without civilian media.[35] It is also

[31] MH 17 Trial, 'Summary of the Judgment of the District Court of The Hague' https://www.courtmh17.com/en/news/2022/summary-of-the-day-in-court-17-november-2022---judgment.html.

[32] Alex Jeffrey, 'Legal Geography III: Evidence', *Progress in Human Geography* 45, no. 4 (2021): 902–13, at 902–3.

[33] Bellingcat, 'MH17—The Open Source Investigation' (2015) https://www.bellingcat.com/news/uk-and-europe/2015/10/08/mh17-the-open-source-evidence/.

[34] Thousands of images and video recordings showing the violence of war are uploaded to the internet every day. Simone Friis, '"Beyond Anything We Have Ever Seen": Beheading Videos and the Visibility of Violence in the War Against ISIS', *International Affairs* 91, no. 4 (2015): 725–46, at 728; Molly Land and Jay Aronson, 'The Promise and Peril of Human Rights Technology', in *New Technologies for Human Rights Law and Practice*, edited by Molly Land and Jay Aronson (Cambridge: CUP, 2018), 1–20, at 9; Mareike Meis, 'Civil-Resistance Videography as Human Rights Practice: The Non-Survivor Testimony and the Striving for Criminal Jurisdiction in Syria and Beyond', *Journal of Human Rights Practice* (2022): 1–19, at 11.

[35] Civilian visual evidence is lauded as an unofficial response to the problems faced by investigators in obtaining timely evidence. Hamilton (n 10) 12.

worthy of note that an important source of valuable images is from the perpetrators themselves.[36]

Delay is no friend of truth-seeking. Destruction and degradation of evidence for want of collection or documentation is a common consequence of delayed investigations.[37] Through democratization, evidence can be gathered expeditiously and preserved, long before investigators arrive on the scene, thereby helping to fill an evidential lacuna that would otherwise exist and to tell a story that might otherwise never be told.[38] This broader scope for visual documentation helps to ameliorate the significant impact of the delayed arrival of official investigators.[39] The availability of pre-existing civilian media may also serve to reduce the risks investigators and forensic experts face when attending conflict zones as they may be able to reduce their time spent on-scene, attend fewer scenes, or attend at a time that offers more safety.

A further favourable attribute of civilian media relates to the importance of viewer perspective. Absent competing civilian visual evidence, the only image-based account of an event might be a skewed combatant or state-produced perspective. Multiple perspectives can precipitate a more encompassing understanding of events and the circumstances leading up to them. Civilian media may corroborate and supplement official narratives of a situation or event and, conversely, it may serve as a strong rebuttal to such narratives.[40] Even though civilian visual evidence falls prey to the choices made by the photographer of what to include in the frame, if there are multiple visual accounts of the same event from different perspectives a more objective view may be achieved.[41]

The ability of eyewitnesses to accurately encode, recall, and narrate memory of an event is fraught with uncertainty and error—a fact not lost by international courts. For example, in *Prosecutor v. Kupreškić et al.*, the Appeals Chamber expressed the need for '… "extreme caution" in relation to visual identification evidence', noting '… the frailties of human perceptions and the very serious risk that a miscarriage of justice might result from reliance upon even the most confident witnesses who purport to identify an accused without an adequate opportunity to verify their observations'.[42] Though the human witness may be unreliable, the camera steadfastly records what occurs within its field of view and even though the images may lack optimum quality and have technical challenges requiring expert interpretation,

[36] Jay Aronson, 'Preserving Human Rights Media for Justice, Accountability, and Historical Clarification', *Genocide Studies and Prevention: An International Journal* 11, no 1 (2017): 82–99, at 87.

[37] Combs (n 6) 245, 249–50.

[38] Levy and Williams (n 1) 454–5.

[39] Hamilton (n 25) 218.

[40] Aronson (n 36) 84; Yvonne McDermott, Alexa Koenig, and Daragh Murray, 'Open Source Information's Blind Spot: Human and Machine Bias in International Criminal Investigations', *Journal of International Criminal Justice* 19, no. 1 (2021): 85–106, at 87.

[41] McDermott, Koenig, and Murray (n 40) 84.

[42] IT-95-16-A, Appeals Judgement, 23 October 2001, para. 34.

they provide a visual perspective independent of the photographer.[43] Sometimes the camera records far more than the witness actually perceived or can recall, and the images can be used to supplement the witness's recollection and at times provide a counterpoint.[44] Beyond the frailties associated with *viva voce* evidence, civilian visual evidence provides an account that offers consistent evidential value, unlike human witnesses who may be threatened, intimidated, or may disappear or be killed before testifying.[45]

By engaging civilians in the collection of evidence, there may be a shift in the balance of control from outside professionals to local people, redistributing or democratizing traditional patterns of authority, thereby improving the capacity of civilians to contribute to accountability and justice.[46] This contribution is achievable because locals are more likely to have access to atrocity crime sites and the people directly affected, as well as knowledge of the prevailing socio-political context, facilitating a more comprehensive understanding of the events and their local impact.[47] Civilian visual evidence may also have a corollary deterrent effect on perpetrators of atrocity crimes by making misdeeds that might previously have been committed under the benefit of metaphorical darkness more visible to the world.[48]

Civilian visual evidence will achieve greater investigative and evidential value if photographers are trained how to properly document events, to preserve the integrity of the media, and to transmit it in a forensically sound manner.[49] Recommendations and best practice guidelines for the proper creation, collection, storage, and transmission of media regarding human rights violations is available with assistance provided by human rights organizations, advocacy groups, the ICC, and the International Bar Association (IBA).[50] In 2013, the Commission for

[43] The term 'photographer' is used in this book to denote the person who records images, whether in still image or video format.

[44] 'International Bar Association Report', *IBA ICL Perspectives: Evidence Matters in ICC Trials* (August 2016) https://www.ibanet.org/document?id=Evidence-matters-in-icc-trials, 19–20.

[45] Hamilton (n 10) 4–5.

[46] ibid; Levy and Williams (n 1).

[47] Levy and Williams (n 1) 462.

[48] Greenfield posits that broader visibility may have a deterrent effect, though I suspect that many criminals fail to look beyond their immediate goals. Greenfield (n 27) 831. See also Heyns (n 26) para. 56.

[49] Transmitting digital media in a forensically sound manner requires that the integrity of the digital file be maintained and verified, which can be accomplished by a hash value verification between the two iterations.

[50] The ICC recently released guidelines intended to provide some standards for civil society organizations that are gathering evidence of crimes within the remit of the ICC. ICC Press Release, 'Documenting International Crimes and Human Rights Violations for Accountability Purposes: Guidelines for Civil Society Organizations' (21 September 2022) https://www.icc-cpi.int/news/icc-prosecutor-and-eurojust-launch-practical-guidelines-documenting-and-preserving-information. WITNESS and other organizations are actively training human rights activists to properly document atrocities to maximize the admissibility and evidential weight of the video collected. Alexa Koenig, Felim McMahon, Nikita Mehandru, and Shikha Bhattacharjee, 'Open Source Fact-Finding in Preliminary Examinations', in *Quality Control in Preliminary Examination*, Vol. 2, edited by Morten Bergsmo and Carsten Stahn (Brussels: Torkel Opsahl Academic EPublisher, 2018), 681–730, at 694–5. See also Heyns (n 26) para. 71; Leyh (n 19) 53; Alexa Koenig, 'From "Capture to Courtroom": Collaboration and the Digital

International Justice and Accountability was formed as a non-profit international criminal investigation organization for the purpose of training Syrians how to visually document their observations in a manner suitable for future international criminal investigations and prosecutions.[51] There are also specific programs designed to train locals to document human rights violations in Iraq and South Sudan.[52] More recently, the *Berkeley Protocol on Digital Open Source Investigations* has emerged as a helpful resource in this regard.[53]

1.2 The Challenges Posed by Civilian Visual Evidence

Few investigators and prosecutors would be inclined to turn away civilian visual evidence given its ability to portray events and draw counsel and the court closer to the truth. Yet this putative digital solution is not an investigative panacea as it brings with it evidential and practical challenges. Objectivity can be a significant concern as civilian visual evidence does not always reveal the complete truth, either by happenstance or by design (a topic that will be developed in Chapter 4).

Risk to the photographer and people shown in the images is another potential downside of civilian media should their identity be discovered by people who may wish them harm, especially if revelation of their identity is required under disclosure rules.[54] Activists and other individuals in conflict zones are frequently subjected to state and non-state surveillance regarding their human rights violation reporting.[55] Beyond the risk of formal disclosure, when first recorded digital media also contains metadata, which may include geographical GPS coordinates at the time the images were recorded, thus posing a surveillance risk to the photographer.[56] Some social media and other internet sites strip metadata when the media

Documentation of International Crimes in Ukraine', *Journal of International Criminal Justice* 20, no 4 (2022): 829–42, at 833–4.

[51] Hamilton (n 25) 217. Training has also been provided by Syrian Archive and WITNESS's Critical and Surge Response Program for the purpose of acquiring effective, safe, and verifiable video recordings. Sandra Ristovska, 'Human Rights Collectives as Visual Experts: The Case of Syrian Archive', *Visual Communications* 18, no. 3 (2019): 333–51, at 346.

[52] Leyh (n 19) 50–3.

[53] The *Berkeley Protocol* was designed to provide guidance to investigators regarding the identification, collection, preservation, analysis, and presentation of digital open source information in international criminal investigations. Berkeley Protocol (n 29).

[54] IBA Report (n 44) 27; Levy and Williams (n 1) 462. Many Syrian civilians and activists have been killed while documenting human and civil rights violations. Meis (n 34) 2.

[55] Deyaa Alrwishdi, 'Reconsidering the Digitalization of International Criminal Justice', *Just Security* 19 (January 2021) https://www.justsecurity.org/74166/reconsidering-the-digitalization-of-international-criminal-justice/; Ella McPherson, 'Risk and the Pluralism of Digital Human Rights Fact-Finding and Advocacy', in *New Technologies for Human Rights Law and Practice*, edited by Molly Land and Jay Aronson (Cambridge: CUP, 2018), 188–214, at 196.

[56] 'Metadata is data about data. The metadata for a digital image includes the camera make and model, the camera settings (eg, exposure time and focal length), the date and time of image capture, the GPS location of the image captured, and much more.' Hany Farid, *Photo Forensics* (Cambridge, MA: MIT

is uploaded, thus ameliorating this risk, but other sites may allow the metadata to remain accessible, placing the photographer at risk, especially in an oppressive state.[57] Therefore, the same evidence that was submitted in an effort to document criminality may be used by perpetrators and their allies to seek retaliation against the photographer or the individuals depicted.[58]

A further perennial concern with civilian media is that of authenticity as digital media is highly vulnerable to manipulation.[59] When the photographer is anonymous and the media is uploaded to social media and other sites, authentication issues are more acute because the ability to access the original data and cross examine the photographer is absent. Indeed, when social media platforms strip anonymous video content of metadata, authentication may be impossible.[60] Absent a proper showing of authenticity, civilian visual evidence may be ruled inadmissible or assigned less weight by the court. While OTP investigators and forensic experts are trained to properly gather and preserve evidence, mindful of chain of custody and authentication requirements, civilians are not bound by the same rules and procedures, nor would they necessarily want to be considering the risks involved. Not all photographers wish to be identified.

A further topic worthy of mention is inequality of arms which is a common issue in criminal prosecutions, as the prosecution typically has more resources and power to collect evidence than the defence, and an abundance of image-based evidence gathered by one side in a conflict may skew the visual story more than may be warranted.[61] The International Criminal Tribunal for the former Yugoslavia (ICTY) and the International Criminal Tribunal for Rwanda (ICTR) defined equality of arms in terms of the court's obligation to provide a level playing field for all parties.[62] The ICC has continued that important obligation, and has elevated the equality of arms principle through codification of the prosecution's obligation to investigate inculpating and exonerating circumstances equally and through the

Press, 2016) 188. It may also include data about image size, pixels, type of compression, frame rate, resolution, aspect ratio, GOP structure, file format, etc. See also Sam Gregory, 'Cameras Everywhere Revisited: How Digital Technologies and Social Media Aid and Inhibit Human Rights Documentation and Advocacy', *Journal of Human Rights Practice* 11 (2019): 373–92, at 379.

57 van der Velden (n 24) 3.

58 Nancy Combs, 'Evidence', in *Routledge Handbook of International Criminal Law*, edited by William Schabas and Nadia Bernaz (London: Routledge, 2013), 323–4. Applications designed to minimize this risk are noted in Section 3. See also Aronson, Cole, Hauptmann, Miller, and Samuels (n 27) 18.

59 van der Velden (n 24); Heyns (n 26) paras. 82–88. The increasing use of deep fake videos only exacerbates authenticity and reliability concerns (see Chapter 5).

60 Greenfield (n 27) 823; McDermott, Koenig, and Murray (n 40) 93.

61 This differential can be compensated in part by the prosecution's obligation to include exculpatory circumstances in its case and the Chamber's power to issue orders, summonses, subpoenas, warrants, and transfer orders.

62 Masha Fedorova, 'The Principle of Equality of Arms in International Criminal Proceedings', in *Defense Perspectives on International Criminal Justice*, edited by Colleen Rohan and Gentian Zyberi (Cambridge: CUP, 2017), 204–34, at 205.

defence's institutional presence in the ICC.[63] Despite these important steps, there remains inequality between the means and resources of the prosecution versus the defence.[64] Dissatisfaction with the availability of resources and funding is a common defence complaint.[65] The ICC has stated that equality of arms is a relevant consideration when assessing the adequacy of defence resources.[66]

It has also been argued that the rise in civilian visual evidence creates a further disadvantage to defendants in that the prosecution accumulates disproportionately more evidence.[67] The defence must factor this evidential imbalance into their trial strategy by combing through prosecution visual evidence for images that may support defence theories and by seeking out media independent of what the prosecution has accumulated. Even though fairness dictates that the defence is equally entitled to obtain evidence in support of their case, it may be that foreign governments are uncooperative, information is destroyed, and witnesses may be uncooperative.[68] Nonetheless, it is a truism that civilian witnesses are more likely to gather incriminating rather than exonerating evidence and so long as the evidence is reliable, the fact that it favours the prosecution is of no moment. Innocent explanations for atrocities are woefully lacking. If dark deeds are being undertaken, the more light that is shone on them the better. The pursuit of justice requires that all available reliable evidence be gathered and assessed for the purpose of determining the truth. Provided exculpatory evidence is disclosed along with the inculpatory, a prosecution that is overwhelming in terms of the weight and cogency of its evidence is not necessarily an unfair one.[69] Nonetheless, counsel and court must be mindful of the lopsided perspective that civilian visual evidence may present and must assess events with the appropriate context.

A further practical concern is that as a result of democratizing a wider array of photographers, voluminous amounts of image-based evidence are gathered and must be catalogued and transmitted to appropriate agencies.[70] Civilian witnesses do not typically have ready access to secure data storage unless using a purpose-built

[63] *Prosecutor v. Lubanga*, ICC-01/04-01/06-1091, Decision on Defence's Request to Obtain Simultaneous French Transcripts, 14 December 2007, paras. 18–19. The Chamber noted that to achieve equality of arms, the minimum rights of the defendant would need to be interpreted generously. See also Fedorova (n 62) 234. Despite these positive steps, inequality remains a concern.

[64] Stefania Negri, 'The Principle of "Equality of Arms" and the Evolving Law of International Criminal Procedure', *International Criminal Law Review* 5, no 4 (2005): 513–71, at 552.

[65] Fedorova (n 62) 219.

[66] See e.g. *Prosecutor v. Ntaganda*, ICC-01/04-02/06-389, Reasons for Review of Registrar's Decision on Defence Resources, 29 October 2014.

[67] The prosecution typically amasses much more evidence than the defence. For an interesting perspective on inequality, see Jeffrey Reiman and Paul Leighton, *The Rich Get Rich and the Poor Get Prison* (New York; Routledge, 2013). See also Hamilton (n 10) 39–40.

[68] James Meernik, 'Equality of Arms? The Individual vs. The International Community in War Crimes Tribunals' *Judicature* 86, no 6 (2003): 312–19, at 316 (commenting on ICTY litigation).

[69] As required by the *Rome Statute*, Art. 67(2). See also Art. 54 and the prosecution's obligation to establish the truth.

[70] van der Velden (n 24) 1; Heyns (n 26) para. 78; Hamilton (n 25) 218.

evidence gathering application.[71] Galvanizing civilian photographers is only part of the process as the evidence must be delivered to people who are able to utilize it in an investigational context, a topic that is covered in Section 2 and Chapter 9.

1.3 A Word of Caution Regarding Democratization and the Use of Intermediaries

The challenges faced by investigators in gaining prompt and sufficient access to crime scenes and other areas of interest have resulted in the OTP relying upon human rights groups, UN agencies, journalists, civilians, and others to gather and supply evidence for consideration.[72] This is not an abdication of the role of OTP investigators but rather is supplemental to the work they already undertake. Human rights collectives that gather image-based evidence range from well-established organizations like Amnesty International and Human Rights Watch (HRW) to smaller entities and university-based research and advocacy centres.[73] The OTP relies significantly upon the assistance of NGO intermediaries working on human rights and humanitarian issues for the investigation of international crimes and other core activities.[74] NGOs such as HRW and Amnesty International collect and catalogue image-based evidence as part of their investigations into human rights investigations.[75] GPS coordinates and satellite imagery have been used by NGOs to visualize situational changes associated with mass violence, displacement of populations, damage to infrastructure, changes in the contours of refugee camps, etc.[76] Collectively, the ability to collect and submit images for consideration means that NGOs, civilians, and others can aid in the fact-finding process by telling their own stories, which might not otherwise be told or might be told in a different way.

[71] Levy and Williams (n 1) 462–3.

[72] Christian De Vos, 'Investigating from Afar: The ICC's Evidence Problem', *Leiden Journal of International Law* 26, no. 4 (2013): 1009–24; Hamilton (n 25) 215.

[73] Ristovska (n 51) 334. Other collectives include NGOs such as WITNESS and Syrian Archive, activist and media groups such as Papo Reto and the Mosireen Collective, and university-based groups such as Forensic Architecture at Goldsmith University in London and UC Berkeley's Human Rights Center. Alice Kohli, 'Data-Driven Human Rights Investigations', in *Digital Investigative Journalism: Data, Visual Analytics and Innovative Methodologies in International Reporting*, edited by Oliver Hahn and Florian Stalph (Cham: Springer International Publishing, 2019), 67–77, at 74–5.

[74] Nicole De Silva, 'Intermediary Complexity in Regulatory Governance: The International Criminal Court's Use of NGOs in Regulating International Crimes', *The Annals of the American Academy* 670 (2017): 170–88, at 171, 178.

[75] A study by New York University's Center for Human Rights and Global Justice, which reviewed all HRW and Amnesty International reports published in 2006, 2010, and 2014, noted increased use of photographs, satellite imagery, and maps. Increased use of this visual data has been made possible by advances in technology and newly available data (e.g. GPS and satellite imagery being more broadly available). John Emerson, Margaret Satterthwaite, and Anshul Pandey, 'The Challenging Power of Data Visualization for Human Rights Advocacy', in *New Technologies for Human Rights Law and Practice*, edited by Molly Land and Jay Aronson (Cambridge: CUP, 2018), 162–87, at 163, 177.

[76] ibid 177–8.

Image-based evidence that is created by trained individuals from established organizations and provided directly to the OTP is likely entitled to greater weight than evidence provided by unknown or untested sources. Authenticity and reliability issues are more amenable to evaluation when dealing with trusted sources, though it would be unwise to assume the absence of such concerns without objective proof. Assessing these important topics is more complex when intermediaries receive evidence from other content providers and in turn forward it to the OTP. When an intermediary organization or individual is involved, that may mean that the person originally creating the images is not part of an established organization and may not be a trained documentarian.

An intermediary layer accentuates potential concerns regarding objective reporting, image reliability, and the ability to authenticate the images as access to the original recording and the photographer may be limited due to the photographer being a further step removed from the OTP. Added to these challenges is the further layer of scrutiny that must be applied to the intermediaries who receive and subsequently transmit the evidence. Have they altered or edited the evidence prior to submitting it to investigators? Have they submitted all the media given to them or only those parts deemed of value? Intermediaries may have agendas and biases that inform their handling of image-based evidence. Intermediaries such as *eyeWitness to Atrocities* are likely of less concern than other less established parties, but the interjection of an additional layer between the original documentarian and the OTP can be problematic.

Democratization is also suggestive of a level playing field in the provision of evidence, but that is misleading. A true democracy would mean that all people are able to participate and have an equal voice. That is not realistic when it comes to the provision of evidence of atrocities. McDermott notes that one of the advantages of open source information is that, '... it provides an avenue through which ordinary people in affected regions can tell their stories and directly influence international fact-finding processes'.[77] This broad statement must be attenuated with access limitation realities. The ability to record and upload images to open source sites is '... heavily mediated by financial, social, educational, technical, political, geographic and physical constraints ... ' meaning that the perspectives of digitally literate, young urban males may be over-represented.[78] Therefore, while ordinary people can provide evidence of value, it is really a subset of those ordinary people that actually do so.

Further, a plausible claim can be made that there is a hierarchy among the entities and individuals who provide image-based evidence to investigators. Human rights organizations and other civil society documentarians are more likely to have the technical resources and necessary training to properly document scenes and

[77] McDermott, Koenig, and Murray (n 40) 93.
[78] ibid 94–5.

events. Qualitatively, their evidence is likely to be given greater consideration than that provided by untested individuals or anonymous submitters to social media. It is reasonable for investigators to prefer evidence provided from sources deemed to be more trustworthy and reliable over untested sources. It would however be ill-advised to relegate evidence from lower-ranked sources as being mere noise, as remarkable evidence can come from the least expected sources.

The OTP relies upon outside resources for some of its evidence gathering and technical assistance.[79] Some organizations may have a stronger voice than others because of relationships that have been developed with the OTP. For example, Bellingcat has provided assistance to the ICC Technology Advisory Board by providing advice as to how open source investigation can be utilized by the OTP.[80] Bellingcat is an independent international collective of researchers, investigators, and citizen journalists who use open source and social media investigation to examine various conflicts and events.[81] Formed in 2014, it focuses primarily on open source investigation regarding the civil wars in Syria and Libya, the downing of Malaysian Airlines Flight 17 (MH17), and the Ukraine/Russian conflict.[82] It is a largely journalistic-based organization and pointedly takes a stance against the military activities of Russia and Syria, amongst others.[83] This is not to suggest that Bellingcat's work is subpar but rather that it is not neutral, as it has a stated agenda. It may constitute valuable lead information but may not be suitable for entry as formal evidence in court.[84] The OTP should be cautious in accepting assistance from Bellingcat and similar organizations without objectively verifying the information provided.

Democratization has demonstrated value because evidence that might otherwise never exist can find its way to the OTP, but along with it comes notions of privatization where investigative functions are delegated to others, and not necessarily in a way that is truly democratic. The OTP must be cautious when receiving evidence from outside sources and must ensure that the evidence is verifiable and

[79] De Vos (n 72) 1009–24.

[80] Bellingcat, https://www.bellingcat.com/about/ (webpage no longer accessible).

[81] ibid.

[82] Aric Toler, 'Crowdsourced and Patriotic Digital Forensics in the Ukrainian Conflict', in *Digital Investigative Journalism: Data, Visual Analytics and Innovative Methodologies in International Reporting*, edited by Oliver Hahn and Florian Stalph (Cham: Springer International Publishing, 2019), 201–15.

[83] ibid 210. Toler is on the Executive Board of Directors of Bellingcat and his statements regarding the focus and perspective of Bellingcat should be accorded *gravitas*.

[84] For example, in relation to the MH17 investigation, Bellingcat conducted an extensive open source investigation and released a report. 'MH17: The Open Source Investigation Three Years Later' (2017) https://www.bellingcat.com/news/uk-and-europe/2017/07/17/mh17-open-source-investigation-three-years-later/. It determined from where the BUK missile launcher originated, how it was transported to the launch site, and who was responsible for its placement. Though Bellingcat's open source investigation may have investigational value for JIT investigators, it would be unlikely to see their work serve as independent proof of the facts alleged. Notably, the Dutch Safety Board's report on the MH17 Crash (October 2015) https://www.onderzoeksraad.nl/en/page/3546/crash-mh17-17-july-2014, makes no reference to Bellingcat's report.

reliable. Partnerships with other organizations cannot be seen to (and cannot) impact the independence of the OTP. Further, the OTP must ensure that all evidence providers are cognizant of the OTP's duty to disclose evidence, whether inculpatory or exculpatory. To that end, the OTP cannot enter into confidentiality agreements or other side-agreements that deviate from this overriding obligation. This may at times prove challenging when the OTP is beholden to others for the provision of evidence.

2. Transmitting the Evidence

Capturing the images is the first step in visually documenting ICC crimes, but without a ready pipeline and repository for them, little use can be made of such evidence in a formal investigation and prosecution. There are four methods by which civilian visual evidence can be transmitted to the ICC. First, it can be given to an OTP investigator directly or through an intermediary via encrypted programs such as Signal or WhatsApp or over messaging platforms such as Facebook, Telegram, Tiktok, etc.[85] Second, civilians can send evidence directly to the OTP in The Hague via the newly created *OTP Link*, which is an advanced evidence submission platform intended to be used for the online and email-based submission of evidence.[86] A third indirect method involves OTP investigative analysts or investigators searching the internet for relevant open source media and causing it to be downloaded by OTP cyber experts for examination.[87] A corollary to this third method is for non-OTP open source investigators to search social media and other sites for relevant media and to forward their findings to the OTP.[88] The fourth method is through the use of internet applications that have been purposefully built to collect evidence of atrocity crimes and human rights violations for use in formal investigations and prosecutions.

The use of evidence gathering applications is worthy of further commentary. The International Bar Association (IBA) established the *eyeWitness Project* and the *eyeWitness to Atrocities* internet application in 2015 for the purpose of collecting, authenticating, and securely storing open source media of human rights abuses and atrocity crimes.[89] The application was developed following consultations with

[85] A substantial volume of media captured by civil society members is sent directly to ICC investigators; Koenig, McMahon, Mehandru, and Bhattacharjee (n 50) 694.

[86] *OTP Link*, https://otplink.icc-cpi.int/. See Section 2 of Chapter 9 for further discussion.

[87] Xabier Aranburu, 'The Contribution of Analysis to the Quality Control in Criminal Investigation', in *Quality Control in Criminal Investigation*, edited by Xabier Agirre, Morten Bergsmo, Simon De Smet, and Carsten Stahn (Brussels: Torkel Opsahl Academic EPublisher, 2020), 117–272, at 124.

[88] Koenig 'From "Capture to Courtroom"' (n 50) 834.

[89] The application was developed after the challenges encountered by the IBA's Executive Director in authenticating footage of Sri Lankan troops executing Tamil prisoners in 2010. Costello (n 26) 279. See also Eleanor Farrow, 'eyeWitness to Atrocities: Verifying Images with Metadata', in *Digital Investigative Journalism: Data, Visual Analytics and Innovative Methodologies in International Reporting*, edited by Oliver Hahn and Florian Stalph (Cham: Springer International Publishing, 2019), 143–55.

lawyers at the ICC and other international and hybrid tribunals.[90] The *eyeWitness* application is designed to record digital video, photographs, and audio, and automatically documents GPS coordinates, date and time, and the location of surrounding cell towers and Wi-Fi networks, constituting three independent sources to confirm date, time, and location.[91] Digital media is stored in an encrypted format on the original recording device in such a manner that it cannot be edited and a hash value is calculated upon recording which can be used to verify the integrity of later iterations. Once the media is transmitted to *eyeWitness*, it is stored in its original format in a secure facility, thereby creating a provable chain of custody.[92] Lawyers then examine the media and provide relevant content to the appropriate investigative authorities. The application is intended to meet the evidential standards required in international criminal litigation.[93] The *eyeWitness* project does not investigate or verify the contents of images or advocate for them, but rather serves to certify image metadata.[94] The images may be suitable for entry as independent evidence in a prosecution or as corroboration of other evidence.

CameraV, developed as part of the *InformaCam Project*, which is a partnership between the software technology group Guardian Project and the video advocacy organization WITNESS, is another application intended for use by people in high-risk situations to record human rights violations.[95] This precursor to the *eyeWitness* application automatically encrypts and password protects recorded media on the local device and claims to capture image and location metadata needed for authentication.[96] Unlike *EyeWitness*, it does not offer a secure repository to which recorded images can be submitted.

Evidence gathering applications are potentially valuable but also have practical limitations. Potential submitters may face personal risk if they have a smartphone in their possession, let alone use it to document events of interest. They need access to a Wi-Fi or cellular network to transmit the images to people who can use them. Assuming these hurdles are overcome and the media submitted through applications such as *eyeWitness* and *CameraV* can be proven to have integrity and authenticity, these applications have clear value. Both applications are designed to generate digital media capable of verification and authentication, and putatively self-authentication.[97] These are robust claims that have not yet been tested by

[90] Hamilton (n 10) 17–19.

[91] See *eyeWitness to Atrocities*, https://www.eyewitness.global/FAQS.

[92] ibid; Costello (n 26) 279–80.

[93] See *eyeWitness to Atrocities*, https://www.eyewitness.global/5-Lessons-Learned-in-5-Years; Levy and Williams (n 1) 463.

[94] Farrow (n 89) 148.

[95] Guardian Project, https://guardianproject.info/archive/camerav/; van der Velden (n 24) 8–9; Hamilton (n 19) 17–19.

[96] Guardian Project, https://blog.witness.org/2013/01/how-informacam-improves-verification-of-mobile-media-files/.

[97] Hamilton (n 10) 4; Gregory (n 56) 382–3. Self-authentication is premised on the view that the media itself provides sufficient metadata to establish authenticity.

experts and counsel in the ICC as no cases have come before the court which have relied upon application-driven media.[98]

Images gathered by the *eyeWitness* application were successfully submitted as crime base evidence by the prosecution and the legal representative for victims before the Military Tribunal in the DRC in 2018.[99] The defence did not mount any technical or legal challenge to the admissibility of the images. The Court found the images to be material and helpful in proving the crime base element of several of the charges. Should such evidence be examined and approved by the OTP and the Trial Chamber, that will be a significant step forward in the use of civilian visual evidence.

Purpose built applications like *eyeWitness* and *CameraV* offer potential evidential protections that other sites are unable to provide because these applications record and preserve metadata. Digital media that is uploaded to sites such as YouTube and Facebook is typically stripped of its metadata, which eliminates the ability to technically verify the integrity of the images and makes authentication very challenging.[100] While civil society members are more likely to use purpose built applications and often have training on how to properly collect and preserve evidence, other civilians may tend to rely upon popular social media sites simply because of name recognition, thus impacting the evidential value of the media submitted.[101] Absent an affirmative legal duty, there is little business incentive for entities such as Facebook, YouTube, TikTok, and Twitter to implement costly programs to help collect and preserve video evidence for eventual use in international criminal trials.[102] Nonetheless, social media organizations have begun to willingly share some uploaded content with investigators in support of international criminal investigations.[103]

Inadvertently, profit-based social media entities have become repositories of evidence in support of international criminal investigations.[104] As valuable as this media may be for global social awareness and to investigators and others with a legitimate claim for access, there is an ever-present risk of it disappearing from the public domain.[105] For example, in 2020, HRW found that 11% of the digital

[98] *eyeWitness* has submitted media obtained by documentation teams to the ICC for consideration in several situations at the preliminary examination stage. How that media will be utilized and whether it will be challenged remains to be seen. See https://www.eyewitness.global/our-impact.

[99] Chiara Gabriele, Kelly Matheson, and Raquel Vazquez Llorente, 'The Role of Mobile Technology in Documenting International Crimes: The *Affaire Castro et Kizito* in the Democratic Republic of Congo', *Journal of International Criminal Justice* 19, no. 1 (2021): 107–30.

[100] Koenig, McMahon, Mehandru, and Bhattacharjee (n 50) 693; Greenfield (n 27) 823; McDermott, Koenig, and Murray (n 40) 93.

[101] *eyeWitness* provides training on basic forensic procedures to its users and partner organizations. https://www.eyewitness.global/our-work. See also Costello (n 26) 280.

[102] Greenfield (n 27) 846.

[103] Digital Lockers (n 25) 9.

[104] Aronson (n 36) 83–4; Hamilton (n 25) 214.

[105] Aronson (n 36) 83; Giancarlo Fiorella, Charlotte Godart, and Nick Waters, 'Digital Integrity: Exploring Digital Evidence Vulnerabilities and Mitigation Strategies for Open Source Researchers', *Journal of International Criminal Justice* 19, no. 1 (2021): 147–62, at 148–9; Lindsay

content it cited in its reports since 2007 had been deleted from available sources.[106] Aronson notes a number of reasons why this may occur, including the creator or uploader becoming concerned about risk to themselves or the community by its remaining online, threats of harm by interested parties if the content is not removed, and unwelcome publicity for the content creator.[107]

Social media organizations may themselves remove content due to violation of community standards, the end user agreement, or copyright law.[108] For example, in 2017, YouTube developed a machine learning algorithm that removed thousands of videos documenting the Syrian conflict by 900 human rights groups, journalists, activists, and eyewitnesses.[109] The deletion of content by social media organizations may result in the only documentation of certain events being lost.[110] Altruistically, the social media accounts of human rights violators may be closed as a means of preventing unwelcome propaganda, but at the cost of eliminating evidence useful for investigators.[111] This is an area in need of some regulation though that is difficult because social media organizations are private entities and are therefore less amenable to national government regulation, let alone international regulation.

3. Civilian Visual Evidence And Atrocity Crimes

Civilian visual evidence of atrocity crimes has changed the investigative playing field considerably. For example, by early 2017, there were reportedly more hours of civilian video recordings documenting the Syrian war than there were hours of war.[112] The use of civilian media as evidence in atrocity crime prosecutions was largely unheard of prior to the early 2010s.[113] Now, crimes that may once have been committed with relative impunity in the confidence there would be no

Freeman and Raquel Vazquez Llorente, 'Finding the Signal in the Noise: International Criminal Evidence and Procedure in the Digital Age', *Journal of International Criminal Justice* 19, no. 1 (2021): 163–88, at 172, 177.

106 Human Rights Watch, '"Video Unavailable": Social Media Platforms Remove Evidence of War Crimes' (10 September 2020) https://www.hrw.org/report/2020/09/10/video-unavailable/social-media-platforms-remove-evidence-war-crimes.

107 Aronson (n 36) 83.

108 Aronson (n 36) 83; Digital Lockers (n 25) 2–3; Fiorella, Godart, and Waters (n 105) 3. See also 'AI: War crimes evidence erased by social media platforms', *BBC News* (1 June 2023) https://www.bbc.com/news/technology-65755517.

109 Ristovska (n 51) 343.

110 Digital Lockers (n 25) 3, 8.

111 Aronson (n 36) 83.

112 Koenig, McMahon, Mehandru, and Bhattacharjee (n 50) 692–3. More than one million videos had been uploaded by perpetrators, journalists, medical professionals, and citizens to social media sites by mid-2017. Aronson (n 24) 134. It is virtually impossible for investigators to view and catalogue this abundance of evidence. Freeman and Vazquez Llorente (n 105) 171–2.

113 Hamilton (n 10) 11.

incriminating evidence available to investigators require more circumspection as the risk of being digitally captured is palpable. The advent of civilian media and the use of social media and other sites constitutes a paradigm shift, replacing or complementing embedded war photographers with civilians willing to document conflict scenes using smartphones and digital cameras and share them locally and via the internet to global audiences.[114] It also marks a shift away from trained investigators with professional obligations to established judicial institutions to private citizens with decreased or no public accountability for their actions.[115]

Many of the video images used in ICTY prosecutions were obtained from Yugoslavian news channels, including targeted documentaries that had been broadcast on television.[116] Additionally, some video evidence was obtained from private sources filmed by or in the presence of the perpetrators.[117] There is some evidence that civilian visual evidence can influence and challenge mainstream news reporting in conflict zones. For example, human rights violations in Syria drew international attention in part due to civilian videos posted on social media sites.[118] Amnesty International, HRW, and the UN Commission of Inquiry have included civilian video recordings obtained through social media in their reports as evidence establishing the Syrian government's use of barrel bombs and chemical weapons against civilians.[119] Greater reliance on civilians acting as journalists in Syria is necessary due to Syria being an extremely dangerous place for foreign correspondents.[120] In 2016, the UN established the International, Impartial and Independent Mechanism (IIIM) for the purpose of gathering evidence for potential future prosecutions in Syria. The IIIM has partnered with civil society groups to gather visual evidence of criminality.[121] Similar UN initiatives have been established to investigate atrocities committed against the Rohingya population in Myanmar, relying on digital content uploaded to Facebook.[122]

A vile and troubling use of video recordings is that of propaganda videos which have been disseminated worldwide by terrorist organizations such as ISIS through the use of social media to inflict terror and to incite violence.[123] These 'terrorist theater' videos are used to document the beheadings of captives and serve as a call

[114] Duffy (n 27) 782. YouTube alone has over two billion monthly logged-in users in over 100 countries, across 80 languages, with over 500 hours of content uploaded every minute. YouTube for Press, https://blog.youtube/press/.

[115] Hamilton (n 25) 219.

[116] Greenfield (n 27) 833.

[117] ibid.

[118] Ristovska (n 51) 352.

[119] ibid 350.

[120] Leyh (n 19) 49; Hamilton (n 25) 216.

[121] Hamilton (n 25) 217.

[122] ibid 217–18; United Nations Human Rights Council, 'Independent International Fact-Finding Mission on Myanmar', Human Rights Council Res. 39/2, U.N. Doc. A/HRC/RES/39/2, ¶ 23 (27 September 2018) https://www.ohchr.org/en/hrbodies/hrc/myanmarffm/pages/index.aspx [perma.cc/M25J-3FAE].

[123] Reading (n 20) 64.

to arms for supporters to engage in violence on behalf of such organizations.[124] The attention devoted to ISIS beheading videos is illustrative of the importance of images in contemporary terrorism and warfare.[125] ISIS has taken particular advantage of this medium throughout its campaign of terror and while co-opting social media has benefitted the growth of ISIS, it also creates a reservoir of video evidence to be used by prosecutors in future trials against the perpetrators.[126] One of the potential benefits of this kind of evidence is that it may spur government action in response to compelling evidence of atrocity crimes.[127] Further, these videos can be used not only to prosecute those involved in producing the propaganda but also as evidence of the crimes themselves.[128]

3.1 International Criminal Court

The establishment of the ICC in 2002 generally coincided with the advent of increasing popularization of mobile phones, social media, and widespread internet access in developed nations and in later years, situation countries, resulting in the eventual gathering of newfound image-based evidence for use by investigating bodies.[129] This fortuitous confluence of technology has been a boon to OTP investigators who benefit from civilian visual evidence in light of their inability to investigate all situations promptly.[130] The OTP's increasing utilization of civilian visual evidence is reflective of the vast amount of information that is provided to investigators directly or uploaded to social media and other sites by witnesses and perpetrators alike, offering visual evidence that may be of considerable value in investigations.[131]

The value of civilian visual evidence is dependent upon its source, photographer identifiability, authentication of the media, and the quality of the media itself. Open source media is a valuable investigative tool which may achieve substantive admissibility if the above factors can be satisfied. Evidence that lacks these hallmarks of

[124] ISIS has 'mastered the art of the intimate kill' and its videos are meant to be polarizing and to provoke a war that ISIS is convinced it will win. Simon Cottee, *ISIS and the Pornography of Violence* (London: Anthem Press, 2019), 4, 7–9.

[125] Friis (n 34) 726.

[126] Greenfield (n 27) 836.

[127] Rebecca Hamilton, 'Atrocity Prevention in the New Media Landscape', *AJIL Unbound* 113 (2019): 262–6.

[128] Heyns (n 26) para. 68; Greenfield (n 27) 838.

[129] Lindsay Freeman, 'Digital Evidence and War Crimes Prosecutions: The Impact of Digital Technologies on International Criminal Investigations and Trials', *Fordham International Law Journal* 41, no. 2 (2018): 283–335, at 287–8.

[130] UC Berkeley School of Law Human Rights Center, 'The New Forensics: Using Open Source Information to Investigate Grave Crimes' (2018), https://humanrights.berkeley.edu/sites/default/files/publications/bellagio_report_july2018_final.pdf, 6 ('New Forensics').

[131] McDermott, Koenig, and Murray (n 40) 86.

reliability may never see the light of a courtroom but may provide valuable investigative leads which can develop other admissible evidence.

Utilizing open source images in investigations may prove advantageous for several reasons. First, it can help to circumvent issues arising from lack of investigator access to areas of interest in a timely fashion and can provide lead, crime base, linkage, and corroborative evidence that might otherwise not exist.[132] Second, it can help democratize the fact-finding process, subject to the caveats discussed in Section 1.3.[133] Third, uploading civilian visual evidence to social media and other sites may reduce reliance upon intermediaries, thus avoiding issues sometimes associated with their use.[134] The OTP readily uses open source information as part of its preliminary examinations and prosecutions and strives to manage the large influx of open source images posted to social media sites.[135] Aware of the value and increasing volume of such evidence, the OTP employs cyber-investigators and analysts to search the internet for relevant open source evidence.[136] For example, the OTP relied upon mobile device video at confirmation hearings and trials for situations in Kenya, Côte d'Ivoire, and Libya.[137] Investigations in Sudan and Mali have relied upon images posted to websites such as Facebook and YouTube, establishing that social media evidence has become part of the prosecution's arsenal.[138]

In 2017, the ICC issued arrest warrants for war crimes of murder for Libyan national Mahmoud Mustafa Busayf al-Werfalli based upon civilian video posted to social media and obtained by the OTP.[139] This is one of the first ICC cases to rely so heavily, at least in early stages, on open source media.[140] At the arrest warrant stage, the applicable evidential standard is reasonable grounds to believe, and the Pre-Trial Chamber was satisfied from the video evidence presented that this relatively low standard had been met.[141] The Chamber's approach to open source evidence may vary depending upon the stage of the proceeding and the applicable standard of proof but that remains to be seen as case law develops. A plausible argument can be made that as the standard of proof increases, so too will the scrutiny applied by the Chamber to the prosecution's evidence, including open source media. There is precedent for the Chamber using civilian media at the trial stage. For example, in *Prosecutor v. Gbagbo and Blè Goudè*, the Chamber considered many open source

[132] ibid 86–7.
[133] ibid.
[134] ibid.
[135] Koenig, McMahon, Mehandru, and Bhattacharjee (n 50) 697–8.
[136] ICC OTP, 'Strategic Plan 2016–2018' (16 November 2015), https://www.icc-cpi.int/iccdocs/otp/070715-OTP_Strategic_Plan_2016-2018.pdf, para. 63.
[137] Freeman (n 129) 289.
[138] ibid 289–90.
[139] *Prosecutor v. Al-Werfalli*, ICC-01/11-01/17-2, Warrant of Arrest, 15 August 2017.
[140] New Forensics (n 130) 3.
[141] *Rome Statute*, Art. 58.

video exhibits which showed speeches made by the defendants as well as civilian witness videos.[142]

In the ICC OTP *Strategic Plan for 2016–2018*, the OTP recognized that it must adapt its strategy to take into account technological advancements, including the 'exponential increase' in the use of electronic devices to document ICC crimes and the fact that victims, witnesses, and perpetrators alike are uploading relevant visual evidence to the internet.[143] The OTP further noted that because evidence can be lost between the time crimes are committed and when the OTP is able to investigate, preservation of such evidence will 'increase the prospects of securing reliable evidence, thereby enhancing the efficiency and effectiveness of investigations and prosecutions'.[144] To this end, the OTP prioritized increasing its ability to collect forms of evidence other than witness statements through continually enhancing its scientific and technology-related capabilities.[145] In the ICC OTP *Strategic Plan for 2019–2021*, the OTP committed to continuing and enhancing these initiatives.[146] It is reasonable to suggest that the volume of visual data that the OTP acquires through the work of investigators and from third parties will most certainly increase and tax the ability of the OTP to effectively process and analyse the evidence.[147] This is reflected in the most recent *OTP Strategic Plan (2023–2025)*, which clearly recognizes that change is needed in the OTP's technological, forensic, and analytical capabilities.[148]

3.2 National Prosecutions for International Crimes

International criminal law has been applied and enforced by international and hybrid criminal tribunals, and national jurisdictions, since the end of the Cold War.[149] National jurisdictions have been conducting prosecutions for international crimes by relying upon the principles of territoriality, active or passive personality, and universal jurisdiction. Territorial jurisdiction is premised on a state having jurisdiction over international crimes when a constituent element of the crime

[142] ICC-02/11-01/15-1263-Conf-AnxB, Reasons of Judge Henderson, 16 July 2019.

[143] ICC OTP Strategic Plan 2016–2018 (n 136).

[144] ibid para. 24.

[145] ibid para. 56.

[146] ICC OTP, 'Strategic Plan 2019–2021' (17 July 2019), https://www.icc-cpi.int/itemsDocuments/20190726-strategic-plan-eng.pdf, para. 14(b).

[147] Freeman and Vazquez Llorente (n 105) 166.

[148] ICC OTP Strategic Plan 2023–2025, available at https://www.icc-cpi.int/sites/default/files/2023-08/2023-strategic-plan-icc-v.2.pdf. At para. 25, the Plan states, 'Effectively harnessing the prolific amount of material and information generated as a result of transformative innovations in digital media, processing and analysis of evidence contained in on-site videos and their distribution through social media, as well as other types of electronic evidence, requires a profound change in the Office's technological, forensic, and analytical capabilities.'

[149] Héctor Olásolo, *International Criminal Law, Transnational Criminal Organizations and Transitional Justice* (Leiden: Brill Nijhoff, 2018), 3.

has occurred within the state, whether that be the initial criminal conduct, intermediate acts, or the eventual effects of the crime.[150] The active personality principle entitles states to exercise jurisdiction over their nationals regarding events or conduct which take place abroad by proscribing its nationals from committing specified crimes abroad even if the conduct is not illegal in the state.[151] The passive personality principle gives the state jurisdiction to punish offences committed against its nationals even when the crime is committed abroad.[152]

The doctrine of universal jurisdiction allows nations to prosecute offenders within their territorial jurisdiction for the core international crimes of genocide, crimes against humanity, and war crimes committed elsewhere, even in the absence of any territorial or national interest.[153] Hybrid criminal tribunals have been actively involved in the prosecution of international crime at the national level.[154] National prosecutions are reflective of the *Global Enforcer* and *No Safe Haven* approaches adopted to combat core international crimes.[155] Most national prosecutions for international crime rely upon territorial and active personality jurisdiction.[156] However, when jurisdiction cannot be linked to territorial or active personality bases, national jurisdictions may rely upon the doctrine of universal jurisdiction.[157] The number of universal jurisdiction trials worldwide has been increasing in recent years.[158] It was on this legal basis that Israel was able to prosecute Adolf Eichmann in Jerusalem in 1961. The jurisdictional right to prosecute

[150] The territoriality principle has been expanded by states to combat international crime. Antonio Cassese, *The Oxford Companion to International Criminal Justice* (Oxford: OUP, 2009), 531–2; Cedric Ryngaert, 'Territorial Jurisdiction Over Cross-Frontier Offences: Revisiting a Classic Problem of International Criminal Law', *International Criminal Law Review* 9 (2009): 187–209, at 208; Michail Vagias, *The Territorial Jurisdiction of the International Criminal Court* (Cambridge: CUP, 2014), 16–17.

[151] This allows states to punish their own nationals for crimes committed abroad, especially when extradition is not available. Cassese (n 150) 228–9.

[152] ibid 451–2.

[153] Luc Reydams, 'The Rise and Fall of Universal Jurisdiction', in *Routledge Handbook of International Criminal Law*, edited by William Schabas and Nadia Bernaz (London: Routledge, 2013), 337–54; Fannie Lafontaine, 'National Jurisdictions', in *The Cambridge Companion to International Criminal Law*, edited by William Schabas (Cambridge: CUP, 2016), 155–77.

[154] e.g. Special Panels for Serious Crimes in East Timor, Regulation 64 Chambers in the Courts of Kosovo, SCSL, ECCC, STL, Extraordinary African Chambers, and the Kosovo Specialist Chambers. Olásolo (n 149) 3. Hybrid criminal tribunals are hybrid because they are neither exclusively international nor national in nature. They involve an international (e.g. the UN) or regional organization (e.g. the African Union) in their creation, their jurisdiction involves national and international crimes, and their staff consist of international and national personnel. Olásolo (n 149) 46.

[155] The Global Enforcer role is illustrated by the domestic implementation of the *Rome Statute* and the creation of war crimes units in Europe, e.g. Germany, Finland, the Netherlands, and Sweden. The No Safe Haven approach is intended to address domestic security concerns regarding foreign fighters returning to or seeking asylum in a non-conflict country. Maximo Langer, 'Universal Jurisdiction is not Disappearing: The Shift from "Global Enforcer" to "No Safe Haven" Universal Jurisdiction', *Journal of International Criminal Justice* 13 (2015): 245–56.

[156] Thousands of international crime cases have been prosecuted at the national level, e.g. Argentina, Bosnia and Herzegovina, Columbia, Uruguay, and Rwanda. Olásolo (n 149) 3, 19–20, 37.

[157] e.g. Belgium and Spain; Olásolo (n 149) 3, 19.

[158] Karolina Aksamitowska, 'Digital Evidence in Domestic Core International Crimes Prosecutions', *Journal of International Criminal Justice* 19, no. 1 (2021): 189–212, at 190.

is premised on the nature of the crimes involved and international treaties and customary international law.[159] Collectively, through these jurisdictional options, international crimes may be prosecuted at the national level rather than relying upon the ICC to assert jurisdiction.

In their 2018 report, the Genocide Network listed several European member state prosecutions for international war crimes that relied upon open source images, primarily of the trophy photo or video recording variety.[160] Prosecutions in Finland, Germany, and Sweden involved defendants sharing trophy images of themselves posing with the severed heads of combatants on social media, desecrating dead bodies, and engaging in assaultive conduct. In many cases, damning images were also found on devices on their possession.

Leiden University's *Digitally Derived Evidence Project* analysed cases from 2007 to 2019 in the Netherlands, Germany, Sweden, Finland, the UK, and Bosnia and Herzegovina, where national prosecutions were conducted of nationals and foreign nationals charged with atrocity crimes in Rwanda, Syria, Iraq, and Afghanistan.[161] The researchers focused on cases in which digitally derived evidence was used as part of the prosecution's case. Examples of such evidence included incriminating video and photographs found on computers and smartphones and more often, uploaded to social media sites such as Facebook and YouTube. In each case, the images were an essential component of proof against the defendants. These cases illustrate the imprudent social practice of perpetrators and their cohorts visually documenting serious criminality and sharing it with a much broader audience only to have their documentarian efforts turned against them.

More recent cases involving image-based evidence of criminality in national prosecutions include an April 2020 prosecution in Germany of two men accused of committing crimes against humanity for the Syrian state. It is believed to be the first case in the world examining the use of torture under President Bashar al-Assad's rule. The defendants were alleged to have worked for Syria's civilian intelligence agency and were accused of torture and other war crimes. Key evidence against them was a large quantity of images captured by a military defector.[162] In

[159] Maximo Langer, 'The Diplomacy of Universal Jurisdiction: The Political Branches and the Transnational Prosecution of International Crimes', *American Journal of International Law* 105, no. 1 (2011): 1–49.

[160] Genocide Network Report, 'Prosecuting War Crimes of Outrage Upon Personal Dignity Based on Evidence from Open Sources—Legal Framework and Recent Developments in the Member States of the European Union' (2018) https://www.eurojust.europa.eu/publication/prosecuting-war-crimes-outrage-upon-personal-dignity-based-evidence-open-sources-legal.

[161] Kalshoven-Gieskes Forum on International Humanitarian Law, 'Prosecution of International Crimes Using Digitally Derived Evidence in National Court' (2019–2020) https://leiden-guidelines.com/assets/National-Courts.pdf.

[162] 'Syrian Civil War: Germany Holds Unprecedented State Torture Trial' *BBC News* (23 April 2020) https://www.bbc.co.uk/news/world-europe-52393402. One defendant was convicted in February 2021; 'Syria Torture: German Court Convicts Ex-Intelligence Officer', *BBC News* (24 February 2021) https://www.bbc.com/news/world-europe-56160486.

December 2020, Azerbaijan charged two of its own soldiers for mutilating the bodies of Armenian soldiers during conflicts in the Nagorno-Karabakh region. The defendants allegedly videotaped their actions and posted the recording on social media.[163] In June 2021, a refugee in the Netherlands went on trial for war crimes over a killing carried out in Syria. He was allegedly identified in a video showing the murder.[164]

Digital evidence has become the bedrock for national prosecutions for core international crimes.[165] The unifying element in these national cases is the utilization of civilian and perpetrator media, often obtained from the defendant's devices, in the prosecution's case. When the evidence emanates from the defendant's own device or consists of images depicting the defendant engaged in criminality, the prosecution's quest for justice reaps the evidential rewards. All civilian visual evidence must be carefully examined for suitability and what use can fairly be made of it by counsel and the court. Evidence of dubious integrity and authenticity may still have investigational value even if it cannot be used as evidence.

4. Civilian Visual Evidence and Fair Trial Concerns

Civilian visual evidence can be evaluated on a continuum where the highest evidential value is ascribed to media when the photographer is known and available to testify as to the circumstances under which the media was recorded, the integrity of the media and its authenticity is established, and the evidence itself is of high quality. Under these circumstances, assuming relevance is established, the court should have little difficulty admitting the evidence and assessing its weight. The lowest evidential value is ascribed to media where the photographer is unknown or unavailable or both, the integrity and authenticity of the media is questionable, and the media is of poor quality. Even assuming relevance is established, the court should be loath to admit such evidence let alone assign any weight to it. Between these ends of the spectrum is media where one or more of these essential elements is missing.

Fair trial concerns are more likely to arise at the low end of this continuum when anonymous image-based evidence emanates from social media and other sites. Photographers who upload media to applications like *eyeWitness* or to social media and other sites may legitimately prefer to remain anonymous for fear of reprisals.

[163] 'Nagorno-Karabakh Conflict: Azeri Soldiers Charged with War Crimes' *BBC News* (14 December 2020) https://www.bbc.com/news/world-europe-55308460.

[164] 'Almad Al K: Dutch Court Tries Refugee over Syria Murder Video' *BBC News* (15 June 2021) https://www.bbc.com/news/world-europe-57481556; 'Syrian Asylum Seeker in the Netherlands Convicted of War Crimes' *DutchNews.nl* (16 July 2021) https://www.dutchnews.nl/news/2021/07/syrian-asylum-seeker-in-the-netherlands-convicted-of-war-crimes/.

[165] Aksamitowska (n 158) 10.

Users of the *eyeWitness* application are given the option to provide contact information, with the warning that it will likely be disclosed to both the prosecution and defence, or the user may choose to remain anonymous.[166] No device related information is collected that could identify the user, nor is the IP address from which the media was transmitted recorded. Users of *CameraV* are not required to make such a declaration but since they can choose to upload the media to any internet site that will accept it, self-identification would likely only occur by happenstance, not design. The same preference to remain anonymous likely applies to civilians uploading media to social media sites in general. Aside from members of civil society groups, there may be little incentive and much to risk in volunteering to testify regarding civilian visual evidence.[167]

Apprehensions about reprisals for providing evidence to investigators and the court are not fanciful. Concern for the safety and well-being of victims and witnesses is an important feature of atrocity crime litigation. The ICTY and ICTR incorporated provisions in their founding statutes for the protection of witnesses and established witness protection programs. The ICC has extensive provisions for the safety of witnesses in the *Rome Statute* and a witness protection program which is dedicated to the needs of witnesses called to testify, but no program can insulate witnesses from all potential risks of violent reprisal.[168] The risks facing civilians recording ICC crime activity are a significant disincentive to assisting investigators.[169] While risk of harm to the photographer is most immediate when actively recording, uploading media to internet sites may not guarantee true anonymity as people depicted may know the identity of the photographer based on its content, rendering violent reprisal a clear and present danger even in supposed anonymity.

The issue then becomes whether civilian visual evidence should be admitted at trial in the absence of the photographer or other source evidence and if so, how it should be evaluated. It may be argued that the use of anonymous image-based evidence is permissible on the basis that once authenticated, the media speaks for itself, the photographer becomes superfluous, and no human sponsor is required.[170] This approach ignores the role of the photographer in choosing what to record and submit for consideration. Questioning photographers may be essential to gain a

[166] See *eyeWitness to Atrocities*, https://www.eyewitness.global/FAQS. Most of the media that *eyeWitness* receives comes from organizations with whom they have partnered.

[167] Tim Welch, Huma Haider, Martin Meenagh, and Yassan M'Boge, 'Witness Anonymity at the International Criminal Court: Due Process for Defendants, Witnesses or Both?', *The Denning Law Journal* 23 (2011): 29–46, at 30.

[168] Art. 68; *Victims and Witnesses Unit*, created pursuant to Reg. 96 of the ICC *Regulations of the Registry*.

[169] In 2018, the Committee to Protect Journalists confirmed the killing of 123 Syrian journalists. Hamilton (n 10) 37. In Leyh (n 19) 50, the author notes that between 2011 and 2013, sixty-five citizen journalists and twenty-four professional journalists were killed.

[170] This is the common law silent witness theory for the admission of video evidence which finds favour in several jurisdictions including Canada, the UK, the US, Australia, and Hong Kong. Though not part of international criminal law, it is a potentially helpful construct.

true contextual understanding of the images. An alternative approach is to admit civilian media as a graphic portrayal of *viva voce* evidence only upon a sponsoring witness testifying that the images fairly and accurately depict what occurred in front of the camera.[171] These competing approaches engage a debate as to whether the camera or the photographer is the true witness.

The Program Director for *eyeWitness to Atrocities* (Wendy Betts) posited that there is a valid legal argument that the application itself is the witness.[172] This perspective misses the mark though because when a photographer is operating the camera, the camera is not the witness—the photographer is the actual witness and the camera merely memorializes what occurred in front of the witness.[173] The images serve as the visual testimony of the photographer.[174] Armed with only the images, the court will receive a story, but not necessarily the complete story. The recording itself can be interrogated by an expert for metadata such as type of camera, location, date, time, camera settings, image size, pixels, compression algorithm, frame rate, resolution, aspect ratio, file structure, and file format, but the media cannot reveal why the recording started and stopped when it did, what happened out of frame, what was heard if no audio is included (and if so, why no audio is included), whether the entire recording was submitted or just selected portions, etc. Only a human witness can give those answers. Should anonymous media be successfully tendered at trial, it could be argued that the court is effectively allowing an anonymous pseudo-witness to testify, and to add insult to injury, one that cannot be cross examined.

Should the camera be viewed as the witness, an approach that I view as incorrect, then anonymous images would be admissible as documentary evidence subject to an assessment of weight.[175] Documentary evidence includes anything in which information is recorded, including digital and other visual media, and can be admitted subject to a later assessment of weight, even when authenticity is in issue.[176] Notional application of the common law best evidence rule, which requires that a party produce the best evidence available, may result in the anonymous visual evidence being deemed admissible, subject to an assessment of weight.[177]

[171] At common law, this is referred to as the illustrative evidence theory. David Watt, *Watt's Manual of Criminal Evidence* (Toronto: Thomson Carswell, 2007), 10.02–10.04. Though not a strict requirement of international criminal law, this approach is wise as it provides necessary context for the evidence shown.

[172] Hamilton (n 10) 46–7.

[173] In circumstances where video images are obtained from an unmanned camera, the camera is by default the true witness.

[174] Paul Lowe, 'The Forensic Turn: Bearing Witness and Thingness of the Photograph', in *The Violence of the Image: Photography and International Conflict*, edited by Liam Kennedy and Caitlin Patrick (London: I.B. Tauris, 2014), 226–54, at 229.

[175] Evidence may be admitted but assigned limited or no weight if found to be unreliable. Mark Klamberg, *Evidence in International Criminal Trials* (Leiden: Martinus Nijhoff Publishers, 2013), 351–7.

[176] *Prosecutor v. Musema*, ICTR-96-13, 27 January 2000, para. 53; Klamberg (n 175) 375–8.

[177] Even though common law rules of evidence such as the best evidence rule do not apply to evidence exclusion in international criminal litigation, they may find favour when assessing the weight of evidence. Klamberg (n 175) 342–3.

Given the tenuous nature of civilian visual evidence that is uploaded to social media and other sites in circumstances where the photographer is unknown, I would expect that counsel would be reticent to tender and rely upon such evidence. Indeed, such evidence should not be admitted unless it can be corroborated by other evidence. Absent corroboration or testimony from the photographer or other supporting witnesses, the court will likely be denied valuable contextual information and context is king.[178] Requiring first person testimony or other corroboration would assist the court in assessing probative value and assigning the appropriate weight to the evidence.

Tribunals and the ICC have been liberal in the reception of evidence on the basis that professional judges can disregard evidence that should not have been admitted or which is assigned no weight, a presumption that research has shown may be unsound.[179] A sounder approach may be to exclude evidence that lacks necessary hallmarks of reliability earlier in the litigation process. Defendants may not be entitled to a perfect trial, but they are entitled to a fair one and the submission of anonymous image-based evidence raises the spectre of unfairness.

Conclusion

The volume of media that may be gathered through the democratization process and ultimately find its way to investigators through direct submission, intermediaries, dedicated evidence gathering applications, or social media and other sites, especially in a longstanding and geographically diverse conflict, is staggering. The most recent example of this is the vast amount of media being created and distributed during the 2022 Russian invasion of Ukraine, some of which may become integral in future prosecutions.[180] As a result, atrocity crime investigations must contend with the double-edged sword of democratization—a vast amount of potentially vital evidence that is likely to be collected for ultimate consideration by the OTP and other investigative agencies, which may not otherwise exist, but with the attendant and often significant challenges associated with this type of free-range evidence.

As a result, there is a corollary need for heightened caution when assessing evidence obtained through the democratization process. It is not akin to manna from

[178] Civilian visual evidence should be secondary evidence used to corroborate evidence gathered by professionals. Hamilton (n 10) 39–42.

[179] Judges are generally unable to avoid being influenced by evidence heard but found to be inadmissible. Anthony Wistrich, Chris Guthrie, and Jeffrey Rachlinski 'Can Judges Ignore Inadmissible Information? The Difficulty of Deliberately Disregarding', *University of Pennsylvania Law Review* 153 (2004–05): 1251–345.

[180] An extensive network of civil society actors commenced visually documenting Russian war crimes and other atrocities in Ukraine for a variety of purposes including gathering evidence for legal accountability in future domestic and international criminal proceedings. Koenig (n 50) 831–2.

heaven. While democratized image-based evidence may ultimately prove to be authentic, reliable, and worthy of inclusion in a trial narrative, it must earn that designation. Achieving that level of confidence is dependent upon investigators, experts, and counsel addressing the issues that are raised in this and subsequent chapters. These issues include assessing the agendas and bias of photographers, evidence submitters, and those who rely upon such images.[181] Assessing image reliability and the need for competent and knowledgeable interpretation are critical steps in understanding what images have to offer.[182] The ability to address any of these issues is premised on determining whether the images are authentic, which can be a vexing process.[183]

It is important for counsel and the court to understand the context in which image-based evidence was obtained, including why certain content was included or excluded during recording. To preserve the integrity of the trial process and the goal of pursuing the truth, the photographer or another supporting witness should testify regarding the recorded event. In practice, that preferred standard may not always be achieved as there are times when the photographer is unknown and the only version of the media that exists is on social media or other sites. In these circumstances, authentication may still be achievable as will be discussed in Chapter 7. Nonetheless, anonymous civilian media denies all parties the ability to question the photographer and severely limits the ability of counsel to challenge the evidence. Rather than deny admission outright in such circumstances, assuming the integrity and authenticity of the media is established, the court should only admit anonymous visual evidence for the limited purpose of secondary or corroborative evidence, not as primary evidence. This approach is liberal in that it admits authentic anonymous visual evidence but at the same time restricts the evidential value that may be placed upon it by relegating it to secondary evidence status, thus preserving trial integrity and addressing fair trial concerns. Even though such evidence may achieve admission and subsequent weighing, cautious appraisal by investigators, counsel, and the court is required as anonymous image-based evidence may be too unreliable to consider.

[181] See Chapter 4.

[182] See Chapters 5 and 6 respectively.

[183] See Chapter 7.

4
Selectivity and Image-Based Evidence

Introduction

Atrocity crime prosecutions come to fruition through the filtering lens of prosecutorial selectivity. At the macro level, selectivity is essential in determining what countries will be investigated, what specific situations will be the focus of investigation, and within those situations, what incidents or events will be targeted. Various criteria are considered when making these assessments, including the gravity of the allegations, the responsibility of the perpetrators, and the availability of evidence. Specific crimes must then be selected for prosecution along with the chosen time frame that will be the focus of the indictment. Finally, it must be determined which defendants should be prosecuted.

Once these decisions have been made, the prosecution must build its trial narrative and in doing so, must consider what evidence should be led before the court. Focusing on image-based evidence, an essential consideration for counsel is the origin of the images being evaluated. Not all evidence accumulated during an investigation is objective, impartial, and independent of partisan interests. The visual narrative of atrocities is influenced by the agendas and biases of the photographer which in turn affect what evidence is framed, collected, and retained. The practical and philosophical implications of relying upon civilian visual evidence in pursuit of the truth must be considered.

The impact of photographer agendas and biases extends beyond image capture to decisions made by photographers as to what images, if any, will be submitted to authorities for their consideration. Prosecutors must then select what images they will include in their trial narrative, cognizant of the fact that while not all evidence that is received is utilized, the prosecution must select and assimilate evidence in a manner that is respectful of the pursuit of truth. Similarly, defence counsel must assess and select images that can be used to counter the prosecution narrative and promote defence theories. Images can be presented to the court by counsel in such a way as to constitute disinformation or misinformation in furtherance of partisan interests.[1] Presentation is impacted not only by image selection but may also be

[1] Disinformation is false information that is deliberately created or disseminated for the express purpose of causing harm. Producers of disinformation typically have political, financial, psychological, or social motivations; Claire Wardle, 'Information Disorder, Part 1: The Essential Glossary' (2018) https://medium.com/1st-draft/information-disorder-part-1-the-essential-glossary-19953c544fe3 accessed 21 December 2020. See also *Lexico Dictionary*, which defines disinformation as false information that

Image-Based Evidence in International Criminal Prosecutions. Jonathan W. Hak, KC, Oxford University Press.
 DOI: 10.1093/oso/9780198889533.003.0004

affected by textual and graphical annotations that may be used as interpretive aids. Trafficking in false narratives emanating from creation, selection, and presentation bias is contrary to the interests of justice. Photographer and party agendas and biases can harm the pursuit of the truth and this conscious and subconscious selectivity is the focus of this chapter.

1. Selectivity in the Creation of Image-Based Evidence

Factored into macro-level decisions involving the selection of cases and defendants are assessments of the nature and quality of the evidence capable of supporting a prosecution. Suppose that investigators receive two video recordings of an incident, each recorded by a different photographer at approximately the same time but from a different vantage point. The first video generally confirms what the investigators believe occurred, but upon viewing the second video a very different picture emerges. If each recording is accurate and reliable, how can the seemingly disparate depictions be reconciled? In such a scenario, the ICC Office of the Prosecutor (OTP) is required to pursue both the inculpatory and exculpatory leads as opposed to only the media that supports the prosecution theory. This accords with the prosecution's duty to pursue the truth and serves to counter the development of tunnel vision. Further, Article 67(2) of the *Rome Statute* compels disclosure of both inculpatory and exculpatory evidence as soon as practicable. Whether the competing versions can be reconciled or not, they must both be investigated and disclosed.

Selectivity and framing are critical interpretive factors in the evaluation of image-based evidence. Investigators and prosecutors may not be cognizant of the origin of all evidence at their potential disposal and whether it fairly depicts relevant events. Many types of evidence are discovered *in situ* by civilians, investigators, and other people, either at a crime scene or at another location that has some connection to the parties involved in the crime. Examples include the victims themselves, blood, fingerprints, DNA, weapons, vehicles, documents, computer files, financial records, computers, and other electronic devices. These are all examples of real evidence, which exist independent of human intervention and are

is intended to mislead, especially propaganda issued by a government organization to a rival power or the media. 'disinformation, n' (*Lexico Dictionary*) http://www.lexico.com accessed 7 August 2023. Misinformation is information that is false, but not necessarily intended to cause harm. For example, individuals may unwittingly share false information on social media. See Wardle. Contrast *Lexico Dictionary* which defines misinformation as false information that is spread, regardless of whether there is intent to mislead; 'misinformation, n' (*Lexico Dictionary*) http://www.lexico.com accessed 7 August 2023. This latter definition is more in keeping with the spirit of misinformation which generally suggests impropriety.

discoverable by anyone who comes upon the scene and those who investigate the suspected crimes.[2]

Certain types of image-based evidence are different from independent real evidence in that they are not merely discoverable, they are *created* by interested parties.[3] For example, images in the form of video recordings and photographs may be recorded (created) by victims, eyewitnesses, third party observers, civil society members, enemy combatants, and others before and during an incident. Images may also be recorded after the crime has occurred by civilians, investigators, forensic experts, and human rights organizations. Examples of image-based evidence created after the fact include photographs, video recordings, satellite imagery, 3D reconstructions, and advanced visual representations. It is because images are created, rather than discovered, that subjective choices are made as to what is ultimately produced, and thus engages a consideration of agendas and biases.

Allegations of political, partisan, ethnic, or national bias are often levied against witnesses in atrocity crime prosecutions.[4] Bias may be defined as being unfairly prejudiced against a particular individual or group or demonstrating an unjustified concentration of interest on a particular target or subject.[5] One type of bias is motivational bias, which involves conscious preferential choices whereas cognitive bias is less overt, often operating at the subconscious level, but no less problematic.[6]

[2] Real evidence primarily consists of objects or things that have material form. 'real evidence, adj and n' Jonathan Law, *A Dictionary of Law*, 9th ed. (Oxford: OUP, 2018). It is evidence furnished by things themselves on view or inspection, as distinguished from a description of them by a witness. 'real evidence, adj and n' Henry Black, *Black's Law Dictionary*, 5th ed. (Minnesota: West Publishing, 1979).

[3] An exception to this general statement would be video evidence that is automatically recorded irrespective of human intervention, including continuously recorded or motion-activated CCTV video, and satellite imagery recorded by passive sensors.

[4] Gideon Boas, James Bischoff, Natalie Reid, and Don Taylor, *International Criminal Procedure* (Cambridge: CUP, 2011), 345–7; Xabier Aranburu, 'The Contribution of Analysis to the Quality Control in Criminal Investigation', in *Quality Control in Criminal Investigation*, edited by Xabier Agirre, Morten Bergsmo, Simon De Smet, and Carsten Stahn (Brussels: Torkel Opsahl Academic EPublisher, 2020), 117–272, at 137–53.

[5] It is described in scientific literature as '[a]ny process at any stage of inference which tends to produce results or conclusions that differ systematically from the truth'. David Sackett, 'Bias in Analytical Research', *Journal of Chronic Diseases* 32 (1979): 51–63, at 51. McDermott et al. adapt the definition of bias in the context of international criminal investigations to '... any systematic distortion or error, due to a design problem, an interfering factor, or a judgement, that can affect the conception, design, or conduct of an investigation, or the collection, analysis, interpretation, presentation, or discussion of the evidence'. Yvonne McDermott, Alexa Koenig, and Daragh Murray, 'Open Source Information's Blind Spot', *Journal of International Criminal Justice* 19, no. 1 (2021): 85–106, at 88.

[6] Motivational biases 'include conscious or subconscious distortions of judgments and decisions because of self-interest, social pressures, or organisational context'. '... judgments are influenced by the desirability or undesirability of events, consequences, outcomes, or choices'. Gilberto Montibeller and Detlof von Winterfeldt, 'Cognitive and Motivational Biases in Decision and Risk Analysis', *Risk Analysis* 35, no. 7 (2015): 1230–51, at 1230–31. Motivational bias, and personal ideology and beliefs impact decision making. Itiel Dror, 'Cognitive and Human Factors in Expert Decision Making: Six Fallacies and the Eight Sources of Bias', *Analytical Chemistry* 92 (2020): 7998–8004, at 8002. Cognitive biases are faulty mental processes that lead to judgments and decisions that violate commonly accepted normative principles, resulting in systematic discrepancies between the correct answer in a judgment-based task and the decision-maker's actual answer. Montibeller and von Winterfeldt, 1230–31.

Cognitive bias includes processes that may lead to inaccurate judgments, interpretations, or decision-making.[7] This impacts not only the veracity and reliability of *viva voce* evidence, where bias is often affiliated, but also any image-based evidence a witness may create.

Bias affects what data is collected and discarded and in the imagery context, what images photographers choose to record and in turn the truth they present to others.[8] Choices must be made when creating images and once a photographer selects a subject within the frame, a bias similar to that of a historian is utilized in that the photographer judges what will become historical evidence.[9] Implicit in every choice to include is the corollary decision to exclude. The images captured reveal the photographer's perception of the event, subjective by nature, even if intending to be objective.[10] Though viewers may believe they occupy the position of witness, the reality is that the photographer is using framing and focus to subjectively interpret the event for the viewer.[11] All images are captured, chosen, limited, and produced for viewing.[12] In short, viewers see what the photographer chooses to show them. Bearing witness through photography is a matter of perspective.[13] Assuming the image is reliable, what is shown may be true, but the broader truth of the image is contextualized through the photographer's eye and framing choice.

When photographers select images to accord with their own beliefs and theories of an event or conflict, they engage in confirmation bias, explicitly rejecting images that stand in opposition to their views.[14] Downstream viewers such as

[7] Glinda Cooper and Vanessa Meterko, 'Cognitive Bias Research in Forensic Science: A Systematic Review', *Forensic Science International* 297 (2019): 35–46, at 35; Carsten Stahn, 'From Preliminary Examination to Investigation: Rethinking the Connection', in *Quality Control in Criminal Investigation*, edited by Xabier Agirre, Morten Bergsmo, Simon De Smet, and Carsten Stahn (Brussels: Torkel Opsahl Academic EPublisher, 2020), 37–66, at 42–3.

[8] Biases can also impact the actual observation and perception of data and how it is tested and interpreted. Dror (n 6) 7998.

[9] Peter Burke, *Eyewitnessing: The Use of Images as Historical Evidence* (London: Reaktion Books, 2019), 29.

[10] ibid 191.

[11] ibid 195. A biased source conveys what is truthful from their perspective, even though the portrayal may not be objectively truthful. Aranburu (n 4) 124.

[12] Immi Tallgren, 'Come and See? The Power of Images and International Criminal Justice', *International Criminal Law Review* 17 (2017): 259–80, at 271.

[13] C. Clarke, 'A Matter of Perspective: Truth, Evidence and the Role of Photography as an Investigative Tool', in *Digital Investigative Journalism: Data, Visual Analytics and Innovative Methodologies in International Reporting*, edited by Oliver Hahn and Florian Stalph (Cham: Springer International Publishing, 2019), 157–69, at 157.

[14] Confirmation bias is one type of cognitive bias. Cooper and Meterko (n 7) 36. It describes a 'tendency to search for and interpret information in ways that are partial to existing hypotheses' and to ignore or interpret opposing information in such a way as to leave the hypothesis intact. Moa Lidén, 'Confirmation Bias in Investigation of Core International Crimes: Risk Factors and Quality Control Techniques', in *Quality Control in Criminal Investigation*, edited by Xabier Agirre, Morten Bergsmo, Simon De Smet, and Carsten Stahn (Brussels: Torkel Opsahl Academic EPublisher, 2020), 461–528, at 462. It occurs when people interpret information or seek new evidence to conform to their preexisting beliefs or assumptions. People observe and give more weight to information which is consistent with their existing beliefs and are less likely to observe and give weight to information which is in conflict. Sarah Stammers and Sophie Bunn, 'Unintentional Bias in Forensic Investigation', *House of Parliament: Parliamentary Office of Science and Technology* 15 (2015): 1–6, at 2.

investigators, counsel, and the court will only see what has been selected by the photographer. When investigators and counsel rely heavily upon images selected by photographers early in the investigation, these selections can frame how the case is viewed, assessed, and developed. Beliefs developed early in a case tend to have an anchoring effect from which all other evidence is evaluated.[15] Prosecutors are not immune from confirmation bias and must engage in critical evaluation of evidence and narratives, mindful of diverse viewpoints and perspectives, to avoid tunnel vision.[16] The dangers of unchecked biases are legion—wrongful accusations, wrongful convictions, and the failure to hold true perpetrators accountable.

The proliferation of smartphones and other consumer grade video recording devices is remarkable.[17] This confluence of technology and eager consumers has engendered a new and generally unregulated generation of civilian documentarians.[18] Witnesses may capture images that supplement or contradict state sanctioned narratives and this digitizing of suffering can provide an evidential windfall.[19] Civilian media can provide information essential for public dissemination and can serve as probative evidence in international tribunals and courts. Paradoxically, this windfall also creates a new problem, namely the opportunity for selective and potentially misleading evidence creation.[20] Visual depictions may represent and misrepresent reality at the same time.[21] Photography as a medium is not the problem, but rather the way the photographer engages with it.[22] Visual documentation is highly subjective.[23]

Photographers have biases that may influence the images they capture, ranging from altruism, where a thorough and fair canvassing of all areas of interest and relevance are included, to the nefarious, where the images captured are

[15] Mirjan Damaška, 'What is the Point of International Criminal Justice?', *Chicago-Kent Law Review* 83, no. 1 (2008): 329–68, at 337–8; McDermott, Koenig, and Murray (n 5) 90.

[16] Developing debiasing techniques to minimize the potential for confirmation bias is essential. Carsten Stahn, *Justice as Message: Expressivist Foundations of International Criminal Justice* (Oxford: OUP, 2020), 412.

[17] The forecasted number of mobile phone users in 2023 is estimated to be 7.33 billion; Statistica, 'Forecast Number of Mobile Users Worldwide from 2020 to 2025' https://www.statista.com/statistics/218984/number-of-global-mobile-users-since-2010/. Internet users are estimated to be 5.03 billion in July 2022, with 4.7 billion being social media users https://www.statista.com/statistics/617136/digital-population-worldwide/.

[18] Sam Gregory, 'Cameras Everywhere: Ubiquitous Video Documentation of Human Rights, New Forms of Video Advocacy, and Considerations of Safety, Security, Dignity and Consent', *Journal of Human Rights Practice* 2, no. 2 (2010): 191–207, at 195.

[19] Aoife Duffy, 'Bearing Witness to Atrocity Crimes: Photography and International Law', *Human Rights Quarterly* 40 (2018): 776–814, at 784–5.

[20] Beyond concerns of photographer selectivity, the widespread availability of digital technology permits the dissemination of manipulated data as well. Office of the United Nations High Commissioner for Human Rights and the Human Rights Centre at the University of California, Berkeley, School of Law, 'Berkeley Protocol on Digital Open Source Investigations' (2020) HR/PUB/20/2, at 4 ('Berkeley Protocol').

[21] Clarke (n 13) 158.

[22] ibid 159.

[23] Clarke notes, 'Whilst the camera can record a moment and provide a "record" of a particular event, situation or person(s), the validity of this record as unadulterated reality is questionable.' ibid 159–60.

highly selective, myopic, and partisan, and reflect disdain for objective truth. Photographers may gather evidence that favours or confirms their perspective and produce a biased visual account that nonetheless retains some evidential value. If enemy forces are pillaging a village and killing its residents, those actions would be the natural focus for anyone attempting to digitally memorialize the event. The photographer's agenda is likely to gather evidence of the attack with the hope of bringing the perpetrators to justice. The presence of an agenda is not necessarily an evil to be eradicated as most people who record images have an agenda.[24] It is when their agenda causes them to create media that unfairly or wrongly depicts an event and the people involved that raises concern.

Viewers must be aware of the impact that agendas can have on image interpretation. Embedded photographers typically have an express agenda, whether to capture images that favour one side in a conflict, to gather material for a book, or to sell media.[25] The images chosen to be framed are not just images awaiting interpretation; the choice to record is an interpretation by the photographer.[26] Even though the National (US) Press Photographers' Association Code of Ethics cautions photographers to avoid presenting their own biases when framing and editing images, putting that into practice is challenging as photographers may not be cognizant of their biases.[27]

Photographers may not know at the time they record images which ones will later achieve significance, though members of civil society, human rights organizations, and NGOs are generally more adept at gathering contextual visual evidence and have some training in this regard.[28] Even investigators may not have a complete understanding of relevance when examining a scene and therefore the absence of image-based evidence due to a failure to visually document certain details is an ever-present risk. The time frame for evidence collection is a relevant evaluative consideration as image-based evidence may be gathered by OTP investigators and civilians years before an indictment is filed and a defence team is formed.

[24] Bouwknegt notes that international criminal justice is grounded in the human rights positivism of the 1990s, when the ad hoc tribunals were formed. He argues that the pursuit of international justice is rooted in part in human rights bias wherein investigations rely upon information provided by human rights lobby groups, impacted by NGO bias. His caution has merit and is reflective of the concern that information gathered by most individuals and groups has a bias attached to it. Thijs Bouwknegt, 'Investigating International Crimes: Pitfalls, Problems and Promises', in *Quality Control in Criminal Investigation*, edited by Xabier Agirre, Morten Bergsmo, Simon De Smet, and Carsten Stahn (Brussels: Torkel Opsahl Academic EPublisher, 2020), 67–113, at 72.

[25] Embedded photographers and videographers are journalists who agree to report only from the perspective established by military and governmental authorities. Judith Butler, 'Photography, War, Outrage', *PMLA* 120, no. 3 (2005): 822–7, at 822.

[26] ibid 823.

[27] Elizabeth Porter, 'Taking Images Seriously', *Columbia Law Review* 114 (2018): 1687–782, at 1761.

[28] Rebecca Hamilton, 'User Generated Evidence', *Columbia Journal of Transnational Law* 57, no. 1 (2018): 1–61, at 41–2; Brianne Leyh, 'Changing Landscapes in Documentation Efforts: Civil Society Documentation of Serious Human Rights Violations', *Utrecht Journal of International and European Law* 33, no. 84 (2017): 44–58, at 50–3; Sandra Ristovska, 'Human Rights Collectives as Visual Experts: The Case of Syrian Archive', *Visual Communications* 18, no. 3 (2019): 333–51, at 346.

Similarly, future defendants and their supporters may amass visual evidence years before the OTP commences an investigation. In either case, photographers must make preliminary assessments as to what should be documented for potential future use. Beyond descriptive *viva voce* evidence, these early images will largely generate the visual backdrop for future litigation.

Photographers consciously and subconsciously decide what to incorporate in the field of view. They may include events, locations, people, and objects they want to memorialize and exclude that which they prefer not to show.[29] In this way, photographers draw upon personal value judgments when deciding what will be visually documented.[30] Even 3D terrestrial laser scanning and the use of drones involves subjective decisions about where to place the scanner and where to fly the drone, thus impacting framing. Selective creation of image-based evidence may result in misinformation. Even in the absence of a deliberate choice to not include items of potential importance, it may sometimes be impractical or impossible to capture all that should be recorded due to lack of scene accessibility, time constraints, adverse environmental conditions, or concerns of personal safety. A detailed 360° view of a scene may simply not be feasible, leaving the downstream viewer at the mercy of the photographer's framing choices.

Once the subject matter has been chosen for memorialization, the photographer must consider how to best document it. Framing the image is itself an interpretive decision about what to capture and present to the viewer, as are the effects of camera angle, focus, and lighting.[31] Partisan dramaturgy may also affect what is included in an image—selecting what seems *right* even though it may not fairly portray the event.[32] The photographer may strategically capture the event, spatially and temporally, so as to present a perspective that accords with their agenda but that may lack objectivity.[33] Strategic framing can produce technically accurate images but may subjectively shape a narrative in such a way as to mislead the viewer.[34] Beyond framing the image, deciding when to commence recording video also influences what the viewer sees and how the event is portrayed.[35] This temporal recording selectivity may produce a vastly different narrative than the actual facts

[29] Naomi Mezey, 'The Image Cannot Speak for Itself: Film, Summary Judgment, and Visual Literacy', *Valparaiso University Law Review* 48, no. 1 (2013): 1–40, at 13.

[30] Butler notes that, '... even the most transparent of documentary images is framed, and framed for a purpose, carrying that purpose within its frame and implementing that purpose through the frame. Butler (n 25) 824.

[31] ibid 823.

[32] Judith Butler, 'Torture and the Ethics of Photography', *Society and Space* 25 (2007): 951–66, at 953.

[33] Hamilton (n 30) 41–2.

[34] Mary Fan, 'Democratizing Proof: Pooling Public and Police Body-Camera Videos', *North Carolina Law Review* 96, no. 5 (2018): 1639–80, at 1662–3.

[35] Fan cites several American cases involving police shootings of civilians where it appears that the police purposely did not activate their body worn cameras until after the fatal encounter, leaving an incomplete visual record. ibid 1659–62.

support. Visual documentation selectivity demands cautious appraisal by investigators, counsel, and the court.

A domestic example may be helpful in illustrating the impact that content selection and framing can have on narratives. Bystanders often record violent interactions between the police and members of the public. On occasion, such recordings may be misleading. Depending on when they begin and end, the vantage point shown, and what is included in the frame, video recordings may show conduct out of context from the entire encounter, unfairly branding justifiable police conduct as criminal. For example, police dashcam video and body worn video may not capture what led up to a violent encounter or may not show events that occurred out of frame during the event. What was said and done before the camera started recording can provide critical contextual information for viewers evaluating police conduct. Additionally, with police video, what is shown is the outward looking police perspective. Cameras may record things the officer did not see and equally, the officer may see things outside of the camera's field of view.[36] Underpinning the adoption of body worn cameras is the quest for unbiased and objective recordings of interactions involving officers, with decreased reliance on human memory and narrative.[37] The same video of police–civilian interactions may in fact reveal a very different narrative interpretation among viewers.[38] Cognitive biases informed by preconceived views of law enforcement can impact how viewers interpret video recordings involving police interactions with the public, illustrating the importance that framing and context play in media evaluation.

Furthering this domestic example, body worn cameras that record police interactions with the public were introduced in part as a check on the exercise of power by the police, with the hope that they would provide additional accurate, objective evidence.[39] Fundamentally, these are tangible benefits yet paradoxically, body worn cameras also set the stage for the creation of evidence by officers who wear them. Officers can use the cameras to manufacture image-based evidence in criminal investigations that casts their conduct in a more favourable light and to show the discovery of evidence that may in fact have been planted by the police.[40] They

[36] Seth Stoughton, 'Police Body-Worn Cameras', *North Carolina Law Review* 96, no. 5 (2018): 1363–1424, at 1403; Morgan Birck, 'Do You See What I See?: Problems with Juror Bias in Viewing Body-Camera Video Evidence', *Michigan Journal of Race & Law* 24, no. 1 (2018): 153–76, at 169.

[37] Fan (n 34) 1662.

[38] In a 2015 research study conducted by University of South Carolina law professor Seth Stoughton, participants were asked to view video from police dashcams and body worn cameras and to articulate their perceptions of the police interactions. All the events had been staged and recordings that captured the entire interaction from a different angle were also viewed. Each scenario showed what appeared to be a violent interaction with a civilian, but the second video shot from a different angle revealed a much different perspective, once far less supportive of the use of force by the police. Timothy Williams, James Thomas, Samuel Jacoby, and David Cave, 'Police Body Cameras: What Do You See? *The New York Times* (1 April 2016) https://www.nytimes.com/interactive/2016/04/01/us/police-bodycam-video.html.

[39] Stoughton (n 36) 1393.

[40] Most images are created but when they are created in such a way as to present a false or misleading narrative, the pejorative term 'manufactured' is a more accurate moniker.

may also narrate their activities and observations to highlight certain aspects of their investigation for later use, whether true or not.[41] Body worn cameras provide valuable evidence that can legitimately assist in criminal investigations, protect the public from abuses of power, and also protect the police from unfair and false complaints of misconduct, yet when strategically abused by the police, they can be used to generate false or misleading evidence, thus feeding into a police-centric agenda.[42] Many countries are increasingly making use of police dashcam video and body worn video. While dashcams record data that is limited in both scope and field of view, recording only events that occur in front of the police vehicle, body worn cameras record wherever the officer is located and in whatever direction the officer is facing. As a result, significantly more police generated video evidence is collected now than ever before, which has created daunting disclosure obligations.

Beyond the law enforcement context, there are many other examples of video recordings which illustrate the impact that content selection and framing can have on narratives derived from the images. Understanding the path of destruction of natural disasters and weather events can be better achieved with broad video coverage. Appropriately framed video images can assist investigators in understanding structural failures such as building, bridge, and crane collapses. They can also assist air safety experts and collision reconstructionists when assessing the dynamics of plane crashes and collisions involving motor vehicles, trains, and ships. Central to these examples is the notion that photographic choices can aid or hinder viewers in their comprehension and interpretation of events depicted.

The focus thus far has been on images created by photographers, yet image-based evidence may also be created from other media, spawning a progeny of new evidence to assist investigators and counsel. For example, as part of the investigation into allegations of human rights abuses by security forces during the Euromaidan Protests in Kiev, Ukraine in 2013–2014, where video images captured weapons being discharged, visual media experts from Carnegie Mellon University and SITU Research were asked to determine whether projectile trajectory could be visualized and whether existing video evidence could aid ballistics experts in

[41] Fan (n 36) 1639–80. Fan cites a Florida example where police bodycam video showed officers struggling with a resistant suspect while yelling at him to stop resisting. Unbeknownst to the police, the encounter was also recorded by a mounted CCTV camera from a higher angle. The static camera showed that the suspect put his hands in the air and then lay down with his hands behind him awaiting arrest. Several officers then kicked and beat him while telling him to stop resisting. This neutral perspective revealed that the police lied about their encounter with the suspect (1672–3). Bellin and Pemberton cite American reports of officers being trained to narrate events to create a favourable audio record. Jeffrey Bellin and Shevarma Pemberton, 'Policing the Admissibility of Body Camera Evidence', *Fordham Law Review* 87, no. 4 (2019): 1425–58, at 1427.

[42] Video evidence can serve as documentation of a good investigation as well as a method of identifying and documenting a poor one. Stoughton (n 36) 1395.

making such a determination.[43] The experts were also asked to identify the locations of specific firearms used as well as the trajectory and potential targets in circumstances where video images showed a weapon being fired but not a corresponding victim being struck. This information could then be used by prosecutors to corroborate or supplement other evidence such as eyewitness testimony, medical reports, media accounts, or GPS location information from the mobile phones of suspects.[44] Image-based evidence created from underlying media may be used as demonstrative evidence or as substantive proof depending upon the accuracy of the underlying data and the analysis undertaken.[45]

Throughout this section and this chapter generally, selectivity is discussed in the context of a human photographer being involved because that is where recording subjectivity is most prevalent. However, some images are recorded on a programmed or automated basis without contemporaneous human input. In the atrocity crime context, satellite photography would be the most apt example. While satellites may be directed by a person to gather certain data, thus triggering the selectivity factors discussed above, this process may also be automated. It is worthy of note that even automation involves a degree of selectivity in that decisions are made as to from where and how much data should be gathered and what resolution is desirable. In the domestic crime context, the most likely source of automated image recordings is a CCTV system. Absent a monitored system wherein someone is directing the camera, decisions will have been made in advance as to where to place the cameras, whether to record continuously or only upon motion activation, what frame rate to record, image resolution, etc. What is common among these automated image recording systems is that even though images of value may be captured by happenstance or fortuitously, there is an element of selectivity involved, albeit one step removed from the moment of image capture.

2. Selectivity in the Submission and Use of Image-Based Evidence

Beyond its creation, image-based evidence faces selectivity in the context of what images are submitted for consideration and what evidence is chosen by counsel for use at trial. While there may be only one ultimate truth as to what occurred in an incident, the criminal trial process often finds the parties promulgating their preferred version of the truth to achieve a desired partisan outcome. Facts can be slippery constructs for truth. They may legitimately support multiple interpretations,

[43] Jay Aronson, McKenna Cole, Alex Hauptmann, Dan Miller, and Bradley Samuels, 'Reconstructing Human Rights Violations Using Large Eyewitness Collections: The Case of Euromaidan Protester Deaths', *Journal of Human Rights Practice* (2018): 1–20, at 1.

[44] ibid 8.

[45] In the Euromaidan example, substantive proof was the goal.

some of which favour one party's perspective over the other. Reasonable doubt can find a foothold in equivocal facts. It is the duty of the defence to raise reasonable doubt regarding the prosecution's allegation of facts, to put forth credible alternative interpretations of those facts, to question whether the truth has been established and even if it has, to argue that it does not sufficiently support the allegations to merit conviction. Beyond the expected reticence to accept facts without robust challenge that is endemic in both the adversarial and inquisitorial approaches, the prosecution and the defence may have independent, sometimes mutually exclusive, perceptions of truth. The agendas and biases of witnesses that influence what evidence they submit to investigators and counsel and those of the parties when selecting what evidence to lead at trial are important considerations in the pursuit of the truth.

Selectivity occurs not only when deciding what images to record and how to frame them, but also when deciding whether to edit the images, which images to retain, and which to submit for consideration. This discretion is more likely to be exercised in the unregulated environment of civilians who are not members of civil society groups, human rights organizations, or NGOs. Images are uploaded to social media or other sites only if the submitter views them as having sufficient merit. This upload discretion is exercised by parties who have agendas, altruistic or otherwise. Dedicated evidence-gathering applications such as *CameraV* and *eyeWitness* also involve selectivity at the submission stage because the photographer decides whether submission is meritorious.

Media uploaded to social media or other sites will only be considered in an investigation if the media comes to the attention of cyber-crime investigators or analysts. Media submitted through the *eyeWitness* application is sent to the International Bar Association (IBA) where lawyers sift through the images, catalogue them, and determine which ones might be useful for a criminal prosecution.[46] Presumably, reviewing lawyers err on the side of inclusion when forwarding evidence to the OTP. Whether evidence is submitted to social media or other sites, the IBA, or investigators directly, it is axiomatic that the submitter chooses what to submit. The court will only know of the media proffered and selected for use by investigators and counsel, even though more images may have been recorded. If media has been edited prior to submission, access to the original will become an issue when assessing the nature of the editing and its impact on content reliability. For example, when the photographer is anonymous, the original may never be ascertained and reliability of the submitted version in the absence of corroboration may be questionable.

When considering the role of counsel in evidence selection, it is important to note that the OTP is both the primary investigative body and a party to the

[46] Hamilton (n 28) 32.

proceedings that has a positive obligation to disclose evidence that is relevant and material to the defence, whether inculpatory or exculpatory, and whether selected for inclusion at trial or not.[47] The prosecution's disclosure obligations regarding evidence which may show innocence, mitigate guilt, or affect the credibility of prosecution evidence is also reflected in the International Criminal Court (ICC) Chambers Practice Manual.[48] In addition to assisting the defence in the preparation of their case, disclosure is also a mechanism that can be used to verify that the prosecution has conducted a thorough investigation.[49] The Trial Chamber in *Prosecutor v. Lubanga* ruled that the prosecution is under a continuing responsibility to disclose potentially exculpatory material throughout the trial.[50] The defence is not generally bound to disclose its case except when it intends to raise an alibi, pursue a ground for excluding criminal responsibility, or when intending to present evidence at a confirmation hearing.[51] Limited defence disclosure is required at the trial stage.[52]

Beyond its disclosure obligations, the prosecution is also tasked with the investigative goal of establishing the truth and a duty to 'investigate incriminating and exonerating circumstances equally'.[53] These significant prosecutorial obligations of

[47] Article 67(2) of the *Rome Statute* compels disclosure of both inculpatory and exculpatory evidence as soon as practicable. Further, the defence is permitted to inspect any books, documents, photographs, or other tangible objects in the possession or control of the prosecution which are material to the preparation of the defence or are intended to be used by the prosecution at trial (RPE Rule 77). A corollary provision provides the prosecution with access to such materials intended to be used by the defence as evidence (Rule 78). These provisions are subject to certain exceptions, Chambers applications, and Chamber orders (Rules 79–84; *Rome Statute*, Art. 64(3)(c)). See also Mark Klamberg, *Evidence in International Criminal Trials* (Leiden: Martinus Nijhoff Publishers, 2013), 287, 291–2, who notes that exculpatory information includes material that tends to show innocence, mitigates guilt, or impacts the credibility of the prosecution's case. See also *Prosecutor v. Lubanga*, ICC-01/04-01/06-1401, Decision on the Consequences of Non-disclosure of Exculpatory Materials Covered by Article 54(3)(e) Agreements and the Application to Stay the Prosecution of the Accused, Together with Certain Other Issues Raised at the Status Conference on 10 June 2008, 13 June 2008, para. 59.

[48] ICC Chambers Practice Manual (2019), https://www.icc-cpi.int/iccdocs/other/191129-chamber-manual-eng.pdf. Para. 21 provides, 'The Prosecutor has the duty to disclose to the Defence "as soon as practicable" and on a continuous basis, all evidence in his/her possession or control which he/she believes shows or tends to show the innocence of the person, or mitigate the guilt of the person or may affect the credibility of the prosecution evidence (cf. Article 67(2) of the Statute), or is material to the preparation of the defence (cf. Rule 77 of the Rules).'

[49] Salvatore Zappalà, 'The Prosecutor's Duty to Disclose Exculpatory Materials and the Recent Amendment to Rule 68 ICTY RPE', *Journal of International Criminal Justice* 2 (2004): 620–30, at 628.

[50] ICC-01/04–01/06-1019, Decision Regarding the Timing and Manner of Disclosure and the Date of Trial, 9 November 2007, para. 28. Late or incomplete disclosure may result in a stay of proceedings or the recalling of affected witnesses for further questioning. Klamberg (n 47) 292. See also Rule 84 which describes disclosure as a continuing process.

[51] RPE Rules 79(1)(a) and (b), 80(1). The defence is required to notify the prosecutor of the witnesses it will call and the evidence it intends to rely upon in support of the defences of alibi or lack of criminal responsibility. *Rome Statute*, Art. 61(6), RPE Rule 121(6). A list of evidence is required to be disclosed to the Pre-Trial Chamber.

[52] Defences relied upon and evidence to be called, as well as witness information, may be disclosable by the defence. This level of disclosure has been found not to violate the defendant's right to a fair trial. Klamberg (n 47) 299–300.

[53] *Rome Statute*, Art. 54(1)(a). The active truth-seeking duty of the prosecution to investigate both inculpatory and exculpatory evidence is a key component in creating a robust case for consideration.

investigation and disclosure have not always been present in international criminal proceedings. For example, the prosecution for the International Military Tribunal for Nuremberg (IMT) and the International Military Tribunal for the Far East (IMTFE) had no duty to investigate or disclose exculpatory evidence.[54] Conversely, the co-investigating judges at the Extraordinary Chambers in the Courts of Cambodia (ECCC) are permitted to '... take any investigative action conducive to ascertaining the truth'. This includes an obligation to conduct their investigation impartially, whether the evidence is inculpatory or exculpatory.[55] For the ad hoc tribunals (the International Criminal Tribunal for the former Yugoslavia (ICTY), the International Criminal Tribunal for Rwanda (ICTR), the United Nations International Residual Mechanism for Criminal Tribunals (MICT), and the Special Court for Sierra Leone (SCSL)), while the prosecution had/has a duty to consider and disclose exculpatory evidence to the defence, there was/is not a corollary duty on the prosecution to seek exculpatory evidence.[56]

The OTP's legal obligation to investigate circumstances and disclose evidence that is inculpatory and exculpatory is an essential component in the broad pursuit of truth and a fair and just result. This objective approach was included in the *Rome Statute* to combine the role of the prosecutor and the investigating judge in the adversarial and inquisitorial legal systems.[57] It helps to safeguard the right of defendants to understand the case against them and to prepare their defence accordingly.[58] The prosecution typically has greater investigative and institutional resources, access to legal compulsion to obtain evidence, and a higher moral authority when conducting its investigation. The obligation of the OTP to disclose exculpatory material is designed to offset the disadvantages faced by the defence.[59] Equality of arms between the parties is essential in ensuring substantive and procedural fairness.[60] The OTP is not tasked with serving two masters, as Chief

[54] Klamberg (n 47) 205. Chief Prosecutor Jackson (IMT) noted '... under the Charter our duty is to present the case for the Prosecution. I do not, in any instance, serve two masters'.

[55] ECCC Internal Rules (Rev. 9), Rule 55(5). The judges are not however required to conduct an exhaustive search for all evidence. Klamberg (n 47) 206.

[56] Klamberg (n 47) 207, 288. The statutory instruments of the ad hoc tribunals (ICTY RPE, Rule 68; ICTR RPE, Rule 68; MICT RPE, Rule 73; SCSL RPE, Rule 68) require the prosecution to disclose to the defence any exculpatory or mitigating information in its possession or knowledge. Exculpatory evidence includes material which may lessen the credibility of prosecution witnesses. David Re, 'Rethinking Disclosure: Embrace the Electronic Disclosure Suite', in *Quality Control in Criminal Investigation*, edited by Xabier Agirre, Morten Bergsmo, Simon De Smet, and Carsten Stahn (Brussels: Torkel Opsahl Academic EPublisher, 2020), 735–90, at 747.

[57] Morten Bergsmo and Pieter Kruger, 'Article 54: Duties and Powers of the Prosecutor with Respect to Investigations', in *Commentary of the Rome Statute of the International Criminal Court* 2nd ed., edited by Otto Triffterer (Munich: Beck/Hart, 2008), 1078.

[58] Xavier-Jean Keïta, 'Disclosure of Evidence in the Law and Practice of the ICC', *International Criminal Law Review* 16 (2016): 1018–47, at 1019. Most exculpatory evidence must be disclosed prior to the confirmation hearing as Art. 67(2) compels disclosure 'as soon as practicable'. Sabine Swoboda, 'The ICC Disclosure Regime: A Defence Perspective', *Criminal Law Forum* 19 (2008): 449–72, at 453.

[59] Keïta (n 58) 1021.

[60] Swoboda (n 58) 450.

Prosecutor Jackson negated in Nuremberg, but rather truth, fairness, and justice. For a conviction to withstand appellate review and public scrutiny, the prosecution must be seen to have honoured these fundamental precepts.

Given the obligation of the OTP to investigate inculpatory and exculpatory circumstances and to disclose to the defence accordingly, it follows that confirmation bias must be guarded against. This means that all relevant evidence, including open source evidence, should be acquired and disclosed in pursuit of the truth, not just the initial prosecution theory.[61] Over the course of a lengthy investigation, voluminous amounts of information are collected, little of which may be used at trial.[62] Regarding image-based evidence, once submitted to the OTP, investigators must assess the media in detail, with counsel ultimately deciding what evidence from the entire media collection will be tendered at trial.[63]

The investigative and disclosure obligations of the prosecution are separate and apart from the tactical decision of the prosecution as to what evidence to tender at trial. Deciding how to frame the prosecution narrative and what evidence to lead in support of it is one of the most important aspects of a criminal prosecution. The role of the prosecution in the selection and presentation of evidence is significant. Prosecutors have considerable discretion in how they construct their case. They must lead evidence on all elements of the offences charged to seek a conviction but are not required to present all the evidence in their possession. Nonetheless, prosecutor selectivity should not be used to exclude exculpatory evidence from consideration by the Chamber. That would violate the prosecution's duty to pursue the truth and to act fairly. Prosecutors must exercise cautious discretion in the presentation of their case and follow important guidelines regarding the use of evidence, including that which is image-based, as suggested below.

First, prosecutors should not lead evidence simply because they possess it. The selection of each item of evidence for inclusion, whether it be *viva voce* evidence, documentary, image-based, tangible, or expert in nature must address an identifiable issue. The evidence must be necessary for the proper exposition of the facts and must relate to an element required to be proven. If the absence of a piece of evidence would have no discernible impact on the final submissions of counsel and the decision of the Chamber, there is merit in not leading it, provided lack of fairness does not result. Prosecution cases should be efficient, surgical, and mindful of time and resource limitations. If a prosecution is so lengthy that a defendant is effectively tried to death, there is little benefit to anyone. Prosecutors are not solely to blame for overly long prosecutions but because they prefer the indictment and

[61] Awareness of cognitive bias is important in the gathering and filtering of evidence as are protocols to safeguard against common bias-related errors. McDermott, Koenig, and Murray (n 5) 12, 14.

[62] Re (n 56) 735, 796. Re colourfully states that 'disclosure is a swamp, like a mire of quicksand that can rapidly swallow the unsuspecting'.

[63] Aronson, Cole, Hauptmann, Miller, and Samuels (n 43) 2–3.

craft their case, they have considerable impact on the length of the proceedings. Evidence selection should therefore be cautiously considered and targeted.

Second, even though prosecutors have a positive obligation to disclose all relevant evidence to the defence whether inculpatory or exculpatory, it does not follow that all disclosed evidence must be led at trial. Prosecutors must exercise their discretion in favour of selecting for presentation at trial the evidence most suitable for proof of the requisite offence elements. If prosecutors are required to present all evidence submitted by investigators and other interested parties, they would be forced to either stop the influx of evidence or conduct interminable prosecutions. Neither approach is in the best interests of justice. All relevant evidence must be available to all parties and each party must then select the evidence that will form part of their case.

Third, defendants are not entitled to a perfect trial, but they are entitled to a fair one. Even though they are a party to the litigation, the prosecution must not be partisan in its presentation of evidence.[64] When selecting evidence for trial, the goal of the prosecution should be to ascertain the truth, mindful that not all parties and the Chamber may view the evidence the same way. Practically, this means that if there are witnesses whose testimony would contradict key prosecution witnesses, so long as there is no demonstrable reason to reject their evidence outright as being wholly false, their evidence should be presented. Regarding image-based evidence, the abundance of such evidence submitted by civilians, human rights activists, and NGOs has resulted in a significant amount of evidence to consider.[65] Multiple video recordings and photographs of an event can provide a multi-perspectival view, enabling investigators, counsel, and the court to understand the event from diverse points of view. This may assist the court when sifting through varied witness accounts of an event and determining how much weight to apply to each account.[66] Filtering by photographers and counsel occurs constantly and ontological norms impact the field of visual representation, where decisions are made about what to record and what to use as evidence.[67] Selectivity and editing during the submission phase are practical realities when a plethora of image-based evidence is involved but objectivity should be the watchword during the culling by counsel for use at the trial phase.[68] When selecting images for use at trial, if there

[64] Prosecutors are held to a higher standard. Luc Côté, 'Independence and Impartiality', in *International Prosecutors*, edited by Luc Reydams, Jan Wouters, and Cedric Ryngaert (Oxford: OUP, 2012), 319–415, at 358. Côté emphasizes that prosecutors must appear to be and must be objective, impartial, and act like ministers of justice.

[65] Hamilton (n 28) 33; Gregory (n 18) 374.

[66] Aronson, Cole, Hauptmann, Miller, and Samuels (n 43) 2.

[67] Duffy described this photographic selectivity process powerfully as deciding 'whose life may be memorialized through seeing and whose life may leave no public trace to grieve'. Duffy (n 19) 783.

[68] A perceived advantage of digital open source information is its 'relative objectivity'. Some open source evidence such as satellite images are not affected by memory problems, the frailties of human perception, self-interest, and bias. McDermott, Koenig, and Murray (n 6) 88. I caution that the 'relative objectivity' of open source visual evidence is highly dependent upon the selectivity, agenda, and bias concerns explored in this chapter.

are multiple sources and perspectives available, most (or all) should be presented by the prosecution for consideration. In short, prosecutorial discretion should not be a vehicle for the exclusion of potentially exculpatory evidence as the goal must be to ascertain the truth, not just the prosecution's conception of it.

Decisions as to what evidence to present are also informed by considerations of unfair prejudice outweighing probative value, needless repetition of evidence, and image-based evidence that may be misleading or of questionable merit, among other considerations, while ensuring a fair and balanced presentation of its case. Targeted evidence selection is equally applicable when the defence constructs its case in furtherance of its narrative. In either case, counsel will decide what images from the entire collection will be presented at trial, subject to any direction from the court. At the terminus of the filtering process by photographers, investigators, and counsel, the court will see only those images that were submitted and presented, not the ones that were never recorded, nor those that were edited out or otherwise discarded.

2.1 The Nuremberg Trial: A Clear and Present Agenda

The tactical collection and use of images can result in a visual presentation used to further a partisan agenda. When the *Nazi Concentration Camps* film was created, it consisted of 6,000 feet of film edited from the 80,000 feet collected.[69] No one could credibly challenge the authenticity of the horrific scenes shown, yet strategic decisions were made when 74,000 feet of film fell to the cutting room floor. The agenda of the US forces was to capture within a reasonable time (approximately one hour) an overview of what the Nazis had done during the Holocaust. Had they chosen to create a two-hour film, there would have been ample material to present an even more evocative rendition. A laudable agenda to expose Nazi atrocities and to seek justice is still an agenda.

The stated motivation of the Americans was to create a visual record of Nazi atrocities, enemy prisoners of war, concentration camps, and their inmates. Deliberately editing out 92.5% of recorded media would sometimes raise legitimate concerns that the media was being selected to accord with the vision of the film's producer and director and might therefore portray scenes that were incomplete or slanted. In this case, setting aside footage that might have been technically inferior (out of focus, off frame, etc.), a conscious choice was made as to what the IMT would be shown and what would become part of history. However, provided the editing was done fairly and with a view to accurately portray the events and scenes recorded, the presence of editing itself is not nefarious. There has been no

[69] Reflected in the certificates and affidavits shown on screen at the beginning of the film and read by the narrator, attesting to the authenticity of the film.

suggestion that the remaining 74,000 feet would have exonerated the Nazis or cast concentration camps in a positive light.

Judicious consideration must be undertaken when selecting images for use at trial. Counsel must be selective when they construct the narrative that will be presented in court, mindful of concerns regarding over-saturation of the point trying to be made, needless use of court resources, and fairness in the presentation of evidence. The IMT clearly absorbed the impact of the shockingly powerful *Nazi Concentration Camps*. Showing an additional twelve hours of similar filmic evidence would not have greatly benefitted the judges. It likely would have served to annoy them and lessen the value of the evidence as the point sought to be made had clearly been made after one hour. The editing employed by the prosecution was respectful of the impact the film would have on the judges yet honoured the truth of what investigators found. It also reflected the fact that powerful visual evidence may reach a tipping point where it becomes more unfairly prejudicial than probative.[70] If the target audience unequivocally gets the message from the media after one hour, there is no value and perhaps irreparable harm in showing hours more of the same imagery.

All photographers have an agenda. The investigators who recorded the footage used to create the *Nazi Concentration Camps* film had an unabashed stated agenda to document evidence of Nazi atrocities. The presence of an agenda may in some cases foretell an attempt to cast a dishonourable or inaccurate light on the scenes portrayed but that was not an issue here. The agenda was to create a snapshot of Nazi atrocities and the suffering they caused for juridical and historical purposes. That mission was accomplished using only a portion of the media available. The American investigators would have had a strong anti-Nazi bias but there is no indication that it affected the soundness and integrity of the final product.

The Nazis also created their own filmic record of the violence they visited upon others. The *Original German Film (8 mm) of the Atrocities Against the Jews* was created by the SS during the liquidation of a ghetto and served as stark evidence of how the SS treated the civilian population. The agenda of the SS in creating the visual record appears to have been one of documenting their racial purification efforts, perhaps with a sense of prideful accomplishment and likely oblivious of the risk that it would later be used to condemn them at trial. Also shown was *The Nazi Plan* which was comprised of propaganda and newsreel films and highlighted Nazi ambitions. The Nazi propaganda films reflected an obvious agenda and bias in favour of the rise to power of the Nazis and served to encourage approval and support from the German people. The accuracy of the *Atrocities* film does not appear to have been affected by the agenda and biases of the SS as it was used to document what they perceived to be positive steps to cleanse Europe. The propaganda

[70] Evidence may be excluded (or accorded less weight) when the prejudicial effect of admitting it outweighs its probative value. *Rome Statute*, Arts. 69(3) and (4).

films were more sanguine in nature, promoting German superiority without fully disclosing the underlying plans to destroy millions of lives. In both cases, the agendas of the photographers were infused in the bravado of the final version.

3. Selectivity in the Presentation of Image-Based Evidence

Once the decision has been made to use image-based evidence at trial, presentation strategy becomes a central consideration. Its interpretation is influenced not only by its content but also by the method of its presentation. Party agendas and biases are capable of permeating presentation methodology and how the media is viewed and assessed by the court.[71] Choices made by counsel regarding the presentation of image-based evidence at trial impact its interpretation.[72] These choices include not only what images are shown but also how they are shown, including the use of graphics and annotations to supplement the visual field.

Multiple interpretations of image-based evidence are ostensibly viable depending upon its context and the purpose for which it is shown.[73] Occasionally, the same images can legitimately be used to bolster diverse perspectives and support party agendas. This illustrates the point that viewers should not look to images alone for meaning but rather at the story and context from which they emanate.[74] Even ostensibly objective visual depictions such as images obtained from a static CCTV camera may invite competing interpretations among viewers.[75] Further, video recordings may not show an entire event from all relevant perspectives, nor will they necessarily negate differing but plausible interpretations.[76] Claims of justifiable homicide by police officers often engender healthy scepticism as not all such claims are proven to be veridical. Video evidence of such actions recorded by witnesses, victims, members of civil society, and combatants alike, shared with investigators, the media, human rights organizations, and the public via social media and other sites may support the proffered justification or show a very different perspective.[77] Assessing the true meaning of image-based

[71] The assignment of meaning to image-based evidence is complex and must take into consideration the individual interests of its creator and the perspective of the viewer. Lisanne van Weelden and Tessa van Charldorp, 'Communications Perspective on the Use of Visualisations in Dutch Court for Minor Felonies', *Utrecht Law Review* 15, no. 1 (2019): 26–37, at 28, 30.

[72] The word 'counsel' is used globally to describe the decision-making process of counsel and the technician or expert who created the court presentation.

[73] Butler (n 32) 957.

[74] Jessica Silbey, 'Evidence Verité and the Law of Film', *Cardozo Law Review* 31 (2010): 1257–99, at 1293–4.

[75] Neal Feigenson, 'The Visual in Law: Some Problems for Legal Theory', *Law, Culture and the Humanities* 10, no. 1 (2014): 13–23, at 18.

[76] '... even authenticated video is an incomplete, mediated view of the world'. Aronson, Cole, Hauptmann, Miller, and Samuels (n 43) 3.

[77] ibid 2.

evidence requires skilful examination of context, purpose, and the fairness of the presentation.[78]

The goal when presenting evidence should be to provide demonstrably objective and reliable evidence. Judge Tarfusser expressed the importance of this goal in *Prosecutor v. Gbagbo and Blé Goudé*, when he criticized the presentation of the prosecution's case, in part referring to the calling of witnesses whose evidence was selective and inferentially biased.[79] Judge Tarfusser said:

> 23. A focused preparation would not only have reduced the risk to spend time in the courtroom on issues outside the scope of the charges, but also prevent the summoning of individuals whose type of knowledge of the facts—as easily ascertainable on the basis of their profile, background, type of knowledge of the facts or connection with either of the accused, or lack of it—could never be suitable to constitute the basis for, or otherwise contribute to, the fundamental determinations as to the innocence or guilt of the accused. The mind goes here to journalists, or staff of international organisation or NGOs, whose knowledge of and connection to the charged events on the ground and charged individuals was tenuous, indirect or inexistent and whose contribution to the trial, if any, should have been limited to tendering their reports and other material as documentary evidence.

In discussing examples of selective and unhelpful evidence, he referred to a particular witness as follows:

> 24 … iv. Witness P-0431 (two hearing days), a British journalist and filmmaker, who—despite the fact that he does not speak French fluently—sojourned in Ivory Coast in 2006 for the purposes of producing a documentary and provided to OTP with selected excerpts of his footage, from which he had excluded those clips which he considered not 'representative of what actually happened on those days'.

The witness was in the Côte d'Ivoire with the stated agenda of documenting ICC crimes, an agenda that has potential value but also gives rise to concerns of selectivity and bias in the presentation of image-based evidence. When journalists and filmmakers edit out footage that does not accord with their view of what happened, a red flag is raised, a concern clearly expressed by Judge Tarfusser.[80] This further

[78] Richard Sherwin, 'Visual Jurisprudence', *New York Law School Law Review* 57, no. 1 (2012): 11–40, at 16; Sandra Ristovska, 'The Rise of Eyewitness Video and its Implications for Human Rights: Conceptual and Methodological Approaches', *Journal of Human Rights* 15, no. 3 (2016): 347–60, at 355.

[79] ICC-02/11-01/15-1263-AnxA, Opinion of Judge Tarfusser, 16 July 2019, paras 23–24.

[80] 'The reality is that photo-journalists everywhere are altering, manipulating and distorting the images that we see every day.' Hany Farid, 'Digital Doctoring: How to Tell the Real from the Fake', *Significance* (December 2006): 162–6, at 163.

illustrates the point made in Chapter 3 that the photographer is the true witness, and the camera merely memorializes what occurs in front of the witness. To combat this photographer selectivity, the entire recording should be presented to investigators and disclosed to the defence. Counsel can then determine what media should be presented in court. Witnesses should not pre-select the visual portrayal to be submitted for consideration but admittedly, the OTP has little input into images that are volunteered for use as evidence though has much more control as to what is used at trial.

In addition to first person images, image-based evidence can also take the form of computer-generated reconstructions designed to posit one party's theory as to how events unfolded and where individuals, vehicles, or other objects were located at relevant times. These reconstructions provide ammunition for counsel to argue their case and, provided there is an evidential basis for the depiction, they are generally admissible and may be helpful.[81] Caution is warranted though as animations are specifically designed to visually depict one party's theory of the case and therefore subtle or overt distortions may occur in what is depicted, giving rise to the potential to mislead and pervert the pursuit of justice.[82] Intentional or inadvertent bias in the creation and presentation of visual reconstructions raises significant fair trial concerns.[83] For example, in the infamous Amanda Knox murder trial in Italy, the prosecution presented an animation which showed avatar Knox killing the avatar deceased, concluding with a crime scene photo showing the deceased's body.[84] Given that Knox was ultimately acquitted through the appellate process, this animation was simply the prosecution's theory given visual form and because it represented only one party's theory, it was by definition biased.

Parties who utilize and instruct the technician or expert who creates the animation have a vested interest in the outcome of the litigation.[85] Accordingly, there may be opportunity and incentive for interested parties to present visual reconstructions in either a subtly or overtly biased fashion.[86] This can lead the court to erroneous conclusions about the true state of affairs.[87] A biased reconstruction can unfairly impact the assessment of the event and should be challenged by opposing

[81] Jennifer Mnookin, 'The Image of Truth: Photographic Evidence and the Power of Analogy', *Yale Journal of Law and the Humanities* 10, no. 1 (1998): 1–74, at 50–1; Vincenzo Sainato, 'Evidentiary Presentations and Forensic Technologies in the Courtroom, The Director's Cut', *Journal of the Institute of Justice and International Studies* 9 (2009): 38–52, at 39; Aronson, Cole, Hauptmann, Miller, and Samuels (n 43) at 17.

[82] Sainato (n 81) 38.

[83] David Tait, 'Rethinking the Role of the Image in Justice: Visual Evidence and Science in the Trial Process', *Law, Probability and Risk* 6, no. 1–4 (2007): 311–18, at 315; Lindsay Freeman, 'Digital Evidence and War Crimes Prosecutions: The Impact of Digital Technologies on International Criminal Investigations and Trials', *Fordham International Law Journal* 41, no. 2 (2018): 283–335, at 319–20.

[84] An avatar is a digital figure representing a particular person in a video game or recreation.

[85] Betsy Fiedler, 'Are Your Eyes Deceiving You?: The Evidentiary Crisis Regarding the Admissibility of Computer Generated Evidence', *New York Law School Law Review* 48, no. 1–2 (2003): 295–322, at 302.

[86] ibid 310–11.

[87] Francis Mootz, 'Law Among the Sight Lovers', *New York Law School Law Review* 57, no. 1 (2012): 61–76, at 63; Sherwin (n 78) 13.

counsel by questioning the creator as to the accuracy and reliability of the presentation, focusing on the integration of selective or incorrect data.[88] In this regard, requiring a thorough audit trail for all aspects of the reconstruction would assist opposing counsel when assessing the evidence.[89] If bias is established, the reconstruction should either be ruled inadmissible or accorded little weight. Courts must be wary of parties whose apparent focus is to prevail without demonstrated concern for the truth or integrity of the legal process.[90]

While the focus tends to be on the images themselves, textual and graphical annotations added to images may be of considerable benefit to the court in developing a fuller appreciation of the images and what conclusions might reasonably be drawn from them, especially considering that while counsel will have seen the images many times before they are presented as evidence at trial, judges may be seeing them for the first time.[91] Despite their potential benefits, counsel and the court should be reticent to simply accept textual and graphical annotations without questioning their objectivity, accuracy, and potential to mislead, as party agendas and biases can be reflected not only in the creation, selection, and presentation of images, but also in the use of these supplemental presentation strategies.

Supplementary textual annotations and graphics may be used to provide interpretive information, clarity, and to enhance believability, but they may also serve to obfuscate and to improperly influence viewers by injecting bias to further an agenda. For example, inserting supplementary annotations that are conclusory in nature such as 'defendant', 'victim', 'attack', along with dates and locations, etc. in a video timeline describing what is being shown is problematic if the issue before the court is whether such conclusions are supportable. Words assigning evaluative meaning to people, objects, and actions are capable of overreaching what the images themselves can really tell us. Textual annotations can affect the perception of an image and can exacerbate interpretive distortion.[92] If textual annotations are to

[88] Jessica Silbey, 'Images in/of Law', *New York Law School Law Review* 57, no. 1 (2012): 171–84, at 176; Damian Schofield and Ken Fowle, 'Technology Corner—Visualizing Forensic Data: Evidence (Part 1)', *Journal of Digital Forensics, Security and Law* 8, no. 1 (2013): 73–90. Sainato cites a US case wherein the prosecution's animation prepared as part of a murder prosecution showed a scowl on the face of the defendant, which was based upon conjecture, not fact. Moreover, the attitude of the defendant towards the deceased was a contentious issue in the case. Prosecutorial misconduct such as this is deplorable, and the Minnesota Supreme Court said that those portions of the animation were improperly admitted. Sainato (n 81) 42–3.

[89] An audit trail documents the creation of the reconstruction from beginning to end, covering all data used and computer processes employed. Audit trails are not a strict legal requirement but are an important attribute of good forensic practice.

[90] Counsel may take on the role of being 'skilled puppeteers' choreographing what is presented in court, as noted in Mootz (n 87) 63–4, referring to the cave analogy in Plato's *The Republic*.

[91] In inquisitorial legal systems and the ICC and other international criminal tribunals, which are quasi-inquisitorial, judges may see visual evidence before the trial commences with or without the benefit of expert assistance.

[92] Annotations can assist with interpretation in the same way framing the image impacts viewer assessment; Duffy (n 19) 782. Textual description of an image influences viewer perception and has been referred to as 'verbal overshadowing'. Porter (n 27) 1755–6.

be used, the words chosen must be neutral, objective, and intended solely to assist the viewer's comprehension, rather than to advance an agenda.[93]

Graphical image annotations include arrows, lines, boxes, circles, and other shapes, all of which are designed to focus attention on a particular aspect of the image. Graphical annotations can also be dynamic, using techniques such as spotlighting, wherein a particular person, vehicle, or object is highlighted by way of increasing brightness and contrast for that portion of the image, ensuring a visual focal point. Motion tracking is another technique that can be used to isolate and follow individuals, vehicles, or other moving objects in dynamic, complex scenes. A blurring effect may also be used to obscure the identity of a person depicted in the images. These techniques are designed to focus viewer attention by supplementing the visual experience with targeted cues. So long as they are applied in a clinical manner for the sole purpose of assisting viewers, graphical annotations are salutary. When they are used to improperly influence viewers, they are problematic. Selectivity in the presentation of image-based evidence is largely unavoidable as choices must be made as to what evidence to utilize at trial. However, counsel and the court must be cognizant of the presence and impact of agendas and biases of the parties in the presentation of image-based evidence and must be on guard against the corresponding risk of interpretive error.

Conclusion

Atrocity crime documentation differs from most domestic crimes because the pool of photographers is likely to be more diverse and may include eyewitnesses, victims, defendants, enemy combatants, broadcast news organizations, and third-party observers such as human rights organizations and other NGOs.[94] Further, there may be more disparate and ardent agendas operating among the photographers, ranging from a desire to accurately document atrocities, to commercializing images of war and tragedy, to creating a false narrative of an event or conflict, or to generating propaganda (e.g. ISIS beheading videos). This is not to say that images emanating from conflict zones should be painted with any particularly broad brush but rather that investigators, counsel, and the court must evaluate these images while cognizant of the potential for a skewed or incomplete visual account implicitly or explicitly being presented.

[93] Annotation colour and word choice can be powerful subliminal persuaders and can result in trial unfairness. The use of red for example can impact assessment of the evidence. Evelyn Marcus, 'The New Razzle Dazzle: Questioning the Propriety of High-tech Audiovisual Displays in Closing Argument', *Vermont Law Review* 30, no. 2 (2006): 361–92, at 385.

[94] The recent example of the 2022 invasion of Ukraine by Russia illustrates the broad-based visual documentation approach that has been implemented to gather evidence of war crimes. This is also readily apparent in the 2023 Israel–Gaza conflict which is being extensively visually documented.

Partisan interests can be the nemesis of learning the truth as ramparts may be built around facts and evidence to obfuscate details. There may be a winnowing of the truth, causing it to be doled out in a measured manner, thereby abrogating any legitimate claim to knowing all there is to know. This veridical winnowing applies to image-based evidence. From its incipiency, the creation of images involves selectivity. The images that are recorded rely upon human judgment as to what to include within the frame and what to exclude and may prove to be inadvertently or intentionally misleading. Judgement influences whether photographers choose to show the ineffable atrocities that otherwise defy verbal description or to further a partisan narrative. Photographers are part documentarians, part storytellers. Their choices to include or exclude influences the visual record. The lens they look through is personal, perhaps inchoate, and serves to promulgate an account that carries some truth, or at least their perception of it. Once the images have been created, human judgement is further applied when deciding what to submit for consideration and in what form. The visual narrative may be selective, where images are edited or presented in a manner that suggests an ersatz narrative.

Professional and amateur variances must also be considered because civilian witnesses and journalists may be less concerned about bias than investigators and forensic scientists, who are required to consider and address bias as part of their workflow and analysis. Parties involved in litigation have agendas. The agendas may be altruistic—a desire to find the truth—or they may be less noble. Context and perspective are paramount in gaining a full understanding of image-based evidence. Bias can be identified and mitigated but cannot be wholly eliminated. Counsel and the court must be mindful of the impact of bias in the creation and submission of image-based evidence, as well as their own biases when assessing the evidence presented. Bias mitigation requires an informed, critical eye that is cognizant of the need for corroboration, and an awareness that extraordinary claims require extraordinary proof.

PART II

ASSESSING THE MEANING OF IMAGE-BASED EVIDENCE

5

Questioning the Reliability of Image-Based Evidence

Introduction

In September 2020, Mozambique Defence Minister Jaime Neto said that video showing people dressed in army uniforms beating and killing a naked woman was edited by 'malicious people' to make the military look bad.[1] In October 2020, anonymous video emerged on social media showing what appeared to be two Armenian soldiers being captured by Azerbaijan troops. A second video showed them being executed. Azerbaijan was quick to dismiss the videos as fraudulent.[2] In March 2021, the BBC reported a remarkable image in which a freighter appears to hover some distance over the sea off the coast of the United Kingdom.[3] In March 2022, a deepfake video shared on Twitter appeared to show Russian President Putin declaring peace with Ukraine.[4] This coincided with deepfake videos found on Meta and YouTube which appeared to show Ukrainian President Zelensky talking about surrendering to Russia. None of the Putin/Zelensky videos were real and were being used by interested parties to spark disinformation and dissent. Powerful images may be fraudulent while seemingly unbelievable images may be true. How can viewers distinguish between fair and false images?

Absent a compelling reason to disbelieve what we see, there is a commonly held default belief in the trustworthiness of what our eyes register—that 'seeing is believing'. In many cases, that belief is justified but given that images emanate from a broad range of sources, some more trustworthy than others, concerns regarding their reliability are not without foundation. Whether images are worthy of belief is a contextual consideration, dependent upon who is presenting them, their source, any narrative attached to the images, and the purpose for which they are being

[1] 'Mozambique Video of Killing Fake, Says Defence Minister' *BBC News* (16 September 2020) https://www.bbc.com/news/world-africa-54179776. The defence ministry said that it would investigate to determine whether the 'horrifying' video was authentic.

[2] 'Nagorno-Karabakh Conflict: "Execution" Video Prompts War Crime Probe' *BBC News* (24 October 2020) https://www.bbc.com/news/world-europe-54645254.

[3] '"Hovering Ship" Photographed Off Cornish Coast by Walker' *BBC News* (5 March 2021) https://www.bbc.com/news/uk-england-cornwall-56286719. The hovering ship was the result of a rare 'superior mirage' weather phenomenon.

[4] 'Deepfake Presidents Used in Russia-Ukraine War' *BBC News* (18 March 2022) https://www.bbc.com/news/technology-60780142.

Image-Based Evidence in International Criminal Prosecutions. Jonathan W. Hak, KC, Oxford University Press.
 DOI: 10.1093/oso/9780198889533.003.0005

shown. The tendency to believe what we see reflects a general lack of critical discernment borne from underdeveloped visual literacy.

Images can be intentionally manipulated or inadvertently altered in such a way as to trick or mislead viewers. The reliability of images is dependent upon how they are recorded, stored, processed, analysed, and presented for consideration. Acquiring the visual literacy needed to properly assess images is essential in searching for the truth that they may offer. Counsel function as evidential gatekeepers. They must have a command of all the evidence to be tendered and this means they must be able to present a blueprint for determining image reliability. Evidence as to the source of the images, the photographer who recorded them, the location of the original media, any image processing or alteration that has occurred, editing, and contextual information surrounding their creation must be pursued. If the lack of some or all these foundational facts results in images that evince tenuous reliability, they will be of little value for counsel in their trial narrative, and of even less value for the court when deciding facts.

1. The Assessment of Images in the Courtroom

Before delving into image reliability, it may be helpful to explore the processes through which images tendered as evidence are assessed in the courtroom. Though the word *evidence* implies a singularity, it in fact describes a relationship between the fact in issue and the evidentiary fact, or material led to support the factual proposition.[5] Fundamentally, the role of the court is to receive evidence presented by the parties, consider it, and make findings on facts in issue. For example, a fact in issue may be the meaning attributed to an image. Who is present in the image? What does it show? Images may be tendered as crime base evidence to help establish the circumstances of the alleged crime or they may be tendered as linkage evidence for the purpose of identifying responsible individuals. Once the court has determined the proven facts from the evidence, it must apply the relevant law to those facts to determine whether the prosecution has proven its allegations beyond reasonable doubt.[6] This section looks at how courts undertake this assessment and the role of the parties in assisting the court.

Most evidence in a criminal prosecution is tendered by the prosecution. This reflects the positive burden on the prosecution to prove their case having made allegations of criminality against the defendant. The defendant is presumed innocent

[5] Henry Wigmore, *The Principles of Judicial Proof, as Given by Logic, Psychology and General Experience, and Illustrated in Judicial Trials* (Boston: Little, Brown and Company, 1913), 5.

[6] Beyond reasonable doubt is the standard applied at trial in common law jurisdictions, the ICC (*Rome Statute*, Art. 66(3)), the ad hoc tribunals (ICTY and ICTR—Rule 87(A)), the MICT (Rule 104(A)), the ECCC (Internal Rule 87(1)), and the SCSL (Rule 87(A)). Lesser standards of proof are applied at certain pre-trial stages.

and need not establish that fact through the presentation of defence evidence.[7] When the prosecution constructs their trial narrative, they must select the evidence that they rely upon for proof, bearing in mind the overriding obligation to present evidence fairly and to seek the truth. When presenting image-based evidence, it falls upon counsel to establish its meaning. This entails leading evidence as to when the images were created, what location is depicted, and an explanation of their content. The interpretation proffered by counsel must be reasonably discernible from the image content.

In some cases, little explanation will be required for the court to comprehend their meaning. For example, beyond the limited narration in the *Nazi Concentration Camps* film, minimal explanation was required by the prosecution for the IMT judges to understand the meaning of the stark images presented to their senses. In other cases, the court will be ill-equipped to comprehend image content without assistance, expert or otherwise. Images may require contextual explanation, or their technical attributes may require expert interpretation for the court to correctly view them. The evidence counsel could lead to establish the meaning of images may consist of *viva voce* evidence from witnesses present at the scene depicted, investigators, experts, or other witnesses with requisite knowledge. Visual evidence in the form of computer-generated reconstructions or advanced visual representations requires expert explanation.

The role of the defence is to challenge the case for the prosecution and when deemed appropriate, to present their own evidence for the court's consideration. The defence may challenge the meaning the prosecution attributes to image-based evidence on the basis that the prosecution is wrong or that other interpretations are reasonably available. For example, during his International Criminal Tribunal for the former Yugoslavia (ICTY) trial, Slobodan Milošević disputed the meaning the prosecution ascribed to certain video recordings and put forth his own competing interpretation.[8] He also requested that other videos be shown to support his interpretation. Should the defence lead their own image-based evidence at trial, they will provide their view as to its meaning and the prosecution will similarly be able to challenge that interpretation.

Beyond the interpretations of image-based evidence by the prosecution and defence, the *Rome Statute* provides that the 'views and concerns' of victims shall also be presented and considered.[9] The Rules of Procedure and Evidence (RPE) established parameters for the involvement of the Office of Public Counsel for Victims in the questioning of witnesses and the provision of oral and written submissions.[10]

[7] *Rome Statute*, Art. 66(1). The presumption of innocence is a longstanding principle of law applied in international criminal prosecutions.

[8] Christian Delage, *Caught on Camera: Film in the Courtroom from the Nuremberg Trials to the Trials of the Khmer Rouge* (Philadelphia: University of Pennsylvania Press, 2014), 14.

[9] *Rome Statute*, Art. 68(3).

[10] RPE Rules 89–93; Mark Klamberg, *Evidence in International Criminal Trials* (Leiden: Martinus Nijhoff Publishers, 2013), 464–9.

The participation of victims may help the Chamber to better understand visual evidence in light of their local knowledge.[11] Further, the interests of victims may conflict with other parties and the RPE allows their voices to be heard. They may disagree with the interpretations of image-based evidence proffered by the prosecution or the defence owing to their more intimate knowledge of local conditions and geography. For example, the prosecution may incorrectly assert that an image depicts a certain location, but victims can correct that interpretation error due to their personal knowledge. There may also be limited scope for victims to present their own evidence at trial, which is a somewhat controversial topic.[12]

Whether counsel for the parties agree on the meaning of image-based evidence or not, the court must ultimately interpret the meaning of all such evidence tendered at trial in its role as fact-finder. Fact-finding describes the process wherein the court evaluates the evidence submitted by the parties to determine a fact in issue.[13] The court must assess the probative value or weight of the evidence and it is the court's interpretive assessment that is authoritative and will guide its ruling on accountability. However, this assessment is not done in a vacuum. The court has the benefit of seeing the evidence for itself and hearing the evidence of relevant witnesses, as well as the submissions of counsel for the prosecution, defence, and sometimes victims as to their interpretation of the evidence and their views as to its meaning.

The court must assess whether the interpretations urged by counsel are reasonable and is not obliged to accept the submissions of counsel or choose between them, though it would be unusual for a court to divine an interpretation not raised by the parties. Beyond the submissions of counsel, the court may have the benefit of other trial evidence that may assist in its interpretation and fact-finding. If independent pieces of evidence have probative value and support counsel's interpretation of visual evidence, the probative value of the questioned evidence should increase accordingly.[14] The ultimate objective is for the court to arrive at sound and reasonable interpretations of image-based evidence.

The interpretation of evidence by counsel and the court can be challenging because a piece of evidence may mean different things to different people. Exploring this thought further by looking at *viva voce* evidence may be instructive. In her provocative work, *Fact-finding Without Facts: The Uncertain Evidentiary Foundation of International Criminal Convictions*, Combs investigated the reliability of eyewitness testimony by studying trial transcripts from the International Criminal

[11] *Prosecutor v. Katanga and Ngudjolo Chui*, ICC-01/04-01/07-1665-Corr, Corrigendum Directions for the Conduct of the Proceedings and Testimony in Accordance with Rule 140, 1 December 2009, paras. 82–91.

[12] This option is discretionary pursuant to RPE Rule 91. See Klamberg (n 10) 464–9 for a helpful discussion of ICC case law on the presentation of evidence by victims.

[13] Henry Black, *Black's Law Dictionary*, 5th ed. (Minnesota: West Publishing, 1979); Klamberg (n 10) 156.

[14] Klamberg (n 10) 178–80.

Tribunal for Rwanda (ICTR), the Special Court for Sierra Leone (SCSL), and Special Panels.[15] Though she noted several testimonial deficiencies, I will focus on those that involve the interpretation of testimonial evidence. In some instances, the answers given by witnesses were not fully responsive to the questions posed by counsel, not because the witnesses were being obstructive but rather because they did not correctly understand the question due to unfamiliar terminology or question format. When the question was asked in a different manner, the witnesses were able to provide a more responsive answer.[16] In other cases, witnesses lacked the linguistic ability to use correct terminology in giving their answers, resulting in unintended attributions of meaning.[17] On occasion, there may be no word in the witness's language that equates with a word used by counsel, making it difficult to provide a responsive answer.[18]

Other testimonial challenges stem from interpretation disparities. Interpretation of witness testimony impedes communication and impairs the fact-finder's ability to assess the credibility and reliability of the witness's evidence.[19] Evidence that is at least one step removed from the witness is more difficult to evaluate. Difficulties arise when interpreters mistakenly use the wrong word to describe what a witness said, thereby changing the meaning of the evidence; omit portions of testimony; incorrectly summarize questions and testimony; or lack the competence to adequately translate the evidence from the witness's language to the court's language, necessitating the use of multiple interpreters with attendant errors along the way.[20] Verbatim translations are virtually impossible when trials involve witnesses speaking radically different languages.[21] Therefore, the evidence given by witnesses is by necessity mediated by interpreters who may not correctly convey what the witness actually said or meant.[22] The net effect may be that the court is not getting a reliable rendition of the witness's evidence because of the vagaries of language and interpretation, thus impacting the essential role of fact-finding by the court due to reliance on secondary evidence.

[15] Nancy Combs, *Fact-finding Without Facts: The Uncertain Evidentiary Foundation of International Criminal Convictions* (New York: CUP, 2010).

[16] ibid 44–62.

[17] ibid.

[18] ibid 76–8. Combs cites several examples of words that have no direct translation and words that have multiple meanings in a witness's language.

[19] ibid 66.

[20] ibid 66–74. Combs noted that at the Special Panels, it was not uncommon for six interpreters to be required from the point the question was asked until the answer was given (ibid 70). The risk of inaccuracy in these circumstances is palpable.

[21] ibid 74.

[22] Almost everyone in the courtroom is at the mercy of interpreters. Beth Lyons, 'Enough is Enough: The Illegitimacy of International Criminal Convictions: A Review Essay of Fact-Finding Without Facts, The Uncertain Evidentiary Foundations of International Criminal Convictions by Nancy Amoury Combs', *Journal of Genocide Research* 13, no. 3 (2011): 287–312, at 289. See also Nancy Combs, 'Deconstructing the Epistemic Challenges to Mass Atrocity Prosecutions', *Washington and Lee Law Review* 75, no. 1 (2018): 223–300, at 285–6.

There is a parallel that can be drawn between fact-finding difficulties stemming from witness testimony that must be interpreted and the interpretation of images. Images can convey meaning but the interpretation of that meaning is dependent upon how the viewer sees the images and understands their content. The meaning and reliability of images is dependent upon the images themselves and the visual literacy of the viewers assessing them. Are viewers sufficiently knowledgeable to understand the technical aspects of the images and how they may impact upon the interpretation of image content? Do viewers require expert assistance to understand the true meaning of the evidence? Might the parties disagree on their interpretation of the images? It is essential that counsel and the court develop sufficient visual literacy to achieve the objective of arriving at sound and reasonable interpretations of image-based evidence.

2. 'Seeing Is Believing': The Default Approach to Images

There is an innate desire to believe that the world in which we live makes sense. When we are young, we tend to believe that what our parents, teachers, and other important adults tell us is true. We want to believe that the words we read and the images we see are things that we can rely upon. This youthful naïveté is not something to be discouraged because we can reasonably trust much of what we are told and what we read and see as we mature. In time, a more discriminating intellectual and visual palate develops, wherein we must reconcile disparate facts that cannot simultaneously all be true. We realize that not everything we were told as children was true and that our parents and teachers are not omniscient.

Focusing in on images, there is sound reason to trust that most images that are connected to our lives in a personal way are worthy of belief and that the people who created them were not trying to trick us. However, the more we venture away from images showing subject matter with which we have a personal connection and into situations and content where our connection is more tenuous, the less that trust may be justified.[23] The question is whether our tendency to believe what we see is warranted.

When we view images that are prima facie realistic, there is a tendency to believe that we have fully absorbed their value, thus obviating the need to make further inquiries.[24] It requires less mental effort and is cognitively more appealing to accept

[23] 'In the contemporary world of manipulable visual images, we are confronted by the brute fact that there are no brute facts: reality is rhetorically structured rather than analytically discerned.' Francis Mootz, 'Law Among the Sight Lovers', *New York Law School Law Review* 57, no. 1 (2012): 61–76, at 64. While Mootz's rather pessimistic view has merit, it is possible to discern many facts involving image-based evidence with the application of expertise, visual literacy, and careful interpretation.

[24] Richard Sherwin, Neal Feigenson, and Christina Spiesel, 'What Is Visual Knowledge, and What Is It Good For? Potential Ethnographic Lessons from the Field of Legal Practice', *Visual Anthropology* 20 (2007): 143–78, at 157.

what is seen as veridical rather than to challenge its veracity. This communicative efficiency is even more prevalent when the images are presented in a motion-based format like video recordings or computer animation as the viewer is more likely to focus on the visual cues presented than to critically analyse their reliability.[25] 'Seeing is believing' is more than a colloquial expression; it describes the construct that the viewer's belief in the subject matter depicted is proportional to the viewer's understanding of the visual palette presented for examination.[26] When we understand what we are looking at, there is a greater tendency to believe in its veracity due to our personal investment in verisimilitude.[27] Yet psychological research shows that in fact it is difficult to know what to believe or when to believe it.[28] Once accepted as true, disbelief surfaces only with effort as images draw power from the personal faith of the viewer that they can believe what they see because they are in fact personally bearing witness to the event depicted.[29] This misperceived belief belies the fact that neither the viewer nor the camera is the true witness. The photographer is the actual witness who uses the camera to memorialize what was observed.

How do images communicate their meaning to viewers? What power do they have to imbue meaning given that they are inanimate, having been created by a photographer? It is well established that the court is more likely to internalize and remember evidence if a visual component is involved and that images are more impactful than non-visual expressions of the same data.[30] Some images may be more complex and laden with interpretive value than words alone can effectively communicate.[31] Visualization economizes viewer understanding as visual information requires less imagination than words alone.[32] Consumption of visual information may be more efficient and may give rise to a perception of increased understanding even if that perception is not supportable.[33] But what meaning should be taken

[25] ibid.

[26] ibid 158; Sherwin further notes that images '... sometimes shimmer with an invisible presence; a strange surplus or aura renders their impact even more vivid to the senses, even more cognitively potent'. Richard Sherwin, 'Visual Jurisprudence', *New York Law School Law Review* 57, no. 1 (2012): 11–40, at 28.

[27] Sherwin, 'Visual Jurisprudence' (n 26) 28.

[28] Sherwin, Feigenson, and Spiesel (n 24) 161.

[29] Jessica Silbey, 'Persuasive Visions: Film and Memory', *Law, Culture and the Humanities* 10, no. 1 (2014): 24–42, at 26.

[30] Betsy Fiedler, 'Are Your Eyes Deceiving You?: The Evidentiary Crisis Regarding the Admissibility of Computer Generated Evidence', *New York Law School Law Review* 48, no 1–2 (2003): 295–322, at 302; Richard Sherwin, *Visualizing Law in the Age of the Digital Baroque* (London: Routledge, 2011), 59; Eryn Newman and Neal Feigenson, 'The Truthiness of Visual Evidence', *Jury Expert* 25, no. 5 (2013): 9–14, at 9.

[31] Sherwin, Feigenson, and Spiesel (n 24) 156; Neal Feigenson and Richard Sherwin, 'Thinking Beyond the Shown: Implicit Inferences in Evidence and Argument', *Law, Probability and Risk* 6 (2007): 295–310, at 297.

[32] See Section 2 of Chapter 1 for further discussion of image visualization.

[33] Sherwin, Feigenson, and Spiesel (n 24) 156; Elizabeth Porter, 'Taking Images Seriously', *Columbia Law Review* 114 (2018): 1687–782, at 1752.

from the images? Some images may convey fundamental meaning with relative ease and require limited human intervention. For example, beyond providing contextual geographical information, any words used to describe the horrific images in the *Nazi Concentration Camps* film would have been mere surplusage and would have added minimal additional meaning for the IMT judges.

Other images may be equivocal in meaning, causing viewers to assign meaning to their content, whether justified or not.[34] Therefore, when images are used as evidence, counsel should not assume that images will convey universal meaning. Counsel must assess what meaning the images are likely to convey on their own and whether that meaning is accurate. They must also consider what additional evidence or explanation is required to ensure that the full meaning of the images is conveyed to the court. In short, counsel should not assign more communicative power to images than is warranted. Meaning must be fully addressed lest the court interpret the images in a way counsel did not foresee. A caveat for the court—experience has shown that images must be scrutinized to determine whether they really stand for the proposition the tendering party urges upon the court.[35]

Images abound in the world and belief in them and what they portray tends to be the default approach of many viewers rather than scepticism.[36] The foundational validity of this belief is in part dependent upon the source of the image being considered. When the image is recorded by or in the presence of viewers or by someone viewers trust or who is objectively worthy of trust, this belief likely has merit. Images also tend to achieve viewer-assessed reliability when viewers believe they were created in the same moment as the event itself, therefore representing an objectively accurate temporal portrayal.[37] When images are found in social media or other sites in circumstances where the photographer is anonymous, disbelief would be a more worthy default. Recognizing the sometimes-precarious position of open source digital media, the *Berkeley Protocol on Digital Open Source Investigations* was designed to standardize procedures and provide methodological guidance to open source investigators on, inter alia, evaluating the reliability of online sources and online image content.[38] Following this protocol should help to elevate the level of image reliability in international criminal prosecutions.

[34] Jennifer Mnookin, 'The Image of Truth: Photographic Evidence and the Power of Analogy', *Yale Journal of Law and the Humanities* 10, no. 1 (1998): 1–74, at 65.

[35] Jessica Silbey, 'Images in/of Law', *New York Law School Law Review* 57, no. 1 (2012): 171–84, at 176.

[36] Sandon refers to this belief more formally as ocular epistemology. Emma Sandon, 'Law and Film', in *Arcs of Global Justice*, edited by Margaret deGuzman and Diane Amann (New York: OUP, 2018), 501–20.

[37] Piyel Haldar, 'Law and the Evidential Image', *Law, Culture and the Humanities* 4 (2008): 139–55, at 142.

[38] Office of the United Nations High Commissioner for Human Rights and the Human Rights Centre at the University of California, Berkeley, School of Law, 'Berkeley Protocol on Digital Open Source Investigations' (2020) HR/PUB/20/2, at 5 ('Berkeley Protocol'). The Berkeley Protocol defines reliability as 'the ability to perform consistently, dependably or as expected' (8). The OED defines reliability as the ability to be relied upon with confidence and trustworthiness. 'reliability, n' (*OED Online*, OUP August 2023), www.oed.com accessed 7 August 2023.

Due to the proliferation of still and video images in our everyday lives, there is a tendency for people to believe that they intuitively know a genuine image when they see it and that they possess the ability to distinguish fair from fraudulent.[39] Even when images enter the evidential paradigm, there is a tendency to take them at face value without examining whether that assessment is merited.[40] This is perhaps reflective of the perspective that seeing is knowing and that sight leads to insight.[41] In short, seeing is believing, especially for those who lack a sophisticated visual literacy. This perpetuates the false security that arises when examining images, namely that there is a clear-cut separation between fact and fiction.[42]

Many images are trustworthy but ocular epistemology should not be the mantra in the criminal justice system. It is a misconception to believe that digital and multimedia evidence possesses inherent reliability and that sound conclusions can be drawn therefrom without further inquiry.[43] Given the current devolution of image manipulation capacity from technical experts to civilians, the chasm between what is seen and what is true deepens, revealing a cognitive dissonance between what we think we see and what we really see. Visual evidence may occupy a foothold in two interconnected realms, providing vast amounts of knowledge far exceeding that obtainable from words alone, yet at the same time providing 'an especially fragile basis for conviction'.[44] The realism that images seemingly convey can make them simultaneously powerful and dangerous; powerful because viewers can examine the event more robustly and with greater confidence, yet dangerous because viewers may regard their own experience with the images as more valid than witness testimony.[45] Images may mean different things to different people in different contexts.[46]

Text-based information, whether in the form of testimony or documents, has a temporal element. Words are often abstractions, and their meaning develops over

[39] Gary Edmond, Katherine Biber, Richard Kemp, and Glenn Porter, 'Law's Looking Glass: Expert Identification Evidence Derived from Photogenic and Video Images', *Current Issues in Criminal Justice* 20, no. 3 (2009): 337–77, at 364.

[40] Naomi Mezey, 'The Image Cannot Speak for Itself: Film, Summary Judgment, and Visual Literacy', *Valparaiso University Law Review* 48, no. 1 (2013): 1–40, at 16. Mnookin and West state that 'the power of visual evidence necessarily relies on a kind of illusion, a willingness to ignore the mechanisms by which visual evidence is made, shaped, and constructed'. Jennifer Mnookin and Nancy West, 'Theaters of Proof: Visual Evidence and the Law in *Call Northside 777*', *Yale Journal of Law and the Humanities* 13, no. 2 (2001): 329–90, at 334.

[41] Christina Spiesel, 'Reflections on Reading: Words and Pictures and Law', *International Journal of Law in Context* 2, no. 3 (2006): 305–20, at 316.

[42] 'Not only can images be manipulated, but all images, fiction or not, are of course captured, chosen, limited, produced.' Immi Tallgren, 'Come and See? The Power of Images and International Criminal Justice', *International Criminal Law Review* 17 (2017): 259–80, at 271.

[43] Elénore Ryser, Hannes Spichiger, and Eoghan Casey, 'Structured Decision Making in Investigations Involving Digital and Multimedia Evidence', *Forensic Science International: Digital Investigation* 34, no. 301015 (2020): 1–10, at 1.

[44] Mnookin and West (n 40) 334.

[45] ibid 387.

[46] Mezey (n 40) 13.

time as the words are heard or read and then considered. Words are the constituent elements of the whole message sought to be delivered. In contrast, images are typically viewed whole first and only then perhaps in more minute detail. Viewers tend to focus on what the image means to them without delving into how the image was created or its context, yet these inquiries are essential to ascertaining the true meaning of an image.[47] A digital image is much more complex than appears at first glance. It is comprised of pixels (picture elements) too small for the human eye to perceive and our brain therefore interprets the sum of the pixels as a single image.[48] Viewers who take in the image holistically, without examining let alone comprehending the constituent parts that make up the whole, risk believing what is seen simply on faith that it must be true; that seeing is believing.

To acquire their true meaning, images must be deconstructed and examined at the constituent level.[49] It is only by looking at images in detail, sometimes with expert assistance, that we can gain a true understanding of what we think we see. It is simplistic to presume that evidentiary images are somehow cloaked with an authoritative and objectively veridical view of what they depict.[50] Naïve realism purports to deliver correct beliefs of the world around us and this inferentially includes images. It would therefore follow that offering proof by images would be the 'ultimate *res gestae*' of what is depicted, a visual representation of the obvious.[51] This perspective is unsophisticated and ill-informed as images are mediated views selected by photographers and designed to convey messages that may or may not be fully justified by their content. Indeed, it has been argued that given the law's increasing dependence on visual evidence, the more legal judgment relies on the visual, the more it may partake in fantasy.[52]

Images may not provide incontrovertible narratives as their true meaning can only be assessed when we understand the context in which they are created.[53] Nor can it fairly be said that images necessarily reflect reality.[54] More effort is needed than just watching images with an uncritical eye. Understanding that images do

[47] Christina Spiesel, Richard Sherwin, and Neal Feigenson, 'Law in the Age of Images: The Challenge of Visual Literacy', in *Contemporary Issues of the Semiotics of Law*, edited by Anne Wagner, Tracy Summerfield, and Farid Vanegas (Oxford: Hart Publishing, 2005), 231–66, at 246–7.

[48] Marie-Helen Maras and Alex Alexandrou, 'Determining Authenticity of Video Evidence in the Age of Artificial Intelligence and in the Wake of Deepfake Videos', *The International Journal of Evidence and Proof* 23, no. 3 (2019): 255–62, at 258. The most common computer display is 1920 pixels wide and 1080 pixels high, meaning that a single digital image would consist of 2,073,600 pixels; Seth Stoughton, 'Police Body-Worn Cameras', *North Carolina Law Review* 96, no. 5 (2018): 1363–424, at 1404.

[49] Haldar (n 37) 140.

[50] Neal Feigenson, 'The Visual in Law: Some Problems for Legal Theory', *Law, Culture and the Humanities* 10, no. 1 (2014): 13–23, at 17–18.

[51] ibid.

[52] Feigenson opines, 'Visual proof that takes the form of movies on screens persuades in part by appealing to largely subconscious desires for ideal knowledge, self-coherence, and community, which it can never really satisfy.' ibid 17.

[53] Mnookin (n 34) 57.

[54] Richard Sherwin, 'Visual Literacy for the Legal Profession', *Journal of Legal Education* 68, no. 1 (2018): 55–63, at 60.

not necessarily represent reality in a complete and unmediated fashion and that they can be manipulated and misleading is part of developing visual literacy. For example, forensic animations create the opportunity for potential abuse as counsel sometimes seek to manipulate details such as lighting and camera angles to support their preferred narrative, resulting in visual evidence that is unreliable.[55] This is problematic if the viewer's default is to believe what is seen.

Some judges view images as merely witness testimony in visual form, sharing many of the frailties that are endemic in eyewitness testimony.[56] There is justifiable merit in this cautious approach, especially in the absence of expert interpretive assistance. There has long been a healthy scepticism as to whether what is displayed in an image should be believed, as case law starting in the late nineteenth century in America has shown.[57] During the advent of photographs being tendered into evidence in nineteenth century American trials, some jurists viewed photographs as being reliable evidence of truth from a mechanism (the camera) that cannot lie, while other jurists were critical that such images were not replications but rather representations, constructed and, therefore, fallible.[58]

Over the past few years, there has been a notable increase in the number of falsified images and videos distributed by governments, state-sponsored entities, and individuals that are in turn further disseminated on social media for the purpose of misleading the public.[59] Fake news, including images of questionable reliability, is a serious threat to society and the pursuit of the truth. While most images tendered in court are likely authentic and reliable, counsel and the court must be on guard for images that appear legitimate but are in fact designed to obfuscate the truth. This includes considering source reliability, the way the images have been framed, and scrutinizing what may have been deliberately omitted by the photographer. A robust visual literacy should cause viewers to attach limited probative value to images of questionable origin that are not materially corroborated.

An informed visual literacy would help to ensure that counsel and the court are aware of the limitations of image-based evidence and the need to exercise caution in ascribing more meaning to the evidence than is justified.[60] Judges in international criminal prosecutions are charged with the responsibility to assess the reliability of images tendered as evidence, a task they may be ill-equipped to carry

[55] Vincenzo Sainato, 'Evidentiary Presentations and Forensic Technologies in the Courtroom, The Director's Cut', *Journal of the Institute of Justice and International Studies* 9 (2009): 38–52, 40.

[56] Mnookin (n 34) 4, 20–1, 58.

[57] Early case law evinces a reluctance by counsel and the court to believe the contents of some images, ibid 27–43. This reluctance may have been borne in part by the novelty of the medium.

[58] ibid 16–18, 23.

[59] Hany Farid, 'Digital Forensics in a Post-Truth Age', *Forensic Science International* 289 (2018): 268–9.

[60] Richard Sherwin, 'Imagining Law as Film (Representation without Reference?)', in *Law and the Humanities: An Introduction*, edited by Austin Sarat, Matthew Anderson, and Cathrine Frank (Cambridge: CUP, 2009), 241–68, at 259.

out without expert assistance.[61] Indeed, attaining visual literacy is a task beyond the ken of most lawyers and judges without expert assistance.[62] Visual literacy requires educating counsel and the court as to how image-based evidence should be approached and providing the necessary expert assistance so as to properly interrogate and interpret the evidence.[63]

Attaining visual literacy gives counsel new communicative powers wherein they are able to present complex visual evidence in a manner that conveys its content accurately, reliably, in greater detail, and with more understanding.[64] Rather than relying on the communicative power of images alone, counsel may find that effective supplemental storytelling is part of conveying a more informed meaning of the images presented.[65] These are tasks that the untrained viewer is generally ill-equipped to perform competently and exemplify subject matter wherein the court may require expert assistance in order to reach an informed judgment. The value that expert assistance brings to the interrogation, interpretation, and analysis of visual evidence is the subject of Chapter 6.

3. Is Digital Image-Based Evidence Reliable?

Almost all image-based evidence that is shown on courtroom monitors today is digital in nature, either because it was originally created in digital format or because the original analogue version was digitized. The early 2000s saw a gradual switch from film-based photograph and analogue videotape formats to digital photographic and video imagery. Digital media provides clear advantages to the photographer and those who utilize the images. It affords processing, analytical, display, and storage efficiencies not realizable with film-based or analogue images.[66] Digital image processing software permits seemingly limitless opportunities to process, modify, and package images for myriad purposes. Robust forensic software programs permit trained analysts to examine digital imagery for authentication purposes and for substantive analysis and interpretation of image content. Digital media can be displayed on screens as small as watches or on large high-definition courtroom monitors and smaller monitors for counsel and the court.

[61] 'International Bar Association Report', *IBA ICL Perspectives: Evidence Matters in ICC Trials* (August 2016) https://www.ibanet.org/document?id=Evidence-matters-in-icc-trials, 20.

[62] Mezey (n 40); Feigenson (n 50).

[63] Interrogating an image involves a detailed examination of the constituent elements of an image both visually and at the metadata level, including the impact of compression, frame rate, resolution, and aspect ratio. Interpretation of an image involves assessing what meaning can fairly be drawn from it.

[64] Spiesel, Sherwin, and Feigenson (n 47) 254–6.

[65] Sam Gregory, 'Cameras Everywhere: Ubiquitous Video Documentation of Human Rights, New Forms of Video Advocacy, and Considerations of Safety, Security, Dignity and Consent', *Journal of Human Rights Practice* 2, no. 2 (2010): 191–207, at 193.

[66] Film-based images can be digitized, thus opening the door to these digital advantages, though there may be some loss of original detail during the digitization process.

Terabytes of data can be stored in a hard drive that fits in a hand. Ensconced within these advantages are nettlesome questions about whether digital media is inherently less reliable than its predecessors.

Critics who inveigh against digital media imply that a Rubiconesque line has been crossed in the process of changing mediums and that the switch from analogue to digital represents a choice of foul over fair. This criticism only has validity if traditional films, photographs, and analogue video are beyond reproach, a proposition that does not have merit. Photographs were criticized for being misleading and deceptive as far back as the nineteenth century in America.[67] There is ample evidence of photographic manipulation long before digital images were even imagined. Stalin, Mao, Hitler, Mussolini, Castro, Brezhnev, and others intentionally caused photographs to be altered by removing or adding people to rewrite history.[68] Countless images across broad sections of society have been modified for subterfuge and less nefarious reasons. Although earlier photographic manipulations required cumbersome, lengthy darkroom processing, for those with the will, there has long been a way to deceive.[69] Arguing that digital media is more pernicious than film-based media has epistemic merit only in the sense that it is easier to manipulate digital images, but not that they are inherently villainous or unreliable.

Unlike film-based images where the image is recorded on a celluloid negative, a digital image has no visual form until it is printed on paper or displayed on a computer screen. A digital image consists of binary data that resides on a digital storage device.[70] It is dependent upon a computer for its visual existence.[71] This digital form of being renders the images highly susceptible to advertent and inadvertent modification after creation.[72] Powerful, low-cost digital technology has made it easier for nearly anyone with a computer to alter digital images in such a way as to make detection very difficult.[73] This widespread ability to deceive viewers

[67] Mnookin includes several examples of photographic trickery in her article; Mnookin (n 34) 16–18, 23.

[68] Hany Farid, *Photo Forensics* (Cambridge, MA: MIT Press, 2016), 1.

[69] ibid.

[70] Digital technology transforms data into a binary format, typically ones and zeros, or in some other binary (two-state) sequence. 'Binary Format', Techopedia https://www.techopedia.com/definition/938/binary-format. Examples of storage devices and other storage locations include smartphones, cameras, laptop computers, tablets, desktop computers, digital video recorders, hard drives, servers, satellites, networks, the internet, etc.

[71] House of Lords Select Committee on Science and Technology: Fifth Report, 'Digital Images as Evidence' (1998) https://publications.parliament.uk/pa/ld199798/ldselect/ldsctech/064v/st0502.htm, para. 1.2.

[72] Jill Witkowski, 'Can Juries Really Believe What They See? New Foundational Requirements for the Authentication of Digital Images', *Washington University Journal of Law & Policy* 10 (2002): 267–94, at 271; Lindsay Freeman and Raquel Vazquez Llorente, 'Finding the Signal in the Noise: International Criminal Evidence and Procedure in the Digital Age', *Journal of International Criminal Justice* 19, no. 1 (2021), 163–88, at 165.

[73] Hany Farid, 'Digital Doctoring: How to Tell the Real from the Fake', *Significance* (December 2006): 162–6. Farid articulates that '... the technology that can distort and manipulate digital media is developing at breakneck speeds'. Farid (n 68) 1; Luisa Verdoliva, 'Media Forensics and DeepFakes: An Overview. Cornell University' (2020) https://arxiv.org/abs/2001.06564v1, 2.

is unprecedented and must be given special consideration in the evidential context. Images can be intentionally modified for the express purpose of deceiving or misleading viewers and such modifications are properly labelled with the pejorative term 'manipulation'.[74] Image manipulation can undetectably modify image content as well as its meaning.[75] This might arise from removing components of an image, adding components, or changing the appearance of existing content.[76] This concern gave rise to incipient suspicion in the early 2000s that digital imagery was inherently a negative game changer in the evidential context.[77] However, digital imagery has entered the criminal justice environment with little fanfare and courts have been able to use existing legal principles to govern their use.

In 1998, the UK House of Lords Select Committee on Science and Technology examined the evidential benefits and challenges associated with digital images in its *Digital Images as Evidence* report.[78] The Committee received submissions from legal, academic, and technical experts on a wide range of digital imagery issues. In its report, the Committee expressed several concerns with digital images, noting that because digital images are visual representations of binary data, they can be altered, deleted, or copied in the same way as other computer data and that subtle but significant and highly convincing image alterations may be almost impossible to detect. The availability of affordable software capable of use by non-experts to implement these modifications made these concerns even more acute.[79] The Committee was shown examples of digitally manipulated images that were believable and convincing even when the alterations were pointed out.[80]

Conversely, the Committee also received submissions on the evidentiary benefits of digital images, including the availability of sound forensic image processing techniques that could enhance the evidentiary value of images by providing more image detail than might otherwise be available.[81] Advice was received regarding methods that could be used to authenticate digital images in ways not available with analogue images. Among its many findings, the Committee recommended that robust authentication techniques be employed as a method of ensuring image

[74] Angelina Gokhale, Preeti Mulay, Dhanya Pramod, and Ravi Kulkarni, 'A Bibliometric Analysis of Digital Image Forensics', *Science & Technology Libraries* 39, no. 1 (2020): 96–113, at 96.

[75] Judith Redi, Wiem Taktak, and Jean-Luc Dugelay, 'Digital Image Forensics: A Booklet for Beginners', *Multimedia Tools Applications* 51 (2011): 133–62, at 134.

[76] New content can be added by copying from a different image (splicing) or from the same image (copy-move). Content can be removed by extending the background to cover where the previous content was located (inpainting); Verdoliva (n 73) 2; Gokhale, Mulay, Pramod, and Kulkarni (n 74) 96–7.

[77] See generally Witkowski (n 72) 267–94.

[78] House of Lords Select Committee (n 71).

[79] ibid paras. 2.5–2.12. This statement was based on the availability of image processing software in 1998. The availability of consumer grade digital media processing software today and its ability to alter images is infinitely greater.

[80] 'We think this technology raises the possibility that people who are not familiar with it can be too easily misled.' ibid para. 5.7. Though the Committee referred to people being misled by digital technology as a 'possibility', I suggest that 'probability' would be a more accurate descriptor in the 2020s.

[81] ibid para. 2.7.

reliability and that fact-finders be warned of potential uncertainties that may exist in digital images in an effort to ferret out questionable evidence.[82] In an early clarion call for improved visual literacy, the Committee further recommended that lawyers and judges receive specialized education on these subjects.[83] The benefits and concerns raised before the Select Committee a quarter century ago remain applicable today. However, concerns regarding the ability to modify digital images without detection are even greater today, exemplified by deepfake technology, which is discussed in Section 3.

Image alteration can occur as part of a deliberate attempt to deceive viewers. Images may be intentionally manipulated by staging image content to produce an entirely fictionalized event, by manipulating image content with Photoshop or other image processing tools for the express purpose of changing the image, and through manipulating metadata by scraping media from one context and repackaging it to appear to be from a different context.[84] The latter scenario is reported by human rights practitioners to be the most prevalent deception.[85] The increasing ability of people to engage in image manipulation will only serve to exacerbate these concerns.[86]

Images can also undergo alteration without malicious intent. For example, YouTube automatically dates videos uploaded to its site according to the date and time uploaded in California's Pacific time zone, thus contributing to disputes about the veracity of some YouTube videos based on alleged timing mismatches.[87] Though presumably done for business reasons, this may have the effect of misleading viewers in situations where date and time is a relevant consideration. Image processing by technically challenged but well-meaning people is also a common cause of image alteration. Absent proper technical training and forensically sound methodology, inadvertent errors in exporting digital media from devices and other sources, formatting, processing, editing, and displaying images can change constituent elements of the media and its meaning.[88] Chief among these errors are compressing images, altering the frame rate, lowering resolution, and utilizing an improper aspect ratio. It is for these reasons that when considering digital image reliability, some of the focus must be on the person processing the images.

Digital image processing has subjective elements in that a person must decide how to process the images, what parts to show, what tools and filters to use, and

[82] ibid para. 5.5.

[83] ibid para. 5.10.

[84] Ella McPherson, 'Risk and the Pluralism of Digital Human Rights Fact-Finding and Advocacy', in *New Technologies for Human Rights Law and Practice*, edited by Molly Land and Jay Aronson (Cambridge: CUP, 2018), 188–214, at 197. The process of scraping media and repackaging it is also referred to as a 'shallowfake'. Gregory (n 65) 384.

[85] McPherson (n 84) 197.

[86] Farid cautions, 'Tomorrow's technology will almost certainly allow for us to manipulate digital media in ways that today seem unimaginable.' Farid (n 73) 165.

[87] McPherson (n 84) 191.

[88] Freeman and Vazquez Llorente (n 72) 9.

how the final product should look. Ideally, a qualified technician or analyst will follow established industry-specific procedures using proven forensic hardware and software tools and will create a proper audit trail documenting all steps undertaken regarding the images, while ensuring that the final product is authentic, forensically sound, and reliable. However, in many agencies and organizations, people performing these tasks may not have the requisite knowledge, training, and tools necessary to correctly undertake this important forensic work, resulting in the situation where unqualified people process and present what is purported to be expert forensic image analysis without possessing the technical competence to do so. Not only do such people lack the requisite technical competence, but they also lack the forensic mindset required to be truly of assistance to the court.

Untrained people, particularly those with only a production video background, are typically more interested in creating a product that is visually appealing and that favours the party who is using them, even if the result is unreliable and lacking in scientific merit. Left unchallenged by people with robust visual literacy, forensically unsound work may find its way into the courtroom far more often than it should. If counsel and the court have sufficient visual literacy to challenge the reliability and veracity of such evidence, it should be ruled inadmissible or assigned no weight.[89] What is more intractable is unreliable media that is admitted on the basis that neither counsel nor the court realize the problems endemic in the evidence.

A further consideration when assessing the reliability of digital images is the purpose for which they are being used. For example, suboptimum images may be adequate when being used to examine an event at a macro level, looking for things like geography, buildings, vehicles, and the movement of people. Yet the same images may be wholly unsuitable when looking for minute geographical, building, or vehicle features, or trying to identify a specific person. Further, though the focus of this section is on intentional and inadvertent image alteration, unaltered images may still be profoundly unreliable.[90] A poorly framed compressed image with limited resolution will provide little in the realm of reliable details.

The method of playback may also impact image reliability depending upon the purpose for viewing the images. When images are viewed frame-by-frame, isolated from their motion video environment, image fragmentation may occur, which may result in images that become abstractions and vitiate the spatial and temporal cohesiveness afforded by real-time viewing.[91] By employing this strategy, counsel may be able to challenge the temporal logic of the event and parse out a different meaning from the images. The differing approaches that may be taken in

[89] Sherwin advocates the need to 'understand how visual images make and convey meaning, both explicitly and implicitly'. Sherwin (n 30) 30. This is part of developing visual literacy; not just looking at images but striving to understand what they truly convey.

[90] Haldar (n 37) 155.

[91] Shulamit Almog, 'Creating Representations of Justice in the Third Millennium: Legal Poetics in Digital Times', *Rutgers Computer & Technology Law Journal* 32, no. 2 (2006): 183–246, at 221.

the analysis of video images may result in interpretations that are starkly different. For example, the prosecution may use real-time video to show the court what it believes happened, but the defence may analyse the video frame-by-frame to show a different theory of what happened.[92] Context and the nature of the inquiry are paramount.

Image reliability relies in part upon considerations of integrity verification and authenticity of the media. Integrity verification is aimed at determining whether an image has undergone any changes from one iteration to the next while authentication focuses on determining whether the images are in fact that which they purport to be. Though integrity verification and authenticity are critical components in establishing the reliability of digital media, they are not necessarily guarantors of reliability. Even expert evidence on these points may not fully establish reliability. For example, even though it can be established that the video file presented in court is a faithful replication of the original media (integrity verification) and does in fact purport to show a particular event (authenticity), the video may be unreliable as evidence because the event portrayed has been staged. By way of illustration, in response to video evidence of alleged war crimes, the Sri Lankan government did not dispute the authenticity of the video evidence but rather claimed that the scene depicted was staged.[93]

In the US, police officers have been known to stage the recovery of a weapon or other evidence of criminality for bodycam documentation, resulting in video evidence that is authentic but not reliable.[94] Whether staged media should be admitted or considered reliable depends entirely upon the purpose for which it is tendered. A computer animation that is designed to showcase one party's theory of a case is generally admissible so long as it is a fair rendition of the evidence presented, but its reliability in depicting the event will be assessed by the fact-finder. When staged content is an issue, counsel and the court will benefit from corroborative evidence when assessing reliability.

A further consideration when assessing reliability is image accuracy. Video images may pass integrity verification and authenticity tests yet may not be accurate and this lack of accuracy impacts the value of the evidence in answering contentious questions. Image accuracy can be affected by temporal and spatial compression, frame rate, aspect ratio, and resolution. These important topics, which affect

[92] Almog asks the question, 'When the normative processes of perception and cognition can be easily challenged or undermined by new forms of digital representations, how can legal rulings rely upon such representations? (ibid 221–2). I suggest that so long as counsel and the court employ a robust visual literacy that permits them to make informed judgments about visual evidence, new forms of digital representation are not a bar to discovering the truth.

[93] Theresa Harris, Jonathan Drake, Jessica Wyndham, Susan Wolfinbarger, Stephen Lott, and Michael Lerner, 'Geospatial Evidence in International Human Rights Litigation: Technical and Legal Considerations', *AAAS Scientific Responsibility, Human Rights and Law Program* (2018) doi: 10.1126/srhrl.aau6090, 15.

[94] Jeffrey Bellin and Shevarma Pemberton, 'Policing the Admissibility of Body Camera Evidence', *Fordham Law Review* 87, no. 4 (2019): 1425–58, at 1427.

both the interpretation and presentation of images, will be discussed in Chapter 6 in the context of expert image analysis.

All images must be assessed for reliability, though concerns of reliability are heightened when the images have been acquired from an open source, especially one where the photographer may be unknown and there is no access to the original media. Several factors impact upon the reliability of digital media including its provenance, the context in which the images were created, the purpose for which they are being tendered, and internal and external markers of reliability.[95] Reliability is also dependent upon how images are recorded, stored, processed, analysed, and presented. The presence of other evidence, visual or otherwise, that can corroborate questioned images may assist in this assessment.

In this chapter, the focus is on media that is recorded and later presented for use as evidence. Intentional or inadvertent alterations to the media can occur between the time of recording and the time the evidence is shown in court. An exception to this scenario is livestreaming, which occurs when an event is filmed live and broadcast near-instantaneously. In these circumstances, there is no opportunity to alter or edit the media, and no possibility to create a deepfake, as these steps require processing time, which is not available with livestreaming. Therefore, should ISIS livestream a beheading for maximum shock value, that video would likely be highly reliable. Further, as the video would constitute an admission against interest, ISIS would find it very difficult to dissociate itself from the video.[96] A word of caution though—livestream video must be captured by someone as a digital file for it to become available for later use as evidence. Many social media and open source entities remove such content as soon as they become aware of its existence. Cyber-investigators therefore need to regularly search for relevant media, mindful of its sometimes-transitory existence.

This section began by asking the question 'Is digital image-based evidence reliable?' A succinct but accurate answer is 'It all depends'. Perspicacious viewers know that the transition from film and analogue video to digital media did not result in forensically unsound imagery by virtue of the transition alone. Digital media can be intentionally manipulated or inadvertently altered in such a way as to mislead the viewer. Central to making informed judgements about the reliability of digital images are two essential prerequisites. First, the processing, analysis, and presentation of images must be performed by competent, properly trained, and qualified people. Second, counsel and the court must possess a robust visual literacy

[95] UC Berkeley School of Law Human Rights Center, 'The New Forensics: Using Open Source Information to Investigate Grave Crimes' (2018), https://humanrights.berkeley.edu/sites/default/files/publications/bellagio_report_july2018_final.pdf, 5 ('New Forensics').

[96] An admission against interest is a statement made by or attributable to a party in litigation which constitutes an admission against the party's interest, and which tends to prove the existence or non-existence of a material fact. Black (n 13).

that allows them to critically analyse media that is tendered for use as evidence.[97] Properly processed, analysed, presented, and considered, digital imagery can reasonably be admitted into evidence for weighing and judgement. Lest I give the impression that this subject has been closed, no discussion about questioning the soundness of image-based evidence would be complete without considering the impact of deepfake technology on the question of digital image reliability, which is the focus of the next section.

4. Deepfake Technology: Should We Be Worried?

When US President Obama gave a speech in which he advocated for the legalization of harmful street drugs, many viewers were justifiably astonished and quick to criticize him. President Obama was likely equally nonplussed, especially given the fact that he never gave that speech, though based on the video it appears that he did. In a similar video, he appeared to speak of the dangers of fake news and mocked President Trump.[98] If all viewers were equipped with robust visual literacy, fraudulent videos like these would be seen for the mischief they represent, but that panacea is not our reality. Given the tendency to believe what is seen absent meaningful input to the contrary, fraudulent videos create the potential for substantial and vexing problems in the criminal justice system.

Software programs utilizing artificial intelligence (AI) and machine learning have created the facility for intrepid individuals to generate deepfake videos that appear genuine for the express purpose of creating a false narrative. No longer the sole domain of Hollywood computer generated imagery (CGI) experts, the increasingly widespread availability of deepfake software sets the stage for the propagation of misleading digital media that causes legitimate scepticism as to whether what is seen is real.[99] Deepfake videos that are created for entertainment purposes likely pose little concern and serve to showcase the software's capabilities. When used to cause political unrest, to falsely implicate someone in criminal activity, or to seek the exoneration of the guilty, the risk of calculable harm and injustice is palpable.[100] This is not just a querulous concern about farfetched possibilities. Questioning whether we can believe what we see takes on increased urgency in an

[97] Sherwin advocates for a more refined capacity for critical visual judgment. Sherwin (n 26) 14. Given that we dissect words to assess meaning, the same critical approach is required when assessing visual evidence.

[98] Mika Westerlund, 'The Emergence of Deepfake Technology: A Review', *Technology Innovation Management Review* 9, no. 11 (2019): 39–52, at 43.

[99] Frederic Chamot, Zeno Geradts, and Evert Hassdijk, 'Deepfake Forensics: Cross-Manipulation Robustness of Feedforward and Recurrent Convolutional Forgery Detection Methods', *Forensic Science International: Digital Investigation* 40, no. 301374 (2022): 1–11, at 1.

[100] Deepfake videos can be used to incite real-world violence through online trickery; Gregory (n 65) 380.

age when image manipulation is taught in YouTube videos and consumer grade deepfake software is readily downloadable.

4.1 An Overview of Deepfake Technology

A deepfake is a synthetic video that merges or superimposes a target image onto a base video using AI, resulting in hyper-realistic but fake imagery.[101] Face-swapping, which occurs when the target (real) face of a person is replaced by the face of another person (source face), is the most widespread category of image forgery.[102] Deepfake videos are the product of AI and machine learning. AI refers to 'computational models of human behavior and thought processes that are designed to operate rationally and intelligently', or in short, computer programs capable of autonomous self-improvement.[103] Machine learning is a type of AI that allows computers to learn directly from examples, data, and their own processing experience, ultimately carrying out complex processes by learning from data, rather than following pre-programmed rules.[104]

Machine learning has the capacity to make increasingly accurate decisions and predictions without the need for constant human input.[105] Computers search for real images on the internet and use that visual data to create a new video with a different face on the virtual subject.[106] Machine learning systems operate in tandem wherein a generative adversarial network (GAN) compares two sets of images or videos. The first system, which is focused on synthesizing image content, attempts to fool the second system, which is designed to probe for image realism. The second machine learning system then provides feedback to the first system indicating when the image appears to be realistic. This feedback allows the first

[101] Synthetic video is created by a computer, rather than occurring in real life and captured by a video camera. Samuel Greengard, 'Will Deepfakes Do Deep Damage?', *Communications of the ACM* 63, no. 1 (2020): 17–19, at 18; Cristian Vaccari and Andrew Chadwick, 'Deepfakes and Disinformation: Exploring the Impact of Synthetic Political Video on Deception, Uncertainty, and Trust in News', *Social Media and Society* (January-March 2020): 1–13, at 2.

[102] Chamot, Geradts, and Hassdijk (n 99) 1–2; Siwei Lyu, 'Deepfake Detection', in *Multimedia Forensics*, edited by Husrev Sencar, Luisa Verdoliva, and Nasir Memon (Singapore: Springer, 2022), 313–32, at 314. Other methods include head puppetry (replacing the head and shoulders) and lip syncing (targeting only the lip region).

[103] Maras and Alexandrou (n 48) 256. John Fletcher, 'Deepfakes, Artificial Intelligence, and Some Kind of Dystopia: The New Faces of Online Post-Fact Performance', *Theatre Journal* 70, no. 4 (2018): 455–71, at 457–8.

[104] The Royal Society, 'Machine Learning: The Power and Promise of Computers that Learn by Example' (2017) https://royalsociety.org/-/media/policy/projects/machine-learning/publications/machine-learning-report.pdf.

[105] Fletcher (n 103) 457–8.

[106] Agnes Venema and Zeno Geradts, 'Digital Forensics, Deepfakes, and the Legal Process', *The SciTech Lawyer* 16, no. 4 (2020): 14–23, at 14.

system to learn and make necessary changes.[107] Thus, deepfake technology is designed to continuously optimize its performance as it learns to improve videos by continually mimicking facial expressions, gestures, and voices, thereby increasing their realism.[108] Though deepfakes are typically thought of in terms of video, deepfake technology can also be used to create audio files.[109]

A *shallowfake* is created by speeding up or slowing down the original video and is easily detectable because the shallowfake can be compared to the original, if available.[110] For example, in the run-up to the 2020 US Presidential election, a shallowfake video emerged of Nancy Pelosi, the Speaker of the House of Representatives, which showed her to be speaking in a manner that evinced confusion or drunkenness.[111] This was accomplished by simply slowing down the frame rate of the video. Since the original media was readily available, the fakery was easily exposed, though many people preferred to believe the shallowfake.

Deepfake technology is advancing at an alarming rate.[112] Deepfakes are becoming easier to create with commercially available downloadable software and can be created on a computer or a cell phone.[113] Immanent with advances in deepfake technology is the likelihood that the images it produces will become increasingly effective and convincing.[114] No longer is a CGI expert required to employ this technology as anyone can download a deepfake application and create 'face-swap videos'.[115] Human faces are the most common target for deepfake technology and because faces display individual biometric traits and convey significant information in relation to identity, the ability of AI software to hijack or substitute facial images for nefarious purposes raises great concern.[116] Recent studies have shown that people cannot reliably detect facial images that are the result of two different faces morphed by computer software into a new fictional face.[117] Even

[107] Greengard (n 101) 18. In a GAN, one algorithm, the 'generator', creates images by drawing upon source data (images) and a second algorithm, the 'discriminator', searches for artificial content. Each algorithm improves its work based on the input of the other, leading to hyper realistic video content.

[108] Maras and Alexandrou (n 48) 255–6.

[109] Venema and Geradts (n 106) 14. Synthesized audio content can make the deepfakes videos appear more convincing Lyu (n 102) 326.

[110] Sometimes referred to as a 'cheapfake'. Venema and Geradts (n 106) 16.

[111] Verdoliva (n 73) 2–3.

[112] Rebecca Hamilton, 'Atrocity Prevention in the New Media Landscape', *AJIL Unbound* 113 (2019): 262–6, at 265; Chamot, Geradts, and Hassdijk (n 106) 1–2.

[113] Home computers have sufficient computational power to create realistic deepfakes using a trained neural network that can be downloaded from the internet; Venema and Geradts (n 106) 14.

[114] Farid (n 59) 268–9.

[115] Examples include FakeApp and Zao per Jan Kietzmann, Linda Lee, Ian McCarthy, and Tim Kietzmann, 'Deepfakes: Trick or Treat?' *Business Horizons* 63 (2020): 135–46, at 136; DeepFake, DeepNude, and FaceSwap, per Gokhale, Mulay, Pramod, and Kulkarni (n 74) 97; and DeepFaceLab, per Chamot, Geradts, and Hassdijk (n 99) 2. See also Maras and Alexandrou (n 48) 256; Jeff Ward, '10 Things Judges Should Know About AI', *Judicature* 103, no. 1 (2019): 12–18, at 17.

[116] Verdoliva (n 73) 9.

[117] Face morphing involves digitally combining images of two or more individuals to create a new person that retains a likeness to the original images. Sophie Nightingale, Shruti Agarwal, and Hany Farid, 'Perceptual and Computational Detection of Face Morphing', *Journal of Vision*, 21, no. 3:4 (2021): 1–18, at 1–3, 14.

state-of-the-art machine learning facial recognition algorithms could not reliably differentiate a face from a midway morphing image of a face.[118] While deepfakes usually require a large number of source images (typically faces) to create a realistic false image, researchers have developed a technique to generate a fake video from only one reference image.[119] This is significant because requiring multiple accessible images of a target would no longer be a prerequisite to creating a deepfake.

4.2 The Impact of Deepfake Videos and Images on Fact-Finding

Unless viewers are prompted and trained to critically assess images, there is a strong tendency to believe what is seen. Images can systematically bias viewers to believe they are seeing truthful images, whether actually true or not.[120] Images can be convincing even if they have been fabricated because visual representations strike us more powerfully than words alone and we intuitively feel the truth of what we have seen.[121] Indeed, deepfake videos can fool even the most discriminating viewer.[122] They are becoming more seamless and more believable.[123] This believability emanates from the quality of the videos coupled with their resistance to forgery detection.[124] Because machine-learning AI learns on its own, it can achieve image accuracy without transparency, which is essential when seeking to avoid detection.[125] Without transparency as to what is real and what is fake, the plight of the visually uninformed is exacerbated.

Deepfake programs can seemingly make people say and do things they neither said nor did and when skilfully created, these videos are observationally indistinguishable from authentic videos for most viewers. When used for entertainment purposes, aside from potentially damaging the subject's reputation, little may be at stake. However, deepfake technology can also be used for far more nefarious purposes centred on wilfully spreading misinformation for disparate uses. If belief is the viewer's default, fraudulent media can be most troublesome, especially when decisions are made based upon it. Deepfake technology can also be used to manufacture evidence as part of a police investigation.

[118] ibid 14.

[119] Westerlund (n 98) 41.

[120] Newman and Feigenson (n 30) 9.

[121] Mnookin (n 34) 66; Porter (n 33) 1694, 1699.

[122] Ward (n 115) 16.

[123] Kietzmann, Lee, McCarthy, and Kietzmann (n 115) 136; Vaccari and Chadwick (n 101) 3; Greengard (n 101) 17–19.

[124] Bobby Chesney and Danielle Citron, 'Deepfakes and the New Disinformation War: The Coming Age of Post-Truth Geopolitics', *Foreign Affairs* 98, no. 1 (2019): 147–55, at 147–8.

[125] 'Deployed carelessly in contexts where transparency matters, such tools may challenge our fundamental need to know, explain, and ensure fairness.' Ward further notes that it may be impossible to know whether the AI tool has incorporated improper biases from its input data; Ward (n 115) 14.

This was fictionally exemplified in a 2019–2022 BBC television series entitled *The Capture*, which drew critical acclaim.[126] In this crime series, the UK Security Service used CCTV images manipulated with deepfake technology to present an alternate reality, which assisted authorities in successfully prosecuting terror suspects when existing admissible evidence was lacking. Referring to this process as 'correction', the falsified CCTV images were described as '... not fake evidence, it is truth re-enacted'. The Security Service claimed legitimacy for their deception on that basis that they only falsified events that actually occurred for the purposes of securing a desired legal conclusion where admissible evidence was lacking. Though only a television programme, the technology showcased is already here and those desirous of creating a false depiction of reality, for altruistic or sinister purposes, have ready access to the necessary software.

Deepfakes contribute to widespread suspicion and mistrust of information prepared for public consumption.[127] They are used to launch credibility attacks, to obscure the truth in an investigation, and as a tool to incite violence against targeted individuals and groups.[128] Relying upon disinformation such as deepfakes to make findings of fact could result in a miscarriage of justice.[129] Deepfakes have the potential to further denigrate trust in the ability of viewers and experts to verify the integrity and authenticity of visual information and raise the spectre of weaponizing open source media sites.[130] For example, terrorist organizations such as ISIS might upload deepfake videos to social media sites showing apparent illegal activities of occupying forces, intended to garner support for their terrorist causes.[131] Should deepfakes become part of the zeitgeist, the public may question the truth of images they view even when they are legitimate.[132] Given the availability of consumer-geared deepfake applications, the potential for mischief is evident, and even more concerning when factoring in the reality that the democratized ability to share deepfake videos is unprecedented.[133]

Deepfakes are problematic not only because they have the potential to mislead. They stand as an anathema to truth and are inimical to the interests of society in seeking justice for abhorrent crimes. Axiomatic in criminal investigations and prosecutions is a concern that deepfakes may be used to create a false visual narrative in court.[134] Using deepfake videos as an offensive tool designed to fool the viewer

[126] 'The Capture' (2019–2022) *BBC TV*.

[127] Fletcher (n 103) 464.

[128] Gregory (n 65) 380.

[129] Alexa Koenig, '"Half the Truth is Often a Great Lie": Deep Fakes, Open Source Information, and International Criminal Law', *AJIL Unbound* 113 (2021): 250–5, at 251.

[130] Social media and other sites provide fertile ground for deepfakes to propagate and take hold. Chesney and Citron (n 126) 150.

[131] Chesney and Citron (n 124) 150–1.

[132] Bobby Chesney and Danielle Citron, 'Deep Fakes: A Looming Challenge for Privacy, Democracy, and National Security', *California Law Review* 107, no. 6 (2019): 1753–820, at 1786.

[133] ibid 1762–8.

[134] Westerlund (n 98) 39.

and avoid detection is an ambitious though not inconceivable play.[135] This trickery raises the spectre of an improper result at trial and a potential miscarriage of justice. Paradoxically, wariness in relying upon images without absolute certainly of authenticity and reliability may have the corollary effect that even legitimate visual evidence may be disregarded for fear of injecting false imagery and narratives, again resulting in a potential miscarriage of justice.[136] Thus, deepfake technology makes it possible to implicate the innocent with fake video while at the same time making it difficult to convict the guilty with authentic video.[137] Though perhaps an unintended consequence, deepfakes may also be used by perpetrators as a liability escape route by claiming that authentic incriminating video is a deepfake.[138] While unlikely to become a standard defence, instead of issuing a flat denial of responsibility, tactical responses of video falsehood may draw some resonance courtesy of the increasing proliferation of deepfakes in popular media.

The volume of visual media uploaded to and available on social media and other sites continues to grow. This can benefit investigators as there is more potentially relevant evidence to consider, but the volume may also create investigative capacity issues. While much of it may be reliable, some of it clearly is not. Given the anonymous nature of many uploaded videos, assessing their reliability requires technical analysis, a topic that will be discussed in Chapter 7. Paradoxically, compelling, authentic, and useful video may get lost among the flotsam and jetsam that describes much of what is publicly accessible on the internet.[139] Further, while this increasing volume provides potential sources of valuable exogenous evidence for investigators, counsel, and the court to consider, it also portends significant challenges in ascertaining the reliability and trustworthiness of such media.

5. Hallmarks of Reliability and Atrocity Crime Prosecutions

The reliability of images tendered as evidence is frequently a matter of concern to counsel and the court in domestic and atrocity crime prosecutions. The level of concern increases if the source of the images is tenuous, if there is no access to the original images, or if the photographer is unknown or not producible. Reliability may still be a concern even if these complicating factors are not present. Image reliability may be a greater concern in atrocity crime prosecutions for several reasons. First, the pool of potential photographers will almost certainly be larger than

[135] Venema and Geradts (n 106) 16.
[136] Chesney and Citron (n 132) 1784.
[137] Fletcher (n 103) 464.
[138] Chesney and Citron (n 132) 1785. The deepfake defence puts the onus on prosecutors to prove a negative, that the video is not a deepfake, and with current technology that may prove to be a very difficult task. Venema and Geradts (n 106) 16.
[139] Gregory (n 65) 384–5.

would be reasonably expected in the domestic context because atrocity crimes frequently involve multiple incidents covering a broad geographic area over a longer period whereas domestic cases tend to be more focused in incidents, area, and time. Additionally, the pool is likely to be larger because of a broader spectrum of potential photographers, as exemplified during the 2022 Russian invasion of Ukraine where soldiers, civilians, government officials, investigators, journalists, human rights organizations, and others have become war photographers sharing smartphone videos and images and live streaming from bomb shelters.[140] Second, a larger pool of photographers will likely generate a greater variety of recordings that range from poor quality and limited reliability at one end of the spectrum to very good at the other. Mathematically, a larger pool is thus likely to produce a greater volume of unreliable image-based evidence.

Third, with such a broad variety of photographers, many of them will be far removed from the OTP and consequently, there may be several steps between the recording of the images and their receipt by the OTP.[141] Professional photographers, investigators, human rights organizations, and NGOs will likely submit their evidence directly to the OTP whereas locally involved or affected witnesses are perhaps more likely to forward their images to an intermediary, a dedicated application, or an open source site. This middle step serves to distance the photographer from the OTP which may impact access to the original media, the chain of custody, and the ability to prove image reliability. Fourth, a greater volume of evidence is administratively much more resource intensive for the OTP, which must review, catalogue, and disclose relevant evidence to the defence. This sifting process is very important as it allows the OTP to separate unreliable recordings of limited or no value from those that bear further consideration for use as evidence in the courtroom, but there must be adequate resources in place to accomplish this task. Fifth, among a large pool of photographers wherein many of them are geographically and otherwise distanced from the OTP, it is expected that many of them may be anonymous submitters and that access to the original images will be nearly impossible. These are not necessarily bars to admission, but they do make establishing authenticity and reliability much more challenging.

Finally, among the many objective and reliable images that are recorded, atrocity crimes are more likely to stimulate the production of altered digital media for the purpose of advancing partisan narratives. For example, early in the 2022 Russian invasion of Ukraine, false or misleading images appeared on social media showing military action from older conflicts (such as the 2014 Crimean conflict),

140 Kazi Stastna, 'The Smartphone War: Soldiers, Civilians and Satellites Give the World a Window onto Russian Invasion' (6 April 2022) *CBC News* https://www.cbc.ca/news/world/ukraine-osint-war-1.6410037. The 2023 Israel–Gaza conflict has similarly engaged a broad number of photographers from a broad range of sources.

141 The same concern arises for prosecutions conducted by Ukrainian authorities.

unverifiable conflicts, military parade flyovers, and online video games.[142] Even deepfakes of Ukraine President Zelensky making false statements have appeared online.[143]

Collectively, these factors serve to accentuate the challenges that counsel and the court must grapple with when assessing the suitability of images for fact-finding in the atrocity crime context. Some challenges may be insurmountable (e.g. where there is no access to the original media, the photographer is anonymous, and there is an absence of corroboration). Other challenges may just require further investigation to confirm image reliability. What is clear is that there is good reason to be cautious when accepting some atrocity crime imagery at face value.

When assessing image-based evidence for reliability, investigators and counsel must determine the presence of hallmarks of reliability. These hallmarks are necessary to develop confidence in what the images portray. Relevant hallmarks include identifying and examining the source of the evidence, determining whether access to the original media is available, identifying and gaining access to the photographer, and evaluating the integrity of the media through metadata and content analysis. The more hallmarks that are present, the more likely it will be to satisfy the court that the evidence is worthy of substantive consideration.

By way of example, the major sources of filmic and photographic evidence of Nazi atrocities during World War II that was presented during the Nuremberg trial were Allied investigators and the Nazis themselves. Focusing on the *Nazi Concentration Camps* film, the film repository that was drawn upon to create it was photographed by American investigators. The photographers did not testify at trial. Instead, the film began with a statement from the Chief Prosecutor that said in part, 'This is an official documentary report compiled from films made by military photographers serving with the allied armies as they advanced into Germany . . . ' His statement was followed by showing the certificates and affidavits of image authenticity. Presumably, had there been a request to produce the photographers, that could have been accommodated. Similarly, the original film appears to have been available for presentation in court if required. The integrity of the film's content was strong as numerous witnesses would have been able to corroborate all the scenes shown.

In summary, the *Nazi Concentration Camps* film bore all the hallmarks of reliability. The source of the film was known, and while there may have been a motive for US investigators to embellish their film accounts, there is no evidence that they did so, nor was there any reason for them to have done so. The images were

[142] Alistair Coleman and Shayan Sardarizadeh, 'Ukraine Conflict: Many Misleading Images Have Been Shared Online' (24 February 2022) *BBC News* https://www.bbc.com/news/60513452; Alistair Coleman, 'Ukraine Conflict: Further False Images Shared Online' (25 February 2022) *BBC News* https://www.bbc.com/news/60528276; Shayan Sardarizadeh and Olga Robinson, 'Ukraine Invasion: False Claims the War is a Hoax Go Viral' (8 March 2022) *BBC News* https://www.bbc.com/news/60589965.

[143] Deepfake Presidents (n 4).

extraordinarily powerful, and it is hard to conceive how they could be embellished. The photographers were known and accessible if needed, the original film was available, and the film's content could be corroborated by *viva voce* evidence. It is worthy of note that the defence did not challenge the reliability of the film, nor did the IMT judges express reservations.

Films produced by the Nazis, including *Original German Film (8 mm) of the Atrocities Against the Jews* and *The Nazi Plan* emanated from Nazi sources.[144] The Nazis would have been motivated to accurately record their actions against civilians and their rise to power. Even though the photographers were not identified or produced, there was no suggestion that the films were unreliable. Further, the content, which was not disputed by the defendants, was capable of corroboration through documentary and *viva voce* sources. Lastly, these films stand as admissions against interest and there would have been no motive for the Nazis to created false filmic evidence of their rise to power and domination of the civilian population.

Similarly, in *Prosecutor v. Ayyash et al.*, a prosecution before the Special Tribunal for Lebanon that lasted from 2014 to 2020, extensive image-based evidence was presented by the prosecution.[145] This complex case, which involved a 2005 truck explosion assassination that killed former Lebanese Prime Minister Hariri and others, relied in part on images of Hariri in meetings at Parliament during the morning and leaving a café immediately before the explosion, crime scene images of the immediate and extended blast area, overall scene and convoy route images, CCTV images showing the explosive laden truck as it approached the site of the assassination, and images of the detailed examination of real evidence.

The sources for these images were Parliament and journalists (Parliament and café images), investigators (crime scene, overall scene, evidence examination), the municipality, a hotel, and a bank (CCTV images of truck), satellite companies (overall scene geography), and forensic experts (detailed evidence examination). These sources all appeared to be trustworthy and without reason to mislead the viewer. It appears highly likely, given the sources, that the original recordings were available for examination. At the very least, faithful copies would have been available. Identification of the photographers and access to the photographers, where applicable, was not an issue as most images were recorded by investigators and forensic experts. The CCTV and satellite images were likely recorded automatically, without the intervention of a human photographer. As to the integrity of the image content, with access to the original media and the photographer, and the automated nature of CCTV video, the images bore the hallmarks of reliability. The

[144] The newsreel films involved other parties in their creation though there was no suggestion that what they selected for inclusion was untrustworthy.

[145] STL-11-01/T/TC-F3839/20200818/R331945-R334626/EN/dm, Judgment, 18 August 2020. This is not an international criminal prosecution for atrocity crimes but is a helpful case on the issue of image-based evidence reliability.

reliability of the images was bolstered by the fact that almost all the tendered images could also be corroborated by eyewitness testimony.[146]

When considering the reliability of image-based evidence that may be tendered in a prosecution, Nuremberg and *Ayyash* are not necessarily outliers, but they do represent a select category of cases wherein the hallmarks of image reliability could be robustly established. These cases could fairly be considered as cases which demonstrate a near panacea for image reliability, certainly at the high end of the spectrum, but it would be erroneous to view them as typical of all cases that involve image-based evidence. More commonly, hallmarks of reliability are missing or difficult to establish. The source of the media, its location, and the identity of the photographer may be unknown. Frequently, some of the media relied upon by counsel may be of questionable reliability.

A case example that resides lower on the spectrum of reliability is *Prosecutor v. Gbagbo and Blé Goudé*.[147] The prosecution relied, inter alia, on video evidence to prove that a FDS convoy intentionally fired upon anti-Gbagbo demonstrators resulting in deaths and injuries. The video evidence relied upon by the prosecution was an unstable video recording of the demonstrators and the approaching convoy. There is no reference by the Chamber to the source of the video evidence, though evidently someone in the crowd recorded the video as the camera moved considerably throughout the event. The photographer is not identified, nor did the photographer testify, though it is unlikely the photographer could have been of much supplemental assistance given the chaos of the event and the specificity of the issue being addressed.[148]

It is unclear how the video recording came to the attention of the OTP, for example, whether the media was provided directly to the OTP, through an intermediary, or whether it was uploaded to an open source site. No reference is made to whether the media was received in its original format.[149] Though *viva voce* evidence was presented to corroborate the video evidence, it proved to be contradictory and of limited value.[150] Collectively, none of the hallmarks of reliability were conclusively established. It is worthy of note that even if the video had been found to be reliable, it would still have been of limited value as '... the video shows only a very limited aspect of the entire incident and even so, the footage is of poor

[146] The CCTV images of the truck were less likely to be corroborated with *viva voce* evidence as there would be no reason for the truck to draw any attention, and so integrity of the CCTV video would need to be established technically.

[147] ICC-02/11-01/15, Judgment, 16 July 2019.

[148] The video recording was being used to determine the timing and number of shots fired during the recorded event and to visualize the approaching convoy.

[149] The defence challenged the authenticity of the video, arguing that the date of the video file did not correspond with the date of the incident. For its decision, the Chamber presumed authenticity. See para. 1775, FN 3962.

[150] ICC-02/11-01/15-1263-Conf-AnxB, Reasons of Judge Henderson, 16 July 2019, paras. 1778–1783.

quality'.[151] When the prosecution relies upon video recorded by non-investigators, reliability may be an issue, as was shown in this case.

This demonstration video is more typical of some of the media that is received through the democratization process. Image quality may be lacking as well as the necessary hallmarks of reliability. These comments are not intended to denigrate the democratization process but rather to illustrate that photographers in highly stressful situations may produce video images of decreased value, especially when the source is unclear and access to the original media and the photographer is not available or even possible. When potential evidence such as the demonstration video is viewed, serious consideration must be given as to whether it is sufficiently reliable to warrant its use in court.

A further example of images that lack hallmarks of reliability are those that are posted anonymously to social media and other sites. In these circumstances, there is no access to the original media or the photographer, nor is there any metadata to evaluate. Absent this vital contextual and technical information, such images could only achieve a measure of reliability if there is independent corroborative evidence to authenticate the content. Given the proliferation of evidence created by the democratization process, a robust quest for reliability is essential.

Conclusion

Should we be worried about unreliable photographic and video images being tendered as evidence in criminal prosecutions, whether created through deepfake technology or other image modification techniques? In a word—absolutely. Unreliable imagery is not a futuristic concern—it is a current issue that is likely to increase in scope. There is ample technical ability and motivation to alter digital images and produce evidence that is neither fair nor reliable. Questionable images that are designed to mislead have a significant impact on the search for the truth. Images may be intentionally manipulated for nefarious purposes, but they may also be inadvertently altered by untrained people lacking the skills needed to process images in a forensically sound manner, unaware that they are altering their integrity.

Reliability is the referent for all types of image-based evidence, whether it is still imagery, video images, satellite images, forensic animations and simulations, or advanced visual representations. Accordingly, when used for the purpose of ascertaining the truth in pursuit of a fair and just result, investigators, counsel, and the court must be satisfied that the evidence relied upon is authentic, accurate, and reliable. These attributes cannot be assumed, they must be proven to exist. Image

[151] ibid para. 1780.

reliability is dependent upon many factors, including subjective choices made by photographers when recording the scene or event, intentional manipulation or inadvertent alteration of images during processing, the context in which the images were obtained, the purpose for which they are being used, and the interpretation and presentation of the evidence in court. Contextually, a benign belief in what is seen may be harmless and justified, but in other contexts a misplaced belief in the trustworthiness of images may result in significant errors of judgment. A notable example in this regard is deepfake videos, which are comfortably located at the higher end of the spectrum of image unreliability and their calculated alteration of imagery represents a clear and present danger to the pursuit of truth and justice. It follows generally that systematic verification and corroboration must be essential procedures for counsel before presenting digital media in court or relying upon it to construct a trial narrative.[152]

Discovery of the truth requires that viewers must be able to discern between images that are fair and trustworthy and those which merit a more cautious appraisal. Reliability does not necessarily co-exist in both paradigms. Unreliable images that are presented as genuine can create cognitive dissonance wherein viewers question what is seen because it does not accord with what is otherwise regarded to be true. Even more problematic is when, owing to insufficient visual literacy by counsel and the court, there is a lack of awareness that a problem even exists. Image-based evidence can be a powerful adjunct in the search for the truth. When processed, interpreted, and presented by properly trained people, and when counsel and the court possess adequate visual literacy to properly evaluate the evidence and assess its meaning, there should exist justifiable confidence in the soundness of decisions based upon image-based evidence.

[152] Koenig (n 129) 254.

6
Pictures Do Not Speak for Themselves

Introduction

The oft cited adage 'the picture speaks for itself' suggests that images possess some sort of innate ability to communicate meaning to viewers. Another adage goes so far as to quantify this communicative ability—'a picture is worth a thousand words'. Both atavistic popular culture references are paradigmatic of the general view that images inherently communicate their content to viewers who can understand their meaning with relative ease. In fact, images rarely speak for themselves. Rather, they must be viewed and interpreted with an understanding of the context in which they were created, the perspective chosen by the photographer, and the narrative they are being associated with by their proponent.

Images do not provide an unmediated objective window on the world.[1] Though it is said that a picture is worth a thousand words, a picture is not a substitute for words. Instead, we must speak for them and through our descriptors we can imbue images with meaning. Not all images have inherent unequivocal meaning, a fact sometimes neglected when counsel rely upon them as propositional proof in court. Depending upon the images and the purpose for which they are being used, reliably assessing their meaning may require evaluation and descriptive interpretation by a person with knowledge about the technical aspects of the images and their content. This may also require an understanding of what is not shown to understand what is shown.

Developing visual literacy includes understanding the complexities of digital images and their interpretation from a technical and content perspective. While *res ipsa loquitur* is a principle with application to some types of evidence, it is not well suited for all images.[2] The uninformed interpretation of images by counsel and the court can lead to erroneous conclusions about their content and meaning. Expert analysis, interpretation, and testimony can bridge the gulf between what might otherwise be an inchoate assessment of image meaning and an evaluation that is fully informed with the benefit of expertise, leading to sound judgement.

[1] Jennifer Mnookin, 'Semi-Legibility and Visual Evidence: An Initial Exploration', *Law, Culture and the Humanities* 10, no. 1 (2014): 43–65, at 53.

[2] Latin for 'the thing speaks for itself', used to suggest that something is self-evident. 'res ipsa loquitur [phr]' (*OED Online*, OUP August 2023), www.oed.com accessed 7 August 2023.

Image-Based Evidence in International Criminal Prosecutions. Jonathan W. Hak, KC, Oxford University Press.
 DOI: 10.1093/oso/9780198889533.003.0006

This chapter explores the importance of improving the visual literacy of all people who are required to evaluate and make decisions based upon the content of images.

1. Understanding Image Content

There exists a commonly held belief that images have the ontological ability to communicate unequivocal meaning to viewers. I advocate instead that images do not necessarily possess inherent meaning, let alone the power to convey it. Images present a tableau for viewers to gaze upon and the ability to understand their content is dependent upon the viewers' personal knowledge of the content and any exogenous information presented to assist with interpretation. The content of an image is a different precept from its interpreted meaning. To truly comprehend the content and meaning of an image, viewers often need more information than meets the eye.

Knowing the five Ws—who, what, where, when, and why—may be essential for full cognition. Seeing an old family photograph may have little meaning unless viewers understand **who** is in the photograph. Images of an alleged perpetrator of atrocity crimes may have added significance depending upon who else is shown in the images.[3] Similarly, when the issue is the age of a depicted alleged child soldier, knowing who the soldier is may be necessary to conclusively determine the age element. Evidence as to **what** is depicted in an image may provide critical contextual information in an investigation. For example, images of victims of genocide and other atrocities, damage to villages and cultural property, the presence of invading forces, weapons, etc. only achieve relevance if their content is understood and relates to the issues being litigated.[4] The location depicted in an image is important when seeking to authenticate it and link it to an alleged crime.[5] Thus, satellite images of a burning village acquire meaning once it can be proven **where** the village is located.

[3] For example, in *Prosecutor v. Lubanga*, ICC-01/04-01/06-2842, Judgment Pursuant to Article 74 of the Statute, 14 March 2012, video images showing the defendant in the presence of alleged child soldiers (paras. 792–93) and in the presence of co-perpetrators (paras. 1209–11) were tendered at trial and used to show criminal complicity.

[4] e.g. proof of physical harm was tendered in part through images in *Prosecutor v. Katanga*, ICC-01/04-01/07, Judgment Pursuant to Article 74 of the Statute, 7 March 2014, paras. 208, 814, 836, as well as the presence of weapons (para. 1207). Video evidence may be led to show the command position of a defendant, exemplified in *Prosecutor v. Ngudjolo*, ICC-01/04-02/12-3, Judgment Pursuant to Article 74 of the Statute, 18 December 2012, paras. 444, 464, 475–82. In *Prosecutor v. Bemba*, ICC-01/05-01/08-2012, First Decision on the Prosecution and Defence Requests for the Admission of Evidence, 9 February 2012, para. 89, video and photographs were tendered to show troop movements.

[5] e.g. video evidence was used to show the location of mass graves in *Prosecutor v. Gbagbo*, ICC-02/11-01/11-656-Red, Decision on the Confirmation of Charges Against Laurent Gbagbo, 12 June 2014, para. 66.

Knowing **when** an image was created is also an essential consideration for gaining a better understanding of the events. For example, in the *Ayyash* et al. trial, images of former Prime Minister Hariri walking out of a cafe have a more sombre meaning knowing that in a few minutes he would be assassinated by a truck bomb.[6] Image timing may have added relevance depending upon the issues being litigated. Sometimes knowing **why** an image was recorded is essential as well. When ISIS records and uploads video of captives being beheaded, they are doing so for propaganda purposes and to foment dissent. Provided authenticity and reliability are established, these video recordings serve as direct proof of the *actus reus* component of criminal culpability of the people depicted. In other cases, exogenous evidence is required to fully understand the context and circumstances under which the images were created. Why do people shown in an image have a particular facial expression? Is it because someone off camera is pointing a gun at them? The meaning of images is dependent upon their content and context, mindful that viewers may have different ways of seeing them.[7] It is for these reasons that not all images *ipso facto* have attendant meaning.

Pictures do not necessarily speak for themselves, no matter how compelling they might be. If they could they would likely speak a language viewers do not understand.[8] We must use words to evaluate their content, with the express caveat that pictures cannot always be reduced to words as they may mean more than words can describe.[9] Even evidence verité requires a narrator to give the images contextual meaning.[10] As persuasive and compelling as images might appear at first glance, they are not unmediated representations of an event, nor will they reveal all they have to offer without varying degrees of viewer effort. They should be viewed with caution and scepticism, as they require testimony for proper context

[6] STL-11-01/T/TC-F3839/20200818/R331945-R334626/EN/dm, Judgment, 18 August 2020, para. 993.

[7] Naomi Mezey, 'The Image Cannot Speak for Itself: Film, Summary Judgment, and Visual Literacy', *Valparaiso University Law Review* 48, no. 1 (2013): 1–40, at 12–13.

[8] Or as Tagg said, '... only qualified experts could read its lips'. John Tagg, *Grounds of Dispute: Art History, Cultural Politics and the Discursive Field* (London: Macmillan Education, 1992), 129. Haldar suggests that '... instead of providing a description of the world, the image in its detail rather explains that world to us'. Piyel Haldar, 'Law and the Evidential Image', *Law, Culture and the Humanities* 4 (2008): 139–55, at 149. I contend that images do not explain their content to viewers but rather make their content available for interpretation. Viewer requires the literacy skills necessary to understand what the images convey.

[9] Neal Feigenson, 'The Visual in Law: Some Problems for Legal Theory', *Law, Culture and the Humanities* 10, no. 1 (2014): 13–23, at 12, 14. Feigenson notes that words are needed to frame the meaning of images so that they can be used for substantive purposes.

[10] Evidence verité is formally defined as a genre of film, television, and radio programmes emphasizing realism and naturalism; OED (n 2). For my purposes, I focus on evidence verité as image-based evidence that captures an event in real time, such as a crime in progress, a crime scene, etc. See also Jessica Silbey, 'Evidence Verité and the Law of Film', *Cardozo Law Review* 31 (2010): 1257–99, at 1294, where the author notes that a photograph's explanatory value arises from its context and its persuasive force is dependent upon the authority of the speaker.

and comprehension.[11] In some cases, expert evaluation, interpretation, and testimony may be essential for these tasks as will be discussed in Section 4.

There is a naïve tendency for viewers to believe that upon seeing an image they can properly understand it. This sense of communicative efficacy is even stronger with sequential moving images which makes video evidence at once appealing and potentially dangerous.[12] Assigning unwarranted credence and meaning to images may arise from the court assuming that the camera delivers unmediated facts without any need for interpretation, and this can lead to incorrect factual findings and potential injustice.[13] Just as a court should not accept *viva voce* evidence without rigorously assessing its reliability, images should similarly be critically examined. Failure to do so risks assigning meaning to images without necessarily understanding them.[14] Visual biases by viewers also influence the meaning drawn from images as they are perceived through a personal rather than objective lens.[15] The phenomenon of illusory causation, which states that camera angle and field of view may impact viewer assessment of meaning, may lead viewers to arrive at unwarranted findings of fact.[16] Absent expert assistance in image interpretation, the court may not see beyond the portion of the image that has garnered its attention. When images are only semi-legible, additional interpretive work and expert assistance are typically required to understand their meaning.[17] Computer generated reconstructions and advanced visual representations are examples of semi-legible displays that can only be fully understood with expert interpretation.

Images may require interpretation when there is an incongruence between viewer expectations and reality, which may lead to inconsistent cognitive results.[18] Unless viewers are suitably sceptical, fully informed, and visually literate, there is a tendency to readily allocate meaning to images when in fact meaning comes from interpretation.[19] Untrained viewers may be aware of the disparate parts of an image

[11] Jay Aronson, McKenna Cole, Alex Hauptmann, Dan Miller, and Bradley Samuels, 'Reconstructing Human Rights Violations Using Large Eyewitness Collections: The Case of Euromaidan Protester Deaths', *Journal of Human Rights Practice* (2018): 1–20, at 3.

[12] Richard Sherwin, Neal Feigenson, and Christina Spiesel, 'What Is Visual Knowledge, and What Is It Good For? Potential Ethnographic Lessons from the Field of Legal Practice', *Visual Anthropology* 20 (2007): 143–78, at 157.

[13] Mezey (n 7) 7.

[14] Alison Young, 'Arrested by the Image', *New York Law School Law Review* 57, no. 1 (2012): 77–84, at 80–1.

[15] Rebecca Hamilton, 'User Generated Evidence', *Columbia Journal of Transnational Law* 57, no. 1 (2018): 1–61, at 49.

[16] ibid. Hamilton cites a study wherein judges were asked to watch a videotaped confession from different perspectives. Owing to illusory causation, judges were significantly more likely to view the confession as voluntary when the camera was facing the suspect as opposed to the interviewer or from a neutral position.

[17] Mnookin (n 1) 65.

[18] Rebecca Tushnet, 'Worth a Thousand Words: The Images of Copyright', *Harvard Law Review* 125, no. 3 (2012): 683–759, at 689.

[19] ibid 689–92; Gary Edmond, Katherine Biber, Richard Kemp, and Glenn Porter, 'Law's Looking Glass: Expert Identification Evidence Derived from Photogenic and Video Images', *Current Issues in Criminal Justice* 20, no. 3 (2009): 337–77, at 337.

and their connection to the whole, but absent sufficient visual literacy, viewers are unlikely to grasp its full significance and this lies at the heart of image misinterpretation.[20] The legibility of images is also dependent upon the knowledge and skill of viewers.[21] For example, counsel may suggest to a witness that an image depicts the witness's village in Mali only to have the witness categorically deny it. Though the witness may have no formal visual literacy training, the witness possesses local knowledge that allows for a critical evaluation of the image's content. In short, the witness may be more informed than counsel.

There is a spectrum across which the need for supplemental interpretive resources will vary. Some images can be properly understood by viewers upon the provision of limited contextual information. Other images will require additional information for viewers to adequately comprehend their meaning. In other cases, expert interpretive assistance will be required as the images themselves are sufficiently complicated or semi-legible such that viewers are highly likely to misinterpret the images or fail to interpret them at all without assistance.

While the assignment of meaning to images is unavoidable, people who must make decisions based upon them should not be left to their own devices to divine image content and meaning. Though it might be suggested that seeing leads to understanding, vision and visual literacy are entirely different precepts. Equating mere vision with sophisticated visual literacy that is intuitively able to understand technical issues and the true meaning of images is fallacious. While vision is a gateway to visual literacy, it is not a substitute. Images are often technically and substantively complex and require more interpretive expertise than average viewers possess.

2. Digital Images Require Technical Assessment

Underlying the belief that pictures speak for themselves is the perception that untrained viewers can effectively decipher image meaning unaided. To be clear, depending on the purpose for which images are being used, unaided viewers can reasonably interpret the content of some images. Nonetheless, there are innumerable examples of images that have undergone extensive analysis to tease meaning from them, beyond what may be readily discernible.[22] While some images are simple and readily amenable to lay interpretation, many are complex and understanding their content will be fleeting and misinformed without guidance. The

[20] Christina Spiesel, 'Reflections on Reading: Words and Pictures and Law', *International Journal of Law in Context* 2, no. 3 (2006): 305–20, at 314.

[21] Mnookin (n 1) 56.

[22] Referring to a well-known American example, film and photographs surrounding the 1963 assassination of US President Kennedy in Dallas, Texas have undergone extensive expert analysis in efforts to either find the truth or fuel conspiracy theories.

following is an overview of selected aspects of digital technology, which is used to create the vast majority of video and still images today.[23]

Cameras do not necessarily capture an event accurately or in a way that allows for informed decision-making without interpretative assistance.[24] Setting aside intentional image manipulation and inadvertent alteration which can render images unreliable, myriad technical issues involving digital images can impact upon the ability of viewers to fully comprehend their content. Viewers who do not adequately understand the complexities of digital images may misinterpret their content and meaning.[25]

Digital images consist of binary mathematical data using discrete values at given sampling points.[26] When digital images are recorded by a camera, a computer assesses constituent lightness and assigns it an algorithmic value which when reconstructed presents a digital image.[27] Motion that is observed in digital video is an illusion achieved by the playback of individual digital images at a suitable frame rate.[28] This individual image feature in digital imagery makes it amenable to forensic analysis on a frame-by-frame basis. Digital images create both epistemic advantages and challenges. The next section provides an overview of key technical issues involving digital images.

2.1 Image Compression

Digital images are made up of binary data which can be reduced in size by decreasing the number of bits required to store or convey images through the process of compression.[29] Image compression is often a practical necessity as it reduces the size of the digital file, allowing for easier storage and electronic transmission.[30] Ideally, compression is used to remove redundancies and reduce the size of the

[23] Comprehensive treatment is beyond the scope of this book.

[24] Sandra Ristovska, 'The Rise of Eyewitness Video and its Implications for Human Rights: Conceptual and Methodological Approaches', *Journal of Human Rights* 15, no. 3 (2016): 347–60, at 355.

[25] Eoghan Casey, 'Editorial: The Epic Story of Scientific Interpretation in Digital Investigations', *Forensic Science International: Digital Investigations* 34, no. 301063 (2020): 1–2, at 1.

[26] Ida Pu, *Fundamental Data Compression* (Burlington: Elsevier, 2006), 189; Richard Sherwin, 'Imagining Law as Film (Representation without Reference?)', in *Law and the Humanities: An Introduction*, edited by Austin Sarat, Matthew Anderson, and Cathrine Frank (Cambridge: CUP, 2009), 241–68, at 262.

[27] Sherwin (n 26) 262; Elizabeth Allen, 'Introduction to the Imaging Process', in *The Manual of Photography*, edited by Elizabeth Allen and Sophie Triantaphillidou (Amsterdam: Elsevier, 2011), 1–18, at 2–3.

[28] Digital video in real-time is comprised of a sequence of 1500–1800 still images per minute; Pu (n 26) 211; Sherwin (n 26) 262.

[29] Compression is the process of reducing data file size using algorithms to reorganize data; Scientific Working Group on Digital Evidence, 'SWGDE Digital Image Compression and File Formats Guidelines' (2016), https://drive.google.com/file/d/1EoT0ZTKtDzahFfyr_2h6uO7UHSBWJIWv/view, 4. Charles Poynton, *Digital Videos and HD: Algorithms and Interface* (Amsterdam: Morgan Kaufman, 2003), 117.

[30] SWGDE (n 29); Poynton (n 29) 117.

dataset without altering the image.[31] When compression is used for non-evidential images, any data loss that does occur may be immaterial. However, when images have probative value, compression that eliminates data is highly problematic. A look at two types of compression, lossless and lossy, is necessary to develop this point.

Image compression is aimed at reducing redundancy in the frequency representation of pixel (picture element) information for the purpose of reducing file size.[32] This is achieved by the use of codecs that examine video images frame-by-frame and remove redundant or irrelevant detail that cannot be perceived by viewers.[33] When this is effected in a lossless manner there is no loss of information and when uncompressed the image retains its original information.[34] Digital video's main compression algorithms tend to be lossy and therein lies the problem.[35] Spatial (intra-frame) compression eliminates redundant pixels within an image, while temporal (inter-frame) compression eliminates redundancies such as repetition or lack of movement among neighbouring frames.[36] With lossy compression, there is a trade-off between the amount of compression achieved and image quality loss.[37] Lossy compression does violence to an image by removing actual content from key or index frames which cannot be recovered in their original form.[38] See Figures 6.1 and 6.2 for illustration. In circumstances where image interpretation is essential, lossy compression is inimical to forensic interests as the first casualty of compression is detail.[39] It is also antithetical to proper forensic imaging which is the process of acquiring a complete and forensically sound copy of digital multimedia files that are intended for evidential use.[40]

The potential impact of compression is dependent upon the purpose for which the images are being used. If images are being tendered to prove the mere presence of a topographical feature, building, vehicle, or group of people, compression may not thwart this broad visual inquiry. However, if the query is focused on the details of a topographical feature, building, vehicle, or group of people, compression will be a nemesis to interpretation and may render the inquiry moot. No amount of computer wizardry and expertise can reveal details that have been lost due to

[31] Allen (n 27) 536.

[32] Tamer Rabie, 'Color-Secure Digital Image Compression', *Multimedia Tools Applications* 76 (2016): 16657–79, at 16659.

[33] 'Codec' refers to compression and decompression algorithms. The aim of the decompression algorithm is to restore the image as close to its original state as possible. Allen (n 27) 537; Edmond, Biber, Kemp, and Porter (n 19) 355; Pu (n 26) 199.

[34] Poynton (n 30) 117; Allen (n 27) 537. The amount of compression achieved in lossless compression is limited given the requirement to reinstate the original image.

[35] Pu (n 26) 198.

[36] ibid 198, 213.

[37] Allen (n 27) 537.

[38] A key or index frame is an image that represents actual content captured by the camera, contrasted with neighbouring images which are predictive of content and created by computer algorithms.

[39] Rabie (n 32) 16658.

[40] ibid.

Figure 6.1 Uncompressed image of bridge. (Jonathan W. Hak (c) 2023)

lossy compression. Aside from data loss, compression can also add digital artefacts, which are visible details that are not part of the original image and whose appearance may cause an uninformed viewer to draw incorrect meaning from the image.[41] For example, viewers may perceive that a person depicted in video images has a weapon in his hand when it might be a compression artefact. There is a paucity of case law about image compression, though it would typically be expected to be a question of weight rather than one of admissibility.[42]

[41] Sophie Triantaphillidou, 'Introduction to Image Quality and System Performance', in *The Manual of Photography*, edited by Elizabeth Allen and Sophie Triantaphillidou (Amsterdam: Elsevier, 2011) 345–63, at 350–1; SWGDE (n 29) 8.

[42] This was the finding in *R. v. Coles*, [2018] EWCA Crim 407. There is no reason to believe that the ICC would treat compression differently.

Figure 6.2 Compressed image of bridge showing loss of image detail. (Jonathan W. Hak (c) 2023)

2.2 Image Resolution

The pixels which give digital images their visual form are the smallest units of information contained therein.[43] Image resolution refers to the amount of spatial detail (pixels) in an image or within a subset of an image.[44] Digital images require a certain number of pixels to show something recognizable by the human visual system.[45] The higher the resolution of an image, the better the quality of the image and the more suitable it will be for interpretation.[46] High-definition images

[43] Hany Farid, *Photo Forensics* (Cambridge, MA: MIT Press, 2016) 320.

[44] John Beaver, *The Physics and Art of Photography, Volume 3: Detectors and the Meaning of Digital* (San Rafael: Morgan and Claypool, 2018), 9.2.

[45] Pu (n 26) 190.

[46] ibid.

accordingly provide more detail than standard-definition images. The ability to display fine detail is dependent upon the number of pixels in an image and the size of the pixels relative to the size of the image.[47]

As valuable as digital imagery can be it nonetheless has data limitations. For example, the ability of digital cameras to record fine detail (resolving power) is often limited because of poor quality optics within the camera and the impact of image compression.[48] Other factors that affect image resolution include incorrect image transcoding, size of the image, pixelization, the distance of the subject from the camera, and recording conditions such as atmosphere, lighting, and movement.[49] Image quality is further affected by tone, colour, sharpness, and image noise (artefacts).[50]

Image resolution is a key feature when striving to obtain details from images. Yet, as remarkable as some forensic image processing techniques are, images cannot yield more information than was recorded by the camera. If viewers primarily rely upon popular media sources to gain visual literacy, they may believe that earth observation satellites can reveal sufficient detail to determine what book a terrorist is reading in a desert camp or that the number plate of a vehicle can be ascertained when the vehicle itself consists of four pixels within an image. The reality is that if the camera did not record an image with sufficiently high resolution, the resultant images may have limited value for ascertaining details though they may offer some value for broader concerns.

2.3 Frame Rate

As noted earlier, digital video consists of a series of single images presented at a suitable frame rate to simulate motion. Real-time video is presented at either twenty-five or thirty frames per second and these frame rates replicate what viewers would observe if seeing the event live.[51] At this frame rate, playback appears generally natural, which allows for reasonable interpretations to be made by visually literate viewers. However, not all cameras record digital video in real-time, either by design or by specified input. When video is recorded at a reduced frame rate, it permits a temporally longer view of an event with reduced file size, especially when coupled with spatial and temporal compression. The problem that arises is that a reduced frame rate results in markedly decreased visual data which can significantly impact

[47] Allen (n 27) 14.

[48] Edmond, Biber, Kemp, and Porter (n 19) 355.

[49] ibid.

[50] Triantaphillidou (n 41) 346–9.

[51] PAL (Phase Alternate Line) is the video format standard used in many European countries and plays at 25 frames per second. NTSC (National Television Standards Committee) is the video format standard used in North America, Japan, and other countries and plays at 29.97 frames per second; Poynton (n 29) 371–9.

the ability of viewers to accurately interpret motion in the images and understand what occurred.[52]

For example, at a frame rate of one image per second, viewers get a snapshot of what occurred on an intermittent basis but are left to guess at what occurred during the 1,475 frames (PAL) or 1,770 frames (NTSC) that would have been recorded per minute in real-time but were not.[53] Reduced frame rate video is particularly troublesome when viewers try to reconcile what they see on video with *viva voce* evidence. A witness may report seeing approximately twenty vehicles pass by a checkpoint, yet a heavily reduced frame rate video may show only five vehicles. Viewers lacking visual literacy may assume that the witness is mistaken, not realizing that the witness may be correct and that the video recording is incomplete having not recorded the entire event.

Reduced frame rate video also makes actions appear unnatural and occasionally more violent than was the case. This can result in viewers misinterpreting the recorded event. A reduced frame rate does not render video evidence inadmissible, but it can impact the meaning that can be drawn from the images and therefore the weight to be attached to the evidence.[54]

2.4 Aspect Ratio

A final consideration in this brief overview is that of the aspect ratio of an image. Aspect ratio refers to the correlation between the width of an image and its height, also known as its proportional representation.[55] A common processing error is the failure to properly calibrate the proportions of an image, resulting in inaccurate images displayed with incorrect dimensions.[56] See Figures 6.3 to 6.5 for illustration.

This becomes an important consideration when seeking to identify topographical features, buildings, vehicles, objects, and people. It further impacts the ability of a forensic imagery expert to conduct a scientific image comparison between questioned and known images because one or both sets of images are inaccurately proportioned.

[52] Dilan Seckiner, Xanthé Mallett, Claude Roux, Didier Meuwly, and Philip Maynard, 'Forensic Image Analysis: CCTV Distortion and Artefacts', *Forensic Science International* 285 (2018): 77–85, at 81.

[53] Only some of these images would be key or index frames as temporal compression would include predictive images.

[54] Frame rate is a higher-level technical issue that has not resulted in many juridical rulings but remains an important interpretive limiter. *R. v. Zoraik*, 2012, CarswellBC 1858, and *R. v. Ferdinand and Others*, [2014] EWCA Crim 1243 assessed frame rate as a question of weight rather than admissibility. I have found no international criminal cases on this point.

[55] Ron Brinkman, *The Art and Science of Digital Compositing* (San Francisco: Morgan Kaufman, 1999), 143–4.

[56] Seckiner, Mallett, Roux, Meuwly, and Maynard (n 52) 78–9.

Figure 6.3 Tower shown with correct aspect ratio. (Photo by Bob van Aubel on Unsplash, 2023)

Figure 6.4 Tower shown with incorrect aspect ratio—too tall. (Photo by Bob van Aubel on Unsplash, 2023; modified by Jonathan W. Hak)

Figure 6.5 Tower shown with incorrect aspect ratio—too wide. (Photo by Bob van Aubel on Unsplash, 2023; modified by Jonathan W. Hak)

3. Courts May Require Interpretive Assistance

Achieving suitable visual literacy requires abandoning the perception that images speak for themselves and that the court is invariably capable of assessing their meaning without guidance. It has been argued that 'I know it when I see it' is the reigning, if not sole, approach to legal visual interpretation.[57] This argument has merit as there is a tendency in the legal community to think that images communicate one correct or predominant interpretation when in fact they may be capable of multiple interpretations. If judges rely on images to decide facts, they must articulate their content interpretation to provide context for their judgment.[58] Reliance upon images will be more defensible and lead to better judgment when the court is afforded the necessary interpretive assistance. It is therefore helpful to explore why the court may require assistance to properly assess images and decide on their meaning.

A common method of presenting video evidence in court is to press play and watch the real-time video en masse in the misguided belief that everyone will perceive the same substantive content and assimilate similar meaning from the images. In this construct where unfounded confidence in image interpretation prevails, video evidence may be misunderstood and misapplied. This occurs in part because viewers bring their own cultural, personal, and experiential biases to

[57] Elizabeth Porter, 'Taking Images Seriously', *Columbia Law Review* 114 (2018): 1687–782, at 1696.

[58] Nancy Marder, 'The Court and the Visual: Images and Artifacts in U.S. Supreme Court Opinions', *Chicago-Kent Law Review* 88, no. 2: (2013): 331–64, at 349, 360–4.

the task of image assessment.[59] Some judges operate under a deeply engrained belief that 'seeing is believing' and that having seen the images, they are quite capable of evaluating their content. Yet judges are no more adept at evaluating images than other types of evidence.[60] Cognitive bias can lead viewers to unconsciously interpret video evidence so as to support their understanding of the event depicted.[61] By doing so, viewers engage in naïve realism, the tendency to identify other people's biases but not their own.[62] The efficiency of conveying information via images includes a tendency by viewers to fill in fragmentary or incomplete images to give them meaning. As a result, viewers assess the meaning of some images oblivious to the need for competent interpretation.[63] Evidence derived from scientific and technologically mediated data does not speak for itself—it requires knowledgeable interpretation to be of meaningful use to the court.[64]

There is a long judicial history of relying upon images to communicate their meaning to the court. A notable domestic example of judges relying upon their own perceived image interpretation skills when assessing the meaning of video evidence is found in the decision of the US Supreme Court in *Scott v. Harris*.[65] In a 8–1 decision that was based in part on the court's interpretation of dashcam video from police vehicles involved in a pursuit, the majority found the video evidence to be dispositive of the issue before them and in a precedent-setting move, the Court posted the video exhibits to its website for public viewing noting, 'We are happy to allow the videotape to speak for itself.'[66] The majority was of the view that the dashcam video showed 'what actually happened', and somehow made the Court an eyewitness to the event.[67] This emboldened the majority to believe that there could be no contrary interpretations and that they were able to assess the facts unaided.[68]

The Court's approach reflects an anchoring cognitive bias wherein a particular piece of evidence achieves dominance, and all other evidence is weighed against it. The fact that the dissenting Justice (and the lower court judges) interpreted the video evidence differently than the majority illustrates that video may say different

59 Denise Barry, 'Snap Judgment: Recognizing the Propriety and Pitfalls of Direct Judicial Review of Audiovisual Evidence at Summary Judgment', *Fordham Law Review* 83, no. 6 (2015): 3343–88, at 3385–6.

60 'The judiciary seems to be not just unaware of their own biases and preferences and the power of video to produce powerful emotional responses, but also its potential malleability.' ibid 3385–3386.

61 Seth Stoughton, 'Police Body-Worn Cameras', *North Carolina Law Review* 96, no. 5 (2018): 1363–1424, at 1406.

62 Richard Sherwin, 'Visual Literacy for the Legal Profession', *Journal of Legal Education* 68, no. 1 (2018): 55–63 at 60.

63 Porter (n 57) 1753–4.

64 Lonneke van der Velden, 'Forensic Devices for Activism: Metadata Tracking and Public Proof', *Big Data & Society* (July-December 2015): 1–14, at 4.

65 *Scott v. Harris*, 127 S.Ct. 1769; 550 U.S. 372 (2007).

66 127 S.Ct. 1775, fn 5.

67 127 S.Ct. 1775; Stoughton (n 61) 1413.

68 Jessica Silbey, 'Cross-Examining Film', *University of Maryland Law Journal of Race, Religion, Gender and Class* 8, no. 1 (2008): 17–46, at 18.

things to different people. Further, it illustrates the point that viewers look through a lens that is formed by their life experiences, social influences, personal values, biases, and perceptions of blameworthiness.[69] It may be that the dissenting Justice employed a more sophisticated visual literacy and recognized that video evidence can be ambiguous and requires interpretation.[70] The majority erred in assuming that the video evidence told the only story available and that no other interpretations were tenable. The judges were not the eyewitnesses they perceived themselves to be. Allowing pictures to speak for themselves does a disservice to the evidence.[71]

At issue is not whether the majority was correct, but rather that they did not appreciate the difficulties endemic in video interpretation, especially the rapid action characteristic of a pursuit. When viewers believe they are correct in their interpretation and that anyone who disagrees is wrong, they engage in cognitive illiberalism, the failure to recognize the relationship between competing factual beliefs and cultural identities.[72] This leads to dissent, both within the courtroom and beyond. *Scott* illustrates that reasonable people can interpret video evidence differently. While we cannot avoid viewers looking at images through their own lens, they must be educated to make more sound, informed assessments by improving the acuity of the lens used. Rather than leaving it to viewers to determine what is shown with limited or no guidance, testimony from an expert who has examined the video evidence and can interpret and narrate it will assist the court to make a more informed judgement, and that is preferable to one borne of limited visual acuity and naïve realism.

International criminal tribunals and courts also wrestle with the interpretation of image-based evidence. A couple of examples follow. In *Prosecutor v. Dordević*, the Chamber received narrated video and photographic evidence describing several deceased victims of crime.[73] The Chamber was satisfied that this evidence could be used for the purpose of identifying the victims. It was also used, amongst other evidence, by an ICC Office of the Prosecutor (OTP) pathologist to comment on the cause of death of several of the victims depicted in the images. The OTP expert was able to discern many visible gunshot injuries to the bodies consistent

[69] Dan Kahan, David Hoffman, and Donald Braman, 'Whose Eyes Are you Going to Believe? Scott v. Harris and the Perils of Cognitive Illiberalism', *Harvard Law Review* 122, no. 3 (2009): 837–906, at 883. Kahan et. al. cautioned against naïve realism, wherein we are adept at finding fault in others for engaging in value-motivated cognition without recognizing that we also form beliefs consistent with our own group commitments (ibid 895).

[70] Mezey (n 7) 26. In William Smith, 'Judicial Opinions and the Digital Revolution', *Judges' Journal* 49, no. 4 (2010): 7–12, the author (a federal judge) viewed *Scott v. Harris* as an endorsement and recognition of the power of visual evidence without noting any of the interpretive challenges involved. This myopic view is troubling and illustrative of the need for visual literacy.

[71] Porter (n 57) 1757. This problem did not start with *Scott*. In *Jacobellis v. Ohio*, 378 U.S. 184, at 197 (1964), Justice Stewart used the image interpretive method 'I know it when I see it'.

[72] Kahan, Hoffman, and Braman (n 69) 843, 896.

[73] IT-05-87/1-T, Judgment, 23 February 2011, para 1412.

with a certain calibre weapon but noted that he could not be certain as he had no scale of reference to measure the wounds. The Chamber limited its reliance on the video evidence to the issue of identification and found that the forensic opinions regarding cause of death were based upon forensic assumptions not supportable by the video evidence alone.[74] Both the OTP expert and the Chamber were aware that the video evidence provided limited data upon which a forensic opinion could be formed and in so doing demonstrated an appreciation of the limited meaning obtainable from the images.

In *Prosecutor v. Lubanga*, the appellant Lubanga argued that it was unreasonable for the Trial Chamber to use video evidence alone to assess the age of individuals for the purpose of determining the presence of child soldiers.[75] At trial, the prosecution chose not to call expert evidence to establish age and instead relied upon lay witnesses, who did not include any family, community, or school witnesses who knew the alleged child soldiers.[76] The Trial Chamber relied upon its own assessment of age from the video evidence rather than the evidence of a lay witness who estimated their ages.[77] The prosecution argued that it was reasonable for the Trial Chamber to conduct this evaluation and had done so cautiously.[78] The Appeals Chamber found that while there was no legal impediment to the Trial Chamber so deciding, the issue was whether the video evidence alone provided a sufficient evidentiary foundation for such a finding.[79]

Relying upon the International Criminal Tribunal for the former Yugoslavia (ICTY) and the International Criminal Tribunal for Rwanda (ICTR) jurisprudence as well as decisions of domestic courts, the prosecution argued that courts can rely upon video evidence because '... the video footage contained therein will usually speak for itself'.[80] The Appeals Chamber agreed that video evidence could be used to establish facts but questioned whether it alone could establish the age of individuals shown in the images.[81] The Appeals Chamber found that the Trial Chamber was aware of the limitations of determining age solely from video and that since it found that only some of the individuals shown were clearly under the age of fifteen, the findings of fact were reasonable.[82] What is unfortunate is that the prosecution perpetuated the belief that images have communicative ability on their own and do not need expert interpretation.

[74] ibid paras. 1413–1416.

[75] ICC-01/04-01/06-3121-Red, Judgment on Appeal, 1 December 2014.

[76] ibid para. 187. The Trial Chamber invited both parties to call expert evidence on the appearance of age yet neither party chose to do so (ibid para. 212).

[77] ibid paras. 188–191.

[78] ibid para. 216.

[79] ibid paras. 218–219.

[80] ibid para. 219; citing *Prosecutor v. Lubanga*, ICC-01/04-01/06-2969-Red, Prosecutor's Response to Thomas Lubanga's Appeal Against Trial Chamber I's Judgment Pursuant to Article 74, 18 February 2013, para. 162.

[81] ibid para. 219.

[82] ibid paras. 222–223.

Though the findings of age by the Trial Chamber were found to be reasonable, the prosecution should have done more to support those findings.[83] The Chamber invited expert interpretation, indicative of a desire to improve its visual literacy, yet counsel declined the invitation, presumably finding it unnecessary. In this case, suitably qualified expert interpretation of the image content (the age of the soldiers) would have been valuable. While judges can make factual findings based upon their unassisted interpretation of video evidence, counsel would be well advised to provide interpretive evidence from a knowledgeable expert instead of relying upon the mantra that images speak for themselves. In short, counsel needs to do the interpretive work with supplemental evidence rather than rely on video images to communicate meaning on their own.

These brief examples reflect a commonly held misconception that images possess inherent reliability and communicative efficiency, and that sound conclusions can be drawn from them without any form of scientific evaluation or interpretation.[84] Depending upon its content and the purpose for which the evidence is being used, image-based evidence may require expert explanation and interpretive assistance for the court and counsel to fully understand it.

There is a misguided tendency to regard the camera, rather than the photographer, as the witness, effectively placing viewers in the position of witness. This was exemplified in *Scott v. Harris* when the majority decided that they were fully capable of interpreting the video evidence as pseudo-witnesses, unaided by testimonial evidence. This is reflective of the naïveté and over-confidence many viewers exhibit when they disavow the need for interpretive assistance or evidential corroboration. This can be dangerous territory as interpretive errors may set the stage for erroneous findings of fact and potential miscarriages of justice. Counsel and the court must be aware that there is more to understanding and critically interpreting images than just viewing them.[85] This in turn requires a measure of humility and acceptance that merely viewing images may not suffice and that expert interpretive assistance would be beneficial. The evidence within images can be of great value if viewers know how to cross examine them.[86] It would therefore be wise to treat

[83] Video and photographic images must be carefully considered for suitability when being used as the main method of proving apparent age as there has been little scientific study on the relationship between apparent age and actual age. See Moa Lidén, 'Child Soldier or Soldier? Estimating Age in Cases of Core International Crimes: Challenges and Opportunities', in *Quality Control in Criminal Investigation*, edited by Xabier Agirre, Morten Bergsmo, Simon De Smet, and Carsten Stahn (Brussels: Torkel Opsahl Academic EPublisher, 2020), 323–460, at 387.

[84] Elénore Ryser, Hannes Spichiger, and Eoghan Casey, 'Structured Decision Making in Investigations Involving Digital and Multimedia Evidence', *Forensic Science International: Digital Investigation* 34, no. 301015 (2020): 1–10, at 1.

[85] Sherwin (n 62) 61; Lisanne van Weelden and Tessa van Charldorp, 'Communications Perspective on the Use of Visualisations in Dutch Court for Minor Felonies', *Utrecht Law Review* 15, no. 1 (2019): 26–37,.

[86] Citing art critic John Ruskin, in at 31–3Peter Burke, *Eyewitnessing: The Use of Images as Historical Evidence* (London: Reaktion Books, 2019), 30.

images in court as being akin to *viva voce* evidence, requiring examination and context, rather than as speaking for themselves.[87] They may need to be cross examined as to their truth, accuracy, and reliability.[88]

Improving the visual literacy of counsel and the court is essential to form sound, informed judgements about images.[89] Visual literacy includes the ability to understand how images are constructed and how to fairly assess and utilize their content in an advocacy context.[90] It also includes knowledge of how images can be modified and presented and the type of expertise required to properly understand their content.[91] Greater visual literacy should lead to more informed interpretation and judgement as to what images fairly mean.[92] Without sophisticated visual literacy, not only might the court misinterpret the evidence, it may be wrongly influenced by partisan interpretations of the images.[93] If neither counsel nor the court understands the technical and interpretive issues that impact image accuracy and reliability when assessing the meaning of images, the risk of erroneous judgement, the failure to find the truth, and unjust outcomes are not just extant but palpable.[94]

The selection, preparation, and presentation of evidence at trial is primarily the role of counsel. When presenting image-based evidence in court, counsel must also assess whether expert assistance is required for the court to fairly understand and evaluate its meaning. While counsel may have spent considerable time extracting meaning from images, the court has not had that luxury. The court must therefore be given time to examine the images and when necessary it should be provided with expert interpretive assistance to do justice to the evidence.[95] The more complex the images, the more time and interpretive assistance are required. When counsel fail to appreciate that image interpretation is a prerequisite to meaningful comprehension, they are less likely to secure interpretive assistance for the court and this failure perpetuates the risk of misinterpretation and errors in judgement. Counsel should resist their instinct to believe that their perception is omniscient when interpreting image-based evidence and seek qualified assistance. Forensic expertise can be utilized to provide such assistance, leading to a more informed and balanced assessment of image-based evidence.

[87] Silbey (n 10) 1290.
[88] Silbey (n 68) 26.
[89] Barry (n 59) 3386.
[90] Sherwin (n 62) 55–63.
[91] Ticien Sassoubre, 'Visual Persuasion for Lawyers', *Journal of Legal Education* 68, no. 1 (2018): 82–91, at 84–5.
[92] Richard Sherwin, 'Visual Jurisprudence', *New York Law School Law Review* 57, no. 1 (2012): 11–40, at 36.
[93] Francis Mootz, 'Law Among the Sight Lovers', *New York Law School Law Review* 57, no. 1 (2012): 61–76, at 63–7.
[94] 'If the legal profession remains visually illiterate and fails to appreciate the many ways images speak, as well as the limitations of what those images can say, it risks sacrificing the crucial role of the law in interpretation, judgment, and justice.' Mezey (n 7) 7.
[95] Spiesel (n 20) 13–14.

4. The Case for Expert Assistance with Image Interpretation

Judges typically do not have scientific training or specialized technical knowledge and are not expected to form independent opinions on matters of science, including forensic science.[96] Many aspects of international criminal litigation are complex, and the court may require expert assistance to correctly find the facts and from them, form a correct judgement. To assist the court in this regard, judges rely upon qualified experts who can provide expert analysis and testimony that will inform judicial decision-making.[97] The role of the expert witness is as pivotal in the pursuit of truth as that of counsel.[98] The importance of expert image interpretation for some image-based evidence cannot be understated.

Image-based evidence must be evaluated for reliability and interpretative meaning to arrive at an informed judgement about its content. Depending on the complexity of the images, the court may be able to undertake this assessment on its own, perhaps coupled with the submissions of counsel, but there will be many cases where the court will benefit from the assistance of a properly trained expert who can technically interrogate the images, evaluate their content, and advise as to what meaning can fairly be drawn from them. The expert can also advise the court regarding image features that limit their interpretive parameters.[99] Absent expert assistance, the court would otherwise be left to conduct its own superficial evaluation.[100] The interests of justice are not served when judges are tasked with discerning image content with minimal or no assistance from expert witnesses. When that occurs, counsel has failed in their responsibility to assist the court.

Forensic analysis of an image requires that the image be confronted by someone with the skills necessary to dissect and reconstruct the image to maximize its evidential value. The result may be an appreciation of the image's true import, far different from that initially held by counsel and the court. Even seemingly benign images can deceive viewers and must be robustly confronted.[101] Forensic video analysis is defined as the scientific examination, comparison, and/or evaluation of video in legal matters.[102] This can be a robust process wherein rather than briefly

[96] Forensic science is not a discrete scientific discipline but rather the application of a broad range of sciences and technical knowledge to legal proceedings. Melanie Klinkner, 'Forensic Science Expertise for International Criminal Proceedings: An Old Problem, a New Context and a Pragmatic Resolution', *The International Journal of Evidence and Proof* 13 (2009): 102–29, at 105.

[97] Artur Appazov, *Expert Evidence and International Criminal Justice* (Switzerland: Springer International Publishing, 2016), 4.

[98] Roger Derham and Nicole Derham, 'From Ad Hoc to Hybrid—The Rules and Regulations Governing the Reception of Expert Evidence at the International Criminal Court', *The International Journal of Evidence & Proof* 14 (2010): 25–56, at 54.

[99] 'International Bar Association Report', *IBA ICL Perspectives: Evidence Matters in ICC Trials* (August 2016) https://www.ibanet.org/document?id=Evidence-matters-in-icc-trials, 20.

[100] Mezey (n 7) 16.

[101] Sherwin (n 92) 18.

[102] Scientific Working Group on Digital Evidence, 'SWGDE Best Practices for Digital Forensic Video Analysis' (2018) https://drive.google.com/file/d/1vXMav2QS8N5iiC7UcW6ZoTsH0OHI7FQi/view, 4. Though aimed at video evidence, this definition also applies to single image analysis.

viewing images and assessing their meaning, an expert may spend many hours interrogating the technical content of images as part of the interpretive process. Expert analysis and image processing may bring out details not otherwise noted and provide a level of understanding unachievable without advanced technical visual literacy, thereby allowing counsel and the court to form informed and rational judgements.

When there are no live witnesses to provide image context and assist with interpretation, understanding the true nature of images and their meaning takes on increased importance. Expert analysis at the pixel level may be necessary for proper interpretation.[103] Looking at an image holistically may provide context and meaning, but since images are a conglomeration of many constituent elements, detailed analysis of those elements may yield additional information, including identification of locations, people and objects, details of movement, the presence of a weapon, infliction of injury, etc.

Drawing meaning from semi-legible images is even more challenging and requires effort and expertise to understand them. By their very nature, semi-legible images may offer multiple inconsistent, though somewhat bounded meanings. Legibility falls within a spectrum ranging from virtually meaningless to images that provide considerable detail and meaning.[104] While lay viewers would be unlikely to interpret DNA profiles, fingerprints, x-rays, and fMRIs images, they may be emboldened to interpret photographs and video images, and thereby claim an innate ability to do so, blissfully unaware of the complexities that may be involved.

Legibility is also dependent upon image context, viewer acuity, and the questions that are asked of the images.[105] Satellite images, for example, requires the assistance of an expert who is able to analyse and interpret the data for the court.[106] Questioning whether a military vehicle was present in a satellite image at a given time and location is different from determining the type of weapon mounted on it. The image may be quite legible for the first inquiry and of limited value for the second due to such image quality issues as lack of resolution, compression, and distance from the camera. The *Leiden Guidelines on the Use of Digitally Derived Evidence in International Criminal Courts and Tribunals* (*Leiden Guidelines*) also provide helpful guidance on the need for expert interpretation of satellite images.[107]

[103] Haldar (n 8) 140, 151.

[104] Even images at the high end of the spectrum still require interpretation. Mnookin (n 1) 51.

[105] Mnookin (n 1) 51–2.

[106] Ben Wang, Nathaniel Raymond, Gabrielle Gould, and Isaac Baker, 'Problems from Hell, Solution in the Heavens?: Identifying Obstacles and Opportunities for Employing Geospatial Technologies to Document and Mitigate Mass Atrocities', *Stability: International Journal of Security & Development* 2, no. 3 (2013), 1–18, at 9–10; Theresa Harris, Jonathan Drake, Jessica Wyndham, Susan Wolfinbarger, Stephen Lott, and Michael Lerner, 'Geospatial Evidence in International Human Rights Litigation: Technical and Legal Considerations', *AAAS Scientific Responsibility, Human Rights and Law Program* (2018) doi: 10.1126/srhrl.aau6090, 11.

[107] Kalshoven-Gieskes Forum on International Humanitarian Law, 'Leiden Guidelines on the Use of Digitally Derived Evidence in International Criminal Courts and Tribunals' (March 2022) https://leiden-guidelines.com/guidelines/. The *Leiden Guidelines* are discussed in more detail in Chapter 9.

4.1 Image Processing and Analysis Techniques

A forensic imagery expert can assist counsel and the court by thoroughly interrogating the images at a technical level and can thereafter interpret them for their discernible meaning and present the evidence so that counsel and the court can make informed judgements about their content. Examples of forensic image processing techniques and analytical work that can be performed by an imagery expert include the following:

4.1.1 Playing Video Recordings Frame-by-Frame

The ability to evaluate video images frame-by-frame (image-by-image) can set the stage for a more detailed assessment of image content and meaning. Utilizing computer software that plays video recordings without the corresponding ability to advance or reverse frame-by-frame deprives viewers of the ability to examine individual images and movement in detail. Frame-by-frame playback also takes out some of the emotionally charged impact endemic in motion video and allows for viewers to assess content more clinically.

4.1.2 Clarifying Image Content

Using forensically appropriate software, experts can clarify the content of some images by adjusting brightness, contrast, and other levels. Clarifying images does not create new content, but rather reveals content already present, much like turning on the light in a darkened room allows viewers to see extant detail more clearly. Frame-averaging, whereby the best qualities of neighbouring images are incorporated into a clarified image, can also be used to reduce image noise (artefacts) and the clarified content can be digitally highlighted to focus viewer attention.

4.1.3 Interpreting Images Considering the Impact of Compression

As noted in Section 2.1, temporal and spatial lossy compression not only change the content of an image through the elimination of redundancies, but it also adds artefacts via predictive algorithms. Expert analysis can assist viewers to understand what parts of an image are reliable notwithstanding the impact of compression and what parts should be disregarded when assessing content, thereby leading to a more informed judgement of image content.

4.1.4 Motion Stabilization

It is difficult to focus on image content and activity within a scene when the video camera that recorded the event was in constant motion. This interpretive problem is common as civilian documentarians are often in danger and therefore in motion when recording active conflict. Image stabilization allows for defined areas within successive images to remain stable while other portions are in motion, allowing for more meaningful evaluation of key content areas.

4.1.5 Motion Tracking

Some video recorded scenes are dynamic and involve significant movement of vehicles, individuals, and objects, and it can therefore be difficult to isolate and follow the movement of individual targets. Motion tracking, which digitally affixes a line, arrow, circle, alphanumeric code, or spotlight to individual targets in the image allows viewers to follow targets continuously throughout the movement. Through this method, viewers are better able to grasp the movement of individual targets within the larger visual palette, while the existing image content remains intact.

4.1.6 Synchronizing Multiple Video Sources

Some scenes are recorded by more than one camera at varying times and from different perspectives. Experts can produce an overhead view of a scene indicating the location of each camera and its field of view to orient viewers to each source. Then each video can be synchronized and played in a single timeline which allows for a forensically sound multi-perspectival view. Camera views can also be played in a split screen format to see an event from two perspectives at once. These methods are more helpful to viewers than watching independent videos unaware of their interrelationship.

4.1.7 Synchronizing Video and Audio Tracks

Not all video recordings have an audio track. Experts may be able to synchronize video and audio files from different recordings to produce a cohesive, informative multimedia portrayal of what was diversely recorded. Accurately syncing audio tracks with reduced frame rate video is more complex but may be feasible depending upon the quality and complexity of the recordings.

4.1.8 Image Comparison and Contrast

Forensic image comparison is defined by the Scientific Working Group on Digital Evidence (SWGDE) as 'an assessment of the correspondence between features in questioned items depicted in images and either questioned or known objects or images for the purpose of rendering an expert opinion regarding identification or elimination (as opposed to a demonstrative exhibit)'.[108] Using this forensic process, imagery experts can undertake a detailed scientific comparison and contrast between questioned and known images of topography, buildings, vehicles, objects, and people to assist with identification. Experts may face restrictions as to whether they can offer an evaluative opinion on identification depending on the subject matter, jurisdiction, and their individual qualifications. For example, the UK Forensic Science Regulator (FSR) issued guidance in 2019 requiring that

[108] Scientific Working Group on Digital Evidence, 'SWGDE Technical Overview for Forensic Image Comparison' (2019) https://drive.google.com/file/d/1m7WO40YJld7i4Aue4JmsHW7OBsN5Bl9r/view, 4.

imagery experts be both technical and subject matter experts to provide an evaluative opinion on identification.[109]

The scientific position espoused by the FSR has merit but does not necessarily reflect case law in the UK, which has ruled such evidence to be admissible even in the absence of expertise in the subject matter being compared.[110] Similar rulings have been made by courts in Canada and the US.[111] In 2021, the FSR mandated that evaluative opinions of multimedia evidence follow an evaluative protocol yet to be developed.[112] I have not found any similar restrictions imposed by international criminal tribunals and courts.

4.1.9 Annotations and Digital Graphics

To better understand image content, an expert can supplement images with digital annotations and graphics. These digital additions may take the form of words, lines, arrows, circles, etc. and are designed to focus viewer attention on certain aspects of images that the expert and counsel wish to highlight, while preserving overall image content.

4.1.10 Narration of Image-Based Evidence

Because images do not necessarily speak for themselves, in addition to the forensic work an imagery expert can undertake to assist counsel and the court, the expert can also narrate the images as they are presented in court. The purpose of the narration is to explain relevant technical issues and to fully explain what is depicted. The expert will have spent many hours examining the images and is in a superior position to that of counsel and the court to convey image content.

4.1.11 Assessing Image Authentication

Image authentication is an essential prerequisite to a court being able to assign any weight to image-based evidence. The role of the expert in this critical area is explored in Chapter 7.

[109] 'FSR Regulatory Notice' (January 2019) https://assets.publishing.service.gov.uk/government/uploads/system/uploads/attachment_data/file/883281/Regulatory_notice_2019.01_-_Imaging__2_.pdf.

[110] See e.g. *Attorney General's Reference (No. 2 of 2002)*, [2002] EWCA 2373; *Coles* (n 42). On this topic, see Jonathan Hak, 'Evaluation of the Forensic Science Regulator's Recommendations Regarding Image Comparison Evidence', *Forensic Science International: Synergy* 1 (2019): 294–7; Gillian Tully and Michael Stockdale, 'Commentary on: Hak. Evaluation of the Forensic Science Regulator's Recommendations Regarding Image Comparison Evidence', *Forensic Science International: Synergy* 1 (2019): 298–301; Jonathan Hak, 'Response to "Commentary on: Hak. Evaluation of the Forensic Science Regulator's Recommendations Regarding Image Comparison Evidence"'. *Forensic Science International: Synergy* 1 (2019): 302.

[111] Case citations for some of these cases appear in Hak, Evaluation (n 110) 152.

[112] The new protocol for evaluative opinions is to be in place no later than October 2026; 'FSR Codes of Practice and Conduct: Development of Evaluative Opinions', FSR-C-118 (2021) https://assets.publishing.service.gov.uk/government/uploads/system/uploads/attachment_data/file/960051/FSR-C-118_Interpretation_Appendix_Issue_1__002_.pdf.

4.1.12 Determining Image Reliability

As discussed in Chapter 5, assessing image reliability is a task for which counsel and the court typically need expert assistance. Forensic imagery experts can interrogate the metadata of images and their overall visual integrity for the purpose of advising the court on the reliability of the evidence being presented. This is not a task for the lay person.

4.1.13 Speed and Height Estimation

Though less likely to be used in atrocity crime prosecutions, in certain circumstances imagery experts may be able to estimate the speed of moving vehicles and objects shown in video recordings and using photogrammetry may be able to estimate the height of people and other items of interest.

4.2 Truth Discovered

The purpose of providing expert assistance is not to train counsel and the court to be experts themselves but rather to equip them to make sounder judgements about the meaning of images. It is the function of counsel and the expert witness to provide robust, objective, and scientifically reliable evidence to the court. Concordant with that duty is the obligation to not overdrive images by attempting to draw more meaning from them than is warranted, and to state any qualifications or limitations to the expert's analysis and conclusions. The role of the expert is not necessarily to give the court the 'answer' but rather to educate the court as to the content and meaning of image-based evidence and set out parameters for reasonable interpretative conclusions.

Acknowledging that truth discovered can be more powerful than truth told, leading the court to the door of discovery with the necessary tools and knowledge to fairly judge images can be rather impactful. Further, cross examination of the forensic expert and the utilization of opposing experts when advisable are central to fully testing the processing, analysis, and interpretation of images. The court must sort through sometimes conflicting information and make determinations of fact where possible. By allowing testimony based on evidence-based research, peer review, and professional credentials, the law becomes more responsive to reason. Expert assistance is thus more likely to contribute scientifically valid truths and aid in the overall assessment of image-based evidence.[113]

[113] David Tait, 'Rethinking the Role of the Image in Justice: Visual Evidence and Science in the Trial Process', *Law, Probability and Risk* 6, no. 1–4 (2007): 311–18, at 313.

5. Applying the Spectrum Approach

Because images contemplated for use in atrocity crime prosecutions may present reliability and interpretive challenges, counsel will generally benefit from an assessment of the proposed evidence by a forensic imagery expert. Using the spectrum approach, images at the low end of the spectrum should be assessed for technical soundness. The purpose of this assessment is to determine whether the images are genuine, whether there is any evidence of editing or questionable alteration, and whether any image processing is necessary. Absent any technical issues arising, images at the low end of the spectrum can be introduced at trial with the requisite contextual information (the 5 Ws) and without the need for expert testimony. At the high end of the spectrum are images that require expert interrogation, interpretation, and narration. Further, some of the analytical methodology set out in Section 5.1 may need to be employed to maximize the interpretive value of the images. Failure to do so may mean that the information the images have to offer may not be fully realized.

An example of image-based evidence at the low end of the spectrum is the filmic evidence led during the Nuremberg trial. Assistant trial counsel James Donovan said, '[T]hese motion pictures speak for themselves in evidencing life and death in Nazi concentration camps . . .'[114] While I disagree with the proposition that pictures speak for themselves, it is true that films such as *Nazi Concentration Camps* would have only needed limited contextual evidence for their meaning to be adequately conveyed to the court. This was accomplished by an unnamed and unseen narrator in the film who briefly described certain aspects of what was depicted, supplemented with some image annotations and commentary from some of the people shown in the film. Competent, knowledgeable narration is a necessary adjunct to most image-based evidence as it assists in securing informed meaning from the images.[115] The brief narration that accompanied the images informed viewers of important references regarding locations and the people shown. The sparing use of narration helped to adequately tease meaning from the images.

The first view of extreme images like those in *Nazi Concentration Camps* is the most offensive, even to a mind prepared for them. Having moved past the initial viewing, it becomes less sacrilegious to critically examine images for structure and meaning.[116] After the initial voyeuristic views of disturbing crime scenes and

[114] Lawrence Douglas, 'Film as Witness: Screening Nazi Concentration Camps Before the Nuremberg Tribunal', *Yale Law Journal* 105, no. 2 (1995): 449–82, at 452.

[115] As Douglas states, '. . . the narration does not simply strengthen the verisimilitude of the image; on the contrary, the voice of the commentary comes ultimately to assert control over the film's images'. ibid 473. Douglas further notes at that '. . . in a trial, even evidence that claims to speak for itself of atrocity ultimately must be spoken for. The legal meaning of such evidence must be secured even as what it shows cannot be denied'. (ibid 481) Douglas's point is sound as interpretation is an essential precondition to understanding.

[116] ibid 465.

other images, sophisticated viewers are able to clinically assess the images with decreased visceral affront. Epistemically, showing moving images to the court without effective narration does a disservice to the images. It assumes an interpretive ability likely not possessed by viewers, let alone one equally possessed by all viewers. Further, it risks a disconnect between what the images show and what unassisted viewers perceives them to show. Counsel for the Nuremberg prosecution understood this and provided the necessary interpretive assistance to aid the court and thus the images had the power to communicate their meaning without supplemental expert interpretation, which would have been superfluous from an interpretive perspective.

An important factor in making this determination is the purpose for which the film was tendered before the IMT. Since it was intended to provide a visual overview of Nazi atrocities, little more than narration was required. Similarly, films produced by the Nazis required only limited narration to provide context. The meaning of the images, once narratively contextualized, was sufficiently apparent. Had the purpose of any of the filmic evidence presented been to identify locations, people, or objects, knowledgeable (and perhaps expert) interpretation would have been required as detailed examination of image content would be involved.

When more is expected of images than simply showing a scene or event, expert interpretation may be necessary. For example, in the *Ayyash* et al. case, once contextualized as to location and time, images of former Prime Minister Hariri in meetings at Parliament during the morning and leaving the café immediately before the explosion required no interpretation to understand their meaning.[117] Little was asked of the images. Images of the blast area and broader environs, overall scene images, and convoy route images required explanation by knowledgeable witnesses as those images did not speak for themselves. Though extensive interpretive assistance was not required, some explanation was necessary, and the prosecution accomplished this primarily through investigators providing *viva voce* evidence. To interpret the specific meaning of image content such as the size of the blast crater, damage to buildings, vehicles, and other objects, technical equipment in convoy vehicles, and discerning human remains among the debris, expert interpretation was required. The Chamber could not comprehend that level of detail without expert assistance. To accomplish this, the prosecution called several experts to explain relevant image content and its significance. Similarly, CCTV images of the explosive-laden truck as it approached the blast site needed to be linked to vehicle parts found at the site. Expert evidence was called for that purpose.

Though not an international criminal prosecution, the *Ayyash* et al. case is a helpful reference as prosecution counsel displayed a sophisticated visual literacy in their use of the video and photographic evidence. The image-based evidence

[117] (n 6).

occupied places along the entire length of the interpretive spectrum. Some of the images required only contextual introduction as to location and timing, some required more detailed investigator narration, while others needed expert interpretation to understand the full meaning of what was shown. The prosecution applied a thoughtful differentiated approach depending upon the purpose for which the images were being used. This was helpful to all counsel and the Chamber in searching for the truth in the case.

An example of a case at the high end of the spectrum where expert image analysis and interpretation was required, though not utilized, is *Prosecutor v. Gbagbo and Blé Goudé*.[118] By way of background on the image-based evidence issue, the prosecution alleged that a FDS convoy intentionally fired upon peaceful female anti-Gbagbo demonstrators in Abobo, killing and injuring several of them.[119] The evidential issue that arose was establishing who fired the shots that hit the victims as there was no direct evidence on this point. Expert ballistics analysis of bystander recorded video of the event identified the audio trace of twenty-seven shots being fired within less than ninety seconds, ten believed to be from a heavy calibre weapon, and the remaining seventeen from a different or lighter calibre weapons.[120] The first three shots were likely attributed to one of the two machine guns mounted on the turret of the BTR-80 that was visible in the video.[121]

After those initial shots, panic broke out and the camera moved rapidly and haphazardly as the photographer likely feared being shot. As Judge Henderson noted, it was thereafter impossible to establish the source of the subsequent shots. Unless the victims were hit by the first three shots, believed to emanate from the BTR-80, it was not known who was responsible for their deaths and injuries.[122] It was noted that the first observation of a fallen victim appeared approximately one minute after the gunfire began. Viewing the video recording in its native format made it very difficult to comprehend what was depicted because of significant camera movement. Owing to the poor quality of the video recording, it was difficult to ascertain where the turret-mounted guns were aimed.[123] It was not possible to determine based on available evidence that the soldiers in the BTR-80 or any other vehicles in the convoy caused the deaths and injuries.[124]

[118] ICC-02/11-01/15-1263, Reasons for Oral Decision of 15 January 2019, 16 July 2019.

[119] Reasons of Judge Henderson, ICC-02/11-01/15-1263-Conf-AnxB, 16 July 2019, para. 1773.

[120] ibid para. 1775. According to the expert, the first three bursts of gunfire occurred within seven seconds, followed by a pause of approximately forty seconds before the next series of shots were fired. By that time, the convoy had already passed the location where the demonstrators were located. According to the Chamber, it could not be determined whether the latter shots caused any of the deaths and injuries (para. 1785).

[121] The BTR-80 is a Russian-built armoured personnel carrier.

[122] Reasons of Judge Henderson (n 119) paras. 1775–1776.

[123] ibid para. 1779.

[124] ibid para. 1787. The Prosecutor appealed this assessment of the Abobo evidence, and in its decision upholding the acquittals the Appeals Chamber was very critical of the prosecution's categorization of this as an error of law. The Chamber did not overturn this finding; ICC-02/11-01/15-1400 01-04-2021 1/166 SL A, Judgment in the Appeal of the Prosecutor Against Trial Chamber I's Decision

An OTP expert primarily trained in ballistics was instructed to analyse the video evidence and to prepare a report of his findings. While the expert opined as to the number of shots heard on the recording during a certain period, it was evident from his testimony that the video recording had not been subjected to analysis by a forensic imagery expert.[125] Therefore, the Chamber was largely left to its own devices to interpret the video evidence and was not favoured with an expert technical analysis of the images.[126] In Judge Tarfusser's concurring opinion, he was critical of the OTP investigation and the prosecution's presentation of evidence at trial.[127] Regarding the video evidence of the Abobo killings, he noted that the OTP expert presented little more than panoramic views of the scene, implying that no helpful analysis had been undertaken.[128]

Presenting panoramic views of a crime scene when the video evidence is central to determining what happened is woefully insufficient. Given that the civilian *viva voce* evidence was contradictory and insufficient to prove the allegations, the video evidence was of critical importance.[129] A forensic imagery expert should have been instructed to engage in a thorough interrogation, interpretation, and analysis of the video evidence. Determining the number of gunshots from video recordings is fraught with uncertainty as video frame rates interfere with audio track syncing. Further, the video evidence in this case was difficult to observe because the camera was in constant motion.[130] Utilizing image stabilization techniques to focus on the area of interest would have allowed for more meaningful interpretation. Thereafter, the ballistics expert would have been in a better position to assess the number of shots heard on the recording. Instructing only the ballistics expert to analyse the recording did not do the evidence justice.

Gbagbo and Blé Goudé struck a blow to the OTP as the Trial Chamber acquitted the defendants of all charges against them and was critical of the conduct of the prosecution and some of the evidence they presented.[131] Proper interpretation of the video evidence would not likely have led to a different result in the case as there were ample other problems with the prosecution's case, but it would have provided the Chamber with a truer sense of the prosecution narrative and what

on the No Case to Answer Motions, 31 March 2021. See also Concurring Opinion of Judge Eboe-Osuji, ICC-02/11-01/15-1400-Anx1-Corr-Red 09-04-2021 1/134 SL A, paras. 226–30.

[125] Transcript of the evidence of OTP Criminalistics Expert CIV-OTP-P-0583, ICC-02/11-01/15-T-185-Red2-ENG, 4 September 2017; ICC-02/11-01/15-T-186-Red2-ENG, 5 September 2017. At p. 36 of the 4 September 2017 transcript, the OTP expert said, 'I am not a signal processing expert, nor am I an audio expert.' And at p. 71, the expert said, '... I'm a criminalistics expert'.

[126] Reasons of Judge Henderson (n 119) paras. 1775–87.

[127] ICC-02/11-01/15-1263-AnxA, 16 July 2019, Reasons of Judge Tarfusser.

[128] ibid para. 31.

[129] Reasons of Judge Henderson (n 119) paras. 1778–1785.

[130] 'Subsequent to these three shots, panic breaks out and the camera swings around violently.' Reasons of Judge Henderson (n 119) para. 1775.

[131] The Appeals Chamber upheld the acquittals (n 124).

occurred regarding the convoy and the demonstrators. In short, the video evidence had more to offer but the Chamber did not have the benefit of this knowledge. The prosecution's approach showed a failure to appreciate the complexity of the evidence and the need to engage properly qualified experts to assist the Chamber.

The approaches taken in these highlighted cases illustrate the important role that counsel have when assessing image-based evidence and how to maximize its value for presentation in court. These three cases were chosen for exposition because they occupy different positions on the spectrum of the need for expert image interpretation. More cases can be cited but space limitations curtail that inclusion. Counsel must achieve a robust visual literacy to ensure that they understand the benefits and challenges of the evidence available to them. This includes seeking the input of appropriate experts and where necessary the presentation of expert evidence at trial. These are vital steps in the truth discovery process.

Conclusion

Images are not sentient—any meaning drawn from them is dependent upon the knowledge and skill of viewers when interpreting them rather than any mystical conveyance of essence by the images. In cases involving image-based evidence, an assessment must be made as to the context in which the images were created and the purposes for which they are being tendered. The exploration of the five Ws is necessary to gain a contextual framework for images, which in turn is a gateway to understanding them.

Properly interpreted and presented legible and semi-legible image-based evidence can be very powerful. Yet irrespective of the knowledge and expertise of viewers, and the assistance of experts, some images will remain semi-legible and of limited value and the court must be very cautious in drawing any conclusions based upon them. In other cases, the details contained within images, properly interpreted, may bring to light aspects of the event that might otherwise be imperceptible to the untrained eye.[132] The value of expert interpretation is that it can assist the court in understanding the parameters of what content images can fairly deliver. It must also be acknowledged that forensic imagery expertise is not a panacea. If the images lack resolution, are heavily compressed, lack metadata, and suffer from other image frailties, there may be little that can be done to extract meaningful content. Details that were never recorded or have been ill-affected by technical complications and limitations cannot be created or resurrected. Still, there is value in knowing what images cannot offer as well as what they can.

[132] Haldar (n 8) 149.

Image comprehension is not an innate skill that all viewers possess—the complexities of images may require technical and scientific assistance to make sound judgements. Educating counsel and the court is essential to raise the level of visual literacy in the courtroom so that they can arrive at sound, informed decisions about image-based evidence.[133] Assessing the reliability and meaning of images requires that viewers possess sufficient visual literacy to understand what is being shown and awareness of the need to seek interpretive assistance from knowledgeable people, expert or otherwise. Only then can meaning be fairly obtained from image-based evidence. Naïveté and misperceived visual literacy may cause viewers to misinterpret images and elevate the risk of errors in fact-finding and judgement and the risk of a miscarriage of justice.

[133] Barry (n 59) 3386.

7
The Authentication of Image-Based Evidence

Introduction

Criminal prosecutions are premised upon the presentation, evaluation, critique, and judgement of evidence. Irrespective of the eloquence of counsel, there must be cogent proof that tendered evidence is authentic for the court to rely upon it. Authentication focuses on whether the evidence is what the proponent claims it to be and whether it is reliable, meaning whether the evidence can be trusted to be used for the purposes intended by counsel. In short, the query centres on what use can fairly be made of tendered evidence at trial. This longstanding authentication requirement applies to all types of evidence though the focus of this chapter is on image-based evidence.

Authentication is not an esoteric topic, nor a mere technicality. Counsel must give due consideration to the question of authentication when contemplating the introduction of image-based evidence. To achieve a just and fair result, courts must be satisfied upon the presentation of adequate proof that the evidence presented and relied upon by counsel in final argument is authentic. Ascertainment of the truth requires nothing less. Authentication is a particularly relevant consideration for digital images and video recordings as they can be easily manipulated.[1] Image alteration no longer depends upon sophisticated, technically adept individuals with state-of-the-art equipment. Commercially available hardware and software provide opportunities for many users to alter digital images in ways that make detection challenging.[2] Viewers frequently do not possess sufficient visual literacy to meaningfully question the authenticity of images and even literate viewers have difficulty detecting cleverly altered digital images.[3] The increasing use of deepfake videos renders this problem even more acute as it may be very difficult to discern

[1] There is ample support for this proposition, e.g. Aida Ashouri, Caleb Bowers, and Cherrie Warden, 'The 2013 Salzburg Workshop on Cyber Investigations: An Overview of the Use of Digital Evidence in International Criminal Courts', *Digital Evidence and Electronic Signature Law Review* 11 (2013): 115–27; Hany Farid, *Photo Forensics* (Cambridge, MA: MIT Press, 2017), 1–3.

[2] Omar Al-Sanjary, Ahmed Ahmed, and Ghazali Sulong, 'Development of a Video Tampering Dataset for Forensic Investigation', *Forensic Science International* 266 (2016): 565–72, at 565–6.

[3] Hany Farid, 'Digital Doctoring: How to Tell the Real from the Fake', *Significance* (December 2006): 162–6.

Image-Based Evidence in International Criminal Prosecutions. Jonathan W. Hak, KC, Oxford University Press.
 DOI: 10.1093/oso/9780198889533.003.0007

real videos from deepfake imposters.[4] Understanding how digital images can be altered and various methods by which those alterations might be detected is part of developing visual literacy.

The legal approach for the authentication of image-based evidence is also a critical consideration. Domestic courts have had a longer history dealing with this topic and much can be learned from how selected courts have grappled with this evidential issue. Some lessons learned domestically can reasonably be incorporated into international criminal prosecutions without the need to start afresh. The approach to authentication by the international criminal tribunals and the International Criminal Court (ICC) along with developments and setbacks in jurisprudence bear examination. As will be seen, there is a dichotomous approach as between domestic and international jurisdictions. Authentication in common law jurisdictions is a prerequisite to admissibility while ICC jurisprudence favours the admission of evidence subject to a final weight analysis, resulting in the court considering evidence that perhaps ought not to have been admitted at all. A new approach to authentication will be offered in this chapter.

1. What is Authentication?

To be authentic means, inter alia, to be genuine, true, real, reliable, or trustworthy.[5] Authenticity is part of common parlance. We look for authentic parts for our vehicle, question whether a shop is selling a real Prada bag or a knock-off, or we desire to have a meaningful, authentic conversation with a friend. Broadly considered, authentication may be defined as the 'decision process attempting to establish sufficient confidence in the truth of some claim'.[6] In the law of evidence, authentication is defined as the provision of evidence sufficient to support a finding that the matter in question is what its proponent claims it to be.[7] To establish that a piece of evidence is authentic, counsel must take positive steps to authenticate it, which means 'to establish [the item] as genuine; to certify to be authentic'.[8] Central to these definitions is the fact that authentication describes a positive action, not a state of being.

4 Bobby Chesney and Danielle Citron, 'Deep Fakes: A Looming Challenge for Privacy, Democracy, and National Security'. *California Law Review* 107, no. 6 (2019): 1753–1820, at 1788.

5 'authentic, adj and n' Henry Black, *Black's Law Dictionary*, 5th ed. (Minnesota: West Publishing, 1979).

6 Elénore Ryser, Hannes Spichiger, and Eoghan Casey, 'Structured Decision Making in Investigations Involving Digital and Multimedia Evidence', *Forensic Science International: Digital Investigation* 34, no. 301015 (2020): 1–10, at 2.

7 Black (n 5). This general legal requirement has been codified in some jurisdictions. e.g. Rule 901 of the *Federal Rules of Evidence* (US) and corollary provisions in US state evidence codes, Section 31.1 of the *Canada Evidence Act*, R.S.C. 1985, c. C-5, as amended.

8 'authenticate, v' (*OED Online*, OUP August 2023), www.oed.com accessed 7 August 2023.

A piece of evidence does not constitute evidential proof in a case simply by the assertion of counsel. Absent an agreement between counsel and approval of the court, the party that tenders evidence has an obligation to authenticate it. Focusing on image-based evidence, authentication requires that counsel establish the location shown in the image so that it can be spatially linked to an incident or event that is relevant to the indictment before the court. Similarly, the date and time the image was recorded are essential components of authentication as they serve to establish a temporal link between the image and the issues raised by the indictment. Beyond geographic and temporal confirmation, the images must also be shown to be reliable.

It is important to distinguish authentication from image integrity and image accuracy as proof of one does not necessarily guarantee proof of another. Integrity verification is a preliminary analytical step where the pertinent question is whether the digital file has undergone any changes from one iteration to the next, e.g. whether the media being presented in court is the same digital file that was first obtained from its original source.[9] The focus at this stage is the digital file structure and metadata. If Image A is technically and visually identical to Image B, integrity verification has been achieved and the second analytical step is assessing authenticity, which focuses on determining whether the images are in fact that which they purport to be.

Suppose an image shows a mass grave and the image has been shown to be a faithful replication of the original media source (integrity verification). To contextualize the image, counsel must authenticate it through the presentation of relevant evidence to establish the location shown and the date of image capture. Note that integrity verification does not inexorably lead to authenticity. By way of illustration, in response to video evidence of alleged war crimes the Sri Lankan government did not dispute the technical integrity of the images but rather claimed that the scene depicted was staged, thus denying legal authenticity.[10] If this claim is true, it would mean that while the video file has technical integrity, it does not actually show what it purports to show because the scene was fictionalized. A further concern is that images may be authentic but misleading because they do not show the entire event and are thereby out of context.[11] Finally, verified and authentic images may nonetheless prove to be inaccurate because of issues related to their content, as discussed in Chapters 5 and 6.

[9] The original source may be the device that first recorded the images (digital camera, smartphone, or other device) or if the original source is unknown, the first iteration of the images found on a device, social media, or another site.

[10] Theresa Harris, Jonathan Drake, Jessica Wyndham, Susan Wolfinbarger, Stephen Lott, and Michael Lerner, 'Geospatial Evidence in International Human Rights Litigation: Technical and Legal Considerations', *AAAS Scientific Responsibility, Human Rights and Law Program* (2018) doi: 10.1126/srhrl.aau6090, 15.

[11] Jay Aronson, 'Preserving Human Rights Media for Justice, Accountability, and Historical Clarification', *Genocide Studies and Prevention: An International Journal* 11, no 1 (2017): 82–99, at 91.

2. Authentication: Technical Considerations

A discussion of technical considerations that may impact image authenticity is instructive. Farid notes the powerful trifecta that affects image integrity and authenticity.[12] First, people create fake content that is very convincing. Second, they distribute it globally through social media and other sites with little or no oversight. Third, there is no shortage of willing consumers ready to believe the worst in people to conform with their world view. Farid aptly refers to this as the weaponization of social media. Though his comments pertain to social media imagery, his concerns can be extrapolated to the courtroom given the increasingly prevalent role of social media images tendered as evidence. He cautions that, 'Tomorrow's technology will almost certainly allow for us to manipulate digital media in ways that today seem unimaginable.'[13] This gives rise to the concern that even experts may not readily discern digital modifications.[14] The more we rely upon digital images for proof purposes, the more important authentication becomes. Technical image authentication, which focuses on image metadata and content analysis, should be undertaken by forensic imagery experts as this level of analysis is beyond the ken of counsel.[15] Even if counsel detect areas of concern, it is the role of experts to evaluate the images and provide expert evidence at trial.

Depending upon the context and purpose surrounding their creation and transmission, there may be no motive for someone to alter digital images. Further, not all people have the necessary software and technical capacity to engage in digital alteration. However, when images are being considered in ICC Office of the Prosecutor (OTP) investigations and prosecutions, depending upon the source, scepticism as to their authenticity may be a logical starting point. Concerns regarding the potential alteration of digital media should be evaluated on a spectrum, ranging from a high likelihood of authenticity at the low end of the spectrum to a high likelihood of image alteration at the high end. At the lower end of the spectrum would be images created by OTP investigators, trusted human rights investigators, and other NGO personnel, and other photographers with a proven record of supplying authentic media. These photographers may be independent photographers or affiliated with reputable news organizations, but both the photographers and the organizations must have earned an established reputation for producing reliable imagery and a

[12] Hany Farid, 'Misinformation Apocalypse', *Stay Tuned with Preet Podcast* (5 March 2020). Farid is a Professor of Computer Science at the University of California at Berkeley specializing in image analysis, digital forensics, and the intersection of technology and society, particularly as it pertains to online imagery.

[13] Farid (n 3) 165. In the years that have passed since this prescient statement, deepfake videos have emerged as a good example of the technology indicated.

[14] Marie-Helen Maras and Alex Alexandrou, 'Determining Authenticity of Video Evidence in the Age of Artificial Intelligence and in the Wake of Deepfake Videos', *The International Journal of Evidence and Proof* 23, no. 3 (2019): 255–62, at 259.

[15] Content analysis refers to the process of examining the content of an image for the purposes of assessing authenticity and reliability.

demonstrated cognizance of the requirement that images must be authenticated before they can be used in any substantive way. Images that are submitted to and archived by a trusted organization would likely be at the low end of the spectrum as it is reasonable to presume that the goal of a reliable archiving organization is to search for and preserve the truth.[16] Additionally, satellite imagery recorded for the express purpose of accurately documenting a target location would likely achieve high authenticity.

At the higher end of the spectrum would be images obtained from social media and other sites where the photographer is unknown and the original media is unobtainable, images that are created by parties adverse in interest to the OTP investigation and for whom verifiable truth may be of secondary interest, and parties who may stand to gain from using images to plant disinformation. Images in this category may be misleading or may have been intentionally altered to trick viewers as part of a disinformation battle. Images intended to subvert the truth have commonly appeared online during the 2022 Russian invasion of Ukraine.[17]

The middle of the spectrum is reserved for evidence that is likely to be authentic due to its source or the manner of recording but requires proper investigation to confirm that fact. Examples of imagery in this category may include images obtained via dedicated applications such as *eyewitness to Atrocities* and *CameraV*. Because of the upfront attention to authenticity, these images are likely to be authentic but still require confirmation. Images obtained from known reputable civilians likely fall somewhere in the middle of the spectrum as well as they are amenable to authentication. Placement within this spectrum of authenticity is not without exception but in general, the more reliable the source and the manner of recording, the more likely authenticity can be established.

This spectrum approach to authenticity applies to images tendered by any party in atrocity crime litigation. The evidential standards required by law and expected by the court must hold the prosecution, defence, and counsel for victims to the same bar. Therefore, all counsel should investigate the source and authenticity of image-based evidence intended for use at trial. This may include the need to supplement the images with expert assessment and testimony as to their soundness.

[16] For example, Syrian Archives authenticates submitted video recordings according to a metadata protocol it has developed in consultation with other human rights organizations. Archivists assess the original title of the video, its source, the original publication link, the recording device, content type, geographical features, language and dialect spoken, and identifiable uniforms and weapons. Archivists do not rely upon one video as proof and instead review multiple videos and images of the same event from different witnesses and perspectives, together with available documentary and *viva voce* evidence; Sandra Ristovska, 'Human Rights Collectives as Visual Experts: The Case of Syrian Archive', *Visual Communications* 18, no. 3 (2019): 333–51, at 341–2, 345.

[17] See Section 5 of Chapter 5.

2.1 Altering Digital Images

In the early days of the ad hoc tribunals and the ICC, it was reasonable to believe that most images were authentic and reliable. In the years since then, the availability of low-cost high-resolution digital cameras and sophisticated consumer grade video editing software such as Adobe Premiere, Adobe Photoshop, Adobe Illustrator, Cinelerra, 3D Max, and Lightworks, and the development of specialized forgery techniques have meant that digital images can be manipulated and altered in such a way as to avoid leaving visible traces of what was done.[18] These digital forgeries may be indistinguishable from authentic images.[19] More troubling is the fact that technology struggles to keep abreast of developments in image forgery.[20]

Intentional digital video manipulations are typically classified as either inter-frame forgeries or intra-frame forgeries.[21] Inter-frame forgeries apply to a series of images and take advantage of the fact that digital video consists of sequential images played back at a visually pleasing frame rate to simulate real time. Inter-frame forgery methods include the insertion or removal of frames from a series of images, frame replication or duplication (cloning, swapping, or copy-move) whereby frames are copied and inserted elsewhere in a video (copy-paste forgeries), and temporal splicing whereby frames from two or more videos are interpolated to create a new video.[22] These methods seek to effect a change in the presentation and overall meaning of the images and to trick viewers into believing that events occurred as shown.

Intra-frame manipulation involves the modification of the content of individual frames. Methods used include copy-paste forgeries in which only a small region of the frame is modified (e.g. the addition or removal of a vehicle, object, or person), cropping frames to remove evidence of what occurred in the margins, adjusting colour and contrast in such a way as to change the meaning of the image, and resizing an image.[23] Digital video can also be altered by intentionally or inadvertently changing the original format to a compressed version, such as JPEG.[24] Machine

[18] Yanjun Cao, Tiegang Gao, Guorui Sheng, Li Fan, and Lin Gao, 'A New Anti-Forensic Scheme—Hiding the Single JPEG Compression Trace for Digital Image', *Journal of Forensic Sciences* 60, no. 1 (2015): 197–205, at 197; Raahat Singh and Naveen Aggarwal, 'Video Content Authentication Techniques: A Comprehensive Survey', *Multimedia Systems* 24 (2018): 211–40, at 211.

[19] Alin Popescu and Hany Farid, 'Statistical Tools for Digital Forensics', in *Information Hiding, 6th International Workshop, IH 2004*, edited by Jessica Fridrich (Berlin: Springer, 2004), 128–47, at 128; Gajanan Birajdar and Vijay Mankar, 'Digital Image Forgery Detection Using Passive Techniques: A Survey', *Digital Investigation* 10 (2013): 226–45, at 226.

[20] Popescu and Farid (n 19) 128.

[21] Singh and Aggarwal (n 18) 211.

[22] Al-Sanjary, Ahmed, and Sulong (n 2) 565–6; Singh and Aggarwal (n 18) 211–12.

[23] Steven Goode, 'The Admissibility of Electronic Evidence', *Review of Litigation* 29, no, 1 (2009): 1–64, at 20; Singh and Aggarwal (n 18) 211–12.

[24] Goode (n 23) 20. This would also include further compressing a compressed video. JPEG (Joint Photographic Experts Group) is a video format that involves compression.

learning artificial intelligence (AI), which learns on its own, may also make changes to media that are not transparent to viewers.[25]

These digital manipulation methods, when effectively deployed, can result in realistic looking images wherein the modifications may be undetectable by human viewers. This is further complicated using anti-forensic techniques, which adapt the forgery process to make the unauthorized alterations inconspicuous to tamper detection methods. For example, researchers are developing JPEG anti-forensic techniques designed to trick existing forensic detection processes by hiding compression artefacts.[26] This would allow for the imperceptible alteration of image content with a corresponding potentially significant impact on truth determination. Since viewers are unlikely to detect these fraudulent images, specialized forensic techniques are required.

2.2 Detecting the Alteration of Digital Images

Any changes to an image constitute an alteration. For example, inadvertently or intentionally compressing an image when exporting it from a device or copying it typically alters the image as data are both discarded and added during the compression process. Similarly, image clarification using forensic software tools for the purpose of drawing out detail constitutes an alteration. Both examples will generate different hashing values as between the two versions. The images may look unchanged to unsophisticated viewers, but they are technically different as their metadata have changed. There is reason to be concerned about image alteration that occurs innocently or inadvertently and that which is done intentionally because in both cases the final product is an altered image. However, I use the word *alteration* primarily to refer to the intentional alteration of images for the purpose of misleading viewers.

Assessing whether digital images are authentic involves determining their source and whether the images are what they purport to be.[27] Image quality alone is not an indicator of authenticity as altered images can look either very realistic or obviously manipulated.[28] Since it is often difficult to visually detect altered images, robust technical methods must be employed to ferret out the false from the factual. Technical authentication methods focus on three different areas: image source (device) identification, image alteration (forgery) detection, and differentiating

[25] Jeff Ward, '10 Things Judges Should Know About AI', *Judicature* 103, no. 1 (2019): 12–18, at 14.

[26] Gurinder Singh and Kulbir Singh, 'Improved JPEG Anti-Forensics with Better Image Visual Quality and Forensic Undetectability', *Forensic Science International* 277 (2017): 133–47, at 134.

[27] Pawel Korus, 'Digital Image Integrity—A Survey of Protection and Verification Techniques', *Digital Signal Processing* 71 (2017): 1–26, at 2.

[28] Mika Westerlund, 'The Emergence of Deepfake Technology: A Review', *Technology Innovation Management Review* 9, no. 11 (2019): 39–52, at 45.

computer generated images from realistic images.[29] Farid classifies authentication examination techniques as being pixel-based, camera-based, format-based, geometry-based, and physics-based.[30] In addition to image authentication, technical examination of images may also reveal hidden data intended to foil alteration detection.[31]

2.2.1 Image Source Identification

Locating a device (camera) in the possession of the defendant, a witness, or third party, or at a specific location that can be linked to distributed images can be pivotal if the original images still reside in the camera's memory. Tracing the history of images back to the camera that recorded them can also be of significant value in an investigation.[32] Algorithms can determine the make and model of the camera that recorded an image. Small artefacts that reside among the different light sensitive elements in camera sensors yield a photo response non-uniformity pattern. Based on this pattern, a digital fingerprint of the sensor can be identified that can link the camera with an image taken by the camera.[33] However, recovery of the camera that recorded images of interest for forensic examination is uncommon. In atrocity crime investigations, much of the media is submitted via social media or other sites, or through intermediaries, placing the photographer far away from the OTP.[34] In these circumstances, the ability to authenticate images back to the device that recorded them is very constrained.

Not only is it unlikely to locate the camera, but it is also unlikely that the original images will be available for examination. When they are available, determining authenticity is more viable as metadata regarding camera settings, location information, and date and time stamps linked to the images can be used to assist in this process. However, when video is obtained through social media sites such as Facebook, Twitter, YouTube, TikTok, WhatsApp, etc., this informative metadata is typically stripped.[35] In these circumstances, authentication must focus on any

[29] Angelina Gokhale, Preeti Mulay, Dhanya Pramod, and Ravi Kulkarni, 'A Bibliometric Analysis of Digital Image Forensics', *Science & Technology Libraries* 39, no. 1 (2020): 96–113, at 98.

[30] Hany Farid, 'Image Forgery Detection', *IEEE Signal Processing* 26, no. 2 (2009): 16–25; see generally Farid (n 1) 2.

[31] Singh and Aggarwal (n 18) 231.

[32] Judith Redi, Wiem Taktak, and Jean-Luc Dugelay, 'Digital Image Forensics: A Booklet for Beginners', *Multimedia Tools Applications* 51 (2011): 133–62, at 137.

[33] Zeno Geradts, 'Digital, Big Data and Computational Forensics', *Forensic Sciences Research* 3, no. 3 (2018): 179–82; Husrev Sencar, 'Source Camera Attribution from Videos', in *Multimedia Forensics*, edited by Husrev Sencar, Luisa Verdoliva, and Nasir Memon (Singapore: Springer, 2022), 89–116.

[34] When media is shared via social media and other sites, access to the original is often impossible. However, original video recordings have been found on the defendant's device in some national prosecutions for atrocity crimes.

[35] This is sometimes referred to as social media laundering. See Alexa Koenig, Felim McMahon, Nikita Mehandru, and Shikha Bhattacharjee, 'Open Source Fact-Finding in Preliminary Examinations', in *Quality Control in Preliminary Examination*, Vol. 2, edited by Morten Bergsmo and Carsten Stahn (Brussels: Torkel Opsahl Academic EPublisher, 2018), 681–730, at 693; Samantha Greenfield, 'Social Media Platforms: Preserving Evidence of International Crimes', *International Comparative, Policy Ethics Law Review* 2, no. 3 (2019): 821–48, at 823; Eleanor Farrow, 'eyeWitness to Atrocities: Verifying Images

available clues in the images themselves.[36] Image metadata is replaced upon uploading with new metadata indicating when the image was uploaded and perhaps from where, but this has limited value for image authentication.[37] For example, YouTube automatically dates videos according to the time of upload in California, using Pacific Time, no matter where the video was uploaded from, thus contributing to disputes about the veracity of uploaded media.[38]

2.2.2 Image Alteration Detection

Image alteration detection consists of active and passive techniques.[39] Active techniques such as digital signatures, watermarks, and steganography require prior knowledge of image content and metadata.[40] This is required to determine whether alteration has occurred and the specific alterations involved. Conversely, passive techniques do not require prior knowledge of image content and metadata. These techniques focus on determining whether an image has undergone forgery operations such as copy-move or spatial alterations of image content.[41] Methods used by forensic experts to ascertain image authenticity typically involve assessing digital signatures, watermark examination, forensic image analysis, and phylogeny reconstruction.[42] An overview of these active and passive forgery detection techniques follows.

A digital image consists of binary data. As a result, it possesses a unique mathematical value which can be ascertained using a digital signature hashing algorithm.[43]

with Metadata', in *Digital Investigative Journalism: Data, Visual Analytics and Innovative Methodologies in International Reporting*, edited by Oliver Hahn and Florian Stalph (Cham: Springer International Publishing, 2019), 143–55, at 145; Yvonne McDermott, Alexa Koenig, and Daragh Murray, 'Open Source Information's Blind Spot', *Journal of International Criminal Justice* 19, no. 1 (2021): 85–106, at 93.

[36] Jay Aronson, McKenna Cole, Alex Hauptmann, Dan Miller, and Bradley Samuels, 'Reconstructing Human Rights Violations Using Large Eyewitness Collections: The Case of Euromaidan Protester Deaths', *Journal of Human Rights Practice* (2018): 1–20, at 2. In the Euromaidan protestor death investigation, social media video was visually linked to authenticated video images, allowing for the synchronization of various video sources.

[37] Aronson (n 11) 92.

[38] Ella McPherson, 'Risk and the Pluralism of Digital Human Rights Fact-Finding and Advocacy', in *New Technologies for Human Rights Law and Practice*, edited by Molly Land and Jay Aronson (Cambridge: CUP, 2018), 188–214, at 191.

[39] William Ferreira, Cristiane Ferreira, Gelson da Cruz Júnior, and Fabrizzio Soares, 'A Review of Digital Image Forensics', *Computers and Electrical Engineering* 85, no. 106685 (2020): 1–9, at 2.

[40] Steganography involves embedding invisible secret information within an image. ibid.

[41] ibid 2.

[42] Korus (n 27). See also the House of Lords Select Committee on Science and Technology: Fifth Report, 'Digital Images as Evidence' (1998) https://publications.parliament.uk/pa/ld199798/ldselect/ldsctech/064v/st0502.htm.

[43] Korus (n 27) 3–4. A hash value is a mathematically unique digital fingerprint used to identify an image and is the prime method of integrity verification. It is constructed from the image's content and structure and is used to confirm that the data has not been altered; Bailey Ulbricht, Christopher Moxley, Mackenzie Austin, and Molly Norburg, 'Digital Eyewitnesses: Using New Technologies to Authenticate Evidence in Human Rights Litigation', *Stanford Law Review* 74, no. 4 (2022): 851–96, at 861. See also Willibald Croi, Fréderic-Michael Foeteler, and Harold Linke, 'Introducing Digital Signatures and Time-Stamps in the EO Data Processing Chain', in *Evidence from Earth Observation Satellites*, edited by Ray Purdy and Denise Leung (Leiden: Martinus Nijhoff Publishers, 2013), 379–98.

Determining the digital signature of an image at the acquisition or pre-processing stage can assist with authentication because if it is determined that a subsequent version of the image has a different hash value from a predecessor, this would furnish evidence of image alteration.[44] This active forgery detection technique is most helpful if the hash value is computed by the camera itself when recording the image.[45] Since hash values are among the metadata typically stripped from an image when uploaded to social media, image authentication can be challenging. One of the benefits of a digital signature system is that no image alteration occurs during the assessment as nothing is added to the image content. When available, digital signatures are a robust method of determining image integrity.

Watermarking is a forgery detection technique used to verify image integrity through the insertion of a digital mark (watermark) or message (steganography) in such a way that the image appears visually unchanged.[46] It is used to identify alterations in an image as between different iterations.[47] Watermarks are used for the varied purposes of data monitoring, copyright protection, and image authentication. Invisible watermarks used for image authentication are irreversibly embedded in an image by means of carefully designed imperceptible changes in image content.[48] Correctly applied, a digital watermarking algorithm should hide enough bits of data without significantly modifying image content.

Authentication is achieved by verifying that the extracted watermark is the same as the originally inserted watermark.[49] A fragile watermark that is applied to the cover image would be destroyed upon image modification, thus providing objective proof of image content manipulation. Removal and re-embedding of a watermark into an altered image without detection would be difficult to achieve.[50] Fragile watermarking is sensitive to any changes in an image and only works in lossless (uncompressed) image formats. However, contrary to a digital signature approach, watermarks are additive as the image is altered through their insertion. Images with and without a watermark will produce a different hash value because the images are different, even if not visually so. This alone may create authentication challenges.

[44] Gokhale, Mulay, Pramod, and Kulkarni (n 29) 98; Birajdar and Mankar (n 19) 227–8.

[45] Popescu and Farid (n 19) 129. Hashing does not address any alterations that may have occurred prior to the hash value being determined. The longer the delay from image capture to evidential consideration, the greater the potential risk of image alteration.

[46] Tamer Rabie, 'Color-Secure Digital Image Compression', *Multimedia Tools Applications* 76 (2016): 16657–79, at 16659; Ferreira, Ferreira, da Cruz Júnior, and Soares Ferreira (n 39).

[47] Scott Craver, Bede Liu, and Wayne Wolf, 'An Implementation of, and Attacks on, Zero-Knowledge Watermarking', in *Information Hiding, 6th International Workshop, IH 2004*, edited by Jessica Fridrich (Berlin: Springer, 2004), 1–12, at 10; Popescu and Farid (n 19) 128.

[48] Korus (n 27) 1–2.

[49] It is uncertain whether this action can be forged; Popescu and Farid (n 19) 129.

[50] Craver, Liu, and Wolf (n 47) 10.

A key limitation with the use of watermarks is that they must be applied upon image acquisition or at the latest upon registration in a media repository.[51] The watermark's digital authentication code must be ascertained before the images are publicly released to determine if subsequent modification occurred. Specialized hardware and software are required to accomplish this authentication task.[52] A further limitation with digital signatures and watermarking is that it may be difficult to distinguish between malicious and inadvertent modifications. Research continues in the use of multiple application specific watermarks to accurately authenticate images as well as recover approximated images, and to differentiate between malicious and incidental attacks.[53]

In the ICC crimes context, investigators and forensic imagery experts typically will not have access to many original images aside from images they recorded as part of their investigation or accessed from a trusted source, thus negatively impacting their ability to utilize active forgery detection methods.[54] Many of the acquired images will be second hand and of uncertain progeny such as images obtained from social media and other sites. As a result, passive forgery detection techniques employed by imagery experts are the preferred approach for determining image authenticity as these techniques do not require information, digital signatures, or watermarks from the original images.[55] Passive techniques are premised on the assumption that while digital forgeries may leave no obvious visual clues, the metadata may reveal such activity as might subtle inconsistencies within the visual image, and these techniques exploit this intrinsic image information and visual content.[56]

Passive forgery detection involves examining the metadata of a digital image. Digital video consists of a series of individual images that are previously encoded and then encapsulated in a multimedia container.[57] Digital video typically operates at a frame rate of twenty-five or thirty frames per second and one minute of digital video at a full frame rate therefore consists of 1,500 or 1,800 images.[58] A small

[51] Optimum authentication via watermarks requires that the watermark be applied upon image capture though not all digital cameras have this capability. Popescu and Farid (n 19) 129.

[52] Birajdar and Mankar (n 19) 227–8.

[53] Rafiullah Chamlawi and Asifullah Khan, 'Digital Image Authentication and Recovery: Employing Integer Transform Based Information Embedding and Extraction', *Information Science* 180 (2010): 4909–28.

[54] Gokhale, Mulay, Pramod, and Kulkarni (n 29) 98.

[55] Birajdar and Mankar (n 19) 226, 228; Ferreira, Ferreira, da Cruz Júnior, and Soares Ferreira (n 39) 2.

[56] Birajdar and Mankar (n 19) 228; Jay Aronson, 'The Utility of User-Generated Content in Human Rights Investigations', in *New Technologies for Human Rights Law and Practice*, edited by Molly Land and Jay Aronson (Cambridge: CUP, 2018), 129–48, at 140.

[57] Carlos Huamán, Anna Orozco, and Luis Villalba, 'Authentication and Integrity of Smartphone Videos Through Multimedia Container Structure Analysis', *Future Generation Computer Systems* 108 (2020): 15–33, at 16.

[58] Charles Poynton, *Digital Videos and HD: Algorithms and Interface* (Amsterdam: Morgan Kaufman, 2003), 117.

percentage of those images are original or reference images with the majority being predictive images. Altering digital video without the benefit of AI and the machine learning associated with deepfakes is a laborious task and therefore manually altering a single image is more feasible.

Image metadata can be a repository of valuable information including resolution, aspect ratio, camera make and model, GPS coordinates, and date and time.[59] Metadata also allows for the reverse engineering of images to detect alterations, such as using the audit trail and history log in Adobe Photoshop CS which reveals image processing steps undertaken after the image was recorded.[60] Metadata analysis can reveal evidence of image cropping and splicing, date and time, and inconsistencies in location, amongst other image specific data. Metadata loss due to uploading means that imagery experts must examine the digital clues that remain to assess image integrity and authenticity.

Passive forgery detection also relies upon image content anomalies to detect manipulation. For example, inconsistencies in light and shadows and pixel incongruencies can be revelatory of copy-paste and cloning alterations.[61] This level of analysis focuses on detecting image alterations such as excising or duplicating frames, splicing, and copy-pasting components of the original image elsewhere in the image. However, high image compression ratios may ill-affect existing footprints so that image processing history may be undetectable. These challenges are more acute when digital media is uploaded to social media and other sites where additional compression is applied. Collectively, this loss of valuable data impacts the ability of experts to assess image integrity and authentication.[62]

Light and shadow inconsistencies may also reveal AI generated imagery. Figure 7.1 was created in seconds using *Midjourney*, a popular tool for creating AI generated images from a simple text prompt, by instructing it to create ('hallucinate') an image of 'a Nikon D50 shoot of a man and a woman hiking on a mountain on a sunny day, snow on the ground, photorealistic, 4:3'.[63]

However, technical analysis of the geometrical and physical properties of the image (the shadows) reveals that the image is not real. Figure 7.2 shows that while the green triangles are consistent in that the shadows link to the light source (sun), the red triangle does not, thus revealing the forgery.[64] Absent a reason to question

[59] Determining the IP address linked to a social media post can also be valuable.

[60] Maras and Alexandrou (n 14) 258.

[61] Farid (n 1). This method is not without challenge as researchers have proposed a way to remove an object from an image as well as its shadow, thus eliminating inconsistency. Justin Hendrix and Dan Morozoff, 'Media Forensics in the Age of Disinformation', in *Multimedia Forensics*, edited by Husrev Sencar, Luisa Verdoliva, and Nasir Memon (Singapore: Springer, 2022), 7–40, at 11.

[62] Maras and Alexandrou (n 14) 258–9.

[63] Email from Marco Fontani, PhD, Forensics Director for Amped Software, Trieste, Italy, to author (June 2023).

[64] Fontani (n 63).

Figure 7.1 AI generated image. (Amped SRL (c) 2023)

such an image, it is likely to be relied upon by viewers as being authentic, even though it is not.

Imagery experts may also employ software programs designed to detect image alteration. *Amped Authenticate* is frequently used to examine image processing history to determine whether an image is original or altered and what device created it.[65] It also permits batch analysis of multiple images at the same time. Figure 7.3 shows an image devoid of any pedestrians on the road and is quite convincing proof of that proposition. However, the image is a forgery.[66]

Figure 7.4 shows the output of a cloning detection algorithm, which identifies portions of the image that are suspiciously similar and marks them with coloured

[65] 'Amped Authenticate', Amped Software, https://ampedsoftware.com/authenticate.
[66] Fontani (n 63).

Figure 7.2 Light and shadow analysis detects forgery. (Amped SRL (c) 2023)

patches, each patch indicating a potentially cloned region. The algorithm does not detect which portions of the image are cloned, only the anomaly.

Figure 7.5 shows a red-green image created by a JPEG-based forensic image algorithm and identifies which pixels were forged. Using both forensic images shows where the forged region is (red) and the type of forgery involved (cloning).

Finally, Figure 7.6 shows the original image.

Using a further example, Figure 7.7 shows a convincing though forged image of a person at a marina.[67]

As with Figure 7.5, the JPEG-based forensic image algorithm identifies which pixels were forged, as shown in Figure 7.8.

Figure 7.9 shows the original image.

[67] ibid.

Figure 7.3 Altered image. (Amped SRL (c) 2023)

Figure 7.4 The coloured patches are indicative of cloning. (Amped SRL (c) 2023)

Figure 7.5 The red-green image reveals the forgery. (Amped SRL (c) 2023)

Figure 7.6 The original image. (Amped SRL (c) 2023)

Figure 7.7 Altered image. (Amped SRL (c) 2023)

Figure 7.8 The red-green image reveals the forgery. (Amped SRL (c) 2023)

Figure 7.9 The original image. (Amped SRL (c) 2023)

Additionally, Hany Farid developed a computer program that will automatically detect cloning within an image.[68] Further, since lighting and shadow differences can indicate image alteration, he also developed a program that automatically estimates the direction of the illuminated light source.[69] Researchers have developed a method that analyses the intrinsic structure of multimedia containers for the purpose of verifying the integrity and authenticity of videos in MP4, MOV, and 3GP formats.[70] It reportedly determines the brand of mobile device that generated the video, the application that was used to transfer it, and the editing program used to alter the images.[71]

Even in the absence of visual clues, forgeries alter metadata and these changes are detectable.[72] To be most effective, image forgery detection software should be passive and require no information about the original image nor access to any digital signatures or watermarks.[73] Along with active and passive techniques, deep learning may also play a role in detecting forgeries.[74] Researchers advise that

[68] Farid (n 3) 164.
[69] ibid.
[70] Huamán, Orozco, and Villalba (n 57) 30.
[71] ibid.
[72] Popescu and Farid (n 14) 129.
[73] Birajdar and Mankar (n 19) 226.
[74] See Section 2.2.3.

countermeasures are likely to be developed for most detection methods but as more authentication methods are developed, it should be increasingly more difficult to alter images in ways that escape detection.[75]

The visual content of geospatial images may also be corroborated by geolocation and landform and structure identification.[76] Support may also come from *viva voce*, documentary, and expert evidence, media reports, open source data, and other evidence.[77] Utilizing geolocation sources such as satellite images obtained from Google Earth, Google Maps, Bing Maps, Terraserver, and other satellite sources, and drone imagery, may permit the circumstantial corroboration of otherwise unauthenticated images.[78] Through this method, a proven image can be the linchpin for authenticating images that are otherwise not independently verifiable. The date and time an image was recorded may be able to be approximated by chronolocation or shadow analysis, weather consistencies, etc.[79] It is also possible to reverse search some images in an effort to determine their origin.[80] Collectively, these passive forgery detection and authentication methods can be quite useful in either detecting evidence of forgery or confirming authenticity.

[75] Popescu and Farid (n 14) 146.

[76] Geolocation describes the process of comparing the content of a questioned location image to known location images to see if sufficient individualizing features can be detected for an evaluative opinion. Office of the United Nations High Commissioner for Human Rights and the Human Rights Centre at the University of California, Berkeley, School of Law, 'Berkeley Protocol on Digital Open Source Investigations' (2020) HR/PUB/20/2, 66 ('Berkeley Protocol'). Geographic and topographical features, buildings, vegetation, and other individualizing features can assist in confirming the location shown in an image.

[77] Alexander Godulla, 'The Content Verification of Digital Photographs', in *Digital Investigative Journalism: Data, Visual Analytics and Innovative Methodologies in International Reporting*, edited by Oliver Hahn and Florian Stalph (Cham: Springer International Publishing, 2019), 171–7, at 1756; Karolina Aksamitowska, 'Digital Evidence in Domestic Core International Crimes Prosecutions', *Journal of International Criminal Justice* 19, no. 1 (2021): 189–212, at 92. For example, in Amnesty International's reporting on human rights abuses and war crimes committed by Boko Haram and Nigerian security forces, video of extrajudicial executions served as powerful proof. These videos were corroborated by other authenticated videos; *viva voce* evidence from witnesses, human rights activists, doctors, journalists, and military sources; government documents; and satellite images. Aronson (n 36) 132, 141–5.

[78] Aronson (n 36) 132; Elliot Higgins, 'Visual Analysis: Verification Via Geolocation and Photographs', in *Digital Investigative Journalism: Data, Visual Analytics and Innovative Methodologies in International Reporting*, edited by Oliver Hahn and Florian Stalph (Cham: Springer International Publishing, 2019), 137–42, at 137. For example, Bellingcat personnel determined that, 'the Russian Ministry of Defense presented digitally modified and falsely dated satellite images to the international public in order to implicate the Ukrainian army in the downing of MH17'. This conclusion was reached by comparing the proffered Russian satellite images to video and still images found at open source sites; Aronson (n 36) 141.

[79] Chronolocation is the corroboration of dates and times of recorded events through shadow analysis and other visual clues; Berkeley Protocol (n 76) 66. For example, in *Prosecutor v. Omae Haisam Sakhanh*, Judgment, 31 May 2017, Svea Court of Appeal, Sweden, paras. 58, 62, shadow analysis by forensic experts determined the length of time between an alleged judicial decision and the execution of Syrian government soldiers shown in YouTube video. The defendant admitted participating in the execution but asserted that he had carried out legitimate death sentences. Shadow analysis revealed that only forty-one hours had passed between the alleged trial and the execution, contradicting the defendant's claim of legitimate due process. Aksamitowska (n 77) 14–15. See also Aronson (n 56) 132.

[80] Using Google Image Search, TinEye, and Chrome; Higgins (n 78) 138.

Two additional approaches to image authentication are worthy of mention: dedicated smartphone applications and phylogeny. Smartphone applications have been developed for the express purpose of allowing people to record verifiable digital images of ICC crimes and human rights violations and submit them directly or indirectly to investigators. According to the developers of the *eyeWitness to Atrocities* application, it automatically documents smartphone GPS coordinates, date and time, and the location of surrounding cell towers and Wi-Fi networks and thereby generates three independent sources to confirm date, time, and location.[81] Digital media that cannot be edited is encrypted on the original device and a hash value is calculated upon recording for integrity verification purposes. Once transmitted to *eyeWitness*, the recording is stored in its original format in a secure facility to preserve its chain of custody.[82] The stated purpose of this application is to meet the evidential standards required in international criminal litigation.[83] An application that makes similar claims is *CameraV* and *Proofmode*, a precursor to *eyeWitness*, created by the advocacy group WITNESS and the Guardian Project.[84] Other applications include International Evidence Locker, Truepic, and Whistler.[85]

In 2015, WITNESS released its *Video as Evidence Field Guide* publication to help photographers gather evidence capable of being authenticated. Other organizations such as Amnesty International and the Open Society Justice Initiative also work towards obtaining media that is authentic.[86] The claims of organizations that created these applications are very robust and have not been challenged in the ICC or any tribunal. Should such evidence be examined and approved by the OTP and the ICC Trial Chamber, that will be a significant step forward in the use of civilian images.[87]

Phylogeny reconstruction is used to identify various versions of an image within a larger collection and to determine the relationship between images and their processing history. Given the staggering number of images on the internet, this is a massive undertaking. Indeed, a recent evaluation of phylogeny reconstruction methods on random images obtained from the internet revealed rather poor

[81] See *eyeWitness to Atrocities*, https://www.eyewitness.global/FAQS. See also Farrow (n 35) 147–8.

[82] See *eyeWitness to Atrocities* (n 81); Róisín Costello, 'International Criminal Law and the Role of Non-State Actors in Preserving Open Source Evidence', *Cambridge International Law Journal* 7, no. 2 (2018): 268–83, at 279–80; Rebecca Hamilton, 'User Generated Evidence', *Columbia Journal of Transnational Law* 57, no. 1 (2018): 1–61, at 4.

[83] See *eyeWitness to Atrocities*, https://www.eyewitness.global/5-Lessons-Learned-in-5-Years; Jessica Levy and Paul Williams, 'Documentation for Accountability', *Case Western Reserve Journal of International Law* 52 (2020): 451–66, at 463.

[84] Hamilton (n 82) 18-19. See Guardian Project's Proofmode, https://github.com/guardianproject/proofmode/blob/master/README.md.

[85] Farrow (n 35) 145.

[86] Brianne Leyh, 'Changing Landscapes in Documentation Efforts: Civil Society Documentation of Serious Human Rights Violations', *Utrecht Journal of International and European Law* 33, no. 84 (2017): 44–58, at 51–2.

[87] This may prove challenging as the OTP's in-house capacity to analyse image-based evidence is rather limited; Greenfield (n 35) 823.

performance and unpredictable behaviour when dealing with random images of unknown origin and processing history.[88] Yet it remains a potential tool in the arsenal of forgery detection.

2.2.3 Differentiating Computer Generated Images from Realistic Images

A deepfake video is a digital video that is generated using a computer algorithm whereas authentic digital video is generated by a camera. When the original video is available for examination, a hash verification or a watermark would be an invaluable tool in the authentication process and for the detection of a deepfake.[89] This is unlikely to be the case in ICC crime investigations. When only the deepfake version is available for examination and no original exists for comparison or when the depicted subject matter is novel, it is more difficult to detect deepfakes. A forensic imagery expert may discriminate between two versions by visually identifying certain attributes of a deepfake video, but human detection cannot be the sole arbiter of reality.[90]

Visual examination by an imagery expert may detect indications of deepfake video.[91] The most important facets of manual detection are searching for evidence of morphing and image creation.[92] Morphing is a combination of image alteration and compositing, e.g. superimposing a new face or facial expression onto an existing face or merging one face with another to create a composite facial image. Visual clues indicative of deepfakes include face wobble and shimmer, image content or boundary warping, smoothness in areas that should have sharp edges, compression artefacts, compression breaks, inconsistencies in speech and mouth movements, inconsistencies in lighting, reflections, and shadows, geographic inconsistencies, lack of breathing, unnatural eye direction, absence of blinking, missing features on people, objects, and scenery, missing hair and teeth detail, misalignment in facial symmetry, inconsistencies in pixel levels and unusual pixel formations, and implausible movement of people and objects.[93] Examining the structure of an image may also detect deepfakes. For example, the metadata of an image may provide valuable clues about image integrity but saving the video

[88] Korus (n 27) 1–2.

[89] Chesney and Citron (n 4) 154; Westerlund (n 28) 46.

[90] Samuel Greengard, 'Will Deepfakes Do Deep Damage?', *Communications of the ACM* 63, no. 1 (2020): 17–19, at 18–19.

[91] Agnes Venema and Zeno Geradts, 'Digital Forensics, Deepfakes, and the Legal Process', *The SciTech Lawyer* 16, no. 4 (2020): 14–23, at 14. Digital manipulation can be traced in varying levels in the falsified media.

[92] ibid. For an example of methodology used to detect face swapped videos, see Paulo Reis and Rafael Ribeiro, 'A Forensic Evaluation Method for DeepFake Detection Using DCNN-based Facial Similarity Scores', *Forensic Science International* (3 June 2023), https://doi.org/10.1016/j.forsciint.2023.111747.

[93] Westerlund (n 28) 45; Greengard (n 90) 18–19; Venema, and Geradts (n 91) 15; Luisa Verdoliva, 'Media Forensics and DeepFakes: An Overview. Cornell University' (2020) https://arxiv.org/abs/2001.06564v1, 3; Siwei Lyu, 'Deepfake Detection', in *Multimedia Forensics*, edited by Husrev Sencar, Luisa Verdoliva, and Nasir Memon (Singapore: Springer, 2022), 313–32, at 319.

in another video format alters the data and hampers this metadata-based investigation.[94] Another method of detecting deepfakes is noise analysis, which focuses on imperfections in images caused by camera sensors which may provide valuable clues, but noise can be forged or deleted with commercially available software.[95]

Despite visual content and metadata-based clues that can assist in deepfake detection, there must first exist the impetus to challenge videos for authenticity. Further, it is not reasonable to expect that imagery experts will be able to detect all deepfakes, nor is it possible to keep up with the increased volume of deepfake videos being disseminated. For these reasons, AI must be employed to examine videos for signs of forgery.[96] For example, software has been developed for the purpose of detecting abnormal eyelid movements, though this in turn encourages deepfake creators to ensure correct blinking in the future.[97] It is in effect a cat and mouse game wherein the publication of new detection methods spurs deepfake content generators to find corresponding workarounds to avoid detection. Reverse image searching to find the earliest available version of a video may assist in authentication.[98] Building upon that, maintaining databases of deepfake and real videos as part of an automated detection system may have some value though it will take time to see how effective automatic detection works in practice.[99]

Other considerations for combatting deepfakes include the use of watermarks on the original video, an automatic authentication process for every video uploaded to the internet, comparing the digital signature of the camera to uploaded video, determining upload source reliability, and the soundness of the website utilized.[100] Forgery detection tools are being manufactured by software developers such as Microsoft's recently announced *Video Authenticator*, which may provide some assistance in deepfake detection.[101] Some researchers caution that forensic software will soon have difficulty detecting digital forgeries.[102] Social media sites could also be required to police their content and remove deepfakes or suspected

[94] e.g. camera make, model, and serial number; date and time of creation or alteration, camera settings, resolution, image size, GPS coordinates and elevation, processing and image history, original file name, lens or flash information, frame rate, thumbnail info, etc. Venema and Geradts (n 91) 15.

[95] ibid.

[96] Westerlund (n 28) 45.

[97] Chesney and Citron (n 4) 152–3.

[98] Aronson (n 11) 92. Videos are harder to find via reverse image searching than photographs, although Amnesty International's YouTube Dataviewer allows for the reverse searching of preview frames from YouTube videos. Higgins (n 78) 138–9.

[99] Venema and Geradts (n 91) 15.

[100] Westerlund (n 28) 46.

[101] Leo Kelion, 'Deepfake Detection Tool Unveiled by Microsoft' *BBC News* (1 September 2020) https://www.bbc.com/news/technology-53984114. See also 'Microsoft on the Issues', https://blogs.microsoft.com/on-the-issues/2020/09/01/disinformation-deepfakes-newsguard-video-authenticator/.

[102] Lindsay Freeman and Raquel Vazquez Llorente, 'Finding the Signal in the Noise: International Criminal Evidence and Procedure in the Digital Age', *Journal of International Criminal Justice* 19, no. 1 (2021), 163–88, at 165.

deepfakes though global regulation of such sites is ambitious and jurisdictionally complicated.[103]

Deepfakes have the potential to amplify existing problems regarding image reliability and serve to weaponize the internet for nefarious purposes.[104] There is no silver bullet that delivers an ideal comprehensive solution to real-world image authentication problems. Digital forgery detection is complex, and the absence of a universally applicable solution exacerbates the situation. What is clear is that imagery experts must be aware of the need for inquiry. They must be well-versed in the targeted use of metadata analysis, content evaluation, machine learning, and AI so that digital forgeries can be more readily detected.[105] Every advance in forgery detection is seemingly matched with advances in anti-forgery detection. Techniques proposed by researchers are generally focused on specific kinds of forgeries, but for videos in general circulation each video becomes a research project that requires time, effort, and expertise to evaluate them in an environment where more videos are uploaded daily.[106]

3. Authentication: The Domestic Legal Approach

Images do not constitute independent direct or circumstantial evidence—they must first be authenticated by the tendering party for them to achieve evidential value. Image authentication is addressed more extensively by some domestic courts than in international criminal tribunals and courts. There is merit in surveying how select domestic common law jurisdictions deal with image authentication as lessons learned domestically may help to develop a more responsive approach to authentication in the international sphere and this contextualization can help gauge the level of authentication robustness at the ICC.

While a broader review of the legal approach to image authentication in common law and other jurisdictions may be valuable, I have limited my review to case law from Canada, the US, the UK, and Hong Kong as these are jurisdictions in which I teach (or have taught) about authentication legal issues. I have found a relative paucity of relevant case law, statutory materials, and scholarly articles in other common law jurisdictions. Case law in Canada and the US is starting to develop some issue depth and includes appellate authority on several image authentication issues. From the jurisdictions selected, a reasonably robust legal landscape

[103] Chesney and Citron (n 4) 154.

[104] Sam Gregory, 'Cameras Everywhere Revisited: How Digital Technologies and Social Media Aid and Inhibit Human Rights Documentation and Advocacy', *Journal of Human Rights Practice* 11 (2019): 373–92, at 384.

[105] Maras and Alexandrou (n 14) 259.

[106] Singh and Aggarwal (n 18) 235.

is evolving that is capable of extrapolation on a principled basis to adversarial systems more broadly.

There is no explicit burden of proof regarding authentication in the inquisitorial system because the collection and evaluation of evidence is conducted by the judge rather than the parties to the litigation, though there is an implicit burden of proof on plaintiffs to produce evidence that will support their claims.[107] The 'free assessment of evidence' approach in the inquisitorial system leaves the standard and degree of proof required to the determination of the inquiring judge.[108] The dichotomy between adversarial and inquisitorial systems is becoming less clear as each system continues to consider and adopt features of the other system, yet it is still helpful to discuss authentication under both systems.[109]

Authentication plays a role in inquisitorial legal systems although there is a greater tendency to admit evidence for final weighing rather than the common law approach of linking authentication to admissibility. For example, the *German Code of Criminal Procedure* permits investigating authorities to take all admissible evidence into account at trial.[110] Regarding documentary evidence, there is a preference in German criminal law to require a human agent to authenticate it rather than admitting such evidence on its own.[111] Extending this approach to image-based evidence, German criminal law recognizes that visual media is not typically self-authenticating and therefore requires *viva voce* evidence as to location, date, time, image integrity, and authenticity.[112] Similarly, in the Netherlands the prosecution is required to prove the authenticity of tendered images.[113] It is reasonable to suggest that in both systems, prudence dictates that the party relying upon image-based evidence should be prepared to fully authenticate it lest it be excluded from consideration on an admissibility basis or given limited weight in the final judgment.

By way of example, the Dutch Public Prosecution Service led image-based evidence during the MH17 trial regarding the downing of Malaysia Airlines Flight MH17 over eastern Ukraine on 17 July 2014 which killed all 298 people on board. The trial began in June 2021 and was held in the Netherlands under Dutch law. The prosecution relied upon video and photographic images of the wreckage, images

[107] Chulyoung Kim, 'Adversarial and Inquisitorial Procedures with Information Acquisition', *Journal of Law, Economics, and Organization* 30, no. 4 (2013): 767–803, at 785.

[108] Martin Oudin, *Evidence in Civil Law—France* (Slovenia: Institute for Local Self-Government and Public Procurement Maribor, 2015), 15.

[109] Anogika Souresh, 'The Adversarial vs Inquisitorial Dichotomy in International Criminal Law: A Redundant Conversation', *International Comparative Jurisprudence* 5, no. 1 (2019): 81–86, at 82.

[110] Section 244(2); Aksamitowska (n 77) 198.

[111] Michael Bohlander, *Principles of German Criminal Procedure* (Oxford: Hart Publishing, 2021), 158.

[112] ibid 162–3.

[113] Aksamitowska (n 77) 198; 'Open Society Justice Initiative Briefing Paper', *Universal Jurisdiction: Law and Practice in the Netherlands* (2019) https://www.justiceinitiative.org/publications/universal-jurisdiction-law-and-practice-in-the-netherlands, 25–26.

showing smoke trails allegedly linked to the firing of BUK missiles at a relevant location and time, and satellite imagery showing specific locations on different dates.[114] For the transportation of the BUK TELAR missile launcher believed to be have been used in downing MH17 from Karsk, in the Russian Federation, to eastern Ukraine, the prosecution relied upon many sources of evidence including visual media showing the convoy.[115]

The authenticity of the image-based evidence relied upon by the prosecution was confirmed by the Joint Investigation Team and the Public Prosecution Service on the basis that they had no reason to suspect image manipulation.[116] However, during the final arguments of the defence, specific mention was made of the smoke trail images and the defence argued that their reliability was highly questionable. They also asserted that images tendered by the prosecution were capable of more than one interpretation and that not all interpretations supported the prosecution's theory.[117] These arguments were ultimately unsuccessful as the Court found the images to be of value in its assessment of the facts in the case and in the convictions of three of the four defendants.[118]

In the selected common law domestic jurisdictions, authentication is a precondition to admissibility and failure to authenticate leads to exclusion. Once authenticated, the images may be weighed and considered by the trier of fact in deciding the case.[119] The traditional approach is to require that images be authenticated by the photographer or someone present at the scene during recording who can attest to the date, time, location, circumstances of the recording, and the accuracy of the images.[120] Recognizing that requiring production of the photographer would be too narrow a ground for authentication, developing jurisprudence confirms that the avenues for establishing authenticity are broad and include the following methods, any one of which may be sufficient for proof depending on the case:

a) A person knowledgeable about the camera's operation can lay the necessary foundation for authentication;[121]

[114] MH17 Official Court Website (9 June 2021) https://www.courtmh17.com/en/news/2021/summary-of-the-day-wednesday-9-june-2021.html.

[115] MH17 Official Court Website (10 June 2021) https://www.courtmh17.com/en/news/2021/summary-of-the-day-in-court-thursday-10-june-2021.html.

[116] ibid.

[117] MH17 Official Court Website (18, 21, 23, and 24 March 2022) https://www.courtmh17.com/en/news/2022/pleadings-by-the-defence_summary.html.

[118] MH17 Trial, 'Summary of the Judgment of the District Court of The Hague', https://www.courtmh17.com/en/news/2022/summary-of-the-day-in-court-17-november-2022---judgment.html.

[119] *R. v. Nikolovski* (1996), 111 C.C.C. (3d) 403; *HKSAR v. Wong Cho Shing and Others* [2017] HKDC 121.

[120] David Watt, *Watt's Manual of Criminal Evidence* (Toronto: Thomson Carswell, 2007), 78; Kenneth Broun, *McCormick on Evidence*, 7th ed. Vol. 2 (St. Paul: Thomson Reuters, 2013), s. 212, at 4–5 (the illustrative evidence theory).

[121] *R. v. Shepherd*, [1993] 1 All E.R. 225; *State of Ohio v. Dzelajlija*, 2008 WL 1903995 (Ohio 2008); *State of Indiana v. Rogers*, 902 N.E.2d 871 (2009); *State of Georgia v. Parks*, 669 S.E.2d 684 (2009); *State of Texas v. Thierry*, 288 S.W.3d 80 (Tex. App. 2009). This is supported by US *Federal Rule of Evidence* 901(b)

b) Images that have been independently authenticated can be used to authenticate other images of the same event;[122]
c) Admissions made by the defendant can confirm image content;[123]
d) Testimony of eyewitnesses and others present in the images;[124]
e) The authentication of objects or people seen in images can serve to authenticate the images globally;[125]
f) Testimony of a witness who viewed the original video, confirmed the accuracy of the time and date stamp, and exported the video from the device for use in court, or photographed monitor images;[126]
g) Testimony of an imagery expert regarding the processing and analysis of the images;[127]
h) Testimony of the photographer;[128]
i) Testimony of an imagery expert regarding the image metadata;[129] and
j) By proving a thorough chain of custody of the images from acquisition to court presentation.[130]

Conversely, case law also provides examples of circumstances which militate against a finding of authenticity, including the following:

a) An unauthenticated YouTube video cannot be used to authenticate a second video;[131]
b) The failure to present the witness who exported digital video from the recording or storage device hampers proof of authenticity;[132]
c) Social media video does not self-authenticate; positive steps are required to establish authenticity;[133]

(9), which allows for evidence describing a process or system that created the evidence and showing that it produces an accurate result.

[122] Anonymous video of an event can achieve authentication when confirmed by other authenticated media. *R. v. Murphy and Another*, 1990 Northern Ireland 306; *HKSAR v. Lee Chi Fai and Others*, [2003] HKCA 233; *HKSAR v. Yeung Ka Ho*, [2013] HKCFA 82.

[123] *R. v. Quinn*, [2011] NICA 19; *Hibbert v. State of Maryland*, 2019 WL 2290320 (2019).

[124] *R. v. Leaney and Rawlinson* (1987), 38 C.C.C. (3d) 263; *Walthall v. State of Georgia*, 636 S.E.2d 126 (Ga. 2006); *R. v. Bulldog*, 2015 ABCA 251; *People of California v. Schmidt*, 2018 WL 4627171 (2018); *Moore v. State of Georgia*, 824 S.E.2d 377 (2019).

[125] *State of Arizona v. Haight-Gyuro*, 186 P.3d 33 (Ct. App. 2008); *Lamb v. State of Florida*, 246 So.3d 400 (Fla. 4th DCA 2018); *United States v. Pettway*, 2018 WL 4958962 (W.D.N.Y. 2018); *R. v. Martin*, 2021 NLCA 1.

[126] *United States v. Hicks*, 27 Fed. Appx. 577 (6th Cir. 2001); *R. v. JSC*, 2013 ABCA 157; *Mills v. State of Maryland*, 2018 WL 3660574 (2018); *State v. Brown*, 229 A.3d 216 (N.J. 2020).

[127] *United States v. Seifert*, 351 F. Supp. 2d 926 (D. Minn. 2005); 445 F.3d 1043 (8th Cir. 2006).

[128] *State of Ohio v. Rogers*, 2018 WL 4182294 (Ohio 2018); *State v. Sassarini*, 452 P.3d 457 (Or. 2019).

[129] *R. v. Andalib-Goortani*, 2014 ONSC 4690.

[130] *Choi Kit Kau v. R.* [1980] HKLR 433. This step alone does not prove that the images accurately depicted the scene.

[131] *R. v. Quinn*, [2010] NICC 27; [2011] NICA 19.

[132] *State of Maryland v. Washington*, 961 A.2d 1110 (Md. 2008).

[133] *Lamb v. State of Florida* (n 125).

d) Editing a video recording so that it no longer accurately shows the event;[134] and
e) When no evidence is presented regarding editing that was performed on a digital video recording and the accuracy of the resultant edited video.[135]

One of the concerns regarding image authenticity is whether video images have been edited in such a way as to render the final version misleading or disingenuous. In practice, editing for the purpose of removing irrelevant content is common as photographers frequently record more than the specific incident of interest. Such editing does not render video evidence inauthentic as long as the edited version remains a fair and accurate depiction of the event recorded.[136] Similarly, alterations which result from image clarification do not render images inadmissible unless the alterations change their meaning, are misleading, or otherwise unreliable.[137] Image clarifications and enhancements should be explained by the person who performed those processes.[138] Inaccuracies in or the absence of a date and time stamp must also be addressed with competent testimony as that could affect authenticity, though more likely is a question of weight only.[139]

Given the increasing number of images being posted to social media and other sites, authentication is a significant concern, especially when the photographer is anonymous and access to the original is not available.[140] When metadata is removed during uploading, other methods of authentication will be required to avoid exclusion for want of proof. Repeated sharing of social media images further exacerbates the inability to determine the source of the data as well as the date, time, and location of the images.[141] For example, civilian video uploaded to social media regarding Syrian atrocities was largely unusable due to an inability to establish authenticity.[142] Social media images that allegedly depict the defendant may be capable of authentication if evidence is presented that confirms that the defendant had an account on the website, used the website, uploaded the images, whether anyone could post on the defendant's account, or whether access was password

[134] *State of Iowa v. Pollard*, 2007 WL 2408114 (2007).

[135] *Torres v. Hickman*, 162 A.D.3d 821 (N.Y. 2018).

[136] *R. v. Solomon* [2007] EWCA Crim 2633; *State of Illinois v. Taylor*, 956 N.E.2d 431 (2011); *HKSAR v. Wong Cho Shing and Others* (n 119); upheld in *HKSAR v. Wong Cho Shing* [2017] HKCA 637 and *HKSAR v. Lau Cheuk Ngai and Others* [2017] HKCA 268; *State of Wisconsin v. Malone*, 384 Wis.2d 413 (2018).

[137] *HKSAR v. Wong Cho Shing and Others* (n 119).

[138] Goode (n 23) 21–2.

[139] *State of California v. D.S.*, 2012 WL 5411556 (2012); *State of New Jersey v. Nieves*, 2013 WL 4104088 (N.J. 2013); *HKSAR v. Jariabka Juraj* [2014] HKDC 1049; *HKSAR v. Cheng Shek Fai and Others*, [2014] HKDC 1518; *State of California v. Colbert*, 2014 WL 4243576 (2014); *Callaway v. State of Maryland*, 2016 WL 7379300 (2016); *R. v. Saddleback*, 2016 ABCA 204; *State of Tennessee v. Long*, 2017 WL 2958700 Tenn. 2017).

[140] Aronson (n 11) 88.

[141] Koenig, McMahon, Mehandru, and Bhattacharjee (n 35) 693.

[142] Hamilton (n 84) 16.

protected.[143] Additionally, a witness familiar with the defendant's social media site could authenticate content, especially when the witness is depicted on the site.[144]

Though the focus of this chapter is on digital video and images, all visual evidence must be authenticated. For example, computer animations must be authenticated by a witness who can establish that the animation fairly and accurately depicts their perception of the event. Computer simulations must be authenticated by establishing the validity of the underlying data and the correct depiction and application of the data with proper hardware and software.[145]

Authentication focuses on people, process, and technology. Questions that must be considered include who recorded the images, what technology was used to capture them, their source, and where and how they have been stored.[146] Proof of authenticity is broadly assessed. The threshold of proof required for authentication is relatively low.[147] Since it can be established many ways, counsel's failure to meet this obligation is generally reflective of poor trial preparation. Indeed, '... the inability to get evidence admitted because of a failure to authenticate it almost always is a self-inflicted injury which can be avoided by thoughtful advance preparation'.[148]

4. Authentication: The Ad Hoc Tribunals and ICC

A thorny issue regarding the authentication of image-based evidence at the ICC is determining when in the trial process a decision on authenticity should be made. The ICC primarily addresses concerns regarding evidence, including expert evidence, in terms of how much weight it will be given when reaching a final decision, rather than ruling on the admissibility of individual items of evidence on an interlocutory basis.[149] For example, in *Prosecutor v. Bemba*, the Appeals Chamber said

[143] *State of New York v. Price* (2017) 29 N.Y.3d 472 (N.Y. 2017); *Hibbert v. State of Maryland* (n 119).

[144] *R. v. Hirsch*, 2017 SKCA 14.

[145] Goode (n 23) 37–9.

[146] Greenfield (n 35) 824.

[147] Reasonable likelihood of authenticity—*United States v. Pettway* (n 125); a prima facie showing—*People in Interest of M. V.*, 432 P.3d 628 (Colo. Ct. App. 2012), *Wilson v. State of Mississippi*, 267 So.3d 264 (2019) (Miss. 2019), *State v. Sassarini* (n 128); balance of probabilities or lower—*R. v. Bulldog* (n 124). Though there is some variance in describing the applicable standard of proof for authentication, it is no higher than the balance of probabilities and therefore much lower than proof beyond reasonable doubt. Section 31.1 of the *Canada Evidence Act* uses the standard 'capable of supporting a finding that ...' a standard found to be lower than the balance of probabilities. *R. v. Martin* (n 125).

[148] *Lorraine v. Markel Am. Ins. Co.*, 241 F.R.D. 534, 542 (Md. 2007).

[149] Hakån Friman, 'Inspiration from the International Criminal Tribunals When Developing Law on Evidence for the International Criminal Court', *The Law and Practice of International Courts and Tribunals* 3 (2003): 373–400, at 383–6; Artur Appazov, *Expert Evidence and International Criminal Justice* (Switzerland: Springer International Publishing, 2016), 2; Geert-Jan Knoops, 'The Proliferation of Forensic Sciences and Evidence Before International Criminal Tribunals from a Defence Perspective', *Criminal Law Forum* 30 (2019): 33–60, at 36. This approach is well stated in *Prosecutor v. Bemba,* ICC-01/05-01/08-2299-Red, Decision on the Prosecution's Application for Admission of Materials into Evidence Pursuant to Article 64(9) of the Rome Statute of 6 September 2012, 08 October 2012, paras. 7–12.

that pursuant to Art. 69(4) of the *Rome Statute*, it had the discretion to decide on the relevance and admissibility of evidence when tendered or to defer those considerations to the end of the proceedings when evaluating the overall case, although it provided no criteria as to when it was appropriate to adopt one procedure over the other.[150]

This is not an academically esoteric point as the absence of an established consistent procedure to challenge tendered technical or scientific evidence and obtain a mid-trial ruling may create unfairness, particularly for the defence. Ruled upon too early, evidence may fail and be ruled inadmissible for want of sufficient proof when supplemental proof might be forthcoming later in the proceedings. Ruled upon too late, the court creates evidential uncertainty for all parties.[151] Counsel can present a more focused final argument when they know what evidence the court will admit, as opposed to being relegated to arguing a series of potential alternatives depending upon future admissibility rulings. Given the monumental volume of evidence that must be considered in ICC cases, mid-trial rulings on admissibility might serve to pare down the evidential palette that must be considered in final judgment. To understand this issue more fully, it is instructive to look at the development of the law in this area in the tribunals and the ICC.

The rules of procedure and evidence utilized in the ad hoc tribunals and the ICC have varied depending upon the tribunal and the make-up of the judiciary. The drafting of the Rules of Procedure and Evidence (RPE) for the International Criminal Tribunal for the former Yugoslavia (ICTY), the International Criminal Tribunal for Rwanda (ICTR), and the Special Court for Sierra Leone (SCSL) was assigned to the judges.[152] When the UN Security Council created the ICTY and the ICTR, the tribunals adopted an approach of liberal inclusivity.[153] Rule 63(2) of the ICC RPE authorizes the Trial Chamber to 'assess freely all evidence submitted in order to determine its relevance or admissibility' while Rule 64 allows for challenges to admissibility and a direction that inadmissible evidence shall not be considered. This flexible or laissez-faire approach is generally viewed as suitable for ICC judges given the complexity of international criminal trials and the absence of

[150] ICC-01/05-01/08-1386 OA 5 OA 6, Judgment on the Appeals of Mr Jean-Pierre Bemba Gombo and the Prosecutor Against the Decision of Trial Chamber III Entitled 'Decision on the Admission into Evidence of Materials Contained in the Prosecution's List of Evidence', 3 May 2011, para. 37.

[151] Lindsay Freeman, 'Digital Evidence and War Crimes Prosecutions: The Impact of Digital Technologies on International Criminal Investigations and Trials', *Fordham International Law Journal* 41, no. 2 (2018): 283–335, at 293.

[152] Göran Sluiter, '*Ad Hoc* International Criminal Tribunals (Yugoslavia, Rwanda, Sierra Leone)' in *The Cambridge Companion to International Criminal Law*, edited by William Schabas (Cambridge: CUP, 2016), 117–36, at 129.

[153] Kai Ambos, 'International Criminal Procedure: "Adversarial", "Inquisitorial" or Mixed?' *International Criminal Law Review* 3 (2003): 1–37, at 20–2; Gideon Boas, James Bischoff, Natalie Reid, and Don Taylor, *International Criminal Procedure* (Cambridge: CUP, 2011), 336.

juries. The judicial interpretation and application of these rules has favoured significant judicial discretion when assessing admissibility.[154]

There are differing approaches to the evaluation of evidence in the ad hoc tribunals and the ICC.[155] Klamberg has identified the steps taken by tribunal and ICC judges as beginning with an assessment of each item of evidence and evaluating whether the totality of the evidence favours the proposition proffered by the tendering party, and then determining whether there is sufficient merit to establish that proposition.[156] This intuitively logical approach has not been uniformly applied, resulting in disparate approaches to evidence, even within the same case.[157] In practice, decisions as to the assessment of evidence follow one of two general approaches.[158] From a timing perspective, under the *admission* approach, evidence is assessed for admissibility when it is tendered by the party. This is the procedure followed in the select common law jurisdictions discussed in Section 3. Conversely, under the *submission* approach, evidence tendered by the party is classified as submitted or produced but the question of admissibility is deferred until the end of the case when the final judgment is rendered by the court.

A further issue beyond the timing of the evaluation is how the court should assess evidence tendered by the parties. In this regard, there are two approaches that must be considered—the *atomistic* and *holistic* approaches. Under the atomistic approach, each piece of evidence is individually evaluated in concert with all submitted evidence to determine its admissibility and weight.[159] Judges must however be mindful not to apply the criminal standard of proof to individual items of evidence as that would be an error of law. Conversely, under the holistic approach evidence is assessed globally rather than individually, serving to lessen the risk of applying too high a standard of proof to each item of evidence. The choice as to which approach to follow is not merely a question of form over substance as an inconsistent approach can cause conflict in the judicial decision-making process.

Tension regarding the interplay of the atomistic and holistic evaluation of evidence in ICC trial and appeal chambers has been evident and has revealed internal

[154] Hakån Friman, 'International Criminal Procedures: Trial and Appeal Procedures', in *Routledge Handbook of International Criminal Law*, edited by William Schabas and Nadia Bernaz (London: Routledge, 2013), 271–87.

[155] Michael Pardo, 'Juridical Proof, Evidence, and Pragmatic Meaning: Toward Evidentiary Holism', *Northwestern University Law Review* 95, no. 1 (2000), 399–442; Jennifer Mnookin, 'Atomism, Holism, and the Judicial Assessment of Evidence', *UCLA Law Review* 60 (2013): 1524–85; Mark Schweizer, 'Comparing Holistic and Atomistic Evaluation of Evidence', *Law, Probability and Risk* 13 (2014): 65–89.

[156] Mark Klamberg, 'The Alternative Hypothesis Approach, Robustness and International Criminal Justice: A Plea for a "Combined Approach" to Evaluation of Evidence', *Journal of International Criminal Justice* 13, no. 3 (2015): 535–53, at 546–7.

[157] See Yvonne McDermott, 'Strengthening the Evaluation of Evidence in International Criminal Trials', *International Criminal Law Review* 17 (2017): 682–702, at 686–7.

[158] Fabricio Guariglia, '"Admission" v. "Submission" of Evidence at the International Criminal Court: Lost in Translation?', *Journal of international Criminal Justice* 16 (2018): 315–39; McDermott (n 157) 687–90; Freeman and Vazquez Llorente (n 102) 19–21.

[159] McDermott (n 157) 687–90.

conflict as to the preferred approach, though a consensus is developing that evidence should be evaluated holistically. In *Prosecutor v. Gbagbo and Blè Goudè*, the Trial Chamber acquitted both defendants at the close of the prosecution case.[160] Each of the three judges wrote separate opinions endorsing and applying the holistic approach in their assessment of the evidence.[161] Their use of the holistic approach was supported on appeal.[162] That approach continued when the Trial Chamber in *Prosecutor v. Ongwen* endorsed the holistic approach for the evaluation and weighing of evidence.[163] The Trial Chamber's use of the holistic approach was also supported on appeal.[164]

The atomistic and holistic approaches are not necessarily incompatible with each other. Individual pieces of evidence can be examined in some isolation, but they cannot be evaluated on a standard of beyond reasonable doubt, nor can other evidence that bears on the evaluation be ignored. Should such evidence be admitted for further evaluation, it must then be evaluated holistically in the final assessment of the case. McDermott argues convincingly that the holistic approach may result in the admission of evidence that may not otherwise merit admission on the basis that individual flaws may be overlooked in the broader evidential context.[165] This leapfrogging assessment must be guarded against. The holistic approach is not intended to cover any manner of sins. A plethora of weak or questionable evidence does not achieve greater weight due to volume. For example, repeated postings of the same altered image on social media does not imbibe the image with evidential strength.

I share McDermott's concern but go one step further and contend that rulings on the admissibility of evidence generally, and the authentication of image-based evidence specifically, should be made during the prosecution or defence case as applicable. For example, if the prosecution cannot sufficiently authenticate a piece of evidence by the time they conclude their case, the evidence should be ruled inadmissible.[166] It is unfair to wait and see if defence evidence will somehow make it

160 ICC-02/11-01/15-1263, 16 July 2019.

161 ICC-02/11-01/15-1263-Conf-AnxB, 16 July 2019, Reasons of Judge Henderson, para. 31; ICC-02/11-01/15-1263-AnxA, 16 July 2019, Reasons of Judge Tarfusser, para. 73; ICC-02/11-01/15-1263-AnxC-Red, Dissenting Opinion of Judge Herrera Carbuccia, 16 July 2019, para. 5.

162 ICC-02/11-01/15-1400 01-04-2021 1/166 SL A, Judgment in the Appeal of the Prosecutor Against Trial Chamber I's Decision on the No Case to Answer Motions, 31 March 2021, paras. 67, 71.

163 ICC-02/04-01/15-1762-Red, Public Redacted Trial Judgment, 4 February 2021, para. 227.

164 ICC-02/04-01/15-2022-Red 15-12-2022 1/611 NM A, Judgment on the Appeal of Mr Ongwen Against the Decision of Trial Chamber IX of 4 February 2021 entitled 'Trial Judgment', 15 December 2022, paras. 78, 83, 320–1.

165 McDermott (n 157) 688.

166 This is similar to the American approach required in respect of expert evidence in *Daubert v. Merrell Dow Pharmaceuticals Inc.*, 113 S. Ct. 2786, wherein trial judges are charged with the responsibility of assessing the admissibility of such evidence in advance of deciding the overall case. Carole Powell, 'Computer Generated Visual Evidence: Does Daubert Make a Difference?', *Georgia State University Law Review* 12, no 2 (1996): 577–600; Dan Kahan, David Hoffman, and Donald Braman, 'Whose Eyes are you Going to Believe? Scott v. Harris and the Perils of Cognitive Illiberalism', *Harvard Law Review* 122, no. 3 (2009): 837–906. The *Daubert* approach has been used broadly in the forensic science community and domestic courts; Knoops (n 150) 49.

admissible. Further, it is undesirable to delay such rulings until final judgment as it creates needless uncertainty for counsel and clutters the record. It also creates an environment wherein the prosecution may be emboldened to tender evidence of questionable admissibility in the hopes that it will somehow inadvertently attach to a count in the indictment without focusing on how it specifically applies.

It is not necessary for a court to choose either the atomistic or holistic approach to evidence evaluation as these approaches are not mutually exclusive. An item of evidence can be subjected to targeted scrutiny yet still be considered in the context of the full evidential record.[167] What is essential is that whatever approach is taken, it must be universally applied by all trial and appellate chambers. In short, the law that is applied in this regard must be consistent and predictable so that all parties coming before court can be confident in the process that will be applied. The current problem with ICC chambers is that judges are choosing the procedure they will adopt either based on what has been decided before or will adopt a new procedure for the case before them. Certainty and predictability are essential cornerstones of a reputable justice system.

In the sections that follow, I will review the approach to the issue of authentication taken by the ICTY, ICTR, STL, and ICC, and will discuss cases dealing with the authentication of image-based evidence.

4.1 ICTY

In *Prosecutor v. Delalić et al.*, the Chamber noted that ICTY professional judges are quite capable of considering each piece of evidence which has been admitted and then determining its appropriate weight.[168] The Chamber asserted that it was not required to decide on the authentication of evidence at the pre-trial motion stage, noting that admission does not equate with a finding of authenticity. Further, factors such as the authenticity of evidence will assume greatest importance when assessing the weight to be given to individual pieces of evidence.[169] The Chamber articulated the standard of proof for the admission of evidence to be prima facie proof, a standard that is not excessively high.[170] On appeal, the Chamber stated, 'The implicit requirement that a piece of evidence be prima facie credible—that it have sufficient indicia of reliability—is a factor in the assessment of its relevance

[167] The Appeals Chamber, in *Prosecutor v. Lubanga*, ICC-01/04-01/06 A5, Judgment on the Appeal of Mr. Thomas Lubanga Dyilo Against His Conviction, 1 December 2014, para. 20, followed a combined approach; See also McDermott (n 157) 689; Pardo (n 155) 438–9.

[168] IT-96-21-T, Decision on the Motion of the Prosecution for the Admissibility of Evidence, 19 January 1998, para. 20.

[169] ibid. See also *Prosecutor v. Blagojević and Jokić*, IT-02-60-T, Judgment, 17 January 2005, para. 29 where the Chamber evaluated evidence holistically and 'did not consider unsigned, undated or unstamped documents, *a priori*, to be void of authenticity'.

[170] ibid para. 31.

and probative value. To require absolute proof of a document's authenticity before it could be admitted would be to require a far more stringent test than the standard envisioned by Sub-rule 89 (C).'[171]

This approach was followed in *Prosecutor v. Brdanin and Talić*, where the Chamber confirmed that authenticity factors into the assessment of weight to be attached to individual pieces of evidence and that at the admission stage only a prima facie case of reliability needs be made out.[172] When objections are raised to the authenticity of documentary and video evidence, the Chamber will admit the evidence and assess its weight at the end of the case.[173] The Appeals Chamber in *Prosecutor v. Prlić et al.*, confirmed this two-step approach wherein prima facie proof of authenticity is required at the admissibility stage, whereas definitive proof of authenticity is applicable at the final weighing stage.[174]

To contextualize the issue of authentication determination, the following cases are presented as selected examples of how image-based evidence was assessed for authentication purposes by the ICTY. In *Prosecutor v. Dordević*, the prosecution showed excerpts of video recordings which showed several bodies to a defence witness in cross examination and thereafter sought to have them admitted.[175] For authentication purposes, the prosecution relied upon the narrator who stated the putative date and location. No evidence regarding the authenticity of the video was presented by the prosecution nor was the video shown to prosecution witnesses who had attended and commented upon the scenes depicted.[176] The defence witness was unable to authenticate the recordings and said that the bodies portrayed in the video were not among the bodies she saw at a nearby mosque.[177] Citing the prima facie standard of proof for admission, the Chamber found that even though the video excerpts were not shown to prosecution witnesses, there appeared to be sufficient correlation between what they described in their testimony and what was shown in the excerpts, together with the video narration, to justify admission.[178]

[171] *Prosecutor v. Delalić et al.*, IT-96-21-T, Decision on Application of Defendant Zejnil Delalic for Leave to Appeal Against the Decision of the Trial Chamber of 19 January 1998 for the Admissibility of Evidence, 4 March 1998, para. 20.

[172] IT-99-36-T, Order on the Standards Governing the Admission of Evidence, 15 February 2002, para. 18. See also *Prosecutor v. Boškoski & Tarčulovski*, IT-04-82, Trial Judgment, 10 July 2008, para. 10.

[173] *Brdanin and Talić* (n 172) para. 19. The same approach was followed in *Prosecutor v. Popović*, IT-05-88-T, Decision on Admissibility of Intercepted Communications, 7 December 2007, paras. 32–36.

[174] IT-04-74-AR73.16, Decision on Prlić's Interlocutory Appeal Against the Decision on Prlić Defence Motion for Reconsideration of the Decision on the Admission of Documentary Evidence, 3 November 2009, para. 34.

[175] IT-05-87/1-T, Decision on Prosecution's Motion for Admission of Video-Recording MFI P1575, 30 March 2010.

[176] The prosecution's disregard of their obligation to authenticate the evidence tendered is lamentable. Showing the video to prosecution witnesses for confirmation or presenting the narrator of the video for examination would have accomplished this task.

[177] *Dordević* (n 175) para. 10.

[178] ibid paras. 13–15.

Therefore, more by happenstance than good case management the video excerpts were ruled admissible subject to a later evaluation of weight.

A more restrictive approach was followed in *Prosecutor v. Prlić et al.* where the defence wished to tender transcriptions of video recordings into evidence but paradoxically did not tender the videos themselves as corollary evidence.[179] The Chamber held that without the video recordings being available to authenticate the transcriptions, they were not admissible.[180] This is a much sounder approach to authentication and admissibility as it puts the onus on the tendering party to authenticate evidence on a prima facie standard to gain admission. The Chamber could not fairly assess the authenticity of the transcriptions without the primary video evidence from which they emanated. This was a self-inflicted injury by counsel. Similarly, in *Prosecutor v. Karadzić*, video evidence that showed a machine gun nest located near a destroyed mosque was tendered.[181] However, insufficient evidence was led by the prosecution as to when the video was recorded which the Chamber found rendered the video evidence unreliable. Therefore, it could not be used to support a finding that machine gun nests were located near mosques at the relevant time.[182] Another self-inflicted injury.

A holistic approach to authentication was applied by the Chamber in *Prosecutor v. Popović*.[183] The prosecution sought to prove the location of mass graves using aerial images provided by the US government. As none of the images contained corresponding site coordinates and the embedded dates had been removed, the defence argued that they should not be admitted, noting a lack of comparative aerial imagery that could link them to the alleged location and satisfy authentication requirements. Despite these notable shortcomings, the Chamber found that sufficient testimonial evidence had been led to establish their authenticity, thus expanding proof of authenticity beyond the images themselves.[184]

Authentication of aerial images provided by the US government also featured in *Prosecutor v. Tolimir*, where the prosecution tendered aerial images for the purpose of establishing the specific locations of gravesites and reburial activities, buildings and vehicles, large groups of prisoners, and bodies.[185] The aerial images were provided to the prosecution by the US government on the express condition that the prosecution '... is not authorized to discuss in courtroom proceedings any information relating to the technical or analytical sources, methods, or capabilities of the systems, organizations, or personnel used to collect, analyse, or produce these imagery-derived products'.[186] The defence challenged the admissibility of

[179] IT-04-74-T, Decision on Praljak Defence Motion for Admission of Documentary Evidence, 1 April 2010.
[180] ibid paras. 54–55.
[181] IT-95-5/18-T, Judgement, 24 March 2016.
[182] ibid para. 1030, fn 3492.
[183] IT-05-88-T, Judgement, 10 June 2010.
[184] ibid paras. 72–75.
[185] IT-05-88/2, Trial Judgment, 12 December 2012, para. 67.
[186] ibid para. 68.

the images on the basis that no evidence had been led as to their origin, method of creation, editing, interpretation, and whether they had been modified prior to being given to the prosecution.[187] Although acknowledging these shortfalls, the Chamber found that they did not impair the credibility of the aerial images in general.[188]

The Chamber looked at the evidence holistically and found that the aerial images were generally reliable and of probative value because the prosecution had led extensive evidence about the use of aerial images in the investigation, had corroborated the locations shown by archaeological and anthropological reports, and led witness testimony as to the location of the gravesites. This approach to authentication is supportable as evidence extraneous to technical image authentication can suffice for a threshold ruling. Regarding other images, the Chamber ruled that video recordings showing people being killed were adequately authenticated by the photographer, video of missing men was authenticated by relatives, and video of a gravesite was sufficiently corroborated by witnesses who attended the location.[189] What is significant about this ruling is that the Chamber effectively stated that without evidence challenging reliability of the images, exclusion was not available, thus placing the burden on the defence to lead prima facie evidence of unreliability and lack of authentication to challenge admissibility.[190] Though not explicitly a reverse onus, its spectre seemed to be lurking in the background.

From the foregoing analysis, it is apparent that the ICTY utilized a two-step approach consisting of a threshold admission requirement followed by a holistic weighing exercise upon final judgment.[191] The Appeal Chamber's decision in *Prlić et al.* reflected earlier ICTY rulings and set a standard for later Chambers to follow.[192] Though the threshold requirement was not conclusive regarding authenticity, it served as a filtering process as evidence that did not meet this test would be excluded from further consideration, as demonstrated in *Prlić et al.* and *Karadzić*.[193] Presumably evidence that met the first threshold admissibility test but ultimately lacked sufficient proof of authenticity during the final weighing process would be disregarded in the final judgment.

[187] ibid para. 69.
[188] ibid para. 70.
[189] ibid paras. 549–550.
[190] Freeman (n 151) 301–2.
[191] The holistic approach was also approved by the ICTY Appeals Chamber in *Prosecutor v. Kupreškić et al.*, IT-95-16-A, Appeal Judgement, 23 October 2001, paras. 135, 202, 334, and *Prosecutor v. Halilović*, IT-01-48-A, Judgement, 16 October 2007, para. 128. The SCSL also adopted this approach in *Prosecutor v. Taylor*, SCSL-03-01-A, Judgment, 26 September 2013, para. 235.
[192] *Prlić et al.* (n 174).
[193] *Prlić et al.* (n 179); *Karadzić* (n 181).

4.2 ICTR

The ICTR's approach to the assessment of evidence and authenticity largely paralleled that of the ICTY. A two-step approach was utilized, consisting of threshold admission being contingent upon proof by the tendering party of relevance, probative value, reliability, and authenticity on the balance of probabilities, followed by a holistic weighing exercise upon final judgment.[194] The *Musema* Chamber relied upon ICTY jurisprudence for setting out principles relating to the assessment of evidence. For example, the Chamber held that relevant and probative evidence must also be shown to be reliable.[195] Reliability was described as 'the invisible golden thread which runs through all the components of admissibility'.[196] The Chamber also adopted the holistic approach to the evaluation of evidence by assessing the weight and probative value of each piece of evidence in the context of all of the evidence presented.[197] Exceptionally, the Chamber said that proof beyond reasonable doubt at the admission stage may be justified if allegations of unreliability about a piece of evidence merit a more exacting standard.[198] This approach is contrary to the general admonition against piecemealing evidence.

Central to establishing the reliability and credibility of documentary evidence is the establishment of its authenticity.[199] The source, form, contents, and purported use of documentary evidence are relevant considerations when assessing their authenticity.[200] Expert testimony may be relied upon to assess authenticity.[201] Finally, the Chamber accepted that corroborative evidence such as testimony and other documentary evidence could be used to establish authenticity.[202]

Consistent with ICTY rulings, video evidence could be authenticated through other corroborative evidence. For example, in *Prosecutor v. Karemera*, video evidence of a rally was in part authenticated by reference to a radio broadcast of the same rally.[203] Similarly, in *Prosecutor v. Bagosora et al.*, witness testimony was used to corroborate video evidence.[204] Radio broadcasts calling for the apprehension of Tutsis were found to be authenticated by an expert witness who testified that following such broadcasts, people hunted Tutsis.[205] In practice, as most tendered

194 *Prosecutor v. Musema*, ICTR-96-13, Judgement and Sentence, 27 January 2000. Rule 89(c) provided that a Chamber may admit any relevant evidence deemed to have probative value.

195 The Chamber described the standard as '... must enjoy some component of reliability. (ibid para. 35).

196 ibid para. 37.

197 ibid para. 41.

198 ibid para. 58.

199 Documentary evidence was defined very broadly as being 'anything in which information of any description is recorded' and included, inter alia, photographs, videotapes, slides, and negatives (ibid paras. 53, 55–56).

200 ibid paras. 61–72.

201 ibid para. 69.

202 ibid paras. 75–79.

203 ICTR-98-44-T, Judgement and Sentence, 2 February 2012, paras. 169, 208, 508.

204 ICTR-98-41-T, Judgement and Sentence, 18 December 2008, paras. 518, 996, 1340.

205 *Prosecutor v. Rutaganda*, ICTR-96-3-T, Judgment, 13 February 1996, paras. 357, 370.

evidence was admitted for consideration, the threshold objections of the parties were primarily to its authenticity.[206] Further, for the ICTR, other tribunals, and the ICC there has been a general tendency to admit evidence challenged on authentication grounds for final weighing.[207]

4.3 STL

Though not an international criminal prosecution for atrocity crimes, reference to *Prosecutor v. Ayyash et al.* is instructive because it helps to confirm a trend in the evaluation of evidence generally.[208] In the final judgment, the Chamber set out the evidential assessment principles to be applied. The Chamber stated that the party tendering evidence must establish its relevance and prima facie reliability, which includes authenticity.[209] Definitive proof of reliability and authenticity is not required at this stage.[210] The threshold assessment of probative value, which evaluates relevance, reliability, and authenticity, is distinct from the final weighing of evidence in the case.[211] Failure to meet the threshold test would result in exclusion on the basis that the evidence would lack probative value.[212] Each piece of evidence found to be relevant, reliable, credible, and probative is then evaluated and weighed against other relevant pieces of evidence in a holistic manner.[213]

The Chamber rejected the atomistic approach, noting that evidence cannot be evaluated in a piecemeal fashion.[214] The Chamber noted that the ICTY, ICTR, MICT, SCSL, and ICC have adopted the holistic approach, avoiding microscopically examining a piece of evidence out of context and on too high a standard of proof.[215] The Chamber noted that the quality of a piece of evidence may not be evident when viewed in isolation and it may be augmented or undermined by other relevant evidence.[216] Notably, a piece of evidence found to be prima facie authentic upon admission may lose that status and found to have no weight when later considered holistically.[217] The Chamber was thus careful to distinguish this weighing process from the prima facie threshold admission, noting that one is not binding on the other.[218] The STL two-step approach carries on the tradition of earlier and

206 Ashouri, Bowers, and Warden (n 1) 118.
207 ibid.
208 STL-11-01/T/TC-F3839/20200818/R331945-R334626/EN/dm, Judgment, 18 August 2020.
209 ibid paras. 177–180.
210 ibid para. 356.
211 ibid para. 181.
212 ibid para. 249.
213 ibid paras. 188, 230, 232, 245.
214 ibid para. 232.
215 ibid para. 233.
216 ibid para. 230.
217 ibid paras. 181, 356.
218 ibid para. 231.

parallel tribunals as well as some ICC Chambers. Requiring prima facie proof upon threshold admission is sound as is the holistic approach to weighing evidence. Caution must be exercised so that the holistic assessment does not imbue a piece of evidence with more weight than it should garner, or as some authors refer to it, paper over cracks.[219]

4.4 ICC

In this section, I examine the ICC's varied approaches as to how and when the authentication of evidence should be addressed. At the conclusion of Section 4.4.1, I recommend a new three-step approach to the authentication of evidence that is designed to accentuate the importance of proving authenticity and to filter out substandard evidence earlier in the proceedings. In Section 4.4.2, I review case examples involving the authentication of image-based evidence.

4.4.1 The Legal Approach to the Authentication of Evidence

There have been varying approaches to the authentication of evidence among ICC Chambers. In *Prosecutor v. Lubanga*, the Chamber stated that pursuant to the *Rome Statute* and the RPE, at the confirmation hearing stage there is a rebuttable presumption of authenticity for all evidence enumerated in the Lists of Evidence provided by the parties.[220] In a later *Lubanga* decision, the Chamber stated that if a challenge is raised to the admissibility of evidence, the party seeking to introduce it must establish its admissibility.[221] The Chamber must be satisfied as to the prima facie relevance and probative value of evidence submitted and the failure by the tendering party to establish reliability may result in exclusion at the outset or during final consideration at the end of the case.[222] Finally, the probative value of the evidence must exceed the prejudicial effect of admission.[223] Thus, authentication does not appear to be a prerequisite for admissibility and may be considered in the final weighing exercise, subject to a probative value assessment.

A different approach was followed in *Prosecutor v. Katanga and Ngudjolo Chui*, where the Chamber addressed an application by the prosecution to tender several documents and video recordings into evidence.[224] Contrary to the more flexible approach in *Lubanga*, the Chamber stated that demonstration by the tendering party of the relevance, probative value, and authenticity of evidence is a precondition to admissibility.[225] Arguments by counsel that its content may prove to be

[219] McDermott (n 157) 688.
[220] ICC-01/04-01/06-803-tEN, Decision on Confirmation of Charges, 29 January 2007, para. 97.
[221] ICC-01/04-01/06-1399, Decision on the Admissibility of Four Documents, 13 June 2008, para. 25.
[222] ibid paras. 27–30.
[223] ibid para. 31.
[224] ICC-01/04-01/07-2635, Decision on Prosecutor's Bar Table Motions, 17 December 2010.
[225] ibid para. 13.

corroborated by other evidence or that the Chamber may subsequently determine its proper evidentiary weight is insufficient.[226] 'Under no circumstances can the Chamber admit unauthenticated documentary evidence since, by definition, such evidence has no probative value.'[227] The Chamber noted that admitting unauthenticated evidence would unjustifiably burden the record of the trial with non-probative material and would serve no purpose in the determination of the truth.[228] As a result, absent self-authentication or a judicially accepted admission, the party tendering evidence must establish reasonable grounds for its authenticity by direct or circumstantial evidence in order to gain its admission.[229]

Regarding videos, films, photographs, and audio recordings, the Chamber required evidence of originality and integrity.[230] Once established, '... this type of exhibit may often be admitted as evidence that speaks for itself and may be regarded, in this respect, as real evidence'.[231] The Chamber mandated the provision of traditional authentication evidence regarding proof of date and location.[232] The Chamber also set out a number of criteria to be considered when assessing reliability including source (bias); the nature and characteristics of the evidence, and if video evidence, whether it was automatically generated, and whether public or private in nature; contemporaneousness—whether the video was recorded at the time of the event, shortly thereafter, or later; the purpose for which the item was created, whether for criminal prosecution or otherwise; whether there is an adequate means of evaluating the evidence and the manner in which it was obtained; and whether it can be independently verified or tested.[233]

This is a sound approach to authentication. Placing the burden of proof on the tendering party is logical as is establishing the standard of proof of reasonable grounds. If the tendering party cannot meet this modest standard, then the evidence is too tenuous to be placed before the Chamber for consideration. While I disagree with the Chamber's statement that visual evidence speaks for itself, I agree with the Chamber's statement that, 'No judgment can be rendered safely if it is based on evidence prepared on behalf of one party which the opponent has not

[226] ibid.
[227] ibid para. 22.
[228] ibid para. 22.
[229] ibid para. 23.
[230] ibid para. 24(d).
[231] ibid.
[232] ibid.
[233] ibid para. 27. The reliability of evidence is considered as part of the assessment of weight, a perspective viewed to be consistent with RPE Rule 63(2), which gives the Chamber the authority to '... assess freely all evidence submitted in order to determine its relevance and admissibility' in accordance with Article 69; *Prosecutor v. Katanga and Njudjolo Chui*, ICC-01/04-01/07-717, Decision on the Confirmation of Charges, 30 September 2008, para. 78. Reliability also factors into the assessment of the probative value of tendered evidence; *Katanga and Chui* (n 224) para. 20. If an item of evidence does not possess sufficient indicia of reliability, it may be excluded (ibid para. 21).

been able to test or verify.'[234] Trial fairness and the pursuit of a just result demands nothing less.

In *Prosecutor v. Bemba*, the Chamber applied a broad approach to establishing the authenticity of documentary evidence by stating that there is no strict requirement that every document be authenticated officially or by a witness.[235] The Chamber stated that items can be self-authenticating, agreed by counsel to be authentic, prima facie reliable, or shown to be authentic by the provision of relevant evidence.[236] This approach should be equally applicable to image-based evidence. When admissibility is challenged, the burden of proof rests upon the party seeking admission.[237] Interestingly, the Chamber stated that admissibility has no bearing on the final assessment of weight.[238] Referring to audio recordings, the Chamber said that unauthenticated recordings were still admissible, subject to an assessment of probative value.[239]

Paradoxically, this suggests that evidence found to be inadmissible or inauthentic might still be afforded weight when deciding the case. Yet regarding the admission of certain photographs, the Chamber noted that the prosecution had led no evidence to support their authenticity and reliability and therefore even though they appeared to be relevant they were ruled inadmissible.[240] These disparate approaches to admissibility in the same decision do little to settle the law or provide guidance to counsel. In a later decision, when deciding on the admissibility of several documents tendered by the prosecution, the Chamber required that there be 'sufficient indicia of authenticity and reliability to warrant its admission into evidence'.[241] This is a stricter standard, requiring at least prima facie proof prior to admission.

In *Prosecutor v. Gbagbo and Blè Goudè*, contrary to the request of all parties, the Chamber declined to adopt an approach wherein admissibility, relevance, and probative value are determined upon submission.[242] The Chamber stated that it is only at the end of the trial that the Chamber can meaningfully assess each item of evidence, though they did acknowledge that when required by the Statute or when otherwise appropriate, an intermediate ruling could be made.[243] The Chamber found that delaying assessment till the end of the case serves to

[234] ibid para. 42.
[235] CC-01/05-01/08-2299-Red, Decision on the Prosecution's Application for Admission of Materials into Evidence Pursuant to Article 64(9) of the Rome Statute of 6 September 2012, 08 October 2012.
[236] ibid para. 9.
[237] ibid para. 10.
[238] ibid para. 11.
[239] ibid para. 120.
[240] ibid para. 159.
[241] ICC-01/05-01/08-2721, Decision on the Admission into Evidence of Items Deferred in the Chamber's 'Decision on the Prosecution's Application for Admission of Materials into Evidence Pursuant to Article 64(9) of the Rome Statute', 27 June 2013, para. 13.
[242] ICC-02/11-01/15-405, Decision on the Submission and Admission of Evidence, 29 January 2016.
[243] ibid paras. 10, 13.

expedite proceedings and avoids the risk of multiple rulings on the same piece of evidence.[244]

Years later, during his final judgment in the case, Judge Henderson disagreed with the majority's approach to the admissibility of evidence and said that relevance and authenticity must be duly established, failing which it would not be appropriate to rely on tendered evidence for fact-finding.[245] Acknowledging that there is no legal mandate to decide on admissibility before final judgment, he noted that delaying such a ruling may not be appropriate.[246] He was of the view that evidence that cannot be authenticated for admissibility purposes also cannot be authenticated for the purpose of assigning evidentiary weight.[247] He did, however, express a general inclination that admissibility rulings should be made earlier in the proceedings, when feasible.[248]

Collectively, these rulings reflect a general judicial preference to address matters of authenticity and admissibility at the end of the case, though the *Katanga and Ngudjolo Chui* requirement that authenticity be a precondition for admissibility certainly creates the environment for rulings earlier in the case. While I appreciate that the end of the case approach may promote judicial economy as it will avoid Chambers having to make interim rulings, it also sets the stage for an evidence pool which may contain a plethora of evidence of sometimes dubious integrity that could have been excluded earlier.

The two-step assessment of evidence which requires prima facie proof upon admission and greater proof upon final weighing is a common though not universally applied approach in international criminal prosecutions. The salutary aspect of this approach is that threshold filtering serves to winnow out evidence at an early stage. The challenging aspect is that it also creates a logjam of evidence at the end of the case for counsel and the court to contend with, some of which could have been filtered out at the end of the prosecution or defence case, as appropriate, where sufficient proof of authentication (more than prima facie proof) was found to be lacking.

I contend that utilizing a three-step approach would address this gap. First, upon tendering the evidence, the party should be required to establish its authenticity on a prima facie basis. Second, any evidence that has not been sufficiently authenticated on the balance of probabilities by the close of the party's case should be excluded. This approach would accentuate the importance of addressing authenticity during the presentation of evidence and help to ensure that only reliable evidence is considered in the final judgment. Failure to meet the first two tests should result

[244] ibid paras. 12–15.

[245] *Prosecutor v. Gbagbo and Blè Goudè*, ICC-02/11-01/15-1263-Conf-AnxB, Reasons of Judge Henderson, 16 July 2019, para. 32.

[246] ibid para. 22.

[247] ibid para. 37.

[248] ibid paras. 20–30.

in the evidence being excluded at an earlier stage and would help to clarify and economize the evidential record for final consideration. It would also put counsel on notice that authenticity must be addressed in a robust manner early in the proceedings rather than waiting to address the issue in final argument. Finally, when the Chamber evaluates all evidence at the close of the case, it must assess each piece of evidence with a view to addressing authenticity and corresponding weight. Any evidence found to lack sufficient authenticity must be disregarded.

The more pivotal the evidence in question is to the prosecution's case, the more important a mid-trial admissibility ruling becomes. For example, if the questioned evidence is a central tenet regarding a count in the indictment and the absence of that evidence would result in the prosecution being unable to maintain their pursuit of that count, then a mid-trial ruling on admissibility would be important and impactful. If the prosecution failed to authenticate evidence necessary to maintain their case on a particular count, the defence could also address this by way of a *no case to answer* motion prior to electing whether to present defence evidence on that count. The main rationale for the no case to answer procedure is to avoid forcing a defendant to answer to a charge when the prosecution's evidence is insufficient to garner a conviction.[249] This stage was expressly included in SCSL Rule 98 and ICTY and ICTR Rule 98 *bis* but the *Rome Statute* and the ICC RPE contain no such provision, though in practice that would not prevent the court from dismissing counts for lack of evidence prior to the defence case.[250] The ICC Appeals Chamber has confirmed this power and it has certainly been applied, as exemplified in *Prosecutor v. Gbagbo and Blé Goudé* where the prosecution's entire case was dismissed on the basis of a no case to answer motion.[251]

4.4.2 Selected Cases on the Authentication of Image-Based Evidence

The purpose of this section is to review selected authentication rulings by ICC Chambers to see how the foregoing legal approaches have been applied in practice. In *Prosecutor v. Gbagbo*, the Chamber preferred to have as much forensic evidence and other material evidence as possible and stated that such evidence should be duly authenticated, along with proof of clear and unbroken chains of custody.[252] The Chamber provided no guidance on how to accomplish this task as this is part

[249] Vladimir Tochilovsky, *Jurisprudence of the International Criminal Courts and the European Court of Human Rights: Procedure and Evidence* (Leiden: Martinus Nijhoff Publishers, 2008), 538.

[250] Robert Cryer, *An Introduction to International Criminal Law and Procedure* (Cambridge: CUP, 2007), 387; Gideon Boas, *International Criminal Law Practitioner Library: Volume 3: International Criminal Procedure* (Cambridge: CUP, 2011), 287–90.

[251] *Prosecutor v. Ntaganda*, ICC-01/04-02/06-2026, Judgment on the Appeal of Mr Bosco Ntaganda Against the 'Decision on Defence Request for Leave to File a No Case to Answer Motion', 5 September 2017, para. 44. A detailed discussion on the use of the no case to answer motion is found in the Reasons of Judge Henderson in *Gbagbo and Blè Goudè* (n 241) paras. 10–19.

[252] ICC-02/11-01/11-432, Decision Adjourning the Hearing on the Confirmation of Charges Pursuant to Article 61(7)(c)(i) of the Rome Statute, 3 June 2013, para. 27.

of counsel's role. How then can a party successfully meet this authentication requirement as it applies to image-based evidence?

There are three approaches that can be followed, depending on the available evidence. First, image-based evidence may be authenticated internally by proving the technical soundness of the metadata and the content of the media. Second, authentication may be proven externally by evaluating other reliable evidence, including *viva voce* evidence, which corroborates the content of the questioned media. At times, a combination of both methods may be used. Third, multiple sources may be able to cross reference and corroborate temporal and spatial narratives reflected in digital media that might otherwise suffer from lack of authentication. This approach does not necessarily directly authenticate the questioned media but provides sufficient contextual confirmation to indirectly achieve that result. Failure to follow any of these methods in support of authentication should result in exclusion of the tendered evidence.

Internal authentication was the approach followed in *Prosecutor v. Bemba*, where the Chamber was satisfied as to the authenticity of a broadcast video interview because it 'bore indicia of reliability, integrity, and originality', including a date stamp, a visible watermark of the TV programme, the image and voice of the known speaker, and no evidence of editing during the entirety of the recorded interview.[253] Similarly, in *Prosecutor v. Katanga and Ngudjolo Chui*, the Chamber opined that video evidence is only fully understandable (and therefore considered disclosed) when the relevant people in the video have been identified; the date, time, and location have been determined as precisely as possible; and a translation into one of the working languages of the Court has been prepared.[254]

An unresolved example is found in *Prosecutor v. Bemba et al.*, where the defence challenged Facebook images tendered by the prosecution on the basis that no evidence had been provided as to their authenticity and linkage to the defendant.[255] The prosecution countered that because the images were found on the open source Facebook site, they were 'thus, prima facie authentic and reliable'.[256] It is hard to conceive of why the prosecution would make such a palpably unsupportable submission.[257] Regrettably, the Chamber did not address this issue,

[253] *Bemba* (n 231) para. 81.

[254] ICC-01/04-01/07-1336, Decision on Prosecution Application to Present Video Evidence, 27 July 2009, para. 11.

[255] ICC-01/05-01/13-1245-Red, Public Redacted Version of Defence Response to Prosecution's Third Request for the Admission of Evidence from the Bar Table (ICC-01/05-01/13-1170), 10 September 2015, paras. 83–6.

[256] ICC-01/05-01/13-1498-Red, Public Redacted Version of the 'Prosecution's Fifth Request for the Admission of Evidence from the Bar Table', 27 November 2015, ICC-01/05-01/13-1498-Conf, 30 November 2015, para. 17.

[257] In the OTP Strategic Plan for 2016–2018, regarding open source media posted to the internet, reference is made to the need for adequate evidentiary details on 'such a dynamic and volatile medium as the internet'; ICC OTP, 'Strategic Plan 2016–2018' (16 November 2015), https://www.icc-cpi.int/iccdocs/otp/070715-OTP_Strategic_Plan_2016-2018.pdf, para. 25.

instead deferring any such decision to the final judgment, where no reference was made to the Facebook images.[258] A further example of internal image authentication is found in *Prosecutor v. Gbagbo and Blè Goudè*, where reference is made to an OTP forensic expert opining that video evidence appeared to be authentic on the basis that no evidence of editing or manipulation was found.[259] Open source images have not faced significant challenges in the tribunals or the ICC. They have undergone very limited forensic analysis and authentication has not been a significantly litigated issue. The default position appears to be admission without detailed examination.[260]

In *Prosecutor v. Al-Werfalli*, the Chamber based its decision to issue an arrest warrant upon, inter alia, video recordings of executions committed by Al-Werfalli personally or ordered by him and committed by others in his presence and subsequently posted to social media sites including Facebook. There may be uncertainly as to where one of the videos was uploaded, which could have impacted authenticity, but that would not have been addressed until later in the proceedings.[261] A full showing of authenticity would have been required at trial but that will not be tested as the ICC withdrew the arrest warrant on 15 June 2022 upon being satisfied that the defendant was dead.[262]

External proof of authenticity was used in *Prosecutor v. Bemba*, where the Chamber admitted video evidence showing troop movements in CAR on the basis that a witness was able to authenticate the image content, it was established that the video was recorded at the relevant time, and it was shown to be an accurate portrayal of the event.[263] Even video that was not authenticated was admitted into evidence as the Chamber noted that lack of authenticity is not a bar to admissibility.[264] External authentication was used in *Prosecutor v. Lubanga*, where a witness depicted in a video recording was able to authenticate the content and location shown by virtue of her presence in it.[265] In *Prosecutor v. Gbagbo*, videos showing

[258] ICC-01/05-01/13-1524, Decision on 'Prosecution's Fifth Request for the Admission of Evidence from the Bar Table', 14 December 2015, para. 3; ICC-01/05-01/13-3343, Judgment Pursuant to Article 74 of the Statute, 21 March 2016.

[259] ICC-02/11-01/15-1263-AnxA, Reasons of Judge Tarfusser, 16 July 2019, para. 31.

[260] Freeman (n 151) 317–19.

[261] ICC-01/11-01/17, Warrant for Arrest, 15 August 2017, para. 22.

[262] See https://www.icc-cpi.int/libya/al-werfalli and https://www.icc-cpi.int/libya/al-werfalli#icc-timeline. There appears to have been adequate proof of authenticity to justify the arrest warrant based upon the content of the second arrest warrant issued by the ICC where reference is made to the key video having undergone a forensic assessment and the presence of additional corroborative evidence; ICC-01/11-01/17, Second Warrant of Arrest, 4 July 2018, paras. 17–19.

[263] ICC-01/05-01/08-2012, First Decision on the Prosecution and Defence Requests for the Admission of Evidence, 9 February 2012, para. 89.

[264] ibid para. 93.

[265] ICC-01/04-01/06-2842, Judgment Pursuant to Article 74 of the Statute, 14 March 2012, paras. 254–257.

FDS troops opening fire on a crowd were found to be authenticated by witnesses who were present at the location of the march and observed the attack.[266]

An example of the failure to authenticate media which resulted in its exclusion is found in *Prosecutor v. Ntaganda*, where the prosecution sought to admit video images showing the presence of alleged child soldiers in Ituri but provided no proof as to when the video was recorded (only when it was broadcast) and no proof of what armed groups were shown. As a result, the Chamber found the probative value of the video to be outweighed by its prejudicial effect and excluded it.[267] Other video evidence was also rejected for want of authentication.[268] Photographs purportedly showing the defendant with members of the UPC/FLPC were tendered but the prosecution failed to provide sufficient evidence as to when and where the photographs were taken, resulting in their exclusion.[269] It is lamentable that the prosecution seemed oblivious to their obligation to authenticate tendered image-based evidence. These injuries to the prosecution case were self-inflicted and with proper planning could have been avoided.

The ICC is aware of the need to authenticate digital media and designs e-Court Protocols to further that goal. While there are general protocols for the electronic submission and disclosure of evidence, evidence-based protocols currently used are case specific and generally set out standards applicable to digital evidence which require metadata to be attached including the chain of custody in chronological order, the identity of the source, the original author and recipient information, and the author and recipient's respective organizations.[270] The Protocols do not provide substantive guidance on evidentiary process or standards.[271] The ICC currently utilizes a set of standards that are specific to digital evidence whereby such evidence must conform to an e-Court Protocol even before it is submitted at the Confirmation Hearing. The Protocol is designed to ensure the authenticity, accuracy, confidentiality, and preservation of the record of proceedings.[272] At present, there is no overriding e-Court Protocol that applies to all cases. A robust e-Court Protocol should require that all digital video and images be authenticated via internal metadata and content verification, external corroboration, or a combination of both.

[266] ICC-02/11-01/11-656-Red, Decision on the Confirmation of Charges Against Laurent Gbagbo, 12 June 2014, para. 47.

[267] ICC-01/04-02/06-1838, Decision on the Prosecution's Request for the Admission of Documentary Evidence, 28 March 2017, para. 63.

[268] ibid paras. 64, 66.

[269] ibid paras. 67–68.

[270] ICC Chambers Practice Manual, para. 20; 'Unified Technical Protocol ('E-court Protocol') for the Provision of Evidence, Witness and Victims Information in Electronic Form', https://www.icc-cpi.int/sites/default/files/RelatedRecords/CR2019_00267.PDF. See also Mark Dillon and David Beresford, 'Electronic Courts and the Challenges in Managing Evidence: A View from Inside the International Criminal Court', *International Journal for Court Administration* 6, no. 1 (2014): 1–8.

[271] Ashouri, Bowers, and Warden (n 1) 117.

[272] ICC Regulations of the Court, Reg. 26(2).

Conclusion

Establishing the authenticity of image-based evidence intended for use at trial is an important consideration in most cases but may be even more acute in atrocity crime prosecutions.[273] When the photographer is known and accessible and when the original media is available for evaluation, authentication is unlikely to be a serious challenge. Such was the case with the *Nazi Concentration Camps* film where internal and external authentication was competently addressed by the prosecution. The original film footage was retained; the photographers, directors, producers, and editors were known; and there were ample witnesses to the recorded scenes. This is the level of authenticity that should be expected when trained professionals are tasked with documenting crime scenes and active criminality. Douglas notes that the film's opening narrative approach to authentication '... supports a novel understanding of the documentary as a privileged witness independently competent to swear to the truth of its own images'.[274]

However, atrocity crime cases are often in a category of their own as they are more likely to draw a larger pool of media that does not meet these preferred criteria. Since atrocity crimes tend to occur over a longer period, over a broader geographic area, and involve multiple atrocity events, the volume of media generated is significant. This increase in volume is also fuelled by the larger pool of photographers expected to be documenting atrocity crime events. Among this broader collection of potential evidence will be media that is suboptimum from an authentication perspective, including images recorded by anonymous or inaccessible photographers where the original recordings are not producible, and images submitted to social media and other sites where metadata has been stripped away. It would be wise to approach all image-based evidence with a healthy amount of scepticism, a far preferable stance over assuming that authentication will not be an issue. Evidence that might be considered novel also garners a heightened need for authentication.[275]

Based on ICC case law to date, it does not appear that the authentication of image-based evidence has been a significant concern for counsel or the court. The prevailing attitude, with noted exceptions, is that almost all evidence will be admitted and holistically sorted out in the final judgment. The danger of this approach is that it fosters a certain amount of complacency regarding authentication, which should instead be a central aspect of admissibility. It is reasonable to predict that increasing amounts of image-based evidence will originate from

[273] Rebecca Hamilton, 'Social Media Platforms in International Criminal Investigations', *Case Western Reserve Journal of International Law* 52 (2020): 213–24, at 218.

[274] Lawrence Douglas, *The Memory of Judgment: Making Law and History in the Trials of the Holocaust* (New Haven: Yale University Press, 2001), 29.

[275] Alex Jeffrey, 'Legal Geography III: Evidence', *Progress in Human Geography* 45, no. 4 (2021): 902–13, at 906.

social media and other sites where photographers may be anonymous, and the original media is absent. These conditions present serious authentication concerns. Understanding that the authentication of image-based evidence is a prescient issue in atrocity crime litigation is an important first step in addressing these concerns. Establishing authenticity requires positive action and counsel must have robust plans to meet these threshold and ultimate proof requirements. Imagery that cannot withstand challenges is a distraction and adds no value to the case. The same internal and external methods that can be used to establish the authenticity of legitimate media can be used to detect media that is untrustworthy and unsuitable for use as evidence. A robust evaluation and filtering methodology is thus essential for maintaining the integrity of evidence tendered by the parties in the search for the truth.

PART III

EMERGING TECHNICAL FRONTIERS IN IMAGE-BASED EVIDENCE AND RECOMMENDATIONS

8
Emerging Technical Frontiers in Image-Based Evidence

Introduction

The use of image-based evidence as methods of proof and didactic tools has been well established in international criminal prosecutions. Film, video, and photographs, whether recorded at ground level, drone level, or by satellites, have found a receptive audience in the courtroom. The familiarity that these images have achieved in the courtroom today occurred incrementally. Each advance in the echelons of technology necessarily attracts scrutiny when intended for use in court because novel forms of evidence are subjected to detailed examination to assess their reliability and accuracy. For example, once considered revolutionary, photographs have long become commonplace, though not necessarily without controversy. Once a general acceptance and level of comfort have settled over counsel and the court, these types of evidence are routinely admitted and used for the purposes intended.

The next significant technological advancement that was considered by counsel and the court was the use of computer-generated representations in the form of animations and simulations which visually depict underlying measurements and visual data to show what happened in a specific event or what is believed to have happened.[1] They may be helpful to visualize events that are technically complex, require an assessment of timing, or when the underlying facts are in dispute.[2] Common concerns for this type of evidence are the validity of the underlying data and the fairness of its presentation. Judicial decisions, primarily at the domestic level, have set out parameters for the use of such representational evidence. Three-dimensional (3D) terrestrial laser scanning and scene modelling represent a further level of technological sophistication and often form part of computer animations and simulations. This 3D approach can provide detailed depictions of static scenes, recreate an occurrence by showing the chronological sequence of events as they unfolded, and may also permit viewers to digitally move throughout

[1] Damian Schofield and Ken Fowle, 'Technology Corner—Visualizing Forensic Data: Evidence (Part 1)', *Journal of Digital Forensics, Security and Law* 8, no. 1 (2013): 73–90, at 83–5. See Chapter 2 for further details.

[2] Carole Powell, 'Computer Generated Visual Evidence: Does Daubert Make a Difference?', *Georgia State University Law Review* 12, no 2 (1996): 577–600, at 581–2.

Image-Based Evidence in International Criminal Prosecutions. Jonathan W. Hak, KC, Oxford University Press.
 DOI: 10.1093/oso/9780198889533.003.0008

the scene to observe it from different perspectives. Three-dimensional scanning and modelling form an integral part of interactive 360° visual representations which have found favour in international criminal prosecutions.

Emerging technical frontiers in the use of image-based evidence and the technical and legal implications for their use in international criminal justice bear further examination. This chapter explores the emerging technologies of virtual reality, immersive virtual environments, and augmented reality since they occupy the next tier of technical advancement with the potential for courtroom application. As with most technologies, they offer advantages and disadvantages in the context of criminal investigations and prosecutions. Legal and practical considerations must be addressed regarding these advanced forms of evidence including an assessment of their probative value weighed against their potential prejudicial effect, along with a recognition that new technologies must have demonstrated merit to achieve inclusion in the judicial environment. We must also consider the role emerging technology should play, if any, in international criminal prosecutions. Just because we may have the ability to provide a hyper-realistic experience for the court, allowing it to virtually walk through a killing field, does not mean that it should be done. Can we go too far?

1. Emerging Technologies: The Path to Virtual Reality

Over the years there has been a steady progression of technologically derived image-based evidence that has found its way into the courtroom. Photographs made their entry in the mid-nineteenth century while film and video arrived in the mid-twentieth century. These now familiar forms of evidence have provided the court with increased comprehension of depicted scenes, superior to that which could be achieved by only narrative testimony. Image-based evidence has also been used to replicate scenes as well as people and objects moving within them in a two-dimensional (2D) format on a digital map. This approach was used extensively in *Prosecutor v. Ayyash et al.*, where analysing the movement of vehicles was essential to understand the vehicle bombing that occurred.[3] The 2D format provides a useful bird's eye view of the scene and events and can also contain digitally embedded links to individual videos and photographs that will show portions of the scene from ground level.[4]

Computer-generated reconstructions in the form of animations and simulations took visual analysis to the next level by allowing witness and expert perspectives to

[3] STL-11-01/T/TC-F3839/20200818/R331945-R334626/EN/dm, Judgment, 18 August 2020.

[4] Jay Aronson, McKenna Cole, Alex Hauptmann, Dan Miller, and Bradley Samuels, 'Reconstructing Human Rights Violations Using Large Eyewitness Collections: The Case of Euromaidan Protester Deaths', *Journal of Human Rights Practice* (2018): 1–20, at 4. These methods are discussed in Section 5.1.

be minutely examined.[5] Once a scene has been digitally constructed by computer scientists using videos and photographs obtained from multiple sources, measurements, spatial analysis, 3D modelling, animation, and interactive visualization, it allows for the creation of a visual narrative of an event, and the corresponding ability of viewers to gain significant information about the location generally and the perspectives of the people involved.[6] Multi-perspectival accounts of the event may be evaluated and tested in spatial (3D) and temporal (4D) reconstructions.[7] These interactive presentation platforms do not necessarily create new substantive evidence but rather generate a new way of examining existing visual data. For a reconstruction to achieve validity and relevance, the images relied upon must be geolocated and synchronized to a global time clock. Some platforms such as those created by SITU Research for the International Criminal Court (ICC) allow viewers to navigate through visual environments using location and time parameters.[8] They also allow for the viewing of embedded synchronized and geolocated still and video images and other evidence by way of augmented reality.[9]

A further advancement in computer-generated reconstructions is to use them not only for demonstrative purposes but as a tool for experts and the court to interpret events within the platform. Building on work performed by SITU Research and Forensic Architecture, Aronson et al. have undertaken projects wherein they have selected key frames from one or more video recordings and used them to model such things as the trajectory of a projectile or the physical reaction of someone who was hit by the projectile.[10] These reconstructions can also be used to evaluate events at a specific place over time. This approach is best understood as a composite one wherein no single video, photograph, or other data is necessarily pivotal, but they may generate new revelations when examined collectively.

[5] Vincenzo Sainato, 'Evidentiary Presentations and Forensic Technologies in the Courtroom, The Director's Cut', *Journal of the Institute of Justice and International Studies* 9 (2009): 38–52, at 40.

[6] Aronson, Cole, Hauptmann, Miller, and Samuels (n 4) 2.

[7] ibid. Reconstructions can show a static scene in 3D but can also show an event over time (4D).

[8] SITU Research is an interdisciplinary applied-research division situated in New York City that works at the intersection of architecture, urbanism, policy, and human rights. One of the tasks it performs is to create 3D reconstructions of scenes and events. Among the work it has done is assisting the ICC OTP for situations in Timbuktu, Mali, and Syria. See https://situ.nyc/research/projects.

[9] e.g. SITU Research, 'Euromaidan Event Reconstruction' https://situ.nyc/research/projects/euromaidan-event-reconstruction. The Euromaidan case is a Ukrainian prosecution, but SITU Research also works on ICC cases. These cases and interactive 360° visual representations generally are discussed in Section 5.1.

[10] Forensic Architecture is a research agency based at Goldsmiths, University of London, that investigates human rights violations worldwide including violence committed by states, police, military, and corporations. It creates architectural evidence of buildings and urban environments in the form of 3D reconstructions using open source investigation, digital modelling, immersive technology, documentary research, interviews, and academic collaboration. Its evidence has been used in various venues. See https://forensic-architecture.org/about/agency; 'Investigations – Virtualreality' https://forensic-architecture.org/methodology/%20virtualreality. See also John Emerson, Margaret Satterthwaite, and Anshul Pandey, 'The Challenging Power of Data Visualization for Human Rights Advocacy', in *New Technologies for Human Rights Law and Practice*, edited by Molly Land and Jay Aronson (Cambridge: CUP, 2018), 162–87, at 179; Aronson, Cole, Hauptmann, Miller, and Samuels (n 4) 4.

Central to the foregoing visualization mediums is the necessity of incorporating reliable scene and event data. For example, when using multimedia visual platforms such as those created by SITU Research, the individual components that are used to create the final representation, including still images, videos, diagrams, and maps, must be independently authenticated and marked as exhibits. The multimedia presentation must also be marked as an exhibit, though it has limited evidential value on its own.[11] The narrative and interpretive testimonial evidence based upon these representations will likely assist the court in understanding various aspects of an event more vividly than by viewing the individual components alone.

The next progression in emerging technologies (and the focus of this chapter) is the use of virtual reality (VR) and immersive virtual environments (IVEs) for the presentation and evaluation of scenes and events. VR describes a digitally constructed artificial environment or medium which the user experiences through sensory stimuli such as sight, sound, and touch that are provided by a computer and in which the user's actions influence what happens in the environment.[12] It is also described as a medium composed of interactive computer simulations that sense the user's position and actions and which replaces or augments the feedback to one or more senses, giving the feeling of being mentally immersed or present within the virtual world.[13] VR environments are also referred to as IVEs and for ease of reference I will generally refer to both collectively as IVEs.[14]

The essence of an IVE is that by using high-resolution stereoscopic projections and 3D computer graphics, the user is physically and mentally immersed in a digitally created world such that the sensory information in the virtual environment is more psychologically prominent as compared to the physical world.[15] In short, the user is situated within the environment rather than viewing it from the outside.

[11] Lindsay Freeman, 'Digital Evidence and War Crimes Prosecutions: The Impact of Digital Technologies on International Criminal Investigations and Trials', *Fordham International Law Journal* 41, no. 2 (2018): 283–335, at 319–20.

[12] Merriam-Webster Dictionary, 'Virtual Reality' https://www.merriam-webster.com/dictionary/virtual%20reality; Damian Schofield, 'Graphical Evidence: Forensic Animations and Virtual Reconstructions', *Australian Journal of Forensic Sciences* 41, no. 2 (2009): 131–45, at 135. Virtual and augmented reality were invented in the 1960s by Ivan Sutherland, an engineer of graphic machines. Martin Warnke, 'On the Spot: The Double Immersion of Virtual Reality', in *Immersion in the Visual Arts and Media*, edited by Fabienne Liptay and Burcu Dogramaci (Leiden: Brill Rodopi, 2016), 205–13, at 206. See also William Sherman and Alan Craig, *Understanding Virtual Reality: Interface, Application, and Design* (Amsterdam: Morgan Kaufmann Publishers, 2003), 25–36 for a lengthy history of VR.

[13] Sherman and Craig (n 12) 13.

[14] Neal Feigenson, 'Too Real? The Future of Virtual Reality Evidence', *Law & Policy* 28, no. 2 (2006): 271–94, at 271; Caitlin Young, 'Employing Virtual Reality Technology at Trial: New Issues Posed by Rapid Technological Advances and Their Effects on Jurors' Search for "the Truth"', *Texas Law Review* 93, no. 1 (2014): 257–74, at 260.

[15] Young (n 14) 260; Jeremy Bailenson, Jim Blascovich, Andrew Beall, and Beth Noveck, 'Courtroom Applications of Virtual Environments, Immersive Virtual Environments, and Collaborative Virtual Environments', *Law & Policy* 28, no. 2 (2006): 249–70, at 250–1; Carrie Leonetti and Jeremy Bailenson, 'High-Tech View: The Use of Immersive Virtual Environments in Jury Trials', *Marquette Law Review* 93, no. 3 (2010): 1073–1120, at 1075–6.

The sense of presence is influenced by the environment's vividness and the user's ability to interact with it.[16] Users may see, hear, perambulate, and interact with simulated objects and people, thereby creating a hyper-realistic sense of being in a real environment, interacting with real objects and people.[17] An ambulatory platform provides seemingly realistic movement through a virtual world in accordance with movement of the user's body.[18] When based upon reliable data, IVEs can provide highly accurate and vivid representations to viewers.[19]

IVEs differ from even highly sophisticated 2D screen-based simulations because they create a 3D experience.[20] Entry into the virtual world is facilitated visually by wearing a head-mounted display that digitally projects scene content from a first person perspective, aurally by wearing headphones which transmit sound seemingly from certain locations within the scene, haptically by wearing gloves that provide mechanical feedback when touching something in the virtual environment, and olfactorily by wearing a nosepiece that releases different smells when the user approaches different locations or objects.[21] Some of these features may not be appropriate to incorporate into an IVE depending upon its purpose and audience (e.g. in an atrocity crime prosecution, visual data would be predominant whereas haptic and olfactory sensations would rarely, if ever, be appropriate).

To achieve virtual movement in the environment, the head orientation and body position of the user are tracked and recorded and the IVE automatically updates the digital environment to respond to such changes.[22] Virtual visualization can permit teleporting (moving the user from one location to another), changing the point of view, and interaction with objects embedded within the environment.[23] An IVE can be set up in multi-user format so that counsel, the court, and the witness can be in the environment at the same time.[24] This would be important if a witness was recreating experiences in an IVE as counsel and the court would need to appreciate the context for the witness's testimony. Beyond the immediate

[16] Feigenson (n 14) 273.

[17] ibid 271.

[18] Sherman and Craig (n 12) 101.

[19] Feigenson (n 14) 271. Virtual worlds that closely resemble the real world are referred to as mimetic (e.g. they mimic the physical world). Sherman and Craig (n 12) 212.

[20] Feigenson (n 14) 273.

[21] The headset presents 3D data by displaying a separate image for each eye, allowing viewers to perceive depth and to look around and move within the virtual environment, delivering a sense of space, scale, and immersion; Bailenson, Blascovich, Beall, and Noveck (n 15) 250–1; Dominic Raneri, 'Enhancing Forensic Investigation Through the Use of Modern Three-Dimensional (3D) Imaging Technologies for Crime Scene Reconstruction', *Australian Journal of Forensic Sciences* 50, no. 6 (2018): 697–707, at 702.

[22] Young (n 14) 261.

[23] Till Sieberth, Akos Dobay, Raffael Affolter, and Lars Ebert, 'Applying Virtual Reality in Forensics—A Virtual Scene Walkthrough', *Forensic Science, Medicine and Pathology* 15 (2019): 41–7, at 43.

[24] Till Sieberth, Dilan Seckiner, Akos Dobay, Erika Dobler, Raffael Golomingi, and Lars Ebert, 'The Forensic Holodeck: Recommendations After 8 Years of Experience for Additional Equipment to Document VR Applications', *Forensic Science International* 329, no. 111092 (2021): 1–7, at 2.

participants, head-mounted display content can be mirrored on other displays for an audience to observe, albeit in 2D.[25]

Movement within an IVE is facilitated depending on the degrees of freedom (DOF) allowed the user. A DOF is defined as a particular way in which a body can move in space.[26] There are six degrees of freedom in unconstrained movement.[27] Movement can be translational along the x, y, and z axes (left-right, forward-backward, up-down) thus defining the user's location within the environment (3-DOF) and rotational, allowing for roll (clockwise or counter clockwise movement), pitch (upward and downward), and yaw (side-to-side), thus defining the user's orientation within the environment (6-DOF when combined).[28] An IVE can be programmed to permit the desired amount of movement and therefore counsel and the expert creating the IVE must determine what amount of movement is appropriate. Judicial direction may also be required in this regard.

Even though movement within the environment is possible, what the user observes is not a photo-realistic depiction of a scene.[29] Viewers are not simply immersed into a scene with the same view as an actual eyewitness. Rather, they observe a highly mediated computer model intended to digitally represent the scene and not the more realistic depictions of a scene provided by high quality video recordings and photographs. Creation of the virtual environment is dependent upon detailed measurements and photographs of the actual scene to accurately replicate the overall scene and objects within it.[30] Terrestrial laser scanners and photogrammetry techniques are used to measure large outdoor areas (up to several kilometres in area), buildings, rooms, and large vehicles.[31] Scanners are able to quickly measure a scene and generate point clouds with millions of points with accuracy to within 1 mm.[32] Smaller scale items such as weapons are documented using high-resolution structured light scanners.[33] An IVE cannot speak for itself and therefore it is essential that an expert explain the technology, underlying data, assumptions, and techniques that were utilized to create the IVE.[34]

[25] ibid.

[26] Sherman and Craig (n 12) 80.

[27] ibid 182.

[28] ibid 80.

[29] Although as technology improves IVEs are achieving more realistic depictions; Gargi Jani and Abraham Johnson, 'Virtual Reality and its Transformation in Forensic Education and Research Practices', *Journal of Visual Communication in Medicine* 45, no. 1 (2022): 18–25, at 22.

[30] Minhua Ma, Huiru Zheng, and Harjinder Lallie, 'Virtual Reality and 3D Animation in Forensic Visualization', *Journal of Forensic Sciences* 55, no. 5 (2010): 1227–31, at 1227. Electronic distance measurement surveying technology and terrestrial laser scanning provide highly accurate measurements which in turn lead to an accurate virtual environment; Schofield (n 12) 133, 135.

[31] Sieberth, Dobay, Affolter, and Ebert (n 23) 41.

[32] Sieberth et al. caution that even though measurements are accurate, current research shows that distances in IVEs are underestimated for large spaces and they recommend that only limited sized scenes such as indoor areas be visualized in an IVE; ibid 46.

[33] ibid.

[34] Leonetti and Bailenson (n 15) 1100.

Augmented reality (AR) is a combination of VR and real-world content (mixed reality) used to create an interactive experience wherein the real-world environment is enhanced by computer-generated perceptual information.[35] The display technology allows the user to combine the physical with the virtual by perceiving the real world with an overlay of additional information, thus augmenting the amount of information available to the user.[36] In practice, the user typically wears a head-mounted display that allows the user to view real-world images with computer-generated images projected on top of them. This can be used to explore the dynamics of an event or a crime scene.[37] For example, a user may explore a virtual crime scene and by clicking on a building within the scene the user will be able to see before and after images showing damage to the building caused by an attack or 360° panoramic photographs of the area. AR is frequently used in interactive 360° visual representations.

VR and the IVE experience effectively recreate a digital, non-photo realistic version of the past by collapsing time and connecting present viewers with a past event.[38] They offer opportunities for observation and interactivity and have the potential to be powerful tools for fact-finding. They may be used for many purposes but the advantages they provide must be tempered by an appraisal of potential disadvantages.

2. Using Virtual Reality in the Courtroom

While photographs, video, and diagrams are certainly helpful in documenting a crime scene, these staid methods may not be sufficient for a full exposition and exploration. Terrestrial laser scanning delivers highly accurate measurements yet when displayed in 2D, viewers only get part of the picture. Being able to visualize a scene or event in 3D provides not only a third dimension but a different and deeper appreciation of the subject matter. VR's 3D environments have been used extensively in various non-forensic contexts including the medical profession for teaching and guiding surgical procedures, tactical military training, flight and driving simulators, training police officers and firefighters, the entertainment industry, computer games, education, and immersive and interactive art installations.[39] VR, IVEs, and AR are also being used in

[35] Ma, Zheng, and Lallie (n 30) 1227–8.

[36] Sherman and Craig (n 12) 18.

[37] Ma, Zheng, and Lallie (n 30) 1227–8.

[38] Renske Vos and Sofia Stolk, 'Courtroom 600: The (Virtual) Reality of Being There', *International Criminal Law Review* 22 (2022): 308–27, at 322.

[39] Leonetti and Bailenson (n 15) 1075–6; Rebecca Pool, 'Virtual and Augmented Reality Tech Joins the Fight Against Crime', *SPIE* (11 January 2019) https://spie.org/news/spie-professional-magazine-archive/2019-january/ar/vr-tech-joins-the-fight-against-crime?SSO=1; Sieberth, Seckiner, Dobay, Dobler, Golomingi, and Ebert (n 24) 1–7; Jani and Johnson (n 29) 20.

human rights journalism to accentuate coverage routinely illustrated with other media.[40]

An interesting recent application of VR is the Courtroom 600 Project in which the University of Connecticut in collaboration with the Nuremberg Trials Memorial and the US Holocaust Memorial Museum has developed a VR rendition of the courtroom used for the Nuremberg Trials at the Palace of Justice in Nuremberg.[41] The purpose of the project is to allow viewers of this travelling exhibition to experience a small portion of these historically significant trials which rely upon archival material for content. VR also has clear application in forensic science, criminal investigations, and the courtroom.

It has been argued that a gradual shift from passive computer-generated animations, simulations, and virtual tours towards interactive VR and AR-based environments is occurring.[42] This shift is likely reflective of the significant value that virtual environments can provide to viewers. IVEs differ from computer animations because of the viewer's perception of being present within the environment which creates a potentially more powerful form of demonstrative evidence.[43] IVEs may allow the fact-finder to take a more active role in the trial, moving from passive receiver of information to active participant.[44] Though one may tend to think of IVEs being used primarily by counsel and the court, they could also be used by witnesses, allowing them to provide more depth to their testimony because of the ability to more effectively visualize scenes in the courtroom.

The use of VR and IVE technology may make the difference between the court gaining a more informed perceptual understanding of a scene and its environs and missing out on this valuable knowledge. It may not be feasible or possible for court members to attend a location for the purpose of viewing a scene for a myriad of reasons.[45] Scenes may be too dangerous for court members to visit, e.g. active atrocity crime locations militate against *in situ* viewing for reasons of personal safety. Some scenes may be largely inaccessible due to distance and remoteness, while others may no longer exist by the time a view is contemplated, or they may have changed substantially due to evidence spoliation or missing evidence, rendering the view of diminished value and perhaps injecting unnecessary confusion.[46]

[40] Sam Gregory, 'Cameras Everywhere Revisited: How Digital Technologies and Social Media Aid and Inhibit Human Rights Documentation and Advocacy', *Journal of Human Rights Practice* 11 (2019): 373–92, at 388.

[41] Vos and Stolk (n 38) 308–27.

[42] Petra Urbanová, Mikolás Jurda, Tomás Vojtísek, and Jan Krajsa, 'Using Drone-Mounted Cameras for On-Site Body Documentation: 3D Mapping and Active Survey', *Forensic Science International* 281 (2017): 52–62, at 60.

[43] Young (n 14) 261.

[44] Feigenson (n 14) 285. There are potential downsides to this more active role, discussed in Section 4.

[45] Feigenson (n 14) 275; Sieberth, Dobay, Affolter, and Ebert (n 23) 42, 46–7.

[46] Sarah Zarmsky, 'Why Seeing Should Not Always Be Believing: Considerations Regarding the Use of Digital Reconstruction Technology in International Law', *Journal of International Criminal Justice* 19, no. 1 (2021): 213–26, at 214.

Government interference may also adversely impact the ability to view a scene as not all state governments welcome outside investigators and other parties. Further, given budget limitations, the cost of an *in situ* view for an ICC panel of judges, counsel, court staff, investigators, and security personnel may be prohibitive.

Even in circumstances where an *in situ* view is possible, the view experienced in person is different from that which can be digitally delivered, and the latter may be preferable. For example, IVEs can be used to recreate scenes and events with the inclusion of significant details that are relevant to the issues being litigated. These details may include the locations of landforms, buildings, people, vehicles, and objects, as well as weather conditions and sounds.[47] They can be used to give the user a first-person perspective of an event or scene by creating a sense of presence at the actual location.[48] By way of illustration, scientists from the Institute of Forensic Medicine in Zurich have developed VR technologies that combine 3D room-scans, video recordings, and autopsy data to produce accurate 3D reconstructions of crimes in a self-styled Forensic Holodeck.[49] This approach has also proved to be valuable in exploring crimes at the domestic level.

Beyond the ability of viewers to be virtually present at a scene, IVEs may also be used to test the veracity and reliability of witness accounts when subjective assessments of perspective are required. Could a sniper have hit a target from the location indicated by a witness? Could a witness have seen what they claimed to have seen?[50] Conspicuity and projectile trajectory are occasionally factual issues in atrocity crime prosecutions. For example, in *Prosecutor v. Milosević*, video and photographic images were used to show the location of sniper nests relative to civilians being subjected to sniper fire.[51] In *Prosecutor v. Dordević*, video and ground-based and satellite photographic evidence was used to corroborate witness testimony regarding the vantage point of certain witnesses.[52] Similarly, in *Prosecutor v. Karadzić*, image-based evidence was used to determine bullet, missile, and mortar trajectories, and the location of sniper nests.[53] The locations of sniper nests and bullet trajectory were also issues in *Prosecutor v. Galić*.[54] In *Prosecutor v. Bemba*, the Chamber relied upon photographic evidence to corroborate the vantage point of a witness who observed a murder take place.[55] Detailed IVEs would likely have assisted these courts in more confidently assessing bullet trajectory and

[47] Bailenson, Blascovich, Beall, and Noveck (n 15) 255.

[48] ibid 256; Marcus Bösch, Stephan Gensch, and Linda Rath-Wiggins, 'Immersive Journalism: How Virtual Reality Impacts Investigative Storytelling', in *Digital Investigative Journalism: Data, Visual Analytics and Innovative Methodologies in International Reporting*, edited by Oliver Hahn and Florian Stalph (Cham: Springer International Publishing, 2019), 103–11, at 103–04.

[49] Bösch, Gensch, and Rath-Wiggins (n 48) 104.

[50] Schofield (n 12) 136–7; Leonetti and Bailenson (n 15) 1076.

[51] IT-98-29/1-T, Judgment, 12 December 2007.

[52] IT-05-87/1-T, Judgment, 23 February 2011.

[53] IT-95-5/18-T, Judgment, 24 March 2016.

[54] IT-98-29-T, Judgment, 5 December 2003.

[55] ICC-01/05-01/08-3343, Judgment, 21 March 2016.

the veracity of witness accounts. By navigating within the IVE and putting themselves in the position of a witness, viewers could see whether a witness's claimed perception was possible or reasonable.[56]

IVEs can also be used to recreate a scene for witnesses to explore and testify to their recollections, thus potentially enhancing the depth and detail of their testimony.[57] An example of this is the Bloody Sunday Tribunal, established in 1998 to re-examine the 1972 killing of Irish citizens by British soldiers in Derry, Northern Ireland. VR views were utilized using 360° views of scenes, allowing witnesses to revisit scenes from different angles and reconstruct their views.[58] This provided added depth and detail for the tribunal to consider.

While IVEs may assist in the investigation of what happened during an incident and may reveal new information not otherwise accessible via conventional methods, they are not necessarily helpful or even appropriate for all scene and event explorations. Indeed, they may only be of probative value for counsel and the court in very limited circumstances. For example, virtual environments could be used as a demonstrative or substantive adjunct to an expert's report wherein the theories of witnesses and forensic experts on such topics as conspicuity, bullet trajectory, impact angles for collisions, and mechanism of injury can be tested and evaluated.[59] Since the expert would be called to testify as to the validity of the underlying data, methodology, and conclusions, the virtual component of the expert's work may prove to be a logical visual extension of the written and testimonial evidence, with added value for the court in terms of comprehending the full extent of the expert's opinion. Some of these issues might not otherwise be subjected to experimentation due to lack of access to the site, subsequent site alteration, or cost. Additionally, a less technically challenging use of virtual environments would be for the depiction of before and after images of scenes, e.g. to show the damage caused to cultural heritage sites. A variation of this has been used by the OTP in interactive 360° visual representations.

An IVE must be created with practical considerations and sensitivities in mind, cognizant of the purpose of the environment. When being used in the forensic context, tailor-making it to the intended audience (counsel, the court, and witnesses) is critical. In the court setting, it is designed to facilitate a slow, cautious, and detailed exploration of scenes and events. It is not intended to be a thrill ride. Similarly, it should be tethered to the real world as far as possible and should not resemble a game. The degrees of freedom and level of immersion afforded viewers must also be assessed so that the optimum forensic experience is offered to viewers while not straying into irrelevancies or potentially prejudicial content. Finally, it

[56] Bailenson, Blascovich, Beall, and Noveck (n 15) 250, 254; Leonetti and Bailenson (n 15) 1077.

[57] Feigenson (n 14) 275.

[58] ibid 274–5.

[59] Ma, Zheng, and Lallie (n 30) 1229; Raneri (n 21) 701; Sieberth, Dobay, Affolter, and Ebert (n 23) 42.

follows that the courtroom must be equipped with the necessary technology to fully utilize and display the virtual environment.[60]

In summary, IVEs provide a sensation of presence not available through other display technologies. They provide the opportunity for enhanced and informative views when other suitable methods may be impractical or impossible, and they create an environment for scene and event exploration, testing eyewitness accounts, and the evaluation of forensic propositions and theories. Ultimately, IVEs can be used by counsel to argue, challenge, and support their position as to key events and scenes, and by the court to make findings of fact. However, they also bear significant and cautious appraisal.

3. Advantages of Virtual Reality

There are advantages that may be leveraged using IVEs for evidential purposes. A useful starting point is to draw parallels and distinctions between a live view versus viewing a scene or event through an IVE. A live view is similar to an IVE in that viewers are physically and perceptually transported to the scene, albeit the latter is in or near the courtroom rather than at a distant location. Both viewing methods present some perceptual challenges in that it cannot be conclusively determined what features of the scene are being viewed and digested as that experience is subjective. A live view carries the palpable risk of the presence of extraneous, irrelevant, or unfairly prejudicial information which may be seen by viewers or overheard in comments made by others present.[61]

Though steps can be taken to guard against this occurring, a scene can rarely be totally controlled. In this respect IVEs offer the advantage that they can be designed to limit the information provided in a way that a live view cannot while at the same time offering interactivity and multi-perspectival views that are harder to achieve in a live view.[62] For example, IVEs can be programmed with gaze-directed steering and locked fields of view which prevent lateral head movement and ensure that all viewers have access to the same views, a control not possible in a live view.[63] Additionally, an IVE can give viewers a more accurate view of a scene or event because it can simulate time of day, atmospheric conditions, the presence of physical evidence, etc. in a way that a live view could never replicate.[64]

[60] Kayleigh Sheppard, Sarah Fieldhouse, and John Cassella, 'Experiences of Evidence Presentation in Court: An Insight into the Practice of Crime Scene Examiners in England, Wales and Australia', *Egyptian Journal of Forensic Sciences* 10, no. 8 (2020), 1–12, at 6–10.

[61] Leonetti and Bailenson (n 15) 1113.

[62] Interactivity refers to the computer responding based upon the input of the user. Sherman and Craig (n 12) 283. See also Feigenson (n 14) 285. For example, an IVE may present a scene that is less gruesome than might be experienced at a live scene, depending upon the status of the scene at the time of viewing.

[63] Leonetti and Bailenson (n 15) 1113.

[64] ibid.

Focusing on fact-finding, IVEs may result in improved legal decision-making. The use of image-based evidence in litigation provides enhanced information to the court that is designed to increase comprehension and retention of the subject matter. IVEs accentuate the use of image-based evidence by creating a sense of vivid presence with more sophisticated visual and aural data delivery, and in some cases, interactivity. They allow counsel and the court to experience the scene more viscerally than using a 2D depiction.[65] This immersive experience may provide the court with a stronger basis upon which to understand scenes and events and to make decisions based upon them.[66] It may fairly be predicted that by increasing the level of engagement of the fact-finder in the assessment of evidence to that of experiencing rather than just observing, IVEs may prompt more attention to the immersive data representations which may in turn lead to more accurate decision-making.[67]

Unlike photographs and video images, IVEs present measured 3D information and can portray scenes from multiple angles and distances and are therefore generally more robust and accurate representations of scenes and events.[68] Further, research has shown that many people have difficulty adequately comprehending 2D spatial information as compared to a 3D environment.[69] Witnesses may therefore find it easier to orient themselves relative to the real world in an IVE and thereby provide more accurate and informative testimony. Combs found in her extensive study of the International Criminal Tribunal for Rwanda (ICTR), the Special Court for Sierra Leone (SCSL), and Special Panels cases that civilian witnesses often had difficulty deciphering 2D maps, owing to lower levels of education and literacy, coupled with an absence of experience using maps.[70] While the court may have no difficulty comprehending a 2D representation, it is not only the court who may be required to use and interpret such data.

IVEs may gain added persuasive value because they are scientifically created demonstratives based upon objectively verifiable scene and event data and may therefore be viewed as portraying objective, reliable truths.[71] To achieve this status the accuracy of the input data must be properly verified, especially given the ability of the environment's creator to alter an IVE to promulgate one party's perception of an event over that of another party. A further advantage is that because IVEs consist

[65] Reshiwaran Jegatheswaran, Chandra Ramachandiran, and Julia Juremi, 'Implementation of Virtual Reality in Solving Crime Scene Investigation', *Journal of Applied Technology and Innovation* 5, no. 2 (2021): 28–32, at 30.

[66] Schofield (n 12) 140; Feigenson (n 14) 283.

[67] Feigenson (n 14) 283, 286. Feigenson suggests that in an IVE jurors may develop more empathy for people involved in a depicted scene or event and that this may be helpful in fact-finding and forming judgments. Whether this would apply to professional judges is more difficult to test as research has focused on the use of mock jurors in domestic cases. See also Young (n 14) 261–2.

[68] Leonetti and Bailenson (n 15) 1090.

[69] Schofield (n 12) 137.

[70] Nancy Combs, *Fact-finding Without Facts: The Uncertain Evidentiary Foundation of International Criminal Convictions* (New York: CUP, 2010), 36–8.

[71] Leonetti and Bailenson (n 15) 1082.

of digital data, they can be stored and archived for later viewing.[72] This would be important from the perspective of creating a record of the evidence presented.

It would be folly to utilize new technology simply because it is available. To earn a place in the courtroom, technology must be found to aid in the search for the truth in a manner that is effective, efficient, and practical. The advantages noted in this section provide scope for the proposition that VR and IVEs may be worthy of consideration, but that must be weighed against potential disadvantages.

4. Disadvantages of Virtual Reality

New technologies often add tangible benefits to the investigational, litigation, and judicial arms of international criminal justice. The benefits of new technologies must be weighed against their potential prejudicial effects so that informed decisions can be made as to their use. While IVEs provide epistemic benefits to counsel and the court, they also have potential disadvantages that must be contextualized for the purpose of sifting the mere risk of prejudice from probable prejudice.

It is reasonable to suggest that IVEs are more cognitively engaging than non-immersive representations of scene and event data because they provide more stimuli for viewer consideration. However, this vividness may cause viewers to be less critical of the data, which may result in the representation being perceived as more persuasive and probative than is merited.[73] Judgmental cognitive processes that reduce complex inferential tasks to simpler forms of judgment may cause viewers to commit inferential errors, that is, to rely upon data that is readily available to their perception and cognition without examining its veracity.[74] As a corollary to this, viewers may be sufficiently persuaded that an IVE is so realistic as to forestall reception of opposing viewpoints.[75] The issue is not whether an IVE can influence the court's assessment of represented facts and subsequent judgment (there is a strong case to be made that this is probable), but whether it might unduly do so.[76]

This concern has been typically raised whenever a new type of image-based evidence is tendered, starting as far back as the 1850s in America when photographs were introduced as evidence. Potentially powerful evidence is not objectionable merely because it may be influential to the fact-finding process and the formation of judgment. Should IVEs be introduced as evidence periodically, they will be less

[72] ibid 1076.

[73] Feigenson (n 14) 282; Young (n 14) 262–3.

[74] Young (n 14) 263–4. The problem arises when factors independent of probative value such as vividness cause information to be more readily accepted by viewers. This type of error becomes unfairly prejudicial when opposing counsel is unable to negate the harmful effects of it.

[75] Bailenson, Blascovich, Beall, and Noveck (n 15) 263–5; Feigenson (n 14) 282; Leonetti and Bailenson (n 15) 1077; Young (n 14) 262–3; Jani and Johnson (n 29) 22.

[76] Leonetti and Bailenson (n 15) 1076.

likely to engender adverse impacts on viewers, similar to the way courts became more accustomed to the introduction of photographic evidence. Courts are quite capable of distinguishing an IVE from other forms of evidence. Even though temporarily in an IVE the court will know it is still in a courtroom.[77] The risk of falling into a 'seeing is believing' mindset and placing undue reliance upon an IVE must be addressed and ameliorated by the expert and counsel.

There is a risk that IVEs may seem more like direct unmediated experiences than indirect mediated experiences and that they may be considered especially persuasive. This persuasiveness may arise due to naïve realism, namely the perception that what is being viewed is an unmediated and objective reality.[78] Viewers may therefore attach a stronger emotional connection with the experience.[79] This is an important consideration should a witness be asked to enter an IVE as part of giving their testimony. For a witness who has experienced traumatic and painful experiences, the virtual environment may simply be too real, too powerful, and may exacerbate existing psychological harm.[80] Ethical considerations might therefore exclude the use of IVEs for some witnesses for fear of further traumatizing the vulnerable. Oversight by counsel and the court on this point is essential.

While the vividness of an IVE may help viewers to better comprehend a scene or event, to the extent that it involves imagery that might be considered gruesome, it may predispose viewers to find in favour of the party tendering the evidence.[81] Graphic imagery may be more persuasive; it may be digested and recalled better than other evidence; and it may generate a sense of moral outrage demanding accountability.[82] The potential impact of graphic imagery on decision-making, whether in an IVE or not, is difficult to measure. Reported research typically relies upon brief mock domestic trials with university students sitting as jurors who claim not to have been impacted by the graphic imagery, yet the results suggest otherwise.[83] An IVE may require more cautious appraisal when being considered for a jury trial as jurors are less likely to have been exposed to actual graphic imagery than a judge.[84] A professional judge would surely deny being affected by

[77] Feigenson (n 14) 279–81; Zarmsky (n 46) 218.

[78] Leonetti and Bailenson (n 15) 1081–2.

[79] Feigenson (n 14) 281.

[80] Carolina Nordin and Adna Zekan, 'Taking Virtual Reality into the Courtroom: An Exploratory Study of How to Implement Virtual Reality Within Swedish Courts' (Master's thesis, Chalmers University of Technology 2021) 99.

[81] David Bright and Jane Goodman-Delahunty, 'Gruesome Evidence and Emotion: Anger, Blame, and Jury Decision-Making', *Law and Human Behavior* 30 (2006): 183–202, at 184.

[82] Kevin Douglas, David Lyon, and James Ogloff, 'The Impact of Graphic Photographic Evidence on Mock Jurors' Decisions in a Murder Trial: Probative or Prejudicial?' *Law and Human Behavior* 21, no. 5 (1997): 485–501, at 487.

[83] ibid 497–500; Bright and Goodman-Delahunty (n 81) 184; Jessica Salerno, 'Seeing Red: Disgust Reactions to Gruesome Photographs in Color (but not in Black and White) Increase Conviction'. *Psychology, Public Policy, and Law* 23, no. 3 (2017): 336–50, at 347.

[84] Most jurors will have been exposed to graphic violence and imagery through film and television but that is not the same as being required to view imagery and make decisions based upon it.

powerful imagery in an immersive environment, yet the risk is that subconsciously this may occur. This is practically impossible to test for and therefore even professional judges must be very cautious when admitting IVE evidence that might objectively be considered overpowering. A solution to this problem may be to redact some of the gruesomeness of a scene in the IVE where it does not add sufficient probative value to outweigh its prejudicial effect.

A related concern that has been raised regarding IVEs is that they may transform fact-finders from objective judges to the role of witnesses or participants as they immerse themselves into a virtual environment, and that this may affect their objectivity.[85] This is a significant concern that must be addressed when an IVE is being contemplated. If an IVE evokes a sense that it is an immersive game for the fact-finder to play, or if the environment is not wholly based upon measured and independently authenticated data, then it would not be appropriate to tender the IVE due to the risk of unfair prejudice outweighing the probative value of the evidence. The gaming risk may be ameliorated by proper instruction from the expert witness, counsel, and judicial self-instruction. Further, though all visual representations can cause viewers to infer meanings unintended by the party tendering the evidence, this potential for cognitive dissonance can be avoided if the intended meaning of an IVE is clearly stated by counsel who rely upon it. Improving the visual literacy of counsel and the court is central to making proper use of image-based evidence, including IVEs.[86]

The concern about fact-finders becoming witnesses or more active participants in the trial process is not without merit and engages a philosophical consideration of the role of the fact-finder. While there must be limits on what the court is asked to do in the name of fact-finding, that does not mean that is there no scope for expanding epistemic boundaries. If a court is asked to undertake a *locus in quo* viewing or look at unpleasant images as part of its fact-finding role, then utilizing a demonstrably accurate IVE is not necessarily a notable extension of the court's role. Arguably, a *locus in quo* viewing may engage more of a concern about the court becoming a witness than by viewing an IVE, yet that is not a reason for denying site visits. If the IVE amounts to another method of providing meritorious and probative data for the court to consider, then the fact that the delivery vehicle is somewhat novel (from a judicial perspective) should not be a bar to its use, provided that the IVE is accurate and based upon verifiable scene data. Presuming proper instruction and use, the court can be trusted to properly utilize this method of evidence assessment.

Caution must be exercised when IVEs are not exclusively founded upon objective measurements and scene-based images. At times, reliance may be placed

[85] Feigenson doubts that the participatory aspect of an IVE will affect the role of the fact-finder, likening an IVE in this respect to live views. Feigenson (n 14) 283.

[86] See also Sheppard, Fieldhouse, and Cassella (n 60) 8.

upon open source and eyewitness accounts to create the environment due to the lack of investigator access to a scene, the absence of accurate measurements, or inadequate photographic and video documentation. In such circumstances, the risk that bias and inaccuracy may be injected into the representation may become exacerbated.[87] Honest but mistaken witness accounts are common and must be viewed with caution for these purposes.[88] Political motives or biases may also impact the objectivity of a virtual environment.[89]

A further concern is whether the IVE would distort or unfairly counter the testimony upon which parts of the virtual representation are based, thus making the medium the message.[90] Ensuring the accuracy of the data used to create the IVE is essential in addressing these concerns. Additionally, the final submissions of counsel and limiting instructions by the court can help to contextualize the assessment of evidence and ensure that IVE evidence is sufficiently mediated.

The International Bar Association opined that visual representations, including 3D computer-generated depictions, are resource intensive to create and may have limited value for the court. They also posit that judges could obtain the same or better information from a *locus in quo* visit. Further, they state that such representations may produce selective data and should be approached with caution.[91] These concerns have merit and must be fully considered. Creating an advanced visual representation is highly resource intensive and can give rise to equality of arms issues.[92] It is also reasonable to conclude that if an IVE has limited value for the court and if a *locus in quo* visit achieves the same result, then that may be the preferred method of fact-finding, subject to the concerns about such visits noted earlier. However, IVEs can accomplish fact-finding tasks that cannot be achieved or replicated by a *locus in quo* visit and it would therefore be incorrect to assume that one is a suitable substitute for the other without a detailed examination of the facts to be assessed and the purpose of a proposed IVE or site visit. While I agree that caution is required when considering 3D depictions of scenes, including the use of VR and IVEs, the IBA's concerns may be painted with too broad a brush. The use of advanced visual representations must always be assessed on a case-by-case basis and any dogmatic pronouncement one way or the other on their value moving forward is doomed to be premature and not fully informed.

87 Zarmsky (n 46) 219.

88 Zarmsky noted that the digital reconstruction of the Saydnaya Prison in Syria by Amnesty International in collaboration with Forensic Architecture was wholly dependent upon the memories of survivors who described the prison to the 3D architect; ibid 222. A court would have to exercise caution when finding facts in such circumstances.

89 ibid.

90 Leonetti and Bailenson (n 15) 1082.

91 'International Bar Association Report', *IBA ICL Perspectives: Evidence Matters in ICC Trials* (August 2016) https://www.ibanet.org/document?id=Evidence-matters-in-icc-trials, 29.

92 Discussed in Section 5.

There are potential disadvantages regarding the use of IVEs in international criminal prosecutions and while some of these concerns may be more theoretical than real, there are some that certainly merit further study. Some of the concerns regarding IVEs may be offset by ensuring that the data used to create the IVE are demonstrably accurate, that the IVE itself is accurate, that all parties have an opportunity to review the data and test the platform, and that expert witnesses fully educate counsel and court as to the intent of the representation and what findings might fairly be made in the virtual environment. Further, counsel must argue what findings can reasonably be based upon the IVE having considered all the evidence in the case.

5. Legal Considerations for Virtual Reality in the Courtroom

When contemplating the use of any technology in the courtroom, counsel must be able to cogently articulate to the court why they propose to use it and how it would benefit the fact-finding and judgment processes. Some questions to consider include the following: What is the aim of the proposed evidence? What questions are being asked of it? Is it being tendered for substantive use or merely as a demonstrative exhibit? Will the technology help to answer questions that are relevant to an issue before the court? Is the immersive nature of an IVE necessary to convey vital evidence? Will it be a benefit or a hindrance? If an IVE is advisable, is interactivity within the environment required? Is the potential for unfair prejudice unjustifiably high? In short, there must be a tangible, articulable purpose for engaging in an immersive virtual walkthrough of a scene.[93] If the same information could be presented to the court in a less technically complex manner, that would generally be preferable. Equally, if it is determined that the use of advanced technology will enhance the search for the truth and will be of benefit to the parties and the court, then it should be pursued and utilized with vigour.

Digital scene and event reconstruction technology has been increasingly used in investigations of mass atrocities by both NGOs and international courts and tribunals, though no specific procedures have been enunciated by courts for the use of digital reconstruction, VR, and IVE platforms.[94] Existing rules of evidence and procedure are quite capable of application to technically advanced and emerging technologies. Article 69(3) of the *Rome Statute* permits the court to receive all evidence it considers relevant for the determination of the truth, but Art. 69(4) qualifies that broad inclusivity by providing for the weighing of probative value and prejudicial effect in respect of any piece of evidence when assessing trial fairness. Probative value refers to the ability of a piece of evidence to help determine

[93] Sieberth, Dobay, Affolter, and Ebert (n 23) 42–3.
[94] Zarmsky (n 46) 214.

the probability of the existence of a fact, taking into account such factors as reliability, accuracy, and authenticity.[95] Prejudice, used in this context, does not refer to the increased likelihood of conviction but rather to evidence that may be used improperly by the trier of fact or in a manner that is considered unfair to the defendant. It includes an assessment of whether admission would unfairly prejudice the parties in the presentation of their cases, would cause undue delay, or otherwise interfere with the rights of the defendant under Art. 67(1).[96] Evidence should be excluded if the potential prejudicial effect of its admission outweighs its probative value. This overriding requirement is well-enshrined in the common law and in ICC jurisprudence.

A ruling on probative value versus prejudicial effect is significant as it constitutes an early assessment by the court regarding the merit of part of the party's case. A favourable ruling which admits disputed evidence may bolster the party's case whereas a negative ruling excluding such evidence may prove to be detrimental to the party depending on the significance of the evidence. Rulings by a Trial Chamber under Art. 69(4) are generally entitled to deference on appeal. Under Art. 83(2), the Appeals Chamber may override the decision on liability by a Trial Chamber only if it finds that the trial decision was 'unfair in a way that affected the reliability of the decision' or that it was 'materially affected by an error of fact or law or procedural error'. Appellate jurisprudence further states that factual errors are not to be interfered with on appeal absent showing that the Trial Chamber committed a clear error, e.g. misappreciated the facts, considered irrelevant facts, or failed to consider relevant facts.[97] The Appeals Chamber will not disturb a Trial Chamber's assessment of facts just because the Appeals Chamber might have come to a different conclusion.[98] Legal errors are similarly subject to reversal only if it is determined that the Trial Chamber would have rendered a different ruling had it not made the error.[99]

This important weighing exercise by the Trial Chamber must be carefully considered by counsel when determining whether to tender IVE evidence. Powerful visual evidence that does not advance the discourse beyond the tangential risks a finding of inadmissibility on the grounds of lack of sufficient probative value or undue prejudice or both. However, if it can be shown that use of the IVE and participation within it will increase the court's ability to view, comprehend, and retain important details about the scene and relevant party narratives, then arguably the probative value of the evidence is likely to outweigh potential prejudicial effects.

[95] *Prosecutor v. Bemba*, ICC-01/05-01/08-2299-Red, Decision on the Prosecution's Application for Admission of Materials into Evidence Pursuant to Article 64(9) of the Rome Statute of 6 September 2012, 8 October 2012, para. 8.

[96] ibid.

[97] *Prosecutor v. Lubanga*, ICC-01/04-01/06-3121-Red, Judgment on the Appeal of Mr Thomas Lubanga Dyilo Against his Conviction, 1 December 2014, paras. 21–27.

[98] ibid para. 21.

[99] ibid paras. 18–19.

Provided counsel have given the court ample justification for the admission of IVE evidence at trial, such admission should be entitled to deference on appeal. In short, when seeking to tender novel or potentially controversial evidence, counsel must present compelling reasons for admission.

IVEs may present evidentiary challenges simply because of their relative novelty. Fundamentally, the threshold requirement for the admission of all evidence is relevance. To establish scene and event relevance, it must therefore be shown that the IVE is substantially accurate when compared to the real environment. Only then is it worthy of further consideration by the court. Further, it must be relevant to an issue that must be decided by the court, one that could be assisted with the use of an IVE (e.g. scene comprehension, assessing witness vantage points, bullet trajectory, event dynamics, etc.).

It might be argued that IVEs offer a vivid sensory palette that is somehow objectionable on that basis alone, but while vividness and interactivity may give the court access to the scene in a way no witness could provide, that privileged perspective is arguably unobjectionable if the data and representation are accurate, although it could heighten the prejudicial effect of the evidence if sufficient safeguards are not established.[100] For example, if the vividness of an IVE caused the court to make unwarranted findings of fact, the prejudicial effect of the evidence may be found to outweigh its probative value, but vividness itself is not a sufficient ground for exclusion. Similarly, vividness may give rise to the risk of viewers committing an inferential error by relying upon the representation without evaluating its veracity. Unless these risks are adequately addressed and mitigated with expert interpretation and instruction, it may rise to the level of unfair prejudice when opposing counsel are unable to negate their negative effects.[101] Necessary safeguards to employ include the testimony of expert witnesses and the submissions of counsel to mediate the IVE in the courtroom and educate the court as to the validity of its underlying data, its creation, and proper parameters for its evidential value. These steps are necessary to ameliorate the 'seeing is believing' default explored in Chapter 5.

An important consideration for counsel and the court is whether a visual representation is being tendered as substantive or demonstrative evidence. Substantive evidence is independent evidence that is tendered for proof purposes. For example, if an IVE is presented to the court as proof of scene measurements and orientation, lines of sight, and the location of specific landforms, buildings, and objects, that would constitute substantive evidence that may be foundational for expert opinions and findings of fact by the court. Conversely, an IVE presented for demonstrative purposes only is intended to display facts that have previously been proven and the demonstrative exhibit itself adds no new facts and does not form the basis

[100] Feigenson (n 14) 277–8.
[101] Young (n 14) 263.

for expert opinions. Tendered evidence is necessarily subjected to more intensive scrutiny when being used as substantive evidence. As a matter of trial fairness and respect for the parties and the court, it is therefore important that the tendering party identify the specific purpose of the evidence.

Irrespective of their classification, IVEs do not speak for themselves and require expert exposition and interpretation. Enhancing the ability of viewers to comprehend complex information is dependent upon properly validating the underlying data and its representation.[102] Therefore, the tendering party must lead evidence from a qualified expert about the technology used to create the IVE and the technology's scientific validity and reliability including the range of measurement error and any peer review that was undertaken. Next, the expert should educate counsel and the court as to the protocols and science employed in the creation and use of IVEs generally as this will help to lay the foundation for the IVE being presented. The input data must be shown to have been complete, accurate, and worthy of inclusion in the virtual representation and, further, that it was properly incorporated into the IVE such that the final product is an accurate representation.[103]

At the data input stage, it may be appropriate to remove certain data which could improperly influence a witness or the court. For example, if a live issue for a witness is the location of certain objects or people, it may be appropriate to remove suggestive content before a witness views an IVE.[104] Any such data reduction and the reasons therefore must be fully disclosed. Collectively, it is essential that expert evidence be presented to address these fundamental foundation facts as the IVE itself cannot be cross examined.[105] Provided these steps are taken, it is reasonable to suggest that a compelling argument may be made for the use of IVE evidence as substantive evidence.

Authenticity, accuracy, and reliability are necessary hallmarks of a trustworthy IVE. An IVE should be designed such that experts are able to validate the virtual environment against the original real-world measurements.[106] The authentication process for an IVE is more involved and technical in nature than for other forms of image-based evidence but the foregoing recommended approach should help to alleviate concerns of data manipulation and unfairness in the representation. Additionally, a sponsoring witness with personal knowledge of the representation's content (e.g. an investigator or eyewitness) may be able to assist in confirming the overall accuracy of the representation, though not necessarily the detailed measurements. Interactive 360° visual representations supplemented with terrestrial laser scanning measurements generate more accurate IVEs compared to those based upon witness recollection, yet there may be a legitimate role for eyewitness

[102] Schofield (n 12) 140–1.
[103] Raneri (n 21) 706.
[104] Sieberth, Dobay, Affolter, and Ebert (n 23) 43.
[105] Feigenson (n 14) 277; Leonetti and Bailenson (n 15) 1097–8.
[106] Schofield (n 12) 134.

input. For example, by the time a scene is photographed and measured, it may have changed in ways that only an eyewitness could address.

Cross examination can be very effective in truth discovery, but one limitation in cross examining experts who create IVEs is that they typically do not have personal knowledge of the representation's content because their role was to incorporate data provided to them by others.[107] Therefore, witnesses who provided foundational data used by the expert are the most direct source for challenge regarding the data, while the expert is the appropriate person to challenge regarding incorporation of the data into the IVE. To the extent that input from witnesses or other people is needed to create an IVE, those people must also be available for cross examination.

Robust authentication is critical for underpinning the probative value of IVE evidence, whether tendered for substantive or demonstrative purposes. To ensure thorough assessment of the evidence, the use of opposing experts may prove essential for testing the IVE's accuracy, veracity, and fairness.[108] Further, from a trial fairness perspective, it may be appropriate that all parties be given the opportunity to modify the IVE to present their viewpoint of the scene, not through direct party modification but through the expert who created the IVE. Objective proof of foundational data accuracy will help the court to discern which proffered IVE is most factually correct.[109] Counsel need to be vigilant and ensure that expert evidence and the IVE do not present scenarios not supported by the case evidence as this would be a misuse of the representation.[110]

Although there is a tendency in the ICC to admit all evidence for assessment of its weight at the end of the trial, I maintain that if the tendering party is unable to adequately establish the accuracy of the data used to create an IVE and the accuracy of the IVE itself by the end of their case, the tendered evidence should be excluded from further consideration by the court. To allow an IVE that does not satisfy these criteria to clutter the evidential record serves no cogent purpose. Further, the requirement of concurrent proof of data and representational accuracy will serve to spur counsel and the experts to address these critical issues up front.

Inequality of arms is an issue that may need to be addressed as inequality generally is a perennial concern for counsel and the court when considering forensic science and technological evidence.[111] Typically the prosecution has access to greater

[107] Young (n 14) 265–8.

[108] Bailenson, Blascovich, Beall, and Noveck (n 15) 263–5; Leonetti and Bailenson (n 15) 1091–2; IBA Report (n 91) 20, 24.

[109] Schofield (n 12) 140. Virtual environments may suffer from a loss of some detail due to necessary data processing prior to visualization and this may therefore impact accuracy. Sieberth, Dobay, Affolter, and Ebert (n 23) 43.

[110] Young (n 14) 268.

[111] e.g. Young (n 14) 269–71; Zarmsky (n 46) 219. Young further argues that an IVE can become in effect a testifying witness that abrogates the opposing party's ability to cross-examine. I disagree with that stance as the expert presenting the IVE can be fully cross-examined on the data used to create it and the data themselves must be independently proven to be accurate by the tendering party.

financial, forensic, and technological resources than the defence.[112] This may place the prosecution at a perceived advantage if they are able to dedicate the resources required to create such representations and the defence does not have the financial or personnel resources to do so, but that fact alone does not make a trial unfair. It is frequently the case that the prosecution has more resources and more evidence than the defence. Similarly, if the defence is well resourced (e.g. the US or UK government, should such a case arise), that does not *ipso facto* lead to unfairness vis-à-vis the prosecution. It would be naïve to suggest that inequality of arms does not exist, but this is not a valid reason to deny a party the right to use probative evidence at trial, including an IVE. The court may be able to alleviate any perceived inequality or fairness concerns by allowing both parties the right to have input into the representation included to help explore party narratives, or by appointing joint experts, or both.

An interesting side effect regarding the use of IVE technology at trial is that it may overtly or subconsciously influence a defendant's decision to testify.[113] The decision to testify is a difficult, strategic, and often vexing one because while testifying allows defendants to state their narrative and position more fully, it also exposes them to cross examination and doors that might otherwise have remained closed are liable to be opened. An effective IVE presented by the defence may provide sufficient information about the defence position such that when considering the risks inherent in cross examination, the defendant will choose not to testify. Equally, a compelling IVE presented by the prosecution may force a defendant to testify to either counter the accuracy of the representation or provide an alternative explanation for it. In either scenario, the use of IVE evidence may influence how defendants respond to the prosecution's case.

A further issue to be addressed is the requirement that all evidence presented at trial be accurately preserved for the court record. The trial court, appellate court, and other interested parties must be able to ascertain what evidence was considered by the court.[114] Therefore, each IVE walkthrough, directional view, teleportation, interaction, and movement should be recorded to create a record.[115] Though it is not possible to precisely capture what viewers saw and experienced because their gaze cannot be discreetly determined or recorded, at least the point of view of the head-mounted display can be captured for simultaneous viewing by others and for

[112] Richard Rogers, 'Assessment of the ICC's Legal Aid System' (2017) https://www.icc-cpi.int/itemsDocuments/legalAidConsultations-LAS-REP-ENG.pdf, 9–10. Rogers found that the defence received less than 10% of the budget of the OTP. In some cases, organizations may donate technology and expertise to the OTP, potentially giving the prosecution an advantage over the defence. SITU Research provided such assistance to the OTP in the Mali case. See also Zarmsky (n 46) 221.

[113] Young (n 14) 271.

[114] Sieberth et al. state that to comply with legal obligations, they record virtual scene walkthroughs for trial and appellate purposes. Sieberth, Seckiner, Dobay, Dobler, Golomingi, and Ebert (n 24) 2.

[115] Sieberth, Dobay, Affolter, and Ebert (n 23) 44.

later examination.[116] As a corollary, we also cannot determine what aspects of a photograph or video image the court focused on, or what aspects of a *locus in quo* visit garnered more attention than others, but these are not impediments to admission. It is essential however that the IVE be entered as an exhibit along with the ability to view the environment in 3D format with a 2D back-up for reference. Video output from the IVE will necessarily be in 2D format which limits the value of the recording because it does not replicate the user's experience.[117] Even though expert assistance will be required for an appellate court and others to view an IVE in 3D, it is at least possible to do so. A 2D reference of the IVE may be sufficient for most post-trial queries.

5.1 Advanced Visual Representations—ICC

I will focus on the use of advanced visual representations at the International Criminal Court (ICC) in this section as the ICC is the predominant adjudicative body dealing with atrocity crimes at the international level. Prior to discussing the use of IVEs, it is important to note that interactive 360° visual representations supplemented with AR features appear to have found a reasonably firm foothold at the ICC and other tribunals. An interactive 360° visual representation typically involves the use of satellite imagery, drone imagery, and ground-based photographs and video.[118]

As described in *Prosecutor v. Katanga and Ngudjolo Chui*, images obtained from satellite, drone, and ground-based cameras all generate GPS data which allows for the accurate geolocation of image content.[119] The 360° panoramic ground-based photos are taken by mounting a camera on a tripod with a specially designed head that is programmed so that every movement of the camera maintains the same angle. Twenty-four photos are typically taken to cover the full 360° view which are then digitally stitched together to create one long, seamless image. Panoramic software is used to curve the photograph and create the 360° image which viewers can pan, tilt, and zoom, replicating the view available had they been standing where the camera was located and simply moved in a circle. Interactive 360° visual representations typically begin with satellite images showing relevant locations and by clicking on each site in the satellite image, the court can view a close-up image of the noted building or feature.[120] By further clicking on digital markings embedded

[116] An eye tracing system within the head-mounted display can be used to record the gaze but even then, it cannot precisely determine what viewers observed. ibid 44–6.

[117] ibid 45.

[118] Eya Macauley, 'The Use of EO Technologies in Court by the Office of the Prosecutor of the International Criminal Court', in *Evidence from Earth Observation Satellites*, edited by Ray Purdy and Denise Leung (Leiden: Martinus Nijhoff Publishers, 2013), 217–40, at 229.

[119] ICC-01/04-01/07-T-90-ENG ET WT 26-01-2010, Transcript, 26 January 2010, 21–5.

[120] As described in *Prosecutor v. Al Mahdi*, ICC-01/12-01/15-T-4-Red-ENG, Transcript, 22 August 2016, 45–9, 52–5, 60–7.

within the images, viewers activate 360° panoramic ground level photographs of the specific area which allows viewers to explore the location in the round. Presentations can also include embedded still photographs, diagrams, and video. The ability to navigate within a visual environment and click on embedded markings to reveal other visual and aural presentations is an example of augmented reality. To illustrate the practical use of these representations, I will review the use of interactive 360° visual representations in three ICC cases.

In *Katanga and Ngudjolo Chui*, which dealt with an attack on the village of Bogoro in the eastern DRC, the prosecution introduced an interactive 360° visual representation prepared by an ICTY technician who had been preparing similar presentations for the ICTY OTP since 2000. To create the visual representation of the village and its immediate surroundings, he relied upon satellite images provided by the OTP, drone images taken of Bogoro at his direction, and ground-based photographs taken by him.[121] The representation employed AR in that by clicking on small symbols within the platform, digitally embedded images showed a more detailed view of the immediate location.[122] The Chamber found that the visual representation may be of assistance to the Chamber and the parties in visualizing relevant locations, but noted that it had very limited evidential value, likening it to a tool used for orientation, like a diagram or drawing.[123] Thus the Chamber treated the visual representation as demonstrative evidence with minimal probative value.

In *Prosecutor v. Al Mahdi*, the defendant was charged with and pled guilty to the war crime of attacking protected objects, specifically mausoleums and mosques.[124] As part of their case, the prosecution used an interactive 360° visual representation prepared by SITU Research for the OTP based upon imagery provided by the OTP to provide a detailed view of the various sites that were destroyed in or near Timbuktu, Mali.[125] Beginning with satellite images showing relevant locations, clicking on each site in the image allowed the court to see the specific mausoleum or mosque with images showing the buildings before and after demolition. By further clicking on digital circles embedded within the images, the court was able to view 360° panoramic ground level photographs of the specific area. The representation also included accessible embedded photographs, diagrams, and video recordings. This representation was very helpful in visually depicting the relevant targets of the attacks and the damage they suffered from an aerial and ground-based perspective.

[121] (n 119).

[122] (n 119) 29–39.

[123] ICC-01/04-01/07-1515, Decision on the Disclosure of Evidentiary Material Relating to the Prosecutor's Site Visit to Bogoro on 28, 29, and 31 March 2009 (ICC-01/04-01/07-1305, 1345, 1360, 1401, 1412, and 1456), 7 October 2009, para. 39. The comments of the Chamber should be read in the context of the application brought by the prosecution to admit evidence filed late in the proceedings. Downplaying the value of the evidence assisted in admitting it on the basis that it would not be onerous upon the defence to address it (para. 40).

[124] ICC-01/12-01/15-171, Judgment and Sentence, 27 September 2016.

[125] ICC-01/12-01/15-T-4-Red-ENG, Transcript, 22 August 2016, 45–9, 52–5, 60–7.

Though it would have been helpful if the visual representation was challenged, defended, and ruled upon, the defence did not challenge the visual representation nor did the Chamber comment upon it in any detail.

A separate prosecution arising out of the same situation in Timbuktu commenced in 2020. In *Prosecutor v. Al Hassan*, the defendant was charged with crimes against humanity and war crimes committed in Timbuktu, including directing attacks against religious buildings and historic monuments, this latter count overlapping with Al Mahdi's war crimes. During their opening statement, the prosecution advised the Chamber that they would be relying upon an interactive platform created by SITU Research which was created based upon visual evidence gathered by the OTP.[126] Though not expressly stated, this interactive 360° visual representation would have been the same or substantially the same as the one used in *Al Mahdi* as the prosecutions overlap in subject matter. The SITU representation was tendered as demonstrative evidence only but was an important part of the prosecution's visual case.

Because the SITU Research interactive platform was created based on images gathered by the OTP, several OTP witnesses prepared reports and some of those witnesses also testified at trial regarding their role in the creation of the underlying images. The purpose of their testimony was to establish the authenticity, integrity, and reliability of the underlying images. This in turn would lend validity to the SITU platform. Amongst the expert evidence presented by the prosecution was an expert in satellite imagery who utilized satellite images to show the location of relevant mausoleums and mosques in Timbuktu and to show images before and after their destruction. Some of those images were used in the SITU representation.[127] An OTP technical witness (P-0631) testified regarding his role in the creation of panoramic images from drone and ground-based photographs resulting in a panoramic horizontal viewing area of 360° and a 40° vertical span.[128] Cross examination of this witness focused on the potential for errors in the creation of the panoramas and the witness confirmed that errors could occur though no errors were specifically identified or acknowledged.[129]

A second OTP technical witness (P-0127) testified regarding the creation of 360° panoramic images utilizing images taken by another member of the OTP, and his reliance upon metadata-recorded GPS coordinates for the individual images.[130] The witness worked on several projects arising from three different missions by other members of the OTP to Timbuktu over a five-year period for the same case.

[126] ICC-01/12-01/18-T-108-Red-ENG, Transcript, 15 July 2020, 13–15. See also Alice Speri, 'How 3D Models and Other Technology Could Make it Easier to Convict War Criminals', *The Intercept* (12 June 2023) https://theintercept.com/2023/06/12/icc-war-crimes-digital-evidence-reconstruction/.

[127] Witness P-0064, Reports MLI-OTP-0017-0029 and MLI-OTP-0021-0006. The reports were entered as trial exhibits though the author did not testify.

[128] ICC-01/12-01/18-T-079-Red-ENG WT, Transcript of P-0631, 28 April 2021, 8–24.

[129] ibid 24–38.

[130] ICC-01/12-01/18-T-087-Red-ENG WT, Transcript of P-0127, 28 May 2021, 6–37.

For one mission, the witness used 3,864 JPEG images to create 201 panoramas for 15 different sites.[131] Another mission generated 7,000 images.[132] The witness was cross examined about the software used to create the 360° panoramas and described the limitations of the software, e.g. the number of images it can evaluate and include in a panoramic display.

The only expert who testified regarding imagery was an expert in geolocation and forensic image analysis (P-0635) who evaluated some of the images used in the SITU platform.[133] The expert was asked by the OTP to perform image analysis and comparison to assist in identifying the locations shown in questioned multimedia files (satellite images, drones images, panoramas, and photographs).[134] In cross examination, the expert was asked about the questioned and known images used for comparison and whether all of the appropriate images had been examined.[135]

At the time of writing, the parties had presented their evidence and closing arguments. The Chamber has issued no ruling on the evaluation of the prosecution case, nor any interim ruling on the SITU platform or the underlying data.[136] Based on the cross examination by the defence of the witnesses noted above, it is reasonable to expect that the defence intends to challenge the validity of the SITU platform by casting doubt on the authenticity and reliability of some of the underlying images relied upon by SITU to create the tendered exhibit. It remains to be seen what comments, if any, the Chamber will make regarding the SITU platform evidence.

The interactive 360° visual representations used in *Katanga and Ngudjolo Chui*, *Al Mahdi*, and *Al Hassan* were not ground-breaking. They have been used by other international tribunals and in different national jurisdictions.[137] However, they do mark a significant step forward from the traditional use of diagrams, and photographic and video images. These representations constitute a method of packaging data that requires technical skill to create and relies upon foundational visual, aural, and measurement data gathered in the field by investigators, experts, and other people in circumstances that are laborious and sometimes dangerous. The ability to view satellite images, before and after images of buildings subjected to destruction, drone imagery, and ground-based still and panoramic photographs and video in one omnibus platform is very helpful to counsel and the court. These representations have not yet faced significant challenge in the ICC though should they be subjected to scrutiny their admissibility should be able to be established

[131] ibid at 17.

[132] ibid at 51.

[133] Witness P-0635, Report MLI-OTP-0069-9281.

[134] ICC-01/12-01/18-T-073-ENG ET WT, Transcript of P-0635, 14 April 2021, 8, 13.

[135] ibid 25–30; ICC-01/12-01/18-T-074-Red-ENG WT, Transcript of P-0635, 15 April 2021, 3–37.

[136] It is unlikely that the Chamber will issue its judgment (which may include commentary about the SITU interactive 360° visual representation) until late 2023 or early 2024.

[137] Some examples are highlighted in Schofield (n 12) 137. Sheppard, Fieldhouse, and Cassella (n 60) 2; Zarmsky (n 46) 216–21.

through the provision of robust expert evidence on authentication and representational accuracy.

While the interactive 360° visual representation approach is less sophisticated than using an IVE, the above cases evince a willingness by the ICC to consider the use of new technology. The next technological step would be to use VR and IVEs to convey vital scene and event data to the court as substantive and demonstrative evidence. Admitting properly authenticated, demonstrably accurate, and explained IVEs is not the equivalent of crossing the Rubicon. Rather, it may plausibly be argued that it is a logical progression in the use of technology in the courtroom.[138] Donning a head-mounted display would certainly be a new experience for the court but the concept of interactivity is not foreign, as evidenced by the interactive 360° visual representations already used. Further, the court is no stranger to participatory activities as evidenced by *locus in quo* visits, but entering an IVE is a different experience, albeit one that can be done in the comfort of the courtroom. The court may be hesitant but also rather intrigued by the IVE experience assuming all evidential requirements and safeguards have been met.

This next immersive step is somewhat of a paradigmatic advancement because it would require the court to go beyond merely observing evidence to participating in the observation of evidence. It will be important to avoid any sense of transforming the court into judicial investigators rather than objective fact-finders. There will be a learning curve in achieving judicial acceptance of this form of evidence but with adequate guidance, education, and instruction by expert witnesses and counsel, the curve need not be insurmountable. Enhancing visual literacy among counsel and the court should be an ongoing goal. The prospect of using VR to examine and navigate within a crime scene was mentioned in an OTP forensic expert's testimony though was not used in that case.[139] VR and IVE technology is not currently being used in any prosecutions at the ICC but is being developed for potential use.

5.2 Advanced Visual Representations—Non-ICC

While the OTP is not currently using VR and IVEs in their prosecutions, other courts and organizations are using them as well as non-VR 3D technology to advance their causes. National courts have relied upon 3D models of key locations and VR, though this is not commonplace. For example, the Bavarian State Criminal Office (LKA) in Munich created a VR version of the Auschwitz concentration

[138] Not all authors agree. Young cautioned that the perception of presence experienced in IVEs poses an exponentially greater risk of unfair prejudice that is different from other forms of demonstrative evidence. His concern justifies a cautious approach by the court, but this risk may be ameliorated as discussed in this chapter. Young (n 14) 257–8, 261.

[139] *Prosecutor v. Gbagbo and Blé Goudé*, ICC-02/11-01/15-T-185-Red-ENG, Transcript, 4 September 2017, 19.

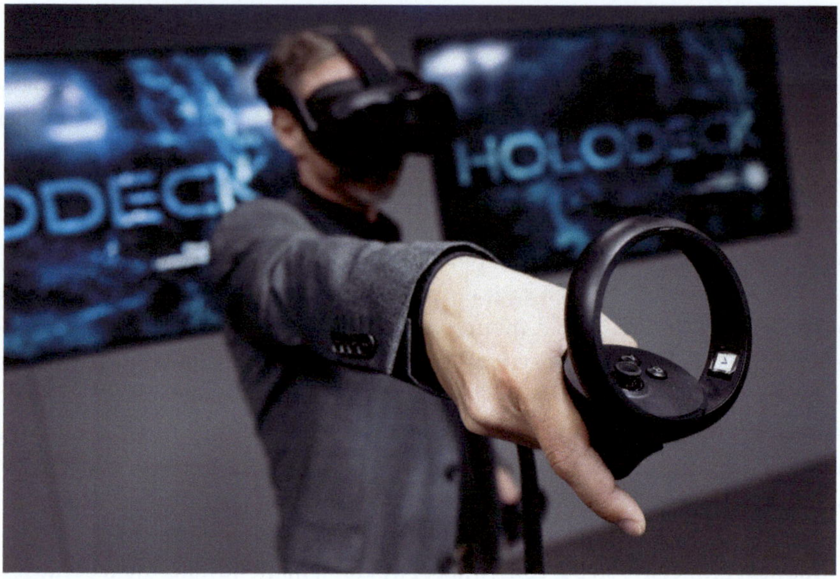

Figure 8.1 Crime scene VR room. (Sven Hoppe/dpa/Alamy Live News (c) 2023)

camp to assist with prosecutions against war criminals.[140] The experts spent five days in Auschwitz laser scanning the buildings and grounds and then created a 3D computer model and a separate VR platform wherein viewers could don head-mounted displays and examine the camp from various angles. Because the SS destroyed all but one of the gas chambers and crematoria in advance of the arrival of opposing forces, the experts relied upon recovered blueprints for all the buildings to accurately recreate them in the virtual environment. The 3D computer model was used in the prosecution of SS camp guard Reinhold Hanning, though the VR platform was not used. The trial judge found the 3D model helpful because it made it possible to understand what Hanning would have been able to see from his watchtower post. This assessment would have been more difficult to make relying only upon 2D images and diagrams.

Figure 8.1 shows Ralf Breker, head of forensic media technology at the LKA, wearing a VR headset in the crime scene VR room (Holodeck) during a press conference. This is the only location in Germany where crime scenes can be precisely created in 3D and walked through by viewers.

In Switzerland, researchers have used VR for visualizing and presenting 3D crime scenes at the investigational and court stage of homicide cases, as a tool for forensic experts to perform 3D reconstructions, and as a vehicle for obtaining

[140] Marc Cieslak, 'Virtual Reality to Aid Auschwitz War Trials of Concentration Camp Guards' *BBC News* (16 November 2016) https://www.bbc.com/news/technology-38026007.

statements from witnesses and experts while in the virtual environment.[141] Further, a Chinese court in Beijing used VR for the first time in 2018 by having a witness don a head-mounted display to re-enact the events leading up to the crime being prosecuted while the court viewed the recreation on a 2D display.[142]

VR has been discussed and used experimentally at the UN Security Council (UNSC). For example, in 2019, in a letter to the UNSC from the Special Advisor and Head of the Investigative Team to Promote Accountability for Crimes Committed by Da'esh/Islamic State in Iraq and the Levant, Karim A. A. Khan (now the ICC Prosecutor) reported on the evidence collected from crime scenes.[143] He noted that comprehensive 3D laser scans had been obtained of key crime scenes '... allowing for the creation of 3D model reconstructions for future integration into a virtual reality platform that will serve both as an investigative tool and as an aid to the presentation of evidence in national courts'.[144] Perhaps now that Khan is the ICC Prosecutor, there will be added impetus to use VR and IVEs where appropriate. More recently, in 2022 the UNSC used VR immersive technology and donned head-mounted displays for the first time to engage in 'virtual diplomacy' for Columbia.[145] This allowed the members to gain a more fulsome perspective of the Columbia situation.

There is a distinction to be made between using VR in the political sphere and a judicial environment. Using VR to inform the UNSC and other organizations about situations of concern in specific regions serves the purpose of a visual tour to orient viewers but does not rise to the level of evidence that is used to make findings of fact and to assess accountability. In this sense, the threshold for the use of VR for political purposes may be less stringent than would be required in a courtroom. While VR can also be used as a demonstrative tool at trial, more attention to the accuracy of the depiction should be expected given that even though demonstrative evidence has no legally probative value, it can impact fact-finders subconsciously as powerful depictions cannot be unseen. Therefore, the use of VR in non-judicial environments should not be conflated as being equally appropriate in the courtroom.

[141] Sieberth, Dobay, Affolter, and Ebert (n 23) 42; Sieberth, Seckiner, Dobay, Dobler, Golomingi, and Ebert (n 24) 1–7.

[142] Liang Chenyu, 'VR Technology Called to the Stand in Beijing Court' *Sixth Tone* (2 March 2018) https://www.sixthtone.com/news/1001846/vr-technology-called-to-the-stand-in-beijing-court.

[143] Letter dated 13 November 2019 from the Special Adviser and Head of the United Nations Investigative Team to Promote Accountability for Crimes Committed by Da'esh/Islamic State in Iraq and the Levant addressed to the President of the Security Council, UNSC S2019/878, 13 November 2019.

[144] ibid para. 36.

[145] Zaini Majeed, 'In a First, UNSC Experiences 3-D "Virtual Diplomacy" to Better Understand Peace-Building' *Republic World News* (21 January 2022) https://www.republicworld.com/world-news/rest-of-the-world-news/in-a-first-unsc-experiences-3-d-virtual-diplomacy-to-better-understand-peace-building-articleshow.html. See underlying UNSC Meeting Coverage and Press Release, 'Upcoming Elections Offer Historic Opportunity to Widen Columbia's Democracy, Special Representative Tells Security Counsel', SC/14770, 8951ST Meeting (20 January 2022) https://www.un.org/press/en/2022/sc14770.doc.htm.

Finally, in national criminal tribunals, 3D evidence has been used for demonstrative purposes primarily to show the court crime scenes and other locations of interest. For example, in *Prosecutor v. Ayyash et al.*, the prosecution presented two 3D digital models of key locations shown before and after the deadly explosion that claimed the life of former Prime Minister Hariri and others. The 3D models were admitted by the Trial Chamber as demonstrative exhibits with the caution that their weight would be later assessed and that the location of non-fixed items such as vehicles and debris would be carefully considered.[146] That approach was confirmed and applied in the Judgment.[147] These exhibits were tendered as Bar Table exhibits, meaning without accompanying expert evidence. These 3D exhibits did not involve VR and the Bar Table approach could never be applied to an IVE which needs accompanying expert evidence and instruction.

5.3 A Final Word of Caution Regarding Outsourcing Forensic Work

The mission of the ICC is at once breathtaking, overwhelming, and inspiring. The preamble of the *Rome Statute* is aspirational and perhaps even Sisyphean in nature. It caters to a global audience and stakeholders who will likely never be fully satisfied or feel that true justice has been achieved, yet despite the significant political, economic, and practical challenges involved, the work of the ICC is important and necessary in the quest for global justice. It is for these reasons that third-party organizations are sometimes willing to lend their technical assistance to the OTP, in some cases at no charge. These organizations often have an unabashed strong human rights and investigative focus and while their contributions are laudatory, it would be naïve to think that their work is purely altruistic. There is no doubt a marketable cache that attaches to an organization which provides services to the OTP, and which may be leveraged to the organization's benefit.

A very small number of organizations have the capacity to provide advanced visual representational services. SITU Research and Forensic Architecture have featured most prominently in this regard. SITU Research describes itself as an organization that investigates and addresses social, legal, and scientific challenges in a collaborative manner through an architectural lens.[148] Their list of clients evinces a strong human rights and investigative focus. Forensic Architecture also has a strong human rights investigative focus.[149] These stated agendas create potential problems in need of solutions. When organizations have a pro-OTP agenda, it

[146] STL-11-01/T/TC, Decision on Prosecution's Motion to Admit into Evidence Photographs, Videos, Maps, and 3-D Models, 13 January 2014, para. 10.

[147] *Prosecutor v. Ayyash et al.* (n 3) para. 386.

[148] See SITU Research, https://situ.nyc/research/profile.

[149] Forensic Architecture (n 10).

creates the risk that their final product may be infused with a bias that impacts objectivity and reliability.

Expert witnesses have a duty to provide fair, impartial, and objective evidence to the court irrespective of which party has hired them or is presenting their evidence. Third-party organizations may not perceive themselves to be beholden to these principles since they are not true forensic science providers whose work is governed by the strictures of quality assurance. I do not suggest that third-party organizations should play no role in OTP work, but rather that red flags should be raised as to their independence and impartiality. Organizations that have a stated agenda are likely to be challenged on the accuracy, fairness, and validity of the evidence they generate. Cautious appraisal is therefore required, and their work should undergo the same rigorous checks and balances as are exacted in the forensic world where the importance of scientific methodology and objectivity is emphasized.

While the OTP has the technical expertise required to create these representations in-house, it does not have the capacity needed to handle the volume of casework it faces. As a result, when the OTP lacks the human, technical, or budgetary resources to create and utilize advanced visual representations, an uncomfortable marriage of necessity and convenience may arise between the OTP and third-party organizations. This is not to suggest that such a marriage is doomed to fail. If the OTP must rely upon third-party service providers, it must be hypervigilant that the high expectations placed upon the OTP by the court are not misplaced by resort to third parties, which must be held to the same high forensic standards wherein data and representational soundness are paramount. This includes testifying to their work in court and facing potentially rigorous cross examination. Any organization that expresses a reluctance to meet these obligations should not be engaged. By utilizing third-party service providers, the OTP is effectively endorsing their work and reputation. That confidence must not be misplaced.

The accuracy, fairness, and validity of an advanced visual representation are dependent upon the validity of the underlying data and the way the data have been incorporated and depicted. If the representation is based solely upon data obtained by OTP investigators and trusted sources, then the soundness of the final product should be capable of independent verification. It follows that if the representation contains open source data not provided or verified by the OTP or if the representation itself is not demonstrably tethered to verified data, the evidence is ripe for challenge because the final product may not be a true representation of provably valid data. If the OTP intends to rely upon advanced visual representations created by third party organizations, then it must ensure that only OTP generated data is included and if other data is sought to be incorporated, it must be fully evaluated for accuracy and reliability.

Finally, advanced visual representations should not be created by people who are primarily focused on production value and visual appeal. The work must be treated as the forensic process that it is, with an emphasis on solid data and representational accuracy. Visual appeal is important but forensic soundness is paramount. The service providers must be fully briefed on the requirements to create a forensically sound visual representation because knowing that they will be fully tested on their work provides a strong incentive to produce a demonstrably robust product. Moving the creative work in-house only solves this issue if the foregoing guidance is followed. If these steps are taken, then this relatively novel evidence can be lead for substantive or demonstrative purposes with the confidence that it should withstand scrutiny. Anything less will cause the parties and the court to engage in a protracted and complex exploration of the tendered evidence with uncertain admissibility results. An unfavourable ruling on the admissibility of such evidence would have a ripple effect that must be avoided.

Conclusion

Technological advancements such as VR and IVEs represent a significant step forward that may provide opportunities for counsel and the court to stretch epistemic boundaries and to consider new ways to observe and examine scenes and events, which may enhance the fact-finding process. International tribunals and courts have not shied away from technological and evidential challenges. They have demonstrated a general willingness to embrace methods of proof that will advance the court's fact-finding role. Non-technical methods such as *locus in quo* visits are reflective of the court's willingness to learn about the cases that come before it. Donning a head-mounted display to enter an IVE would be a significant step forward for the court. I do not suggest that IVEs should be routinely used; in fact, their use would likely be the exception rather than the rule. Fundamentally though, if the court is satisfied that such an approach will aid in the search for the truth, then novelty alone should not be a bar to admission.

Photographs and video recordings are virtual environments in that they represent a mediated environment wherein subjective choices have been made as to what to include in the frame and how to display it.[150] Interactive 360° visual representations have thus far found a favourable audience in the ICC and other tribunals. IVEs are arguably the next logical step in sensory representation. They constitute a clear advancement in mediated environments and offer benefits that are likely preferable to a *locus in quo* viewing of a scene that will almost always be out of date and of limited value, assuming a site visit is even possible to undertake. Depending on the case and the issues being litigated, IVEs may prove to be far more effective, informative, and efficient.

[150] Leonetti and Bailenson (n 15) 1079.

I would be remiss if I did not acknowledge that the topic of advanced visual representations and in particular the use of IVEs may be controversial, but controversy can spark research and healthy discussion. Pushing technological and epistemic boundaries has merit if the result is a more robust and informative method of appreciating scene and event details, and therefore providing a platform for enhanced fact-finding. More research is needed on the accuracy and efficacy of IVEs and their potential impact on fact-finders. For example, if it is determined that an IVE can only be generated with some measure of artistic licence and that the represented environment is more of an approximated reality than a measured reality, that would militate against its use based on decreased probative value and the risk of unfair prejudice. Conversely, if the environment can be verified as accurate, the probative value of the depiction may take precedence. Further research is needed on whether the types of scenes that could arise in an atrocity crimes context would be suitable subject matter for an IVE. It may be that larger outdoor scenes may not be adequately replicated in an IVE, as Sieberth et al. have noted.[151] The use of IVE technology must be tethered to scenes that can be properly represented. A cautious stance is therefore merited but measured appraisal and robust research may yield an evidential windfall or at least an evidential benefit.

To profitably use IVEs in international criminal justice they must be thoroughly tested to ensure that they have incorporated verified data and that they generate an accurate and reliable virtual environment. Significant expert evidence may be required to fully present the IVE and to teach counsel and the court about the technology and the data used to generate it, including commentary on the value of using IVEs and any potential interpretive concerns that may arise. These are important building blocks in improving the visual literacy of counsel and the court so that they can competently consider and apply IVE evidence. The court would also need to be satisfied that the time, effort, and expense involved in the creation of IVE evidence will yield sufficient probative value regarding relevant issues to merit its introduction. A related consideration is whether the introduction of such evidence will cause significant delay due to any request by the opposing party to explore the IVE with their own experts.[152] These are likely not insurmountable challenges.

An IVE could be used in a variety of contexts and for different purposes.[153] In its role as gatekeeper, the court must exercise caution when considering the admission of such advanced visual representations. A balance must be struck between going too far in admitting new forms of evidence and hindering the proper reception of valuable evidence. All visual representations can cause viewers to infer meanings unintended by the party tendering the evidence. Therefore, the intended meaning

151 Sieberth, Dobay, Affolter, and Ebert (n 23) 46.

152 Some authors suggest that the use of VR may have the effect of shortening trials because of their ability to convey information comprehensively to the court. Whether that economy would be achieved at the ICC remains to be seen. Sheppard, Fieldhouse, and Cassella (n 60) 2.

153 Leonetti and Bailenson (n 15) 1099–1101.

of an IVE should be clearly stated by the experts presenting them and by counsel relying upon them, including an evaluation of whether an IVE should be tendered as demonstrative or substantive evidence. Evidence should not be tendered as demonstrative evidence and then relied upon for the purposes of proof.

International criminal law is sufficiently well developed to address advanced technological evidence. Adequate legal safeguards are in place to allow counsel and the court to consider the admissibility and assessment of weight assigned to VR and IVE evidence. An omnibus judicial pronouncement on IVEs would be neither wise nor appropriate. Rather, concerns should be assessed on a case-by-case basis. Courts must always be cautious in admitting new forms of evidence without a robust showing of authenticity, accuracy, and reliability. Powerful and evocative sensory evidence that has marginal probative value risks a finding of inadmissibility on the grounds of undue prejudice. In a case where the virtual exploration of a scene or event is likely to yield epistemic value, it is reasonable to argue that there is a place at the table for VR and IVE evidence. Once an inaugural use of this evidence has been made in a trial, counsel and the court will be able to comment on the efficacy and value of the evidence and that feedback and judicial commentary will be useful moving forward.

9
Conclusions: Charting a Path Forward

Introduction

Image-based evidence has long been part of the search for the truth and the pursuit of justice in international criminal prosecutions, starting as early as the Nuremberg trial. Ranging from the use of film, photographs, and video images to advanced visual representations, image-based evidence has been shown to be a potentially powerful method of proving (or disproving) allegations of wrongdoing and for presenting complex data in a more meaningful way in the courtroom. Despite its seemingly ubiquitous role in international criminal justice, comparatively little has been written about the use of image-based evidence. For example, while there has been a reasonable amount of published discourse on the power of images and the challenges they may present, the focus has been mostly on the images themselves and less about their use as evidence in a courtroom. Similarly, though advanced visual representations have been used for proof and didactic purposes, there has been limited guidance on how and when such evidence should be utilized. This book seeks to fill those gaps and to provide substantive guidance and recommendations for the use of image-based evidence in international criminal prosecutions.

Other researchers, authors, and organizations have provided some guidance on discrete relevant topics. For example, the *Leiden Guidelines on the Use of Digitally Derived Evidence in International Criminal Courts and Tribunals (Leiden Guidelines)*, produced through the International Humanitarian Law Clinic of the Faculty of Law at Leiden University in The Netherlands, and which are based upon an analysis of jurisprudence emanating from international criminal tribunals and courts, are designed to aid international criminal law practitioners in their use of digitally derived evidence in (primarily) International Criminal Court (ICC) prosecutions.[1] The *Leiden Guidelines* focus on the use of video recordings, photographs, aerial and satellite images, intercepts of audio communications, call data records, and audio recordings as evidence. The guidelines are targeted at foundational procedural topics such as relevance, admissibility, authentication, the assessment of probative value, disclosure, and expert reports, and are grounded in international jurisprudence and statutory provisions such as the ICC Rules of

[1] Kalshoven-Gieskes Forum on International Humanitarian Law, 'Leiden Guidelines on the Use of Digitally Derived Evidence in International Criminal Courts and Tribunals' (March 2022), https://leiden-guidelines.com/guidelines/ ('Leiden Guidelines').

Image-Based Evidence in International Criminal Prosecutions. Jonathan W. Hak, KC, Oxford University Press.
 DOI: 10.1093/oso/9780198889533.003.0009

Procedure and Evidence (RPE). The *Leiden Guidelines* do not, and were not intended to, provide an in-depth exploration of the types of evidence referenced and the challenges involved with them. Nonetheless, these guidelines provide helpful procedural advice to counsel dealing with such evidence.

The University of California (Berkeley) School of Law Human Rights Center has also produced several helpful reports on open source investigations and the use of social media and open source evidence. The *Berkeley Protocol on Digital Open Source Investigations (Berkeley Protocol*) was '... developed to provide international standards and guidance for investigators in the fields of international criminal justice and human rights'.[2] It is intended to be a reference for open source investigators and focuses on the '... identification, collection, preservation, analysis, and presentation of digital open source information and its use in international criminal and human rights investigations'.[3] A subsequent report entitled *Digital Lockers: Archiving Social Media Evidence of Atrocity Crimes* focused on the preservation of such evidence.[4] These documents are helpful for investigators focusing on open source evidence. Similarly, *Digital Witness: Using Open Source Information for Human Rights Investigation, Documentation, and Accountability* by Dubberley et al. recommends best practices in open source investigations.[5] Open source evidence is one of the topics that is addressed in this book though with more of an emphasis on the democratization of evidence gathering and the challenges involved in the use of images obtained from social media and open sources from an authenticity and reliability perspective. The UC Berkeley and Digital Witness publications are valuable resources on this discrete topic. What the *Leiden Guidelines*, *Berkeley Protocol*, and the work of Dubberley et al. have in common is a demonstrated desire to offer concrete guidance on certain aspects of digital evidence to specific audiences in varying degrees of specificity. They are not intended to be comprehensive works that tie in the legal, procedural, and practical challenges associated with image-based evidence.

Even with these helpful resources, what is apparent from the existing literature is that the use of image-based evidence in international criminal prosecutions has not received the critical attention it deserves. While image-based evidence features in every prosecution, it is not necessarily afforded the interpretive and narrative focus that is required to develop and profit from what it may have to offer, or to realize the challenges that it may portend without adequate examination. The risks

[2] Office of the United Nations High Commissioner for Human Rights and the Human Rights Centre at the University of California (Berkeley) School of Law, 'Berkeley Protocol on Digital Open Source Investigations' (2020) HR/PUB/20/2, Executive Summary, vii ('Berkeley Protocol').

[3] ibid at 3.

[4] UC Berkeley School of Law Human Rights Center, 'Digital Lockers: Archiving Social Media Evidence of Atrocity Crimes' (2021) https://humanrights.berkeley.edu/sites/default/files/digital_lockers_report5.pdf, 2 ('Digital Lockers').

[5] Sam Dubberley, Alexa Koenig, and Daragh Murray, *Digital Witness: Using Open Source Information for Human Rights Investigation, Documentation, and Accountability* (Oxford: OUP, 2020).

associated with misinterpretation and misapplication are inimical to the search for the truth. This book argues that more can, and should be, done to make effective use of image-based evidence in the courtroom. Merely showing images should not be the predominant method of utilizing this evidence as there are better ways to convey scene and event data to the court. To the visually literate, image-based evidence has much to offer.

This final chapter coalesces and identifies the macro themes that have emerged in previous chapters and sets out targeted practical recommendations for the use of image-based evidence in international criminal prosecutions. It also identifies which stages of the proceedings are engaged, whether it be the preliminary examination, the investigation, the confirmation hearing, the trial, or all four stages. New content and specific recommendations for the ICC Office of the Prosecutor (OTP) regarding the development and refinement of a formal repository for the acquisition, assessment, and archiving of image-based evidence submitted by individuals and organizations other than OTP investigators are presented, along with restrictions and guidelines that would be required for such a repository to be successful and the practical and budgetary considerations involved. Given that the expected volume of media would exceed the ability of human personnel to evaluate, a case is made for the further incorporation of machine learning and artificial intelligence to aid in this monumental task. Disclosure ramifications of a social media and open source repository are also considered.

I contend that the use of image-based evidence in international criminal prosecutions is at a tipping point. This chapter evaluates the *status quo* regarding the use of this evidence and makes three broad recommendations for how to transcend the *status quo* to push the use of image-based evidence out of the liminal space it currently occupies to the next level in international criminal justice.

1. Recommendations for the Use of Image-Based Evidence in International Criminal Prosecutions

Previous chapters have undertaken an in-depth exploration of substantive topics pertinent to image-based evidence and its role in international criminal prosecutions. As a result of the academic, technical, and legal research that has been presented, recommendations for the effective and strategic use of this evidence by counsel and the court have been developed. These recommendations are intended to assist counsel for the prosecution, defence, or victims in the preparation and presentation of image-based evidence and to assist the court in evaluating the evidence presented. While some of these recommendations are tethered, at least in part, to jurisprudence and procedural rules, most are based on experience given that comparatively few international rulings have been issued about image-based evidence. Unless otherwise stated, all these recommendations are applicable to international criminal prosecutions.

Cases that make it to trial in the ICC proceed through a series of stages. The preliminary examination phase assesses whether there is sufficient evidence of crimes within the court's jurisdiction and whether opening a formal investigation is merited (Art. 15). During this phase, the OTP analyses the information it has gathered, and may seek information from other entities and receive testimonial evidence at the seat of the Court. If the preliminary examination phase dictates that an investigation is warranted and the Pre-Trial Chamber authorizes it, then a formal investigation is undertaken wherein the OTP collects and examines evidence from myriad sources including on-site investigations (Art. 54), and may pursue unique investigative opportunities to examine, collect, or test evidence (Art. 56). Should the investigation support bringing specific defendants to trial for specific charges, the Pre-Trial Chamber must confirm the charges. During the preliminary examination, investigation, and confirmation stages, evidence is gathered and undergoes a preliminary assessment, but it is not until the trial stage that evidence is subjected to robust testing and assessment by the parties and the Chamber.

Some of the following recommendations are geared towards the trial stage, while others are applicable at earlier stages as well. For each broad topic, I will identify the stages that are engaged.

1.1 Constructing a Visual Trial Narrative

Fundamentally, criminal trials involve storytelling. Though the subject matter is often deeply disturbing, counsel is effectively presenting a trial narrative (story) for opposing counsel to critique and for the court to evaluate. Weaving image-based evidence into the trial narrative has a long history in international criminal justice. As far back as the Nuremberg trial, filmic images such as those shown in *Nazi Concentration Camps* were effectively used for probative and didactic purposes as were maps within the film for the depiction of concentration and death camp locations. Relevant and probative image-based evidence has been a common part of the trial narrative in the post-Nuremberg tribunals and courts, particularly during the prosecution's case. The following recommendations are aimed at the trial stage.

Recommendation 1.1.1 When constructing trial narratives, counsel should strategically incorporate image-based evidence to corroborate the evidence of witnesses and as independent proof of alleged facts.

It would be hard to imagine an atrocity crime case being presented in court without reliance upon image-based evidence for some aspects of the trial narrative and ultimately the search for the truth. Image-based evidence may be used as direct evidence to independently prove (or disprove) a fact or contention or as circumstantial evidence to corroborate or rebut other forms of evidence, in particular *viva voce* evidence. Counsel's case should take the form of a well-crafted and supported narrative of their contentions and the evidence presented in support thereof. The strategic incorporation of image-based evidence as a form of proof can be pivotal in the exposition of the case and is consistent with counsel's pedagogical role to teach their case in an effective and compelling manner to the court.

Recommendation 1.1.2 Counsel must be explicit as to the purposes for leading image-based evidence at trial.

Tendering image-based evidence at trial requires that there be an express reason for doing so because all evidence must have as its central purpose the ability to advance the discourse before the court in a tangible and articulable manner. Counsel must therefore consider what specific factual propositions will be advanced through the tendering of the evidence. For example, counsel must query what work is being asked of the images and determine whether they are rationally capable of meeting those objectives. When considering the use of advanced visual representations, counsel must be able to articulate cogent reasons for dedicating the time and expense required to create and present them, including how their use will advance the search for the truth.[6] Asking these frank questions in advance of trial and realistically assessing the potential value of image-based evidence for selection will lead to a more compelling narrative.

A related question that must be answered is whether the evidence is being led for substantive proof purposes or as demonstrative evidence. If it is being led for proof purposes, then the requirement to prove the authenticity, accuracy, and reliability of the image-based evidence is triggered, which will be expanded upon in later recommendations. This requirement applies to all types of image-based evidence but is particularly apt when considering advanced visual representations. Evidence led for demonstrative purposes must still have an authenticated factual basis to have propositional value for counsel and the court but arguably less is expected of the evidence as it has no overt probative value. The word 'overt' is used advisedly because it would be naïve to suggest that evidence expressly led for demonstrative purposes only and with no legally probative value does not carry weight in the eyes of the court. Powerful advanced visual representations, even when led for demonstrative purposes, cannot be unseen and may accumulate intrinsic *gravitas* even though not expressly referred to in the final judgment.

The concern regarding the power of demonstrative evidence is not just academic. There is a tendency to believe that we can fully absorb the meaning of prima facie realistic images.[7] The more we think we understand, the less likely we are to

[6] For example, 3D modeling, animations, simulations, interactive 360° visual representations, virtual reality, immersive virtual environments, and augmented reality.

[7] Richard Sherwin, Neal Feigenson, and Christina Spiesel, 'What Is Visual Knowledge, and What Is It Good For? Potential Ethnographic Lessons from the Field of Legal Practice', *Visual Anthropology* 20 (2007): 143–78, at 157.

question what we see. This tendency can reasonably be extended to other forms of image-based evidence such as advanced visual representations as they draw upon the inclination of viewers to believe what they are shown. Herein lies the potential danger involved in categorizing image-based evidence as demonstrative in nature as it may cause counsel and the court to be less vigilant as to the accuracy of the evidence and the propositions it is being used to support.

Tendering image-based evidence as demonstrative evidence must not cause counsel and the court to be more accepting of the evidence and less critical of its content. Vigilance must remain the watchword for all forms of image-based evidence, even when tendered in a demonstrative capacity. The summative value of the final product is only as good as the data upon which it is based.[8] Counsel must therefore be clear on the categorization and stated purpose of image-based evidence and ensure that it is led and argued in the correct context, less the spectre of trial unfairness and appellate intervention arise. Evidence led under either classification must be robustly defensible and only used for the purposes tendered.

Recommendation 1.1.3 Counsel should ensure that image-based evidence is presented in the courtroom in its optimal form using suitable display technology.

All the work that goes into the creation, evaluation, and analysis of image-based evidence may be severely compromised if the version that the court sees does not fully display what the evidence has to offer. Chief among these impediments is when the court is given a printed version of image-based evidence that contains fine detail, or a substandard electronic display is used in the courtroom. While printed versions may be appropriate for some graphical representations of data (e.g. charts, tables, graphs, and maps), it would rarely be suitable for photographs, video recordings, advanced visual representations, and other images. Even high-quality printers are not designed to accurately capture and reproduce fine details and when those details matter, counsel and the court may be left with inferior evidence. Printed versions should only be used as a desk reference and never as substantive evidence. The standard method of displaying digital and filmic evidence should be to use high-definition monitors accessible to all court participants. Finally, as there is sometimes a lack of aspect ratio congruence between how the evidence should be displayed and how it is actually displayed in the courtroom, a qualified technician should confirm this spatial arrangement prior to the evidence being presented.[9]

[8] Alexa Koenig and Lindsay Freeman, 'Cutting-Edge Evidence: Strengths and Weaknesses of New Digital Investigation Methods in Litigation', *Hastings Law Journal* 73 (2022): 1233–54, at 1252.

[9] For example, images that should be displayed in a 4:3 width to height aspect ratio (full screen) may be converted by the monitor to 16:9 (wide screen) and thereby incorrectly stretch the image.

1.2 Assessing the Sources of Image-Based Evidence

When contemplating whether to tender image-based evidence, it is essential that counsel consider the reliability and trustworthiness of its source given that source integrity is an important component of its foundational validity. Potentially viable sources of image-based evidence include OTP investigators, civilians, local intermediaries, civil society members, NGOs, journalists, researchers, and other interested parties, all of whom may be well positioned to provide probative crime base and linkage evidence. On occasion, even the defendant may have recorded relevant video and photographic images that could shed needed light. While source consideration is linked to other important factors discussed in later sections, it is properly siloed as an independent preliminary inquiry given its foundational character. The recommendations in this section are fully engaged at all pre-trial stages as well as the trial itself. Identifying and evaluating the source of image-based evidence and the ability to access original evidence must be undertaken long before trial so that informed decisions are made during the pre-trial phases. This will also assist in reducing the number of meritorious evidential issues at trial.

Recommendation 1.2.1 Evaluate the source of the evidence using a spectrum approach.

Sources of image-based evidence may be evaluated using a spectrum approach wherein sources in the trustworthy range would generally include OTP investigators, human rights investigators, and other sources with a proven track record for objectivity and integrity. Conversely, sources in the prima facie untrustworthy range would be anonymous contributors of images to social media and other sites. Beyond these ends of the spectrum is a potentially vast middle ground containing sources who must be thoroughly evaluated to assess how their evidence should be treated. Locating a source within this spectrum will dictate whether further investigation is required. Though this categorization is not legally mandated, in practice the fewer steps geographically and technically between the source and the OTP, the more trustworthy the evidence may be though that must be objectively established. In this context, trustworthy means that the source's evidence is authentic, accurate, and reliable. Part of the requisite source assessment is whether the media has been intentionally or inadvertently altered such that the proffered version is incomplete or misleading.

Recommendation 1.2.2 Efforts should be made to identify and interview human sources of image-based evidence that is being considered for entry at trial.

Though it would be ideal if OTP investigators were able to gather all relevant image-based evidence in a timely manner, the reality is that their ability to obtain sufficient evidence at most atrocity crime scenes and events is severely limited.[10] Key impediments facing investigators include delays in attendance, government interference, lack of resources, and security risks in active conflict zones. These impediments contribute to an evidential vacuum which has precipitated a partial reliance by the OTP upon the democratization of evidence gathering wherein the need for relevant evidence may be filled in part by documentarians other than OTP investigators and forensic personnel. Increasing the scope of potential contributors will often generate an evidential windfall yielding disparate perspectives and content otherwise unattainable by investigators.

Central to evaluating the reliability of tendered evidence from untested sources is identifying the original source where possible. This typically means identifying the photographer and securing the original media (the images first recorded to the relevant camera or connected device). Doing so will usually assist with the assessment of authenticity, reliability, and bias. If the source is identified, steps should be taken to interview that person for the purpose of understanding the context in which the images were created, the fairness of their content, and whether the images have been edited or otherwise altered to make them unreliable. Adopting a policy of obtaining this source information will assist with the legal obligation to authenticate image-based evidence provided by the source. Securing this witness account is particularly important given that the images may not be tendered into evidence for years and in a location far from where the photographer is located. Where the direct source is an intermediary, steps should be taken to identify the original source. In both cases, given the security risks applicable to evidence providers, steps must be taken to safeguard the identity of any such witness.[11]

[10] The 2022 Russian invasion of Ukraine is somewhat of an exception to the norm in that OTP staff were in Ukraine relatively early in the conflict familiarizing themselves with the conflict and gathering forensic and other evidence. Still, they cannot be at all relevant locations nor on an ongoing basis and thus their ability to gather evidence is constrained. 'ICC Prosecutor Karim A.A. Khan QC Visits Kharkiv, Ukraine on 15 June 2022' (17 June 2022) https://www.icc-cpi.int/news/icc-prosecutor-karim-khan-qc-visits-kharkiv-ukraine-15-june-2022; 'Press Conference of the ICC Prosecutor and Eurojust with Joint Investigation Team on Alleged Core International Crimes in Ukraine' (27 May 2022) https://www.icc-cpi.int/news/press-conference-icc-prosecutor-and-eurojust-joint-investigation-team-alleged-core; 'ICC Prosecutor Karim A.A. Khan QC Announces Deployment of Forensics and Investigative Team to Ukraine, Welcomes Strong Cooperation with the Government of the Netherlands' (17 May 2022) https://www.icc-cpi.int/news/icc-prosecutor-karim-aa-khan-qc-announces-deployment-forensics-and-investigative-team-ukraine; 'Statement by ICC Prosecutor, Karim A.A. Khan QC: Office of the Prosecutor Joins National Authorities in Joint Investigation Team on International Crimes Committed in Ukraine' (25 April 2022), https://www.icc-cpi.int/news/statement-icc-prosecutor-karim-aa-khan-qc-office-prosecutor-joins-national-authorities-joint.

[11] The ICC offers protective measures for vulnerable witnesses including the use of pseudonyms, face and voice distortion, and the use of private and closed sessions. See, e.g. *Prosecutor v. Kani*, ICC-01/14-01/21-537-Red, Decision on the Prosecution's Request for Reconsideration of the In-Court Protective Measures for Witness P-0435, 8 November 2022.

Recommendation 1.2.3 Image-based evidence obtained from social media and other sites requires careful consideration.

In an ideal world, the human source of image-based evidence would be identified and interviewed, and access to the original media would be available. In the real world, that is frequently not the case. A considerable amount of photographic and video images is uploaded to social media and other sites which are largely unregulated. Some evidence gathering sites such as *eyeWitness to Atrocities* serve as valuable intermediaries with an attention to detail and a desire to gather robust evidence, but that is the exception rather than the rule. One of the biggest challenges with social media and other open source images is that the repository platforms to which they are submitted do not necessarily share the same concerns that counsel and the court have regarding the authenticity and integrity of the images. Identification of the photographer is dependent upon the input of the submitter and access to the original images is rarely obtainable. As a result, experience has shown that hypervigilance is required by investigators and counsel when evaluating the suitability of social media and other images for court purposes because much of the information needed to properly evaluate the source and the images is absent.

Recommendation 1.2.4 Access to the original images must be addressed expeditiously before the evidence is lost or compromised.

Every effort should be made to obtain the original images from the source and failing that, the most technically complete version of them should be obtained before the original or best evidence is destroyed or lost. This is not a legal requirement but as a matter of policy, the more intact the evidence, the easier it is to authenticate. Further, given the precarious lifespan and unpredictable stability of images and video recordings uploaded to social media and other sites, images and recordings should be downloaded as soon as possible. Koenig and Freeman note the evidential losses that occur when social media content moderators or users remove content prior to investigators being able to capture it. In the absence of lay investigators gathering that evidence, its content will never be known or available for use.[12] More vexing is the reality that the volume of uploaded media is such that investigators cannot possibly examine all content. The *Berkeley Protocol* provides detailed guidance on the preservation of uploaded media.[13]

[12] Koenig and Freeman (n 8) 1241. See Bailey Ulbricht, Christopher Moxley, Mackenzie Austin, and Molly Norburg, 'Digital Eyewitnesses: Using New Technologies to Authenticate Evidence in Human Rights Litigation', *Stanford Law Review* 74, no. 4 (2022): 851–96, at 860, who note that YouTube's content moderation algorithms have removed thousands of video recordings of human rights violations that were uploaded by individuals and civil society organizations. See also Jack Goodman and Maria Korenyuk, 'AI: War Crimes Evidence Erased by Social Media Platforms' *BBC News* (1 June 2023) https://www.bbc.com/news/technology-65755517. Koenig also notes the dynamic nature of social media platforms and the need for evidence preservation. Alexa Koenig, 'From "Capture to Courtroom": Collaboration and the Digital Documentation of International Crimes in Ukraine', *Journal of International Criminal Justice* 20, no. 4 (2022): 829–42, at 835.

[13] See *Berkeley Protocol* (n 2) section on preservation of digital content, 60–3.

Recommendation 1.2.5 Image-based evidence obtained from an anonymous source or a source that cannot be examined should not be relied upon or admitted in the absence of material corroboration.

Anonymity fosters the substantial risks of mischief, compromised fact-finding, and unfairness at trial. In circumstances where the source of image-based evidence is unknown, or known but unavailable to be produced and interviewed, counsel should not factor such evidence into their trial narrative unless it can be robustly corroborated by admissible and independently proven evidence.[14] Such evidence may consist of eyewitnesses or other images recorded by a different photographer present at the same location at the relevant time, documents, and other physical items of evidence. Similarly, lack of access to the original media or a trustworthy version of it should militate against its use.

1.3 Accounting for Agendas and Biases in the Creation of Image-Based Evidence

All image-based evidence is intertwined with, and potentially influenced by, the agendas and biases of its creators. Though it is often said that the camera is the witness, I contend that the photographer is the true witness and that the camera merely memorializes what the photographer chooses to include in (and exclude from) the frame. Images are created by interested parties and contextualizing their creation is important because it alerts viewers to the fact that subjective choices by the photographer must be considered when evaluating image content. It is reasonable to suggest that all photographers are biased in the way they choose to record scenes and events. Biases may operate overtly in favour of accurately and objectively documenting what is observed. Conversely, they may cause photographers to capture the vision they wish to present to others irrespective of whether it is accurate. Agendas and biases may also operate at a subconscious level and may unintentionally skew the visual record. The recommendations in this section are relevant to pre-trial decisions made based upon image-based evidence and the proper assessment of the evidence at trial where the failure to account for agendas and biases may lead to unfavourable fact-finding.

Recommendation 1.3.1 Images should not be accepted at face value without questioning the photographer about their content.

Because photographic and video images represent a subjective choice by the photographer, viewers must carefully evaluate their content and the narrative they are alleged to support or contradict. Questioning the photographer to gain

[14] ICC law is unsettled on this point but as a matter of practice this would be the prudent approach to follow.

contextual information could be of significant assistance when assessing what meaning should be attributed to the images. While questioning the photographer will not generate images that were not recorded or retained, there is value in asking contextual questions and exploring the presence and impact of agendas and biases. Questions may include the following: Why was this image recorded? What did the photographer intend to capture within the frame? What was occurring outside of the frame and why was that not memorialized? Why did the recording begin and end when it did? If a video recording contains no audio, why was the choice made to record visual evidence only or, if applicable, why was the audio track subsequently edited out? Were all the recordings submitted for consideration? Were any recordings edited prior to submission? It follows that when the photographer can be identified and questioned, agendas and biases can be explored. When the photographer is anonymous or unavailable for questioning, this can prove to be a significant impediment to image evaluation, especially in the absence of external corroboration.

Recommendation 1.3.2 Corroborative evidence should be sought to assist in the evaluation of photographer agendas and biases.

Whether the photographer is known and available for questioning or not, corroboration in the form of images from a different proven source or perspective, or *viva voce* evidence, should be pursued as a means of teasing out and contending with the subjectivity of the image creation process. Photographer agendas and biases can best be assessed when other evidence is available to provide context for the images. The presence of corroborative evidence may enhance the robustness of the images under consideration and equally, the absence of corroboration might justify caution when evaluating their soundness. Image corroboration is not required as a matter of law, but when more information is available to counsel and the court, one can predict a more informed assessment of the tendered images.

Recommendation 1.3.3 Advanced visual representations must be assessed for underlying data soundness and accurate visual depiction.

Advanced visual representations are created based upon foundational scene measurements and other data. Whenever choices are involved in the visual representation of underlying data, the potential for creative agendas and biases to skew the final depiction exists. Therefore, these methods of data representation should not be taken at face value. Rather, good practice dictates that counsel and their experts should take steps to assess whether the foundational data is correct and whether it has been fairly represented in the tendered visual display.

Recommendation 1.3.4 Counsel must ensure that their selection of images and other visual representations fairly depict the scene or event.

While the impact of agendas and biases is primarily focused on photographers and those who create visual representations of data, counsel are not immune from making subjective choices that can impact the creation of their trial narrative.[15] Counsel's selection of images for use at trial and visual representations of data must reflect a fair depiction of the scene, event, or underlying data. When tendered by the prosecution, competing and perhaps exculpatory images and data should also be presented, especially considering the prosecution's goal to ascertain the truth. Similarly, when image-based evidence is supplemented with textual or graphic annotations, counsel must ensure that such supplemental data are objectively fair and accurate. The fairness of the prosecution's case should not become a live issue at trial.

1.4 Authentication of Images

Counsel have a positive obligation to authenticate images tendered as evidence. From a legal perspective, authentication means establishing that the images are indeed that which they purport to be. While related to assessing the accuracy, reliability, and meaning of image content, authentication is a standalone foundational step that serves as a gateway for these further assessments. At its core, image authentication is focused on proving the location portrayed, the date and time of the portrayal, and overall image integrity. There is a tendency to think of authentication as a trial level responsibility but that belies the importance of establishing image authentication at the outset. Images should not be used as part of pre-trial stages unless their authenticity can be firmly established. The first and second recommendations are applicable at all pre-trial stages of a case and the trial phase while the last recommendation applies only to the trial phase.

Recommendation 1.4.1 Counsel must take positive steps to present a solid blueprint of authenticity for the court to consider.

One of the biggest challenges that counsel must face when they deal with image-based evidence is establishing its authenticity. A seminal consideration in an authentication inquiry is the source of the images. When the images have been created by an OTP investigator or other trustworthy source, authentication should not be challenging as the creator of the images is able to provide location and temporal data as well as evidence regarding the method of recording, the integrity and accuracy of the content, details of any editing undertaken, and a full chain of custody. Additionally, the original media will often be available for examination. In

[15] Nor are investigators who search for social media and open source evidence. Koenig and Freeman (n 8) 1240. The *Berkeley Protocol* (n 2) 57–8 briefly addresses the significance of online investigator bias.

these circumstances it is unlikely that additional authentication evidence will be required including expert evidence.

When the source is unknown or untrustworthy, authentication is typically much more challenging as there may be no access to the source of the media, the photographer, or the original recording. Images uploaded to social media and other sites are frequently stripped of essential metadata during the uploading process which adversely impacts the ability of experts and counsel to assess them for integrity.[16] Further, vital information regarding the recording process and the integrity of the content may never be available. Therefore, in cases where the source is unknown or untrustworthy, a forensic imagery expert should be engaged to conduct a thorough technical evaluation of the media's metadata (when present) and visible content. Employing relevant forgery detection techniques to assess the integrity and authenticity of the digital media can yield valuable results. Because authenticity should be a legal and practical prerequisite to substantive consideration by the court, opposing counsel should raise authenticity concerns as soon as they become apparent and preferably prior to trial.

Recommendation 1.4.2 Corroborative evidence should be presented to supplement proof of authenticity.

Even though not expressly required by law, experience dictates that beyond undertaking the foregoing foundational authentication steps of proving location, date, time, and overall integrity, counsel would be wise to seek and present external independent corroborative evidence to bolster authenticity, especially when the source is unknown or untrustworthy. External corroborative evidence may consist of witness testimony, third party verification, documents, admissions of the defendant, other authenticated media, expert evidence, etc.[17] This will assist in bolstering authenticity from a legal and technical perspective by aligning the images with other aspects of the case.

Recommendation 1.4.3 There should be a new legal approach to authentication.

Contrary to many domestic jurisdictions which link authenticity to admissibility, there is demonstrable tension in the ICC with different Chambers recommending and adopting disparate approaches to authenticity. Some Chambers advocate that authenticity should be a prerequisite to admission while others relegate it to the weighing process at the end of the case. I advocate a new three-step approach to the legal evaluation of authentication. First, there should be a requirement that the tendering party provide prima facie proof of authenticity when the

[16] This metadata provides valuable information about the technical content of the images and may also include location and temporal indicators.

[17] Authenticated media can be used to authenticate questioned media; Ulbricht, Moxley, Austin, and Norburg (n 12) 891–2.

evidence is first presented to the court. Second, a stronger confirmation of authenticity (balance of probabilities) should be established at the close of the party's case to ensure that the preliminary admission was warranted. Third, the court should engage in a final assessment of authenticity during the judgment phase. Failure to meet the first two tests would result in the evidence being excluded at an earlier stage and would serve to clarify and economize the evidential record for final consideration. This approach would also put counsel on notice that authenticity must be addressed in a robust manner early in the proceedings rather than waiting to address the issue in final argument.

1.5 Assessing the Meaning and Reliability of Images

Viewers often have unrealistic expectations regarding the power of images, including the belief that they speak for themselves and that their meaning will be obvious to all people. In fact, images do not necessarily possess inherent meaning, nor do they have a concordant ability to communicate their meaning in equal measures to all viewers. Viewers must do some interpretive work, and this includes learning to ask the right questions of images. For example, to competently assess the meaning of selected images, viewers would benefit from understanding the context in which they were created and why the photographer chose the depicted perspective. A further consideration is what trial narrative the images are being associated with by counsel. It follows that positive steps must be taken towards gaining a comprehensive and informed understanding of the meaning and reliability of images that are being contemplated for use as evidence or those that have been tendered by the opposing party. The following recommendations are founded on practical experience and are designed to assist in gaining this understanding. They are primarily directed at the presentation of evidence at trial, but they evoke important considerations that are relevant to earlier stages as well given that the failure to properly assess image meaning and reliability at the outset will have a cascading negative effect on the value of the evidence.

Recommendation 1.5.1 Counsel should lead contextual evidence that establishes the 5Ws for tendered images.

Fundamentally, for each image selected, counsel should be able to answer the following five questions through the presentation of knowledgeable and reliable evidence to the court. *Who* is depicted in the image? For images that contain people, this question may not always be answerable with a specific name but there must be a valid descriptor, e.g. 'an unidentified child soldier'. *What* is depicted in the image? Bearing in mind that different viewers may interpret an image in different ways, counsel should state what they believe the image shows, e.g. damage to a mausoleum caused by shelling. *Where* is the location in the image situated?

Contextualizing an image by location is central to establishing relevance and authenticity, and therefore the location must be stated and provable. *When* was the image recorded? A bedrock feature of image relevance and authentication is establishing temporal parameters and counsel must therefore be able to prove when an image was recorded to meet these objectives. *Why* was the image recorded? The response to this question may be factually established when the photographer is known and can provide this information or it may be obvious from the image's context, but in cases where this origin story is missing counsel may have to posit their theory as to why an image was created.

Not only will addressing the five Ws prior to tendering images as evidence help to ultimately establish their relevance, authenticity, and probative value, it will help to infuse the images with necessary context and meaning. Following this five-step rubric for evaluating images will help to engender a protocol for cautious appraisal in the early stages of developing a trial narrative and may serve to expose the basis upon which an image's meaning may be contentious, thereby highlighting the need for further inquiry to answer these questions. Dissension at the pre-trial stage is likely to portend challenges in the trial courtroom. Following the five-step rubric does not mean that other interpretations may not be tenable, but it provides counsel with a solid foundation for arguing their interpretation. Alternative interpretations must be factored into counsel's narrative so that the court has the benefit of counsel's interpretive commentary. Addressing the five Ws with cogent and reliable evidence will likely be sufficient for the defensible interpretation of most images, though for others a full analysis by a qualified imagery expert may be necessary.

Recommendation 1.5.2 Counsel should use a spectrum approach when assessing image reliability and look for relevant hallmarks.

Reliability is a fundamental issue when dealing with image-based evidence. When assessing images for their meaning and reliability, both counsel and the court should employ a healthy amount of scepticism. Unnecessary paranoia is not advocated, nor is every photographer trying to fool viewers, but the default stance should be to question images rather than to accept them at face value. The need for reticence can reasonably be evaluated using a spectrum approach. The more trustworthy the source of the images, the less need there may be to seriously question their reliability. For example, images created by OTP and human rights investigators, and other sources with a proven track record for integrity are likely to be more reliable than social media images with no identifiable photographer. This is not to suggest as a blanket proposition that images at this latter end of the spectrum have no evidential value. In fact, they may prove to be authentic and reliable, but that designation should be earned, not awarded without inquiry.

Assessing images for their suitability in advancing the trial narrative should include evaluating the presence or absence of hallmarks of reliability. These hallmarks include identification of the source of the images, the likelihood of image manipulation, and any motive and capacity of the source to do so. Further hallmarks include determining whether access to the original media is available, whether the photographer has been identified and is accessible, and determining whether the integrity of the image content is robust or questionable. The more hallmarks of reliability that are present, the more likely it will be that counsel can satisfy the court that the evidence is worthy of substantive consideration.

Recommendation 1.5.3 Expert assistance may be required to assess image reliability.

Image reliability need not be determined in a vacuum. Though an untrained eye may perceive images to be trustworthy, there is merit in engaging a forensic imagery expert to interrogate and technically evaluate them. An imagery expert can use multiple content-based methods to examine the images and this approach can serve to either confirm counsel's initial perception or contradict it. Assessing image content can include an examination of image metadata (when available and trustworthy), time of day and shadow inconsistencies, weather and geography anomalies, etc. Attempting to geolocate the image using other proven imagery may also be of considerable assistance.[18] Expert confirmation or contradiction will bolster counsel's decisions regarding the use of images as evidence. The goal of robustly assessing image reliability in advance of entering images as evidence at trial is to forestall the need for any serious inquiry by opposing counsel or the court as to the soundness of the images tendered.

1.6 Image Interpretation and Expert Assistance

Once counsel have achieved an informed understanding of the content and meaning of the images they have selected for use at trial, and have articulated a valid purpose for using them as evidence, consideration must then be given to how their content can be most effectively conveyed to the court. This task which may involve counsel, witnesses, or imagery experts, or a combination thereof could be approached using a spectrum analysis, the purpose of which is to determine what supplemental interpretive resources are required. These recommendations are primarily aimed at the trial phase while the second recommendation may also have application at earlier stages to ensure that images are correctly interpreted during the investigation.

[18] These content-based methods of assessing image reliability are found in Chapter 5. See also Koenig and Freeman (n 8) 1249.

Recommendation 1.6.1 Counsel should use a spectrum approach when determining what resources are needed to convey the content and meaning of images to the court.

Some images may be entered from counsel table via bar table motion with a brief explanation by counsel as to their meaning. These images would be reflective of those that are at the low end of the spectrum, and do not require supplemental interpretive assistance. Given that images should rarely be allowed or expected to speak for themselves, comparatively few images would occupy this end of the spectrum. More frequently, using a mid-spectrum approach, images should be accompanied by the appropriate supplemental explanatory evidence that is needed to fully explain to the court the context in which the images were created, their meaning, and the purposes for which they are being tendered. This may be achieved by counsel leading *viva voce* and other evidence from eyewitnesses, third party observers, investigators, or other suitably informed individuals who can provide direct proof on image interpretation and meaning to adequately cover the five-part rubric discussed above (the five Ws). If direct proof is not possible via this approach, witnesses may be able to provide *viva voce* or other evidence that may be able to corroborate counsel's theory laterally. At the higher end of the spectrum, expert interpretive assistance will be required when the images themselves are sufficiently complicated or semi-legible such that the viewer is highly likely to misinterpret the images or fail to interpret them at all without assistance. This policy recommendation is designed to ensure that counsel evaluates the evidential support needed for each piece of image-based evidence.

Recommendation 1.6.2 Forensic imagery experts should be retained to evaluate and analyse image-based evidence prior to it being included in the trial narrative.

A common element in the spectrum approach to image interpretation is that except at the low end of the spectrum, some form of explanatory evidence from an informed witness is essential to develop a proper understanding of image content. It is therefore important that counsel develop a plan for how to best present image-based evidence to the court. Beyond the five-step rubric discussed above, counsel should not undertake image evaluation on their own as counsel who choose to interpret images without technical assistance do so at their peril. Even the sharpest of counsel may discern the apparent meaning of an image but not comprehend technical issues that may impact that assessment. This is not a failing by counsel but rather a reflection of the fact that different people can bring additional light to bear upon image interpretation commensurate with their qualifications. All images that counsel intend to tender as evidence should undergo a technical assessment by a forensic imagery expert.

The purpose of this preliminary assessment is twofold. First, the expert can determine whether there are any technical issues such as image compression and associated data loss and artefact additions, image resolution deficiencies, frame rate anomalies, and aspect ratio errors that might impact the interpretation of the images. These features frequently accompany digital imagery and can significantly influence the meaning attributable to images and can lead to viewer misinterpretation. The courtroom is not the place to discover these issues—they must be proactively addressed prior to images being relied upon for proof (or disproof) of any proposition.

Second, the expert can advise counsel as to whether targeted analytical processes should be undertaken to assist in maximizing the value of the images for the court's consideration and judgment.[19] Depending upon the complexity of the images, the court will likely benefit from the assistance of an expert who can technically interrogate the images, evaluate their content, and advise as to what meaning can fairly be drawn from them after conducting a full technical analysis. Absent this expert assistance, the court would otherwise be left to conduct its own superficial evaluation.[20] Further, expert analysis may bring out details not otherwise noted or observable and provide a more sophisticated level of understanding, thereby allowing counsel and the court to form more informed and evidence-based judgments. The expert can also advise the court regarding image features that serve to limit their interpretive parameters which can help to avoid counsel and the court overdriving image content.[21] Further, there are categories of semi-legible images such as satellite photographs and complex video and still imagery that mandate expert analysis and interpretation to form a correct judgment.

Depending upon the images, the interests of justice may not be served when judges are tasked with discerning image content with minimal or no assistance from experts. When that occurs, counsel have failed in their responsibility to assist the court. The purpose of this recommended policy of utilizing a two-step preliminary assessment is to cause counsel to engage in the meaningful evaluation of image content at the earliest stages by relying upon not just their own perception but the input of imagery experts. It bears noting that for this approach to have merit, there must be sufficient expert resources in place to provide this assistance.

[19] These analytical processes include breaking down video images to a frame-by-frame level of analysis, clarifying image content, evaluating the impact of temporal and spatial compression, motion stabilization, motion tracking, synchronizing multiple video sources, synchronizing video and audio sources, image comparison and contrast, assessing image authenticity and reliability, speed and height determination, etc. See Section 5 of Chapter 6 for further details.

[20] As was the case in *Prosecutor v. Gbagbo and Blé Goudé*. See Section 6 of Chapter 6.

[21] Overdriving an image means drawing more interpretive value from an image than it can fairly provide. See also 'International Bar Association Report', *IBA ICL Perspectives: Evidence Matters in ICC Trials* (August 2016) https://www.ibanet.org/document?id=Evidence-matters-in-icc-trials, 20.

1.7 Presenting Complex Data with Image-Based Evidence

Complex visual depictions can take millions of data points and create a method of understanding them that would otherwise render the data largely unintelligible to counsel and the court. Advanced didactic visualization methods include the use of 3D scene and event modelling, and computer generated data visualizations in the form of animations or simulations. The question that must then be addressed is how this evidence can best be used to assist in the search for the truth. These recommendations are applicable to the trial stage of proceedings.

Recommendation 1.7.1 Forensic experts or other suitably qualified technical witnesses are required to present complex data in court.

The essence of presenting complex data in visual form is to make it more understandable to counsel and the court. However, the visual presentation itself may have limited stand-alone value and is not a substitute for the explanatory *viva voce* evidence needed to explain the data. As a matter of practice, a two-stage process is therefore recommended for presenting such data. The first step is for the expert or other suitably qualified witness to use data visualization as a primer to explain the relevant science or technical methodology to the court in a case neutral manner. After laying this *viva voce* and visual foundation, the second step is to present the case specific data in visual form. This two-step approach has a didactive and pedagogical basis wherein the court is more likely to find value in the case specific evidence if is first afforded a basic understanding of the underlying science or technical details. The goal is not to elevate the court to the expert level or to teach the court how to do the proverbial math but rather to show how the results were obtained in such a way that the court can have faith in the methodology employed. The court is more likely to accept and properly utilize the case specific evidence if it has a suitable understanding of how the evidence was obtained, how it was analysed, and its meaning in the context of the case.

Recommendation 1.7.2 Advanced data visualization methods may be required to present complex or compendious data points.

Some scenes or events cannot be adequately depicted using more traditional photographic, video, or diagram-based approaches. For example, when accurate measurements are critical to evaluating and understanding a scene or event, 3D terrestrial laser scanning may be employed to capture millions of measurement points and to thereafter create a 3D digital model for counsel and the court. Given the transient nature of some scenes, the sooner the measurements are obtained, the better. Similarly, computer generated visualizations in the form of animations or simulations may be helpful for recreating a dynamic event. While animations are demonstrative tools only and are typically used to illustrate a party's case theory, they will be more probative if they are grounded upon accurate measurements. Conversely, simulations can be classified as substantive evidence when they are based upon proven precise mathematical and physics data and formulas and are particularly helpful as they can be used to show different dynamic permutations. All methods of presenting complex or compendious data to the court are only as good as the data relied upon and therefore all underlying data must be independently proven to be accurate to give the visual representation *gravitas*.

1.8 Advanced Visual Representations

Advanced visual representations in the form of interactive 360° visual representations, virtual reality, immersive virtual environments, and augmented reality can be very effective methods for presenting compendious, complex, or dynamic data, thus giving the court a more robust platform from which to find facts. While these platforms typically rely upon measurements obtained through 3D scanning, that is not always the case and thus these advanced representations are addressed separately in this section. The preliminary issue that must be addressed is whether they should be used at all. Properly prepared and on the right case facts, there is legal support for using advanced visual representations, but the OTP may wish to develop a policy on the use of this type of evidence. The following recommendations would be relevant to developing such a policy and are primarily directed at the trial phase. To the extent that advanced visual representations are used before the Pre-Trial Chamber to seek authorizations or confirmation, these recommendations would apply as well.

Recommendation 1.8.1 Advanced visual representations should only be used when they add tangible value to the search for the truth.

Due to the time and expense required to create advanced visual representations and concerns of judicial trial economy, advanced visual representations should only be used if they will enhance the ability of counsel and the court to determine critical facts. If the same objective can be achieved by using more traditional 2D methods such as maps, diagrams, and photographic or video images, that would be preferred. In short, advanced visual representations should be additive evidence, not merely complementary. It follows that when these representations are used, counsel must be clear on the purposes for which they are being tendered. When tendered as substantive evidence, a higher authentication threshold is engaged as the evidence can be used in argument by counsel on liability and by the court to make findings of fact. Demonstrative evidence serves a different (lower) purpose, primarily serving as a tour of a scene. Both have merit but a conscious choice must be made and communicated to opposing counsel and the court as to categorization. In either case, the representation must be a fair and objective representation of underling data and the probative value of the representation must exceed its prejudicial effect.

Recommendation 1.8.2 Advanced visual representations do not speak for themselves and require expert narrative interpretation.

Advanced visual representations have limited probative value without supplementary expert narrative. Only then can their content and the purposes for which they have been led be fully communicated to opposing counsel and the court. If the choice is made to present an advanced visual representation as evidence, counsel must present a solid basis for its admission including leading the evidence through a qualified expert, scientifically validating the platform used, authenticating and establishing the accuracy of the underlying data (measurements, video, photographs, diagrams, etc.), and showing that the data have been correctly incorporated into the representation. Data accuracy is critical because these representations are primarily a visually summative form of pre-existing evidence—a representation based upon underlying data. It must therefore be proven that the final product has properly incorporated and displayed the underlying data and that it is collectively sound, valid, accurate, and reliable for use by counsel and the court for the purposes stated.

Should the OTP or any other party rely upon third-party service providers to create advanced visual representations, the same high standards required for this type of evidence must be maintained. The service provider must be given all relevant measurements, photographs, video images, and other requisite data. Counsel must ensure that clear instructions are provided, and that the final product is accurate and reliable. To the extent that the service provider makes any assumptions or generalizations in the creation of the representation, those must be reported to and approved by counsel and fully disclosed.

A related consideration in utilizing an advanced visual representation is the choice made by counsel and the expert as to what content will be included, the level of engagement available to viewers, and whether the representation is intended for use only by the court or also by counsel, experts, and perhaps witnesses. These considerations are unique to this type of representation because of the level of viewer participation that is potentially available. Lastly, a suitable record of the representation must also be prepared for exhibit purposes. This may be in the form of a recorded 3D viewing or a 2D representation, the former being the preferred method.

1.9 Visual Literacy

Visual literacy refers to developing a suitable level of competence in, and knowledge of, image-based evidence. While visual literacy is not part of the job description of an investigator, counsel, or the judiciary, it is an important component in the evaluation and interpretation of images and is needed to form sound and informed judgements about their meaning. Merely viewing an image does not equate with understanding what the image has to offer (and its technical and epistemic limitations), nor does it lead to visual literacy as vision and visual literacy are entirely different precepts. Achieving suitable visual literacy requires abandoning the perception that images speak for themselves, and that viewers can comprehensively digest and interpret their content without guidance. Visual literacy causes viewers to exercise more critical discernment when assessing images and is ultimately needed to ensure that the court can correctly assess the legibility of images and render judgment upon them with a full understanding of what propositions they support or refute. Deficient visual literacy can give rise to the risk of erroneous judgement, the failure to find the truth, and miscarriage of justice. The following recommendations are applicable at all stages of a case, whenever image-based evidence is being considered in the decision-making process.

Recommendation 1.9.1 There is a need to improve the visual literacy of people who must assess and ascribe meaning to images.

Images that have been selected for consideration progress through an evidential filtering process. Investigators and other people who initially evaluate images must determine whether they possess content that is relevant and merit consideration by counsel. Counsel must then interpret the meaning of the images and determine if and how they factor into the trial narrative. Once tendered as evidence to support or contradict the propositions of counsel, the court must determine how to factor the images into the fact-finding process. These steps require a level of visual literacy that is not adequately being addressed in international criminal litigation. This is not intended as a criticism of these important players in the criminal justice system but rather it reflects the fact that focused on-the-job training is needed to effectively contend with evidence that can be both deceptive and revelatory. Visual literacy is needed at all stages of a case. Investigators, counsel, and the court must question what the images portray, what those portrayals mean, and how they are relevant to the issues being litigated.

The OTP should adopt a policy whereby investigators, counsel, and the court would receive expert training about digital imagery generally, covering such topics as how images are created; the impact of temporal and spatial compression, frame rate, resolution, and aspect ratio, the elements involved in image authentication and the challenges involved in the authentication process, image reliability, and the ability of people to intentionally manipulate image content, etc. Training should also include more advanced topics such as the detection of deepfakes, including digital discovery and verification techniques. The goal of this expert training is not to elevate the audience to the expert level but rather to help make them more aware of the need for inquiry when interpreting the content and meaning of images. 'The picture speaks for itself' and 'I know what I see' should not be opening salvos to image interpretation. Instead, the objective interrogation and interpretation of images will engender a more informed assessment of their meaning by investigators, counsel, and the court.

Further, an effort should also be undertaken to educate counsel and the court generally about the technology involved in advanced visual representations and their application in the judicial context. This should include a discussion and demonstration of the technology used to create such representations including the relevant advantages and potential disadvantages involved in its use as well as the need for expert interpretation. This illustrative education could be undertaken outside of the context of any specific case as part of the general education of counsel and the court.

Recommendation 1.9.2 Images should be didactically presented to the court, not merely shown.

Once it has been determined by counsel that images have evidential value, the images should be taught to the court, not merely presented for consideration. Images do not necessarily mean the same thing to all viewers. A fulsome didactic approach to images requires presenting evidence on the five-part rubric (the five Ws) through eyewitnesses, third party observers, investigators, or other suitably informed individuals who can provide direct proof on these interpretive issues. It may also require the presentation of other evidence that can corroborate the propositions which counsel urge emanate from the images. Where technical image interrogation and interpretation are required, then the use of imagery experts will be necessary. This is particularly important when necessary to highlight limitations in the images to avoid more meaning being ascribed to them than is warranted. Should counsel choose to employ advanced visual representations as part of the trial narrative, counsel and the expert witness must educate the court on the record as to the creation of the representations and their proffered interpretation of the case specific evidence. Collectively, this didactic presentation approach should not only result in the more comprehensive and informative use of image-based evidence, but it can also vicariously serve to elevate the visual literacy of the court.

2. Considerations for the ICC OTP Regarding Open Source Images

One of the challenges involved in obtaining image-based evidence through the process of democratization is the number of steps that frequently exist between the photographer and the OTP.[22] The more steps that exist between the photographer

[22] Though this section focuses on the ICC OTP because it is the predominant institution that investigates and prosecutes atrocity crimes, these comments also apply to other institutions that target atrocity crimes, internationally and domestically.

and the end user, the greater the likelihood of evidential complexities. For example, when photographers upload images and video recordings to social media and other sites, they may intentionally or inadvertently inject a measure of anonymity into the process which can affect the ability of the parties to authenticate the images.[23] Further, the process of uploading images to internet sites often results in the stripping of essential metadata which adversely impacts the ability of experts to assess authenticity and integrity. There is also no guarantee that such images will ever come to the attention of investigators or counsel because scouring open source sites is extremely resource intensive and the lifespan of such media uploads is often tenuous.[24] Even dedicated evidence gathering applications such as *eyeWitness to Atrocities* and *CameraV* represent a step between the photographer and the OTP, albeit for altruistic reasons. Finally, reliance upon intermediaries for the receipt and transfer of image-based evidence creates its own host of problems.[25]

One way to address these delivery and authenticity obstacles is for the OTP to develop its own secure method of acquiring, assessing, and archiving image-based evidence submitted by individuals and organizations other than OTP investigators. Though the OTP receives a considerable amount of unsolicited information on situations under investigation or situations that may be worthy of investigation, a more formal repository specifically intended for image-based evidence would be a potentially valuable evidential resource. The goal of such a repository would be fourfold. First, it should help to reduce the current partial reliance upon social media and other sites for the provision of image-based evidence in that it would create a portal dedicated to atrocity crimes. Second, it should minimize the necessity for intermediaries to submit evidence to the OTP and the attendant complications that are associated with that procedure. Third, by setting parameters for direct uploads, it may result in a higher degree of image integrity. Fourth, it would ultimately vest more control in the process with the OTP.[26]

To achieve this goal, the OTP would need to establish the necessary technical resources to receive, document, and archive the data, and the technical and human capacity to evaluate it. With the continued proliferation of atrocity crimes that are being committed in varied locations and new situations developing therefrom, this will be a monumental and costly endeavour. Notably, in May 2023, the OTP launched *OTP Link*, which it describes as an advanced evidence submission

[23] Photographer anonymity occurs when social media and other sites do not require photographers to identify themselves or do not verify provided information on identity.

[24] Researchers have been experimenting with blockchain technology to help preserve and verify open source images and recordings and have submitted their results to the ICC for consideration. This method of preserving open source images is dependent upon finding the images before they are removed from the site; Julia Horowitz, 'A Crypto-Based Dossier Could Help Prove Russian Committed War Crimes' *CNN Business* (10 June 2022) https://www.cnn.com/2022/06/10/tech/ukraine-war-crimes-blockchain/index.html.

[25] See Section 1.3 of Chapter 3.

[26] Currently, open source evidence may be held by various investigative organizations which may in turn share such evidence with interested parties; Koenig (n 12) 838–9.

platform.[27] It is intended to be used for the online and email-based submission of evidence by external stakeholders and witnesses. There are several issues that must be considered in the early days of *OTP Link* and the balance of this chapter addresses these issues.

Despite the laudatory aspects of developing in-house OTP capacity to receive, process, and evaluate submitted media, there are clear practical and legal challenges to overcome. First, becoming a worldwide repository of submitted visual evidence of atrocity crimes may prove to be the legal equivalent of opening Pandora's box. By unleashing this evidential floodgate, the volume of media received may prove to be crippling and may cause *OTP Link* to struggle under the weight of the very thing it sought to collect. Domestically, many police agencies have created portals for the receipt of publicly submitted image-based evidence and have set rules for the submission of such media, but the volume received is jurisdictionally limited. Conversely, the jurisdiction of the ICC is exponentially larger, and it would be very difficult to predict how much media would be submitted to an OTP repository rather than or in addition to social media and other sites. Given the willingness of so many people to capture evidence of atrocities, especially in situations where most people have smartphones (e.g. the Russian invasion of Ukraine and the Israel–Gaza conflict), the volume is reasonably expected to be high.[28] Other organizations are currently looking at the feasibility of creating a repository of evidence for international conflicts.[29] Any project, whether through *OTP Link* or an outside organization, would be vast.

One way to ameliorate this capacity challenge would be to limit the volume of evidence received by establishing strict guidelines for submission. Such guidelines could include requiring verified identification of the photographer, access to the original media, an accompanying witness statement to provide context for the media, restrictions on file format, etc. Acquiring media under these circumstances

[27] OTP Link, https://www.icc-cpi.int/news/icc-prosecutor-karim-aa-khan-kc-announces-launch-advanced-evidence-submission-platform-otplink; https://otplink.icc-cpi.int/. See also Hayley Evans and Mahir Hazim, 'Digital Evidence: Collection at the International Criminal Court: Promises and Pitfalls', *Just Security* (5 July 2023) https://www.justsecurity.org/87149/digital-evidence-collection-at-the-intl-criminal-court-promises-and-pitfalls/.

[28] The volume of potential cases to investigate is substantial. In July 2022, Ukraine's Prosecutor General said that Ukraine was investigating 21,000 war crimes and crimes of aggression. Yaroslav Lukov, 'Ukraine War: 21,000 Alleged War Crimes Being Investigated, Prosecutor Says' *BBC News* (6 July 2022) https://www.bbc.com/news/world-europe-62073669. By January 2023, the Prosecutor General stated that more than 62,000 war crimes had been recorded. James FitzGerald, 'Ukraine War: Putin Should Face Trial This Year, says Top Lawyer' *BBC News* (1 January 2023) https://www.bbc.com/news/world-europe-64138851. See also Jay Aronson, 'Computer Vision and Machine Learning for Human Rights Video Analysis: Case Studies, Possibilities, Concerns, and Limitations', *Law and Social Inquiry* 43, no. 4 (2018): 1188–1209, at 1188.

[29] The UC Berkeley Human Rights Center, the IBA, and the University of Oxford Institute for Ethics, Law and Armed Conflict are partnering with relevant organizations with a view to developing such a repository. Koenig (n 12) 839.

would be highly beneficial for image integrity and authentication purposes but not all submitters are likely to comply or be able to comply with what may be viewed as administratively intrusive though evidentially sound hurdles. What should the position of the OTP be under these circumstances? Should it reject valuable evidence that has been submitted because not all boxes could be checked off? Would it program the system in such a manner as to prevent the uploading of media unless these conditions are met and risk losing valuable evidence? As limiting as these restrictions may seem at first glance, an open forum wherein all media is received without filters would be untenable and may lead to the collapse of the repository. Regulating the receipt of submitted evidence is therefore essential. At present, *OTP Link* has adopted an open forum approach and does not utilize any such restrictions on the submission of evidence through its platform. Submitters are not required to formally identify themselves and can choose to be anonymous. They are not required to provide original media and all types of electronic file formats appear to be acceptable. This open forum approach is likely to pose significant volume and authentication concerns.

Second, the OTP must ensure that it has sufficient qualified personnel to administer *OTP Link* and must amass the requisite software and hardware needed to perform these functions.[30] The OTP already employs investigative analysts who search the internet for relevant open source media and cause it to be downloaded by in-house cyber experts for examination.[31] A dedicated repository such as *OTP Link* will accentuate the need to increase the resources currently available, though even with the addition of personnel and regulating the submission of media to the OTP via upload restrictions, the volume of images and recordings that would be required to be assessed would likely be larger than human personnel could ever manage.[32] The potential for a veritable treasure trove of evidence is undeniable and institutions such as the OTP are only beginning to grasp the task before them. The human labour and expense required to evaluate such a large collection of images would be prohibitive, let alone the human cost incurred by the people required to watch images of horrific events.[33]

[30] The technology used by the OTP is not as robust as it should be, and the ICC is chronically understaffed and underfunded. 'Independent Expert Review of the International Criminal Court and the Rome Statute System: Final Report' (IER Report) (30 September 2020) https://asp.icc-cpi.int/sites/asp/files/asp_docs/ASP19/IER-Final-Report-ENG.pdf, para. 632.

[31] Xabier Aranburu, 'The Contribution of Analysis to the Quality Control in Criminal Investigation', in *Quality Control in Criminal Investigation*, edited by Xabier Agirre, Morten Bergsmo, Simon De Smet, and Carsten Stahn (Brussels: Torkel Opsahl Academic EPublisher, 2020), 117–272, at 124.

[32] Owing to smartphone technology and social media and other sites, more information is generated today than ever before. An investigation may involve thousands of incidents over several years, generating a potentially extensive library of video and images. Nema Milaninia, 'Biases in Machine Learning Models and Big Data Analytics: The International Criminal and Humanitarian Law Implications', *International Review of the Red Cross* 102, no 913 (2020): 199–234, at 200, 226, 231.

[33] The vicarious trauma occasioned by those tasked with watching disturbing video recordings and images is becoming more recognized. See e.g. Sam Dubberley, Elizabeth Griffin, and Haluk Bal, 'Making Secondary Trauma a Primary Issue: A Study of Eyewitness Media and Vicarious Trauma on the Digital Frontline', Eyewitness Media Hub Report (2015) http://eyewitnessmediahub.com/uploads/browser/files/Trauma%20Report.pdf.

Under these circumstances, there is a vital role for machine learning and artificial intelligence to play in doing some of the work that humans would otherwise be tasked with doing. The solution is not necessarily to work harder but rather better and more efficiently.[34] Machine learning is the science of programming computers to arrive at logical conclusions about the world due to being programmed and exposed to relevant data.[35] Algorithms, which are a series of rules or processes performed sequentially, are used to sort through large amounts of data and search for targeted commonalities, e.g. vehicles, buildings, landforms, people, or events, often from multiple sources and perspectives.[36] Being able to identify additional media sources and perspectives can help to ameliorate the epistemic challenges that may be faced when only sparse imagery is available, and when its context may be equivocal. A single source may favour one party's narrative, but additional sources may call that narrative into question. Context is often critical.

Machine learning occurs when computer scientists give the system training data from which it can learn patterns and use that newly acquired knowledge to examine questioned data. Used in conjunction with computer vision, which is the analysis of digital images to detect objects and related scenes, machine learning assists with the identification of relevant image content and the ability to generate corresponding investigational leads.[37] Computer scientists are currently developing machine learning and artificial intelligence products that are designed to automate the evaluation and categorization of images for later review by a human analyst.[38]

For example, researchers at Carnegie Mellon University in the US have developed a machine learning video analysis system called Event Labelling through Analytic Media Processing (E-LAMP), which is designed to detect specified objects, sounds, speech, and events in video recordings, potentially reducing work that might have taken years to days.[39] Through the use of training videos that depict objects or events of interest to researchers, E-LAMP evaluates the videos for

[34] Aronson (n 28) 1188–9. Using E-LAMP, Aronson estimates that it would cost under US $2,000.00 to evaluate eight hundred hours of video (at 1197).

[35] ibid 1193.

[36] ibid 1190, 1193.

[37] Methods used for image content detection include colour, shadow, and light analysis, geometrical analysis of curves and edges, and photogrammetry. ibid 1190, 1194, 1195. In the international criminal law context, machine learning can be used to detect visual data such as tanks, missiles, helicopters, aircraft, military vehicles, specific types of buildings, camouflaged soldiers, crowds of peoples, bodies, bridges, landforms, terrain, etc. It can also be used to detect aural data such as gunshots, explosions, cries, or screams. See also Milaninia (n 32) 201; Elena Radeva, 'The Potential for Computer Vision to Advance Accountability in the Syrian Crisis', *Journal of International Criminal Justice* 19, no. 1 (2021): 131–46.

[38] e.g. Magnet Axiom's Magnet.AI, Griffeye, and Cellebrite's Physical Analyser. Stuart Hall, Amin Sakzad, Kim-Kwang Choo, 'Explainable Artificial Forensics for Digital Forensics', *WIREs Forensic Science* 4, no. e1434 (2022): 1–11, at 3–4.

[39] Jay Aronson, Shicheng Xu, and Alex Hauptmann, 'Video Analytics for Conflict Monitoring and Human Rights Documentation: Technical Report', Carnegie Mellon University (2015) https://bit.ly/2LXJhiH; Aronson (n 28) 1196; Milaninia (n 32) 201.

targeted content and then examines a larger collection of non-training videos to look for examples of the targeted content. It then returns a set of videos that it thinks matches the targeted content to the E-LAMP operator who confirms whether E-LAMP is correct or not, and using this feedback the computer examines more videos. The result is the development of a 'classifier' or event kit, which can be visual, aural, semantic, or a combination of the three, and which is then used to search for targeted content in large video collections. It can also be used to detect duplicates or near-duplicate images.[40]

Aronson notes that E-LAMP has thus far proven most useful as a filter for removing irrelevant video from an analyst's workflow and for identifying videos that bear further examination. It has not developed to the point where it can generate a collection of relevant videos that do not require significant analyst evaluation.[41] The algorithms are probabilistic, though not necessarily conclusive. Thus, a human analyst would still be required to evaluate images identified by the computer to see if they bear any relationship to one another and are relevant to the investigation. The computer would be trained to look for certain types of image content and the analysts would be trained to evaluate the proffered images, with the primary goal being reducing the need for human-centred manual review, though not its elimination.[42]

E-LAMP's efficacy is dependent upon the quality of the video images selected for evaluation and the refinement of its algorithms. It will likely not replace human knowledge and judgement.[43] Further, E-LAMP does not assess the authenticity of images (that work must still be performed by an imagery analyst), nor does it mediate poor quality images or biased perspectives. The real value in machine learning is finding potential evidence that might otherwise be overlooked due to sheer volume. Nonetheless, analysts would need to guard against automation bias which is the tendency to favour results generated by a computer over those generated otherwise, irrespective of the error rate.[44]

One of the more common domestic uses for machine learning and computer vision is for the detection of child pornography. It also plays a role in the detection of deepfakes.[45] This technology is significant and as it improves it should be of tremendous assistance to investigators, but it should be viewed as an investigative tool, not a method of proof. E-LAMP and similar tools are just that: tools. They do not generate new evidence in isolation, rather they wade through vast swaths of media and identify images that require human analysis. The identification and

[40] Aronson (n 28) 1196–9.
[41] ibid 1199.
[42] Hall, Sakzad, Choo (n 38) 5.
[43] Aronson (n 28) 1205.
[44] Milaninia (n 32) 215.
[45] Marie-Helen Maras and Alex Alexandrou, 'Determining Authenticity of Video Evidence in the Age of Artificial Intelligence and in the Wake of Deepfake Videos', *The International Journal of Evidence and Proof* 23, no. 3 (2019): 255–62.

evaluation of relevant image content through machine learning may form part of the case narrative that will require expert and other corroborative testimony.

Undertaking a robust machine learning approach to media repositories, which is contemplated by *OTP Link*, requires significant technical and human resources. Should the OTP choose to house the media repository but offload the assessment and evaluation of some or all the submitted media to a third-party service provider, it must ensure that the same high standards expected of OTP personnel are followed. Objective verification is essential when utilizing third party assistance, especially given that such providers may have vested interests in promoting their own organizations and may inadvertently demonstrate less adherence to the accuracy and reliability of the assistance provided.

The foregoing practical challenges are significant and detailed study will be required to assess the volume of media submitted to *OTP Link*; the restrictions that should be imposed on submissions; and the cost and logistics involved in receiving, processing, and evaluating media, whether by humans, machine learning and artificial intelligence, or more likely all three methods. A corresponding legal problem that may arise from the creation of a large media repository such as *OTP Link* is the ability to sort through it and comply with disclosure obligations.[46] This is significant because the OTP is both the primary investigative body and a party to the proceedings that has a positive obligation to disclose evidence that is relevant and material to the defence, whether inculpatory or exculpatory, and whether selected for inclusion at trial or not.[47] The prosecution is under a continuing responsibility to disclose potentially exculpatory material throughout the trial.[48] These disclosure obligations regarding evidence which may show innocence, mitigate guilt, or affect the credibility of prosecution evidence are also reflected in the ICC Chambers Practice Manual.[49] In addition to assisting the defence in the preparation of their case, disclosure is also a mechanism that can be used to verify that the prosecution has conducted a thorough investigation.[50] The obligation of the OTP to disclose exculpatory material is designed to offset the disadvantages faced by the defence, and reflects the fact that equality of arms between the parties is essential in ensuring

[46] Lindsay Freeman and Raquel Vazquez Llorente, 'Finding the Signal in the Noise: International Criminal Evidence and Procedure in the Digital Age', *Journal of International Criminal Justice* 19, no. 1 (2021), 163–88, at 178.

[47] *Rome Statute*, Art. 67(2). See also the right of defence inspection under RPE Rule 77.

[48] *Prosecutor v. Lubanga*, ICC-01/04–01/06-1019, Decision Regarding the Timing and Manner of Disclosure and the Date of Trial, 9 November 2007, para. 28. Late or incomplete disclosure may result in a stay of proceedings or the recalling of affected witnesses for further questioning. Mark Klamberg, *Evidence in International Criminal Trials* (Leiden: Martinus Nijhoff Publishers, 2013) 292. See also RPE Rule 84 which describes disclosure as a continuing process.

[49] ICC Chambers Practice Manual (2019) https://www.icc-cpi.int/iccdocs/other/191129-chamber-manual-eng.pdf, para. 21.

[50] Salvatore Zappalà, 'The Prosecutor's Duty to Disclose Exculpatory Materials and the Recent Amendment to Rule 68 ICTY RPE', *Journal of International Criminal Justice* 2 (2004): 620–30, at 628.

substantive and procedural fairness.[51] Beyond its disclosure obligations, the prosecution is also tasked with the investigative goal of establishing the truth and has a duty to 'investigate incriminating and exonerating circumstances equally'.[52]

The OTP's disclosure obligations are significant in this context because if the OTP is unable to assess, categorize, and disclose all submitted media which may be relevant as soon as practicable due to volume, then a disclosure problem is sure to arise.[53] Under those circumstances, the OTP would be unable to meet its ongoing obligation to disclose evidence because it would not be able to confirm that it has reviewed all the information in its possession and control. Further, this issue may be exacerbated if evidence continues to be submitted during trial. These disclosure issues could lead to trial delays and the spectre of potential injustice. Accordingly, the OTP must ensure that it has the capacity to process media submitted to *OTP Link*.

3. Some Cautionary Comments About the Use of Image-Based Evidence

Can counsel go too far in the use of image-based evidence? Are there risks involved when counsel and the court rely upon image-based evidence to argue and decide a case? Can it be used improperly by counsel and the court? Can the use of image-based evidence be counterproductive to the search for the truth? Each of these questions draws an affirmative response. Fundamentally, all evidence must be led for the purpose of advancing or challenging a party's narrative propositions in a case, and ultimately in furtherance of the search for truth. It must be relevant to an issue before the court and must further the discourse between counsel and the court. Choosing image-based evidence that meets these goals requires a full understanding of the meaning of the evidence and the propositions it is intended to address.

Attaining suitable visual literacy is integral to meeting these objectives, as is the wisdom needed to decide what evidence should be led and for what purposes. For example, it would be inappropriate to lead video and photographic images primarily for their shock value because the prejudicial effect of the images upon the fairness of the trial would likely exceed their probative value. However, the fact that images have shock value does not make them inadmissible provided they have supplemental articulable probative value. The *Nazi Concentration Camps* film shown

[51] Sabine Swoboda, 'The ICC Disclosure Regime: A Defence Perspective', *Criminal Law Forum* 19 (2008): 449–72, at 450; Xavier-Jean Keïta, 'Disclosure of Evidence in the Law and Practice of the ICC', *International Criminal Law Review* 16 (2016): 1018–47, at 1021.

[52] *Rome Statute*, Art. 54(1)(a). The truth-seeking duty of the prosecution to investigate both inculpatory and exculpatory evidence is a key component in creating a robust case.

[53] Koenig (n 12) 840–1.

by the prosecution to the International Military Tribunal for Nuremberg (IMT) judges during the Nuremberg trial was most certainly shocking. To this day, it remains a very powerful film, even after decades of direct and vicarious exposure to other shocking and graphic images in news broadcasts and popular media. The graphic Holocaust images were likely without precedent for viewers at the time and given the reaction of the judges, members of the gallery, and some of the defendants, the film hit the desired mark. Yet despite its graphic nature, the dominant purpose of leading the filmic evidence was to provide proof of the atrocities that the defendants were directly or indirectly involved in perpetrating. It had articulable probative value. If the prosecution could not articulate this value, it would have been an error for counsel to lead it and for the judges to admit it as its prejudicial effect upon the fairness of the trial would achieve predominance.

Powerful images can impact everyone in the courtroom and not always in ways that are salutary. Before subjecting court participants to such images and turning them into virtual witnesses, it must be asked whether doing so is necessary and whether the same point could be made in a less graphic way. Shock and gore have a place in the courtroom, but its presentation must be governed by principled necessity and probity. As a result, where video and photographic images are supplemental to other forms of evidence, and the point sought to be made could be made without resort to disturbing images, there is merit in avoiding their use. Even within a collection of media, there may be a gradation of images and it may be appropriate to select images that are less graphic for use at trial if there is no cogent reason for using more visceral images. Conversely, where the video evidence constitutes the bulk of the factual foundation for the case, it must form part of the party's narrative.

Other risks that may arise from the use of image-based evidence include the inability of viewers to comprehend its content, misinterpretation of content, and disengagement from the task at hand. To counteract these risks, images must not be allowed to speak for themselves. They must be supported with knowledgeable *viva voce* (and in some cases written) explanations and narration by qualified witnesses in the courtroom that are designed to fully explain image content and meaning as both elements are necessary to achieve informed comprehension. The interpretation advanced by counsel must be explained to the court together with competing interpretations. Since counsel cannot give evidence themselves, their interpretation must be supported by the image-based evidence and the supplemental *viva voce* and expert evidence presented. Provided counsel fully comprehend the content of the evidence and the available interpretations, and they lead the necessary explanatory evidence, the risk of the court failing to comprehend the evidence or misinterpreting it is very low, as is the risk of the court totally disengaging due to lack of understanding.

On occasion, it may be appropriate to present a more condensed and simplified explanation to the court to convey the main points of the evidence, e.g. not showing complex data when the point could be made more simply. Nonetheless, any explanation provided must have a solid data-supported foundation. This is not to suggest that a court cannot handle complex image-based evidence, but rather it acknowledges that there are different ways to teach complex material. In this regard, counsel should consider themselves to be teachers, who together with qualified witnesses present the necessary information to the court. Properly presented image-based evidence should never be too much for a court to consider, nor are counsel incapable of acquiring the necessary knowledge and technical assistance to properly evaluate, understand, and use image-based evidence in the presentation of their case, but these goals are achieved through strategic planning, not happenstance.

A further risk associated with image-based evidence is its ability to mislead the viewer, either intentionally owing to an agenda on the part of its creator or unintentionally because of the way the evidence has been processed or presented. This risk can be substantially mitigated if not virtually eliminated if the recommendations presented in this work are implemented. Further, evaluation by opposing experts and competent cross-examination should serve to ferret out any misleading aspects of the evidence. The questions identified at the beginning of this section acknowledge that there are risks associated with the use of image-based evidence, but these risks are known. One of the goals of this book is to chart a path forward for addressing image-based evidence proactively, thereby mitigating the risks associated with its use, and providing a sounder basis upon which to argue and decide cases.

4. Is Image-Based Evidence at a Tipping Point?

The use of image-based evidence in international criminal prosecutions has expanded over the years commensurate, though at a lagging pace with, advances in technology and the willingness of counsel and experts to test the judicial *status quo*.[54] When the *Nazi Concentration Camps* film and related Holocaust atrocity films were shown to the IMT in the Nuremberg trial, the imagery was revolutionary, but the medium was not. Films and photographs had long since occupied a comfortable place among developed countries in a non-judicial context. The use of filmic, video, and photographic images, whether recorded at ground level, drone level, or by satellites has found a receptive audience in the international courtroom.

[54] Technological advancements can spur legal innovation but there tends to be a significant lag in their practical implementation. Rohan Grey, 'Digital' in *Tipping Points in International Law: Commitment and Critique*, edited by John Haskell and Jean d'Aspremont (Cambridge: CUP, 2021), 116–31, at 120.

Provided the images are shown to be authentic and reliable, they have earned that recognition.

A caveat to the general acceptance of video and photographic images in the courtroom is the use of social media and other open source images. The potential value to be gained from such free-range images must be weighed against the challenges associated with their authenticity, trustworthiness, and reliability. There has been some use of social media images in international criminal prosecutions and national prosecutions for international crimes, but these images represent a small percentage of the overall images tendered. For example, in *Prosecutor v. Al-Werfalli*, the Chamber issued an arrest warrant based in part on video recordings of executions that were posted to social media sites including Facebook. Authenticity may have been an interesting triable issue, but the ICC withdrew the arrest warrant upon the death of the defendant, thus bringing the proceedings to an end.[55] Nonetheless, this case evinces a willingness by the ICC to look beyond traditional sources of images. What remains to be achieved is the establishment of a track record for using such images at trial. Much more work is required to integrate social media images into the trial narrative. The recommendations developed throughout this book are designed in part to assist in this task.

This section began by questioning whether we are at a tipping point in the use of image-based evidence in international criminal prosecutions. Attempting to answer this rather vexing question requires understanding what constitutes a *tipping point*. Haskell describes a tipping point as a stage where what came before is either about to change or is in the process of changing and where we have yet to fully appreciate what the new environment will look like and what its effects will entail.[56] In perhaps starker terms, d'Aspremont describes a tipping point as 'an extraordinary moment in the present' and likens it to a 'revolution, crisis, metamorphosis, watershed moment, breaking point, rupture, fall, etc.'.[57] He asserts that this level of categorization is necessary to justify the stated need for change now and in the future. Tipping points highlight existing and new challenges and constraints, but also foretell avenues for change. Haskell asserts that if there is a current crisis with significant challenges, the proposed solutions need to be equally significant.[58] Identifying a tipping point first requires a critique—identifying what is wrong, troubling, or inadequate about the current situation. It follows that if the status quo is not broken or otherwise in need of substantial repair, there is no urgent need to

[55] ICC-01/11-01/17, Warrant for Arrest, 15 August 2017, para. 22. See https://www.icc-cpi.int/libya/al-werfalli; https://www.icc-cpi.int/libya/al-werfalli#icc-timeline.

[56] John Haskell, 'Experiencing Tipping Points in International Law', in *Tipping Points in International Law: Commitment and Critique*, edited by John Haskell and Jean d'Aspremont (Cambridge: CUP, 2021), 1–25, at 5.

[57] Jean d'Aspremont, 'The Literary Performances of the Tipping Point', in *Tipping Points in International Law: Commitment and Critique*, edited by John Haskell and Jean d'Aspremont (Cambridge: CUP, 2021), 26–36, at 27–8.

[58] Haskell (n 56) 6.

fix it. If the critique identifies problems in need of solution, then the second step is to articulate the commitment needed to carve out a new and better path.[59]

Tipping points are not a new phenomenon. There are tipping points in scientific discovery, the economy, politics, crime, armed conflict, etc. Gladwell popularized this notion in *The Tipping Point: How Little Things Can Make a Big Difference* by using fashion trends, crime, and epidemics as his subject matter.[60] Tipping points have also found a place in international law conferences.[61] Commonalities are found in the status quo which gives rise to the need for a new equilibrium. d'Aspremont cautions that declaring an extraordinary moment in the present to exist must be the result of a series of sophisticated moves and postulations because the net effect is to declare that what has been ordinary is now defunct.[62] He also argues that identifying a tipping point serves the interests of those who declare it.[63] Further, he notes that a tipping point necessarily involves hesitation to change and promotes self-reflection and some rehabilitation of the past.[64]

In asking the question whether the use of image-based evidence in international criminal prosecutions has reached a tipping point, I am not striving to find problems where there are none. In critiquing the status quo, I must identify what is wrong, troubling, or inadequate, such that change is necessary. The status quo approach has been to use film, video, and photographs from varied sources primarily to show scenes and events. This has generally worked well although images have not always been used to their full advantage, thus leaving some visual evidence (and truths) undiscovered. There has also been some use of 3D terrestrial laser scanning and modelling, and interactive 360° visual representations but the use of these methods of presenting data has been sporadic at best. The status quo is not inherently bad and has been of value in ascertaining the truth. Thus, I cannot fairly invoke d'Aspremont's 'extraordinary moment in the present' classification, nor can I declare the existing use of image-based evidence to be in crisis or at a breaking point. However, I believe that it is reasonable to postulate that the use of image-based evidence is at a stage where what came before is either about to change or is in the process of changing and we have yet to fully appreciate what the new environment will look like. My assessment is not that the current approach is inherently wrong or troubling but rather that it is fundamentally inadequate for truth seeking purposes, the core business of the court. It would not be a stretch to say that the

[59] ibid.

[60] Malcolm Gladwell, *The Tipping Point: How Little Things Can Make a Big Difference* (New York: Little, Brown and Company, 2000).

[61] Haskell (n 56) 14, 20.

[62] D'Aspremont (n 57) 28–30. He argues that the tipping point is not ready to leave the past behind nor is it ready to embrace the present; it is a moment caught in the continuing past and a present that has yet to begin.

[63] ibid 29.

[64] ibid 31–2.

current approach risks being wrong and troubling by virtue of it being inadequate. Change is needed.

At present, potentially valuable evidence is being overlooked, under-analysed, or not analysed at all, and the presentation of image-based evidence in the courtroom leaves something to be desired. While images serve an important expository purpose, they should be used for more than merely depicting a scene or event: they should be used to help analyse the scene or event and to extract details that might otherwise go unnoticed. If the status quo is merely maintained, then valuable evidence will be left on the table, and this may impact the ascertainment of the truth and the dogged pursuit of justice. Further, some image-based evidence may never make it to the table because the OTP cannot possibly identify and assess all relevant imagery posted to social media and other sites. Existing epistemic and technological paradigms need to be stretched to take greater advantage of what image-based evidence has to offer. Accomplishing this will also require the use of imagery experts to interrogate, interpret, and analyse images for use in the courtroom. For these reasons, I believe that the use of image-based evidence in international criminal prosecutions is at a tipping point. So much more can and should be done to maximize this evidential resource.

If my critique is correct and there is an identifiable problem in need of a solution, then the next step is to articulate the commitment needed to carve out a new and better path. In this regard, I make three broad recommendations for how to transcend the status quo and make more effective use of image-based evidence. First, the OTP must capitalize on the current and future prominence of social media images. The availability of images ripe for the plucking is an evidential boon that should not be squandered. Achieving this goal will require considerable effort as well as significant human and technical resources. The OTP presently has some capacity for this open source work through its cyber investigators and analysts, but more can and should be done. The creation of *OTP Link* for the acquisition, assessment, and archiving of submitted media is a significant step forward, but guidelines will likely be needed to govern submissions. The use of machine learning and artificial intelligence must be fully engaged as human personnel cannot possibly do all that is required to evaluate submitted images, let alone address disclosure obligations. Undertaking these tasks is likely to result in an evidential windfall to the OTP and the search for the truth. Substantial ICC and OTP commitment will be required to achieve these goals, through *OTP Link* and otherwise.

Second, there should be a measured expansion in the use of more technically advanced image-based evidence for scene and event analysis. Courts are rarely vanguards when it comes to the use of new technology. This conservative tendency is generally borne from the desire to see new technology tested by researchers and other organizations so that the court can be satisfied that it is fit for purpose. Counsel also tend to be conservative regarding the use of cutting edge technology that has not achieved a solid track record. There is wisdom in the court and counsel exercising patience and caution. Appellate intervention for the improper use of technology must be avoided. Despite this seeming reticence, the ICC has shown a willingness to accept technical assistance that accentuates the value of image-based evidence. For example, the use of interactive 360° visual representations supplemented with augmented reality features appears to have found a reasonably firm foothold at the ICC, though they have been used sparingly. These technical explorations of scenes can be very informative for the court as it allows for an in-depth view from different angles and locations which are drawn from different types of media. The use of 3D terrestrial laser scanning and modelling, and animations and simulations, could be used more often to posit and explore the theories of counsel and experts as to how certain events occurred. An ambitious leap forward would be the use of immersive virtual environments for scene and event exploration. For a case with the right facts, I believe that the ICC would be receptive to the use of these more advanced technologies provided counsel can articulate their probative value and the reliability of the depiction.

Third, forensic imagery experts must be more fully engaged by the OTP. Image-based evidence must be evaluated for authenticity, reliability, and interpretative meaning to arrive at an informed judgement about its content. Depending upon the complexity of the images, the court may be able to undertake this assessment on its own, perhaps coupled with the submissions of counsel, but there will be many cases where the court will benefit from the assistance of an expert who can technically interrogate the images, evaluate their content, and advise as to what meaning can fairly be drawn from them. Most images should not be woven into a trial narrative without evaluation by an imagery expert. This evaluation would begin with a technical interrogation of the images aimed at assessing the soundness of their purported content. This will assist in determining whether the images are authentic, whether they have been modified, whether they are deepfakes, etc. Next, the expert can advise as to the interpretation of the images and what meaning can fairly be drawn from them based on their content and quality. This role is fully supportive in the quest for the truth.

This level of knowledge cannot be achieved by counsel and the court merely looking at the images. Expert analysis at the metadata and pixel level may be necessary for proper interpretation. Forensic analysis of images requires that they be confronted by someone with the skills necessary to evaluate and enhance their evidential value. Looking at an image holistically may provide counsel and the court with superficial context and meaning, but technical analysis can serve to unlock details and interpretations that may otherwise remain hidden. Image interrogation and interpretation are tasks that must be performed by imagery experts, failing which the court may not have all the information that could have been available to it. Exemplified in *Gbagbo and Blé Goudé*, the images relied upon by the prosecution cried out for expert interpretation, yet the court was effectively given no support. Indeed, the court was critical of the prosecution's failure to properly analyse the video evidence. The court should not have to tell the OTP how to properly analyse and present its evidence—yet such commentary is instructive. If the OTP does not have sufficient forensic imagery experts on staff, they must either retain such staff or outsource the work to qualified experts. The status quo is insufficient.

Haskell notes that when assessing the presence of a tipping point, it is important to determine whether what is observed is merely a 'blip' or something that will be longstanding.[65] The former could perhaps be ignored while the latter cannot. A further consideration is whether the identified concerns are subject to human control and if so, what can be done to address them.[66] Given the ever expanding volume of images from myriad sources that document atrocity crimes and offer potential crime base and linkage evidence, the concerns outlined throughout this book about the authenticity, reliability, and trustworthiness of images, the difficulties involved in correctly interpreting images, the lack of sufficient visual literacy among counsel and the court, and the continued need for expert assistance, it can reasonably be postulated that current concerns regarding the use of image-based evidence in international criminal prosecutions are not a blip. Current concerns will continue to be operative and are likely to increase in scope as more images are created and mined for evidential value. Second, addressing these concerns are subject to human control and this work has set out what may be done to address them.

When advocating change, it is important to recall and reinforce bedrock principles. The OTP has expanded its capacity to receive evidence using *OTP Link* and must correspondingly increase its ability to evaluate, analyse, interpret, and incorporate submitted image-based evidence for use throughout the various stages of a case, including the trial, mindful of the goal to pursue objective truth. The OTP is required to investigate both incriminating and exonerating circumstances equally and must disclose evidence that is relevant and material to the defence, whether inculpatory or exculpatory, and whether selected for inclusion at trial or not. When assessing newly acquired evidence, the OTP must guard against engaging in confirmation bias wherein potential evidence is assessed for its value in strengthening existing prosecution hypotheses.[67] Confirmation bias can result in misguided investigations, wrongful convictions, and the failure to prosecute responsible parties. As Lidén notes, the ability to eliminate alternate hypotheses is undermined if investigators fail to see other reasonable hypotheses and therefore do not investigate them.[68] Anticipated or known defence perspectives must be considered throughout the investigation and not only at trial. The goal of preventing

[65] Haskell (n 56) 16.

[66] ibid 18.

[67] Moa Lidén, 'Confirmation Bias in Investigation of Core International Crimes: Risk Factors and Quality Control Techniques', in *Quality Control in Criminal Investigation*, edited by Xabier Agirre, Morten Bergsmo, Simon De Smet, and Carsten Stahn (Brussels: Torkel Opsahl Academic EPublisher, 2020), 461–528, at 462.

[68] ibid 469.

or mitigating confirmation bias is to promote a cautious appraisal of evidence and the hypotheses it may support or detract from, whether they support the prosecution theory or not. Defence perspectives should be top of mind for the prosecution when assessing evidence and developing trial narratives.

Conclusion

International criminal tribunals and courts have recognized the value that image-based evidence brings to fact-finding and truth discovery and have shown a willingness to receive a variety of such evidence upon being satisfied that it is worthy of consideration. Image-based evidence currently occupies a liminal space wherein the status quo approach has merit and has advanced the search for the truth, but more can and should be done to promote the use of this important category of evidence in international criminal justice. I assert that it is at a tipping point, not in the sense that there is an existential crisis afoot, but rather that the current approach is fundamentally inadequate for truth-seeking purposes. This chapter is the culmination of the expansive groundwork laid in earlier chapters and the recommendations put forth are intended to accentuate and maximize the value and use of image-based evidence in international criminal prosecutions. To accomplish these achievable goals, there must be dedicated efforts in improving the visual literacy of counsel and the court and a corresponding improvement in the ability of the OTP to receive, evaluate, analyse, and profit from image-based evidence. The status quo does not currently meet these objectives. The OTP and the ICC generally should strive to be the world leader in the use of evidence that advances the truth inquiry. Accomplishing this will require dedicated focus, further evolvement within the OTP, and the requisite funding. These are tall but not insurmountable obstacles.

Mapping out how these changes can be achieved is beyond the scope of this book, but some commentary may be beneficial. The OTP has the authority to establish a formal repository for the broad-scale submission and acquisition of image-based evidence relating to atrocity crimes within its jurisdiction.[69] This authority has been evidenced by the creation of *OTP Link*, which is a significant step forward in gathering relevant image-based evidence. Through *OTP Link* and public statements, it is readily apparent that the Prosecutor is aware of the volume and importance of image-based evidence.[70] The Prosecutor seeks to establish technological

[69] RPE Rule 10 mandates that, 'The Prosecutor shall be responsible for the retention, storage and security of information and physical evidence obtained in the course of the investigations by his or her Office.' It does not dictate how that evidence should be collected, nor would the RPE be the appropriate mechanism to do so. Receiving, processing, and analysing evidence is already addressed by OTP Reg. 23 which requires the OTP to maintain an evidential database with an expressed preference for digital evidence.

[70] The ICC Prosecutor noted, 'Conflicts and international crises now generate audio, visual and documentary records on a massive scale. The commission of international crimes leaves a significant

infrastructure that would include an expansion of existing digital storage capacity, the introduction of tools for the automatic transcription and translation of video and audio files, and a customized evidence lifestyle management system to centralize evidence.[71] A comprehensive repository for the acquisition, evaluation, and archiving of image-based evidence such as *OTP Link* is essential and in keeping with the Prosecutor's stated intentions. However, gathering image-based evidence cannot be done with half measures—this is a significant undertaking that must be done correctly and on the appropriate scale. Refinement of the inaugural version of *OTP Link* will likely be needed to control the volume, quality, and authenticity of submissions, but with sufficient public outreach it can gain traction and become the go-to location for the submission of image-based evidence of atrocity crimes.

A further consideration is whether the OTP should also partner with appropriate organizations for the acquisition of publicly submitted media. Other organizations have experience with receiving, evaluating, archiving, and transmitting image-based evidence of atrocity crimes.[72] However, partnering with other organizations or any measure of outsourcing the collection of valuable evidence would require careful consideration. Should any partnering or outsourcing occur, the agendas and biases of non-OTP participants in the gathering, evaluation, and processing of evidence must be addressed and policed. Given the importance of the chain of custody, authentication, and processing of digital evidence, it is preferable that such work be done primarily in-house using OTP infrastructure and facilities and staffed by OTP cyber investigators and analysts. Qualified personnel are already employed by the OTP to do this kind of work though many more will be required to accommodate a comprehensive repository like *OTP Link*. To the extent that State Parties second personnel to assist the OTP in this work and to the extent the OTP welcomes such assistance, the OTP must be in complete control of the endeavour.

As with all recommendations for improvement and advancement, it is reasonable to inquire as to the cost of implementing them. Many of the recommendations do not require much in the way of additional resources. For example, improving the visual literacy of counsel so that they are better equipped to appreciate the value of image-based evidence for probative and didactic purposes, to understand image content and assess its reliability, to be able to factor in the potential impact of photographer and party agendas and biases, to assess the purpose for leading

digital footprint.' 'Statement of ICC Prosecutor, Karim A.A. Khan QC: Contributions and Support from States Parties will Accelerate Action Across our Investigations' (28 March 2022) https://www.icc-cpi.int/news/statement-icc-prosecutor-karim-aa-khan-qc-contributions-and-support-states-parties-will.

[71] ibid. This is further reflected in the ICC OTP Strategic Plan 2023–2025, available at https://www.icc-cpi.int/sites/default/files/2023-08/2023-strategic-plan-otp-v.3.pdf, at para. 26.

[72] See e.g. *eyeWitness to Atrocities*, discussed in Chapter 3. I am not suggesting that *eyeWitness* is the only organization that handles such evidence or that the OTP should partner with them, but rather note them to illustrate that similar work is already being done.

image-based evidence, and to plan for effective evidence presentation in the courtroom would largely fall upon the existing cadre of counsel. These recommendations do not necessarily significantly impact the workload of counsel or require more counsel to be appointed, but rather they highlight the need for focused attention and expert training on these topics. To accomplish visual literacy training, imagery experts would be required, and the OTP would need to bolster its expert resources accordingly.

Other recommendations such as improving the visual literacy of the court, adopting a more robust approach to image authentication, the use of advanced visual representations (whether outsourced or in-house), and elevating the level of forensic image analysis that is required to properly evaluate and interpret image-based evidence clearly require the appointment of additional forensic imagery experts. Utilizing a robust in-house repository such as *OTP Link* for publicly submitted image-based evidence, together with the necessary analytical personnel and machine learning and artificial intelligence resources, will be resource intensive. While the ICC does not have unlimited resources, I am also cognizant of the ambitious remit of the ICC and the optics of linking the amount of justice achieved to the amount that can be afforded. Through the establishment of the *Trust Fund for Advanced Technology and Specialized Capacity*, the Prosecutor has sought capital and other investment from State Parties to support three priority initiatives, the relevant one for these purposes being the 'Use of new advanced technological tools and equipment in the collection, analysis and processing of evidence.'[73] This is a promising start though more is needed than tools. For example, a substantial increase in the number of qualified cyber investigators, analysts, and imaging experts, and the infrastructure needed to operate at this higher level are essential.

Throughout these chapters, I have sought to be comprehensive in my approach to the selected topics and although I have strived to produce an extensive study of image-based evidence in international criminal justice, there are limitations to what can be accomplished within the allotted space. Future research could include targeting a broader cross-section of domestic civil and common law jurisdictions to study their use of image-based evidence in the prosecution of serious and violent crime, how issues such as authenticity and admissibility are addressed, and what lessons might be extrapolated to the international arena. Practical examples of the use of specialized forensic image analysis techniques to draw out further details and content from video and still images would be of benefit as a means of showcasing what can be accomplished by imagery experts. Further, expanded technical content regarding image reliability, authentication, and advanced visual representations would be instructive. These aspirations for future study are reflective of the fact that the use of image-based evidence is a complex and evolving topic both at the international and national criminal justice levels.

[73] (n 69).

Index

For the benefit of digital users, indexed terms that span two pages (e.g., 52–53) may, on occasion, appear on only one of those pages.

Figures are indicated by *f* following the page number